高 橋 和 希

TO ALL OF YOU WHO'VE SUPPORTED
ME...YOU HAVE MY DEEPEST THANKS.

—KAZUKI TAKAHASHI, 2004

Artist/author Kazuki Takahashi first tried to break into
the manga business in 1982, but success eluded him
until **Yu-Gi-Oh!** debuted in the Japanese **Weekly
Shonen Jump** magazine in 1996. **Yu-Gi-Oh!**'s themes
of friendship and fighting, together with Takahashi's
weird and wonderful art, soon became enormously
successful, spawning a real-world card game, video
games, and two anime series. A lifelong gamer,
Takahashi enjoys Shogi (Japanese chess), Mahjong,
card games, and tabletop RPGs, among other games.

YU-GI-OH!: MILLENNIUM WORLD VOL. 7
SHONEN JUMP Manga Edition

STORY AND ART BY
KAZUKI TAKAHASHI

Translation & English Adaptation/Anita Sengupta
Touch-up Art & Lettering/Kelle Han
Design/Sean Lee
Editor/Jason Thompson

In the original Japanese edition, YU-GI-OH!, YU-GI-OH!: DUELIST and YU-GI-OH!:
MILLENNIUM WORLD are known collectively as YU-GI-OH!. The English YU-GI-OH!:
MILLENNIUM WORLD was originally volumes 32–38 of the Japanese YU-GI-OH!.

Printed in the U.S.A.

Published by VIZ Media, LLC
P.O. Box 77010
San Francisco, CA 94107

10 9 8 7 6 5 4 3
First printing, February 2008
Third printing, January 2014

PARENTAL ADVISORY
YU-GI-OH!: MILLENNIUM WORLD is rated T for
Teen and is recommended for ages 13 and up.
It contains fantasy violence.

ratings.viz.com

www.viz.com

THE WORLD'S
MOST POPULAR MANGA

SHONEN JUMP

www.shonenjump.com

SHONEN JUMP MANGA

YU-GI-OH! Millennium World

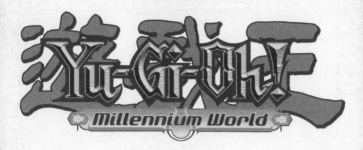

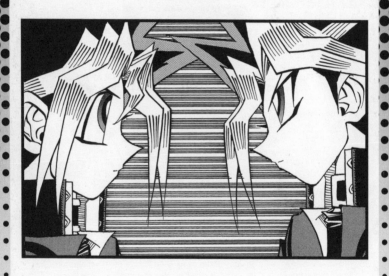

Vol. 7

THROUGH THE LAST DOOR

STORY AND ART BY

KAZUKI TAKAHASHI

THE MAIN CHARACTERS

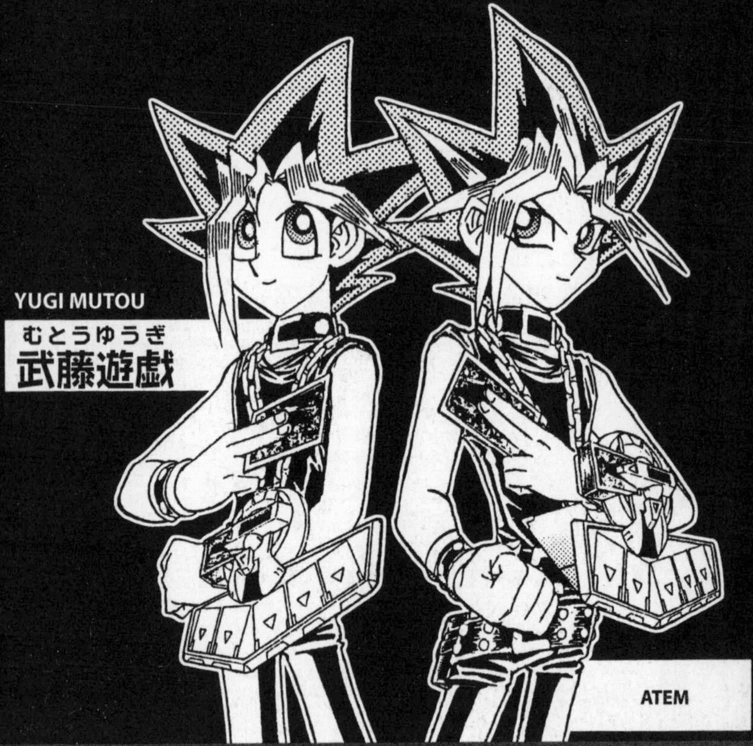
YUGI MUTOU
むとうゆうぎ
武藤遊戯
ATEM

Soon Akhenaden surrendered to the dark side and summoned Zorc Necrophades, who attacked Egypt with an army of the dead. Then Bakura revealed the truth: the "world of memories" is a simulation, a shadow role-playing game based on Yu-Gi-Oh's memories of the past! Yu-Gi-Oh and the priests (including Akhenaden's son Seto) fought bravely against Zorc and Bakura, knowing that only the winner could escape the role-playing game alive. All hope seemed lost, until Yugi's friends followed Yu-Gi-Oh into the game. There, they found the key to victory: the pharaoh's true name, which had been forgotten for 3,000 years.

The ancient Egyptians believed that magic dwelled in a person's name. When Yu-Gi-Oh spoke his true name, "Atem," the three Great Gods of Egypt appeared. Merging into one, the creator god Horakhty, they blasted Zorc with a beam of light…!

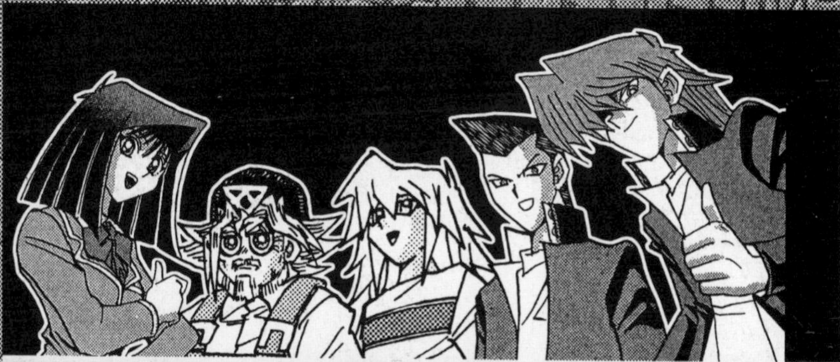

まざきあんず 真崎杏子 ANZU MAZAKI

むとうすごろく 武藤双六 SUGOROKU MUTOU

ばくら りょう 獏良 了 RYO BAKURA

ほんだ 本田ヒロト HIROTO HONDA

じょうのうちかつや 城之内克也 KATSUYA JONOUCHI

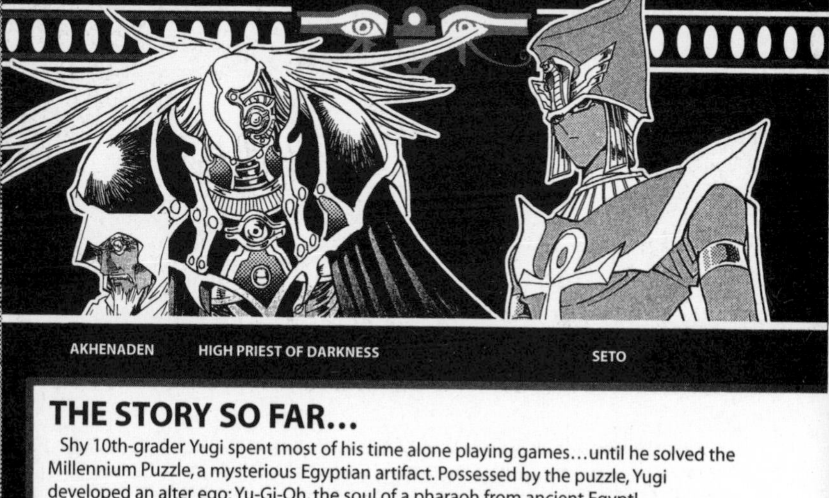

AKHENADEN

HIGH PRIEST OF DARKNESS

SETO

THE STORY SO FAR...

Shy 10th-grader Yugi spent most of his time alone playing games...until he solved the Millennium Puzzle, a mysterious Egyptian artifact. Possessed by the puzzle, Yugi developed an alter ego: Yu-Gi-Oh, the soul of a pharaoh from ancient Egypt!

Discovering that the card game "Duel Monsters" was of Ancient Egyptian origin, Yu-Gi-Oh collected the three Egyptian God Cards and used them to travel into the "world of memories" of his own life 3,000 years ago. There, he found that he was the pharaoh, served by priests who used the seven magic Millennium Items.

But unbeknownst even to the pharaoh, the Millennium Items were stained with blood. Created by the high priest Akhenaden, the Millennium Items owed their power to a mass human sacrifice! Their bloody origin had infused the Millennium Items with an evil spirit: the dark god Zorc Necrophades, who tempted Akhenaden with untold power. In the modern world, Zorc's servant was Bakura, a piece of Zorc's consciousness who dwelled in the Millennium Ring.

Yu-Gi-Oh! Millennium World

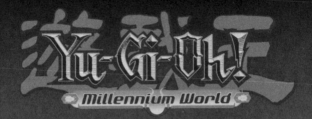

Vol. 7

CONTENTS

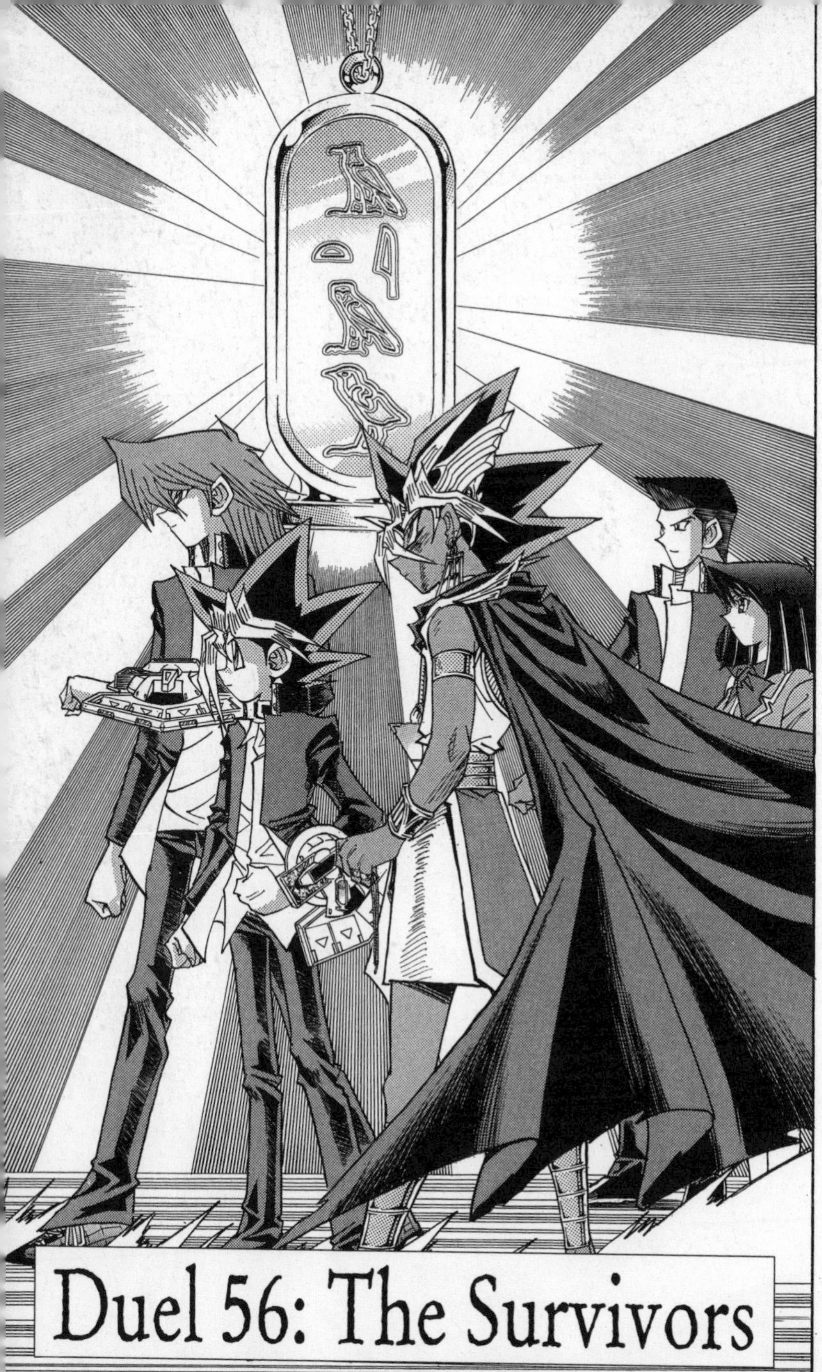

Duel 56: The Survivors

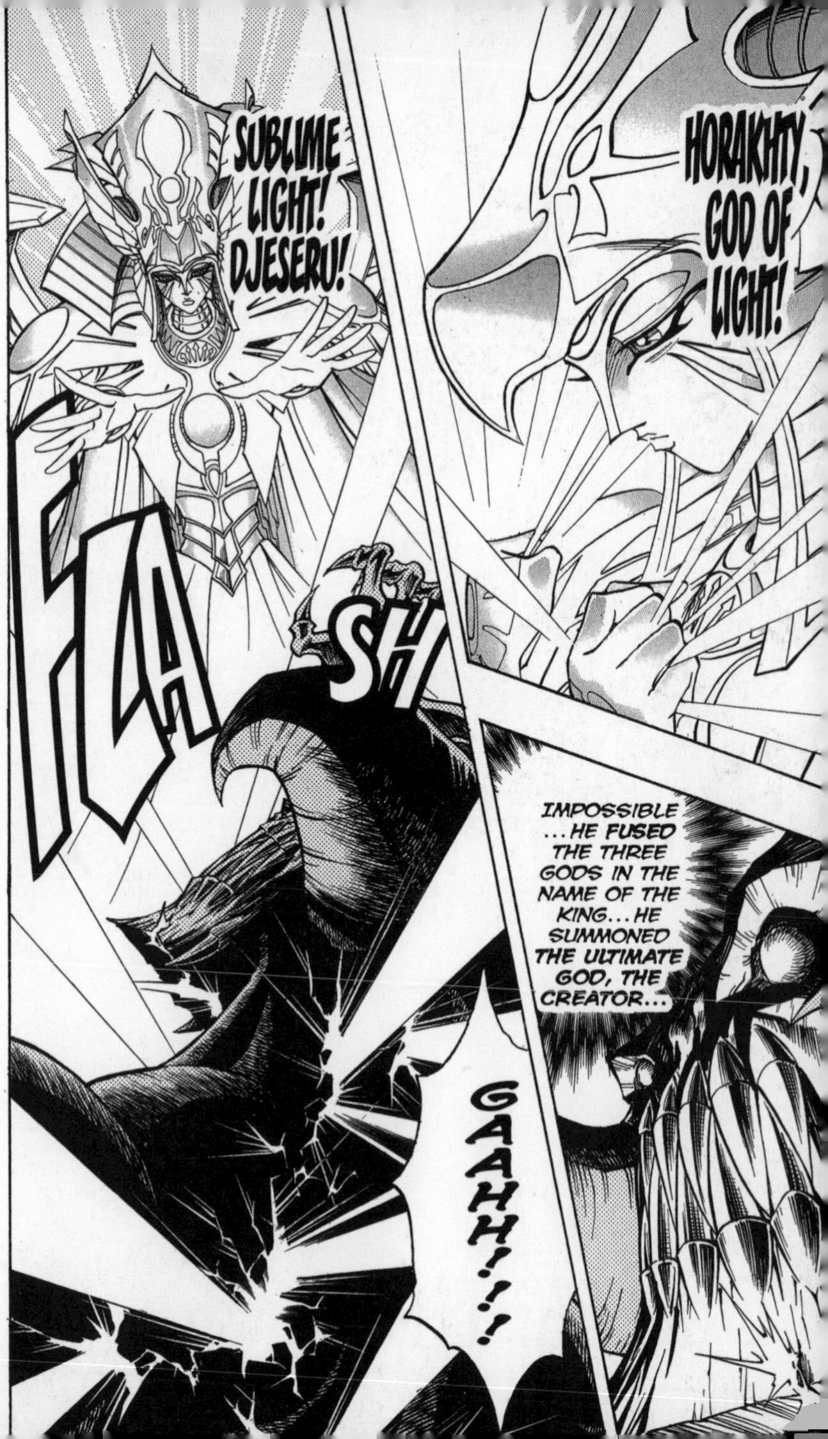
HORAKHTY, GOD OF LIGHT!
SUBLIME LIGHT! DJESERU!
FLASH
IMPOSSIBLE ...HE FUSED THE THREE GODS IN THE NAME OF THE KING... HE SUMMONED THE ULTIMATE GOD, THE CREATOR...
GAAHH!!!

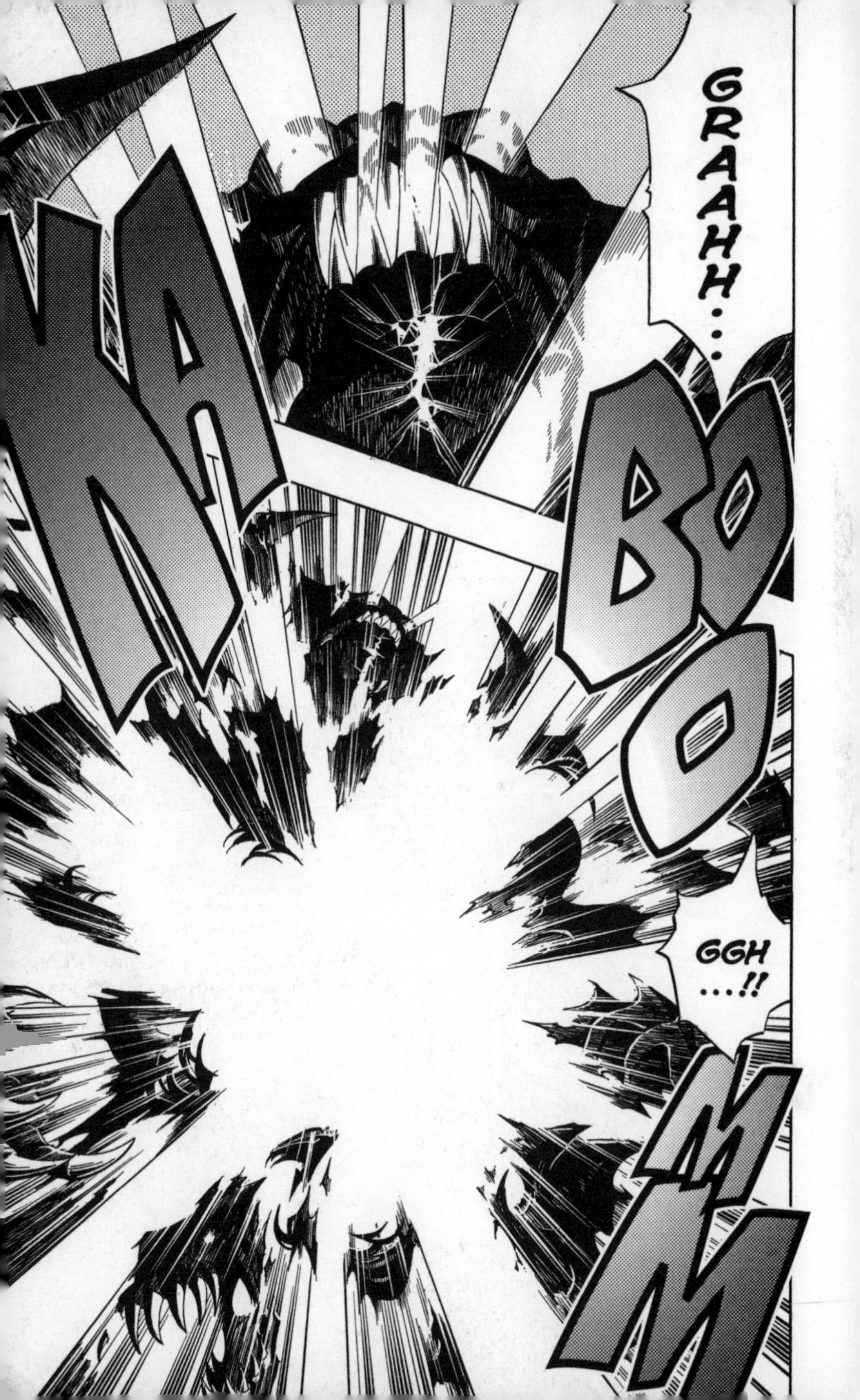
GRAAHH...
KABOOMM
GGH ...!!

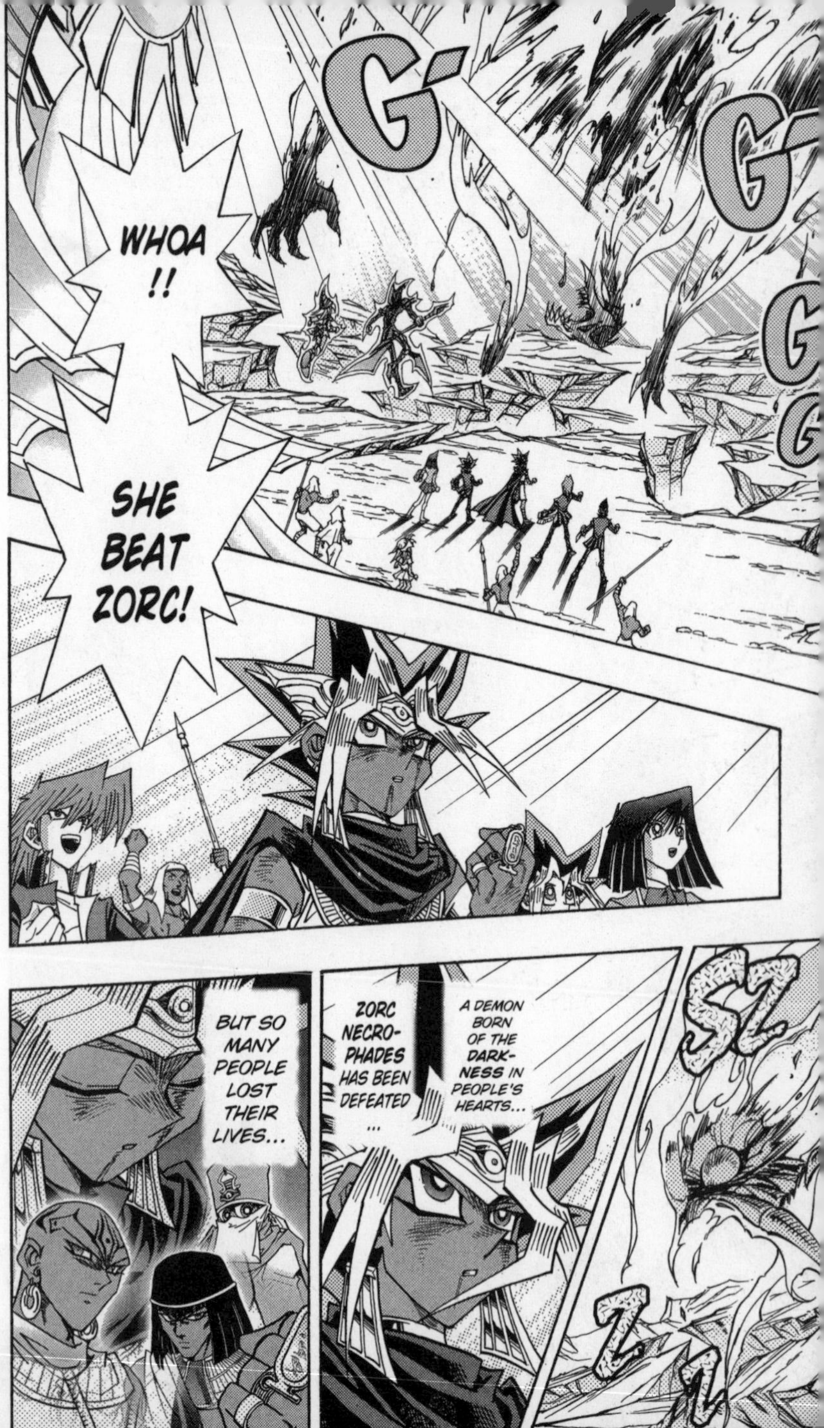
G-
G-
G
G
WHOA !!
SHE BEAT ZORC!
SZ
A DEMON BORN OF THE DARKNESS IN PEOPLE'S HEARTS...
ZORC NECROPHADES HAS BEEN DEFEATED ...
BUT SO MANY PEOPLE LOST THEIR LIVES...

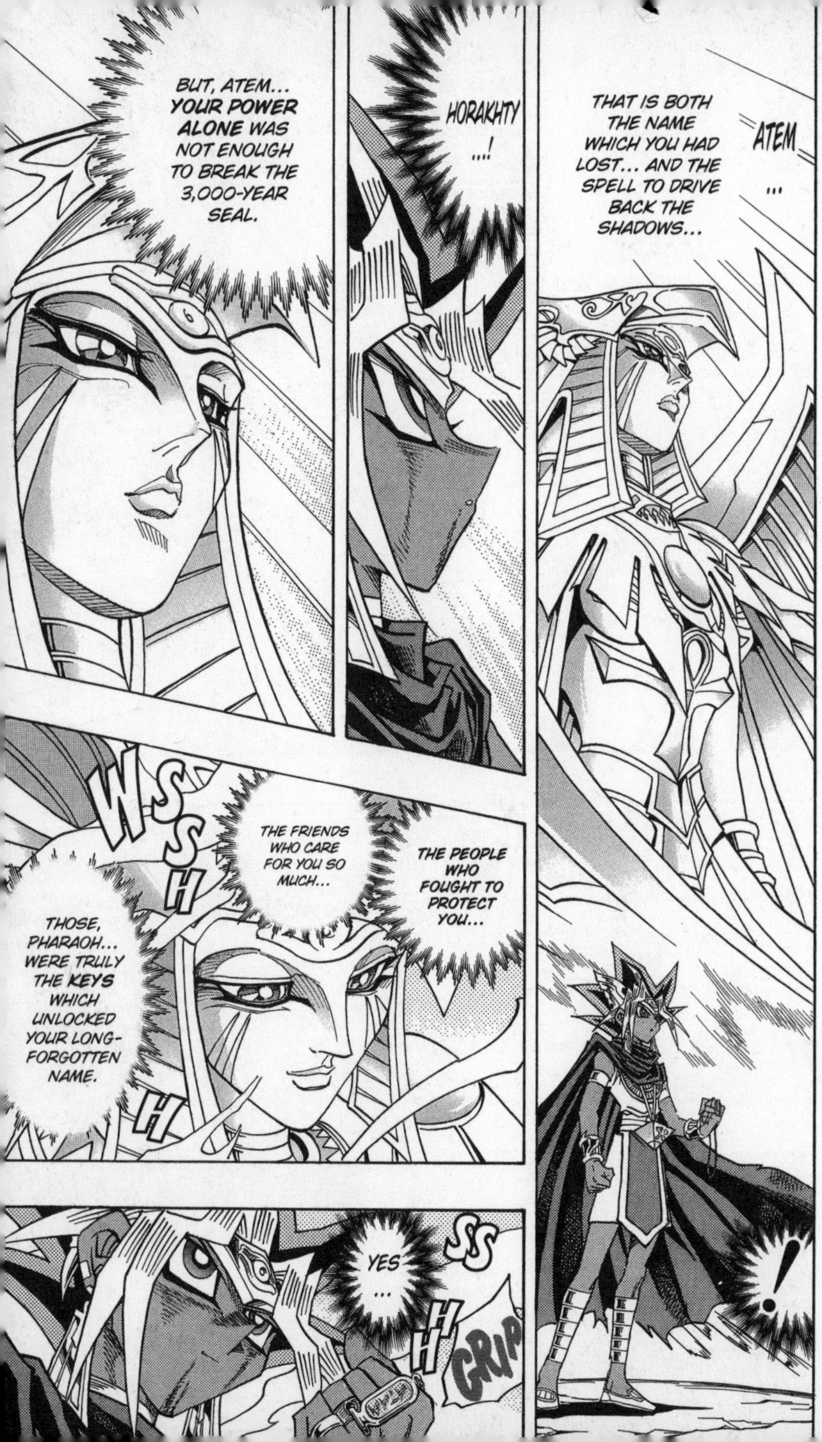
ATEM ...
THAT IS BOTH THE NAME WHICH YOU HAD LOST... AND THE SPELL TO DRIVE BACK THE SHADOWS...
HORAKHTY ...!
BUT, ATEM... **YOUR POWER ALONE** WAS NOT ENOUGH TO BREAK THE 3,000-YEAR SEAL.
!
THE PEOPLE WHO FOUGHT TO PROTECT YOU...
THE FRIENDS WHO CARE FOR YOU SO MUCH...
WSSH
THOSE, PHARAOH... WERE TRULY THE **KEYS** WHICH UNLOCKED YOUR LONG-FORGOTTEN NAME.
H
SS
YES ...
HH
GRIP

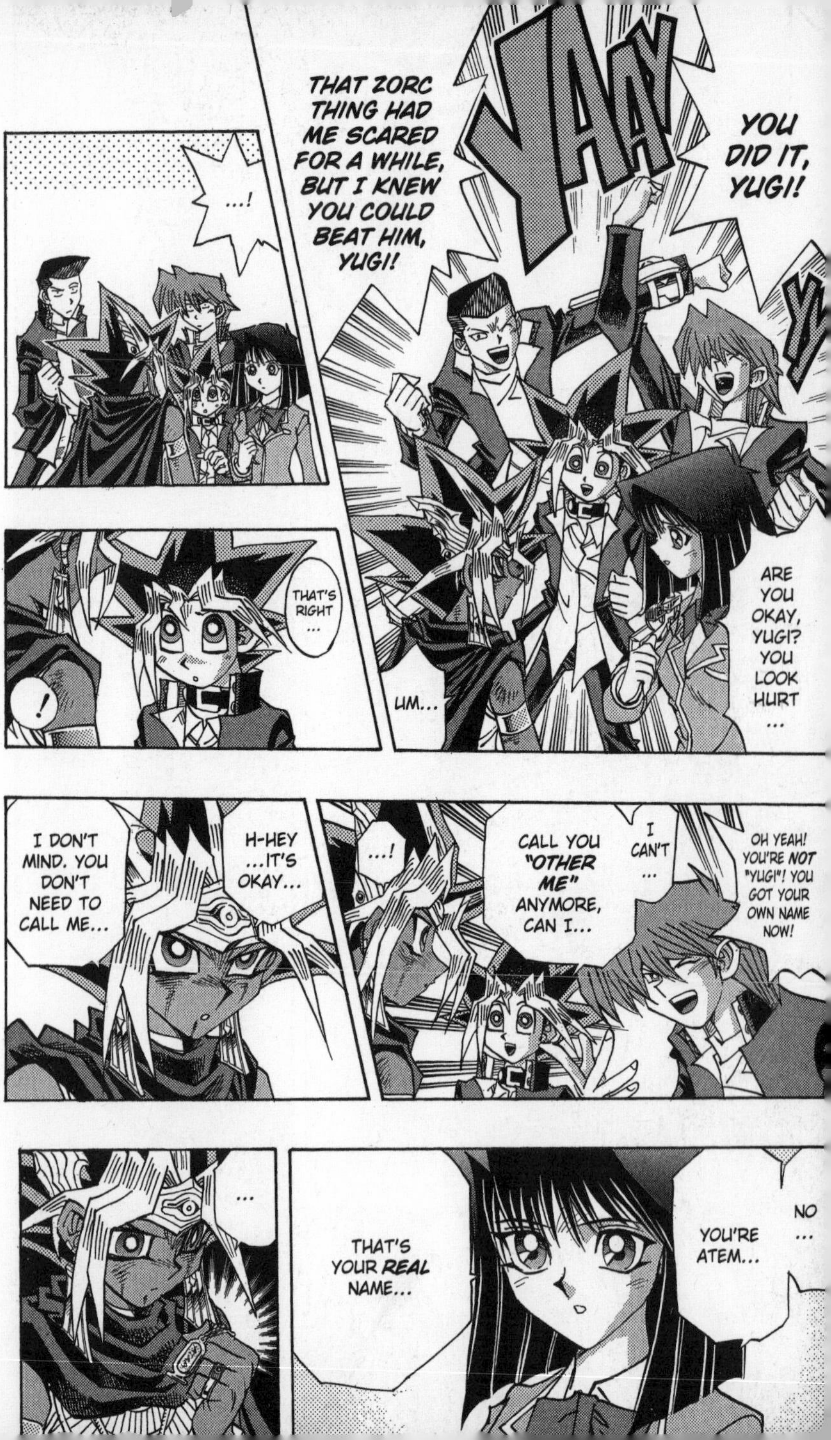
YAAY
YOU DID IT, YUGI!
THAT ZORC THING HAD ME SCARED FOR A WHILE, BUT I KNEW YOU COULD BEAT HIM, YUGI!
ARE YOU OKAY, YUGI? YOU LOOK HURT...
UM...
...!
THAT'S RIGHT...
!
OH YEAH! YOU'RE NOT "YUGI"! YOU GOT YOUR OWN NAME NOW!
I CAN'T...
CALL YOU "OTHER ME" ANYMORE, CAN I...
...!
H-HEY ...IT'S OKAY...
I DON'T MIND. YOU DON'T NEED TO CALL ME...
NO...
YOU'RE ATEM...
THAT'S YOUR REAL NAME...
...

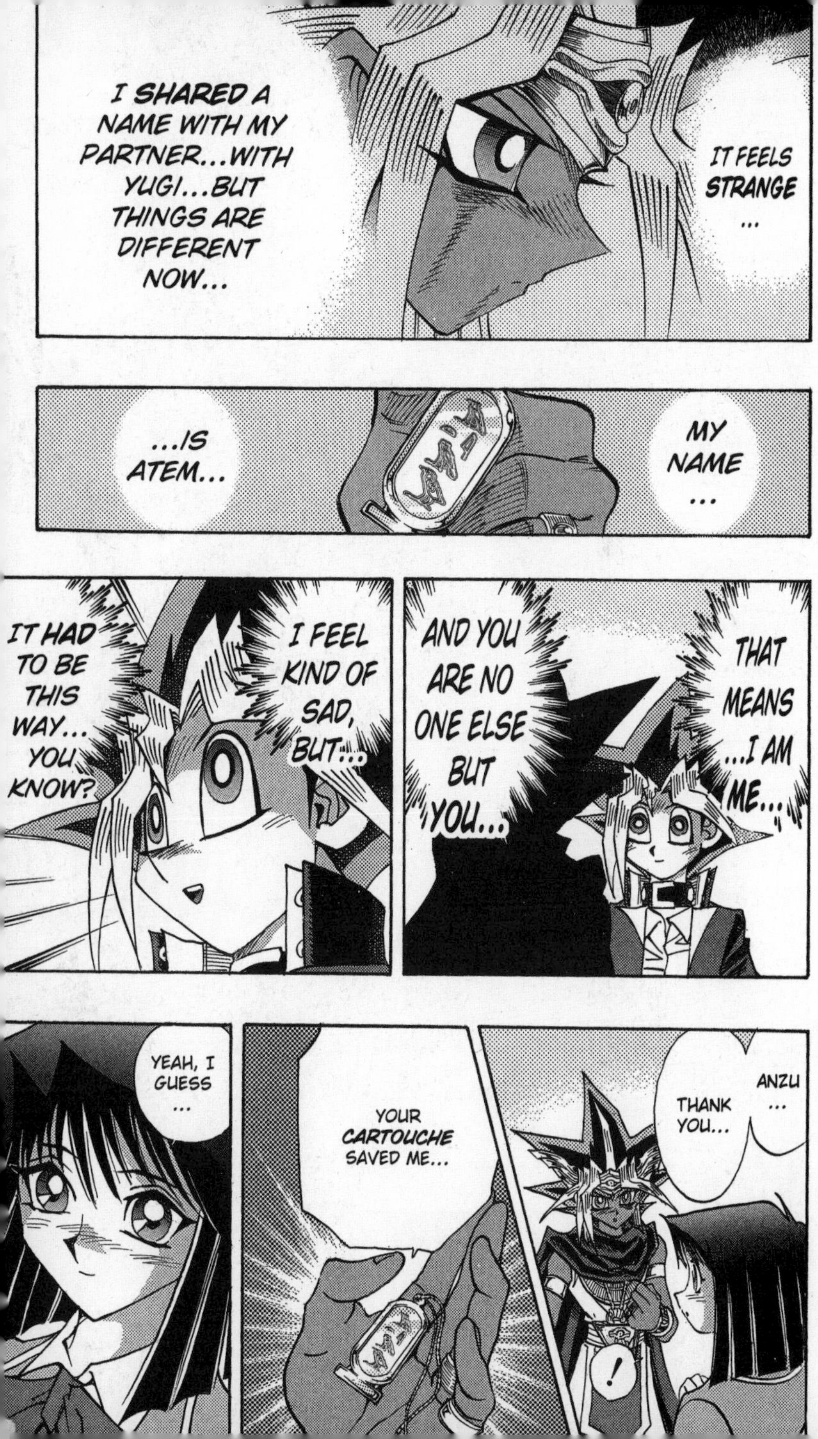
IT FEELS STRANGE ...
I SHARED A NAME WITH MY PARTNER...WITH YUGI...BUT THINGS ARE DIFFERENT NOW...
MY NAME ...
...IS ATEM...
THAT MEANS ...I AM ME...
AND YOU ARE NO ONE ELSE BUT YOU...
I FEEL KIND OF SAD, BUT...
IT HAD TO BE THIS WAY... YOU KNOW?
ANZU ...
THANK YOU...
!
YOUR CARTOUCHE SAVED ME...
YEAH, I GUESS ...

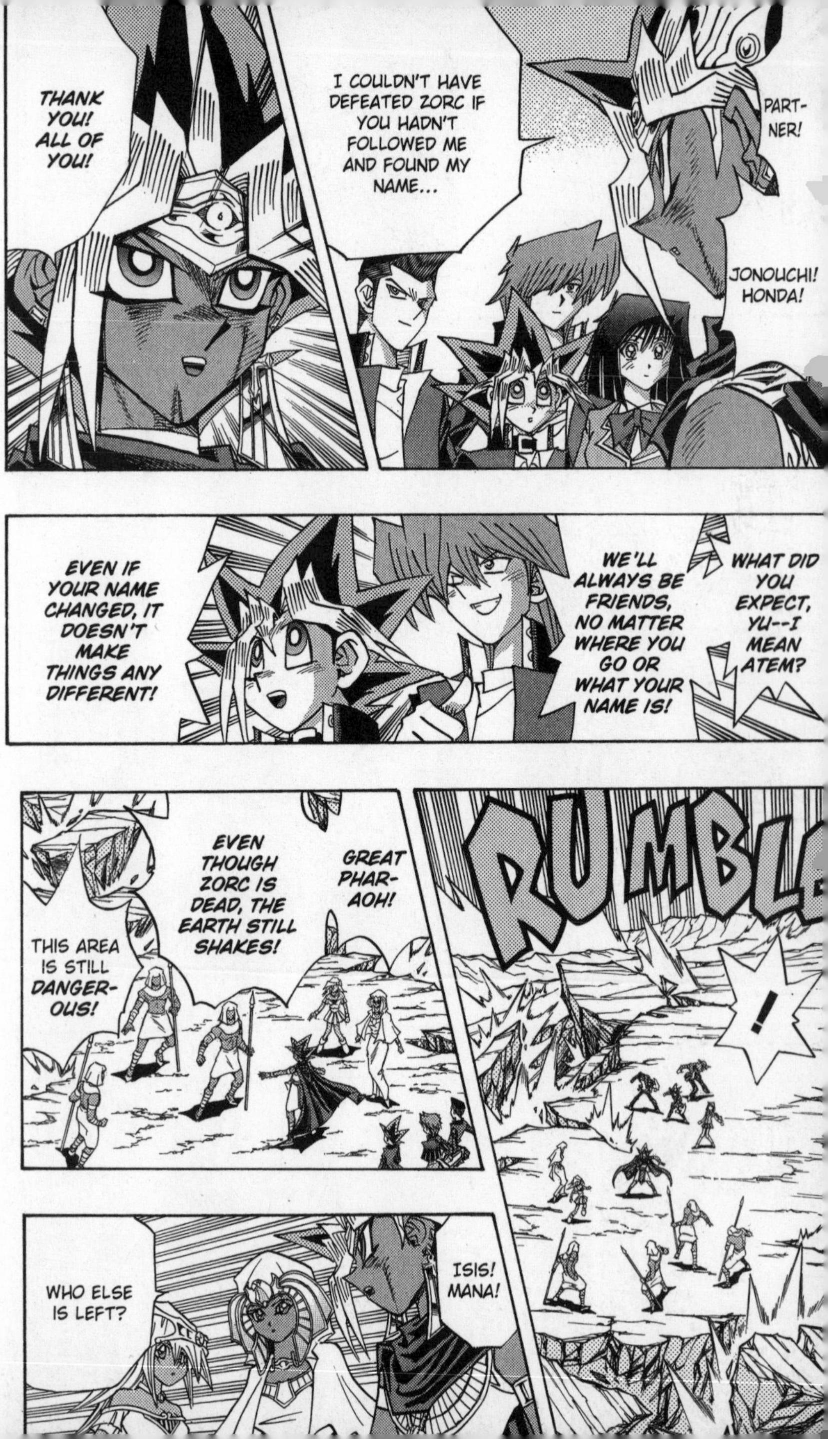
PART-NER!
JONOUCHI! HONDA!
I COULDN'T HAVE DEFEATED ZORC IF YOU HADN'T FOLLOWED ME AND FOUND MY NAME...
THANK YOU! ALL OF YOU!
WHAT DID YOU EXPECT, YU--I MEAN ATEM?
WE'LL ALWAYS BE FRIENDS, NO MATTER WHERE YOU GO OR WHAT YOUR NAME IS!
EVEN IF YOUR NAME CHANGED, IT DOESN'T MAKE THINGS ANY DIFFERENT!
RUMBLE
!
GREAT PHAR-AOH!
EVEN THOUGH ZORC IS DEAD, THE EARTH STILL SHAKES!
THIS AREA IS STILL DANGER-OUS!
ISIS! MANA!
WHO ELSE IS LEFT?

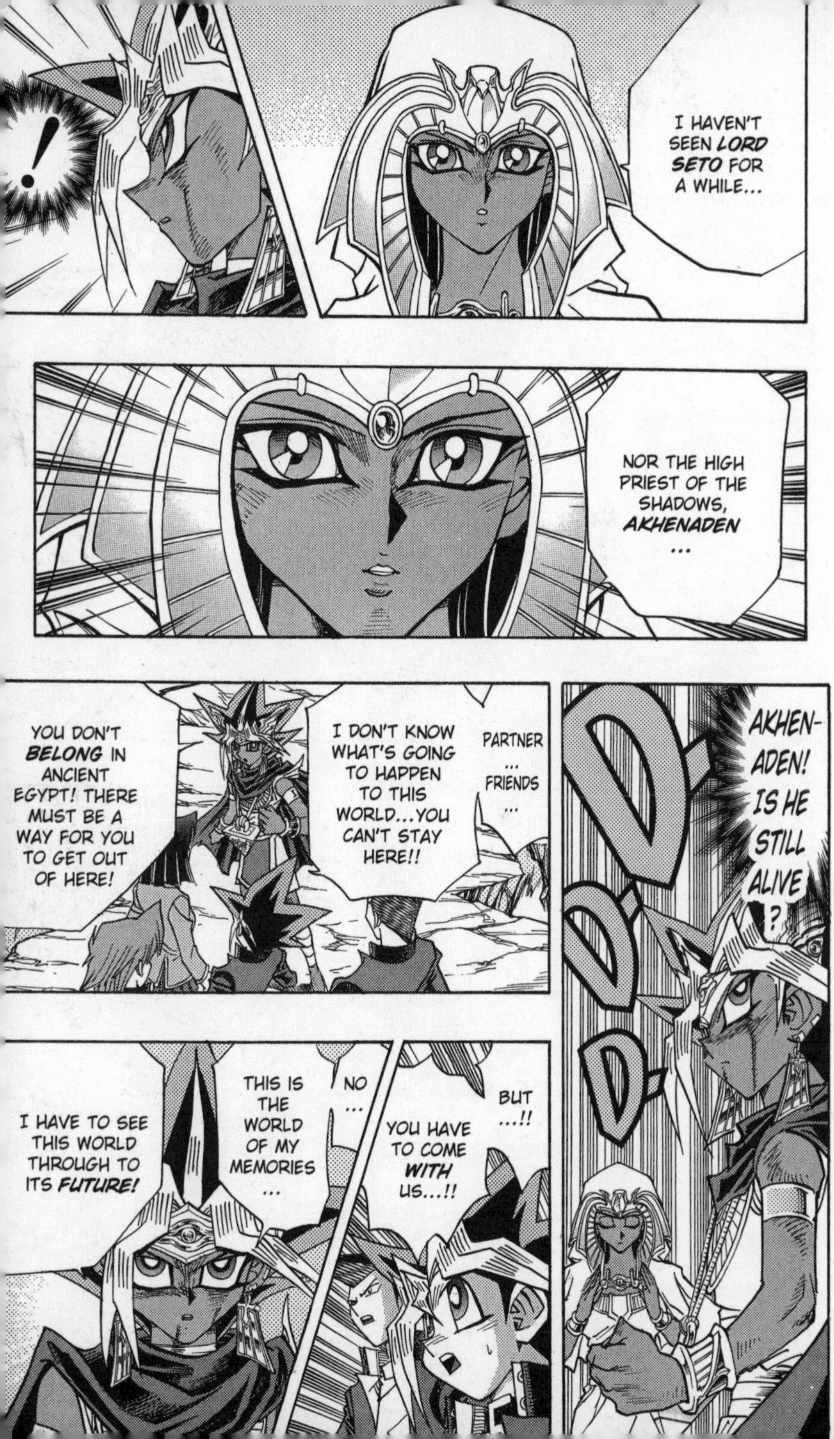
I HAVEN'T SEEN LORD SETO FOR A WHILE...
!
NOR THE HIGH PRIEST OF THE SHADOWS, AKHENADEN ...
AKHEN-ADEN! IS HE STILL ALIVE?
PARTNER ... FRIENDS ...
I DON'T KNOW WHAT'S GOING TO HAPPEN TO THIS WORLD...YOU CAN'T STAY HERE!!
YOU DON'T BELONG IN ANCIENT EGYPT! THERE MUST BE A WAY FOR YOU TO GET OUT OF HERE!
BUT ...!!
YOU HAVE TO COME WITH US...!!
NO ...
THIS IS THE WORLD OF MY MEMORIES ...
I HAVE TO SEE THIS WORLD THROUGH TO ITS FUTURE!

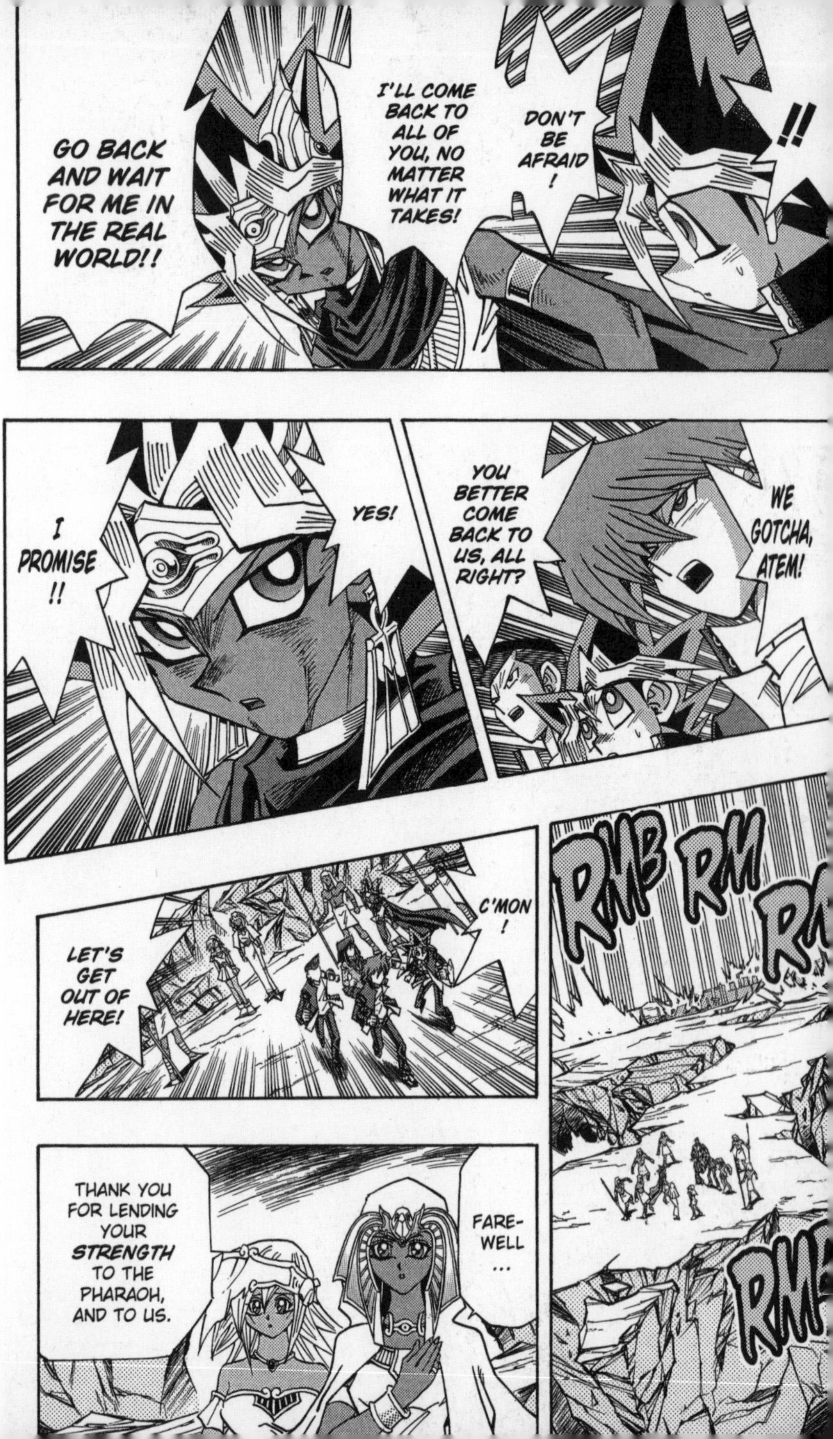
!!
DON'T BE AFRAID!
I'LL COME BACK TO ALL OF YOU, NO MATTER WHAT IT TAKES!
GO BACK AND WAIT FOR ME IN THE REAL WORLD!!
WE GOTCHA, ATEM!
YOU BETTER COME BACK TO US, ALL RIGHT?
YES!
I PROMISE!!
RMB RM
C'MON!
LET'S GET OUT OF HERE!
FARE-WELL...
THANK YOU FOR LENDING YOUR STRENGTH TO THE PHARAOH, AND TO US.

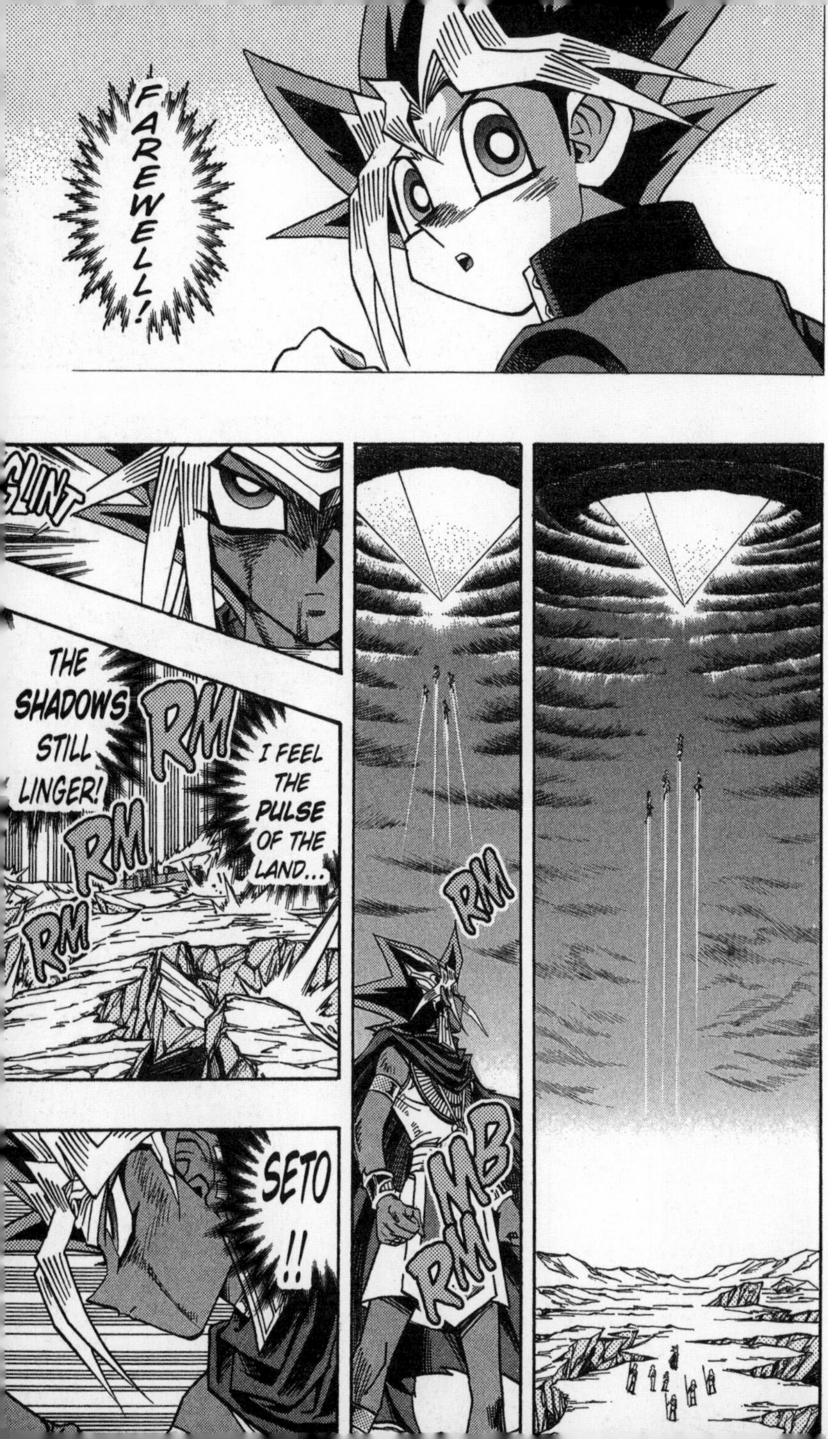
FAREWELL!
RM
RMB
RM
GLINT
I FEEL THE PULSE OF THE LAND...
THE SHADOWS STILL LINGER!
RM
RM
RM
SETO!!

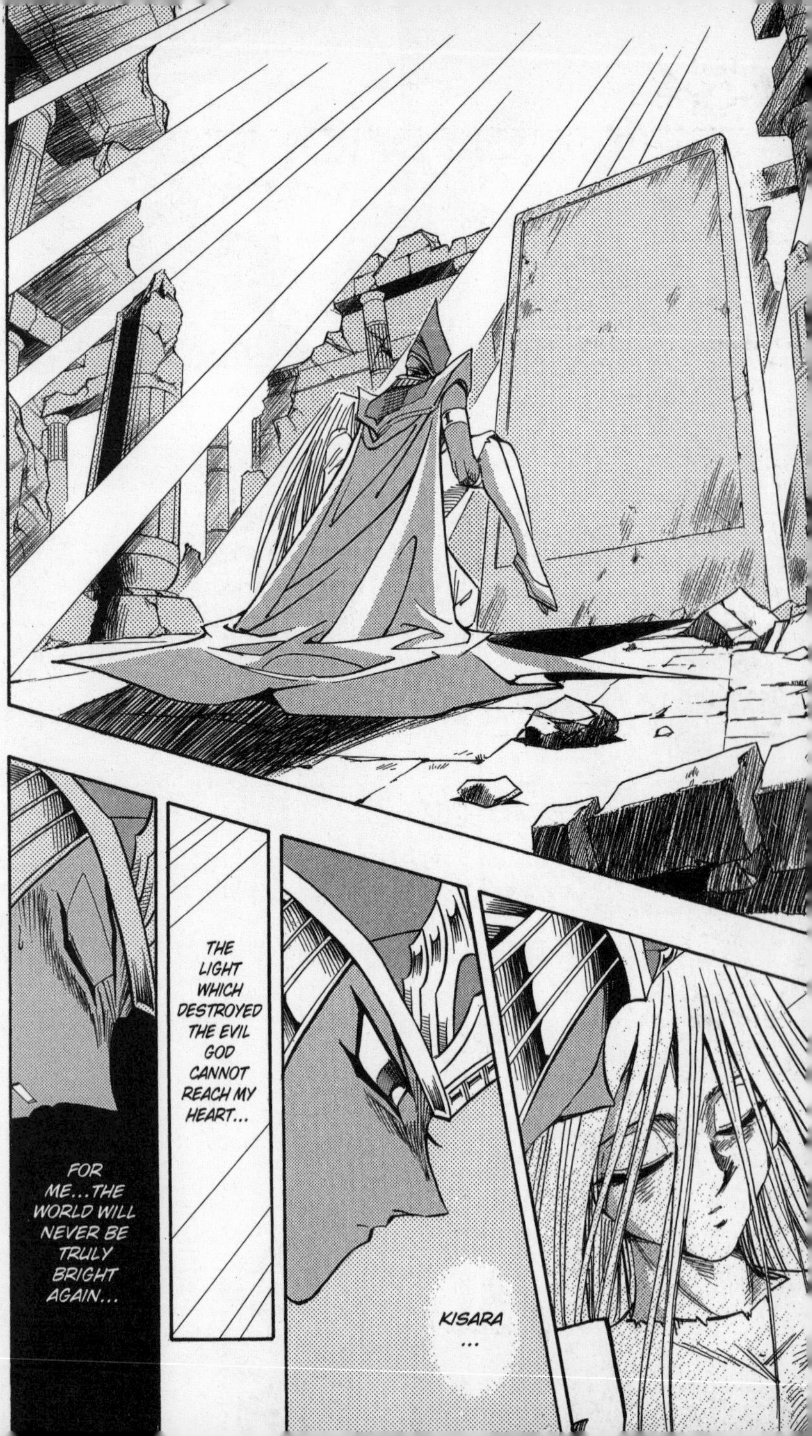
KISARA ...
THE LIGHT WHICH DESTROYED THE EVIL GOD CANNOT REACH MY HEART...
FOR ME...THE WORLD WILL NEVER BE TRULY BRIGHT AGAIN...

READ THIS WAY

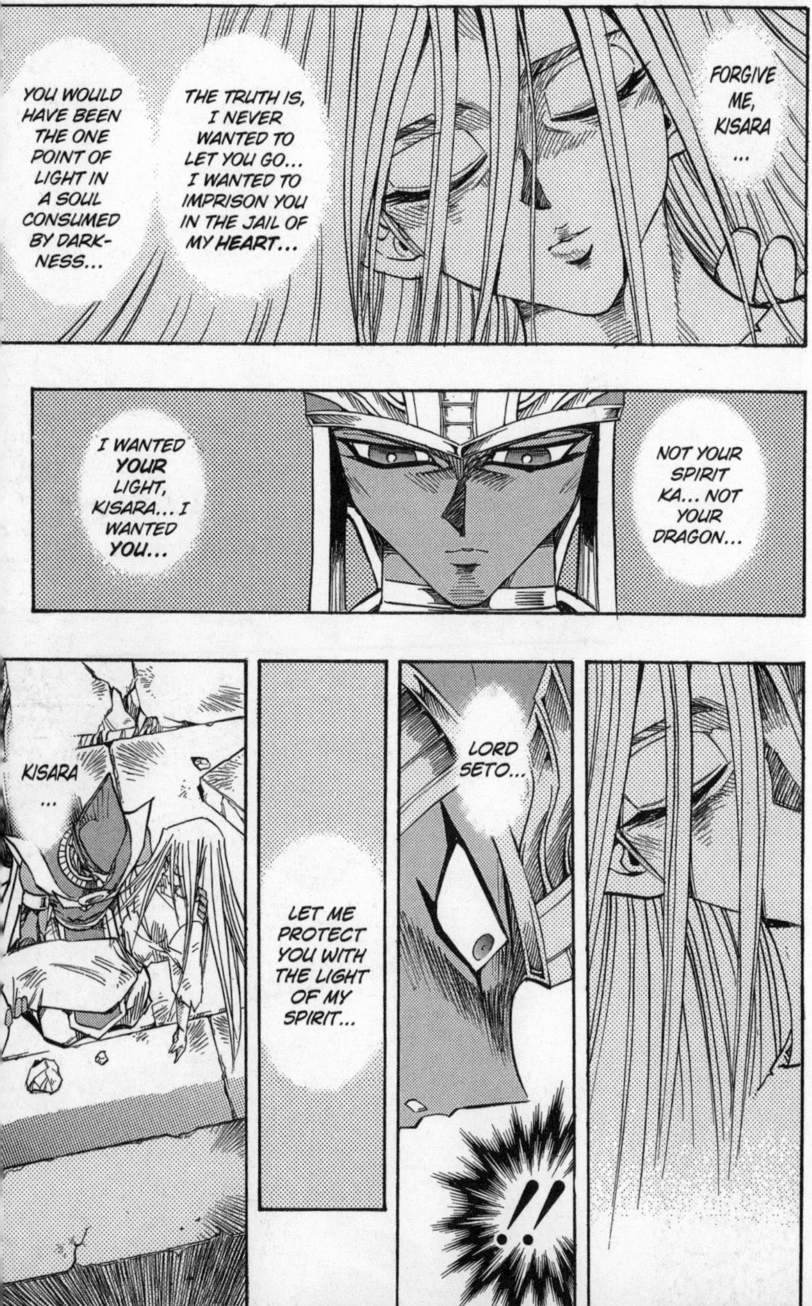
FORGIVE ME, KISARA...
THE TRUTH IS, I NEVER WANTED TO LET YOU GO... I WANTED TO IMPRISON YOU IN THE JAIL OF MY HEART...
YOU WOULD HAVE BEEN THE ONE POINT OF LIGHT IN A SOUL CONSUMED BY DARK-NESS...
NOT YOUR SPIRIT KA... NOT YOUR DRAGON...
I WANTED YOUR LIGHT, KISARA... I WANTED YOU...
LORD SETO...
!!
LET ME PROTECT YOU WITH THE LIGHT OF MY SPIRIT...
KISARA...

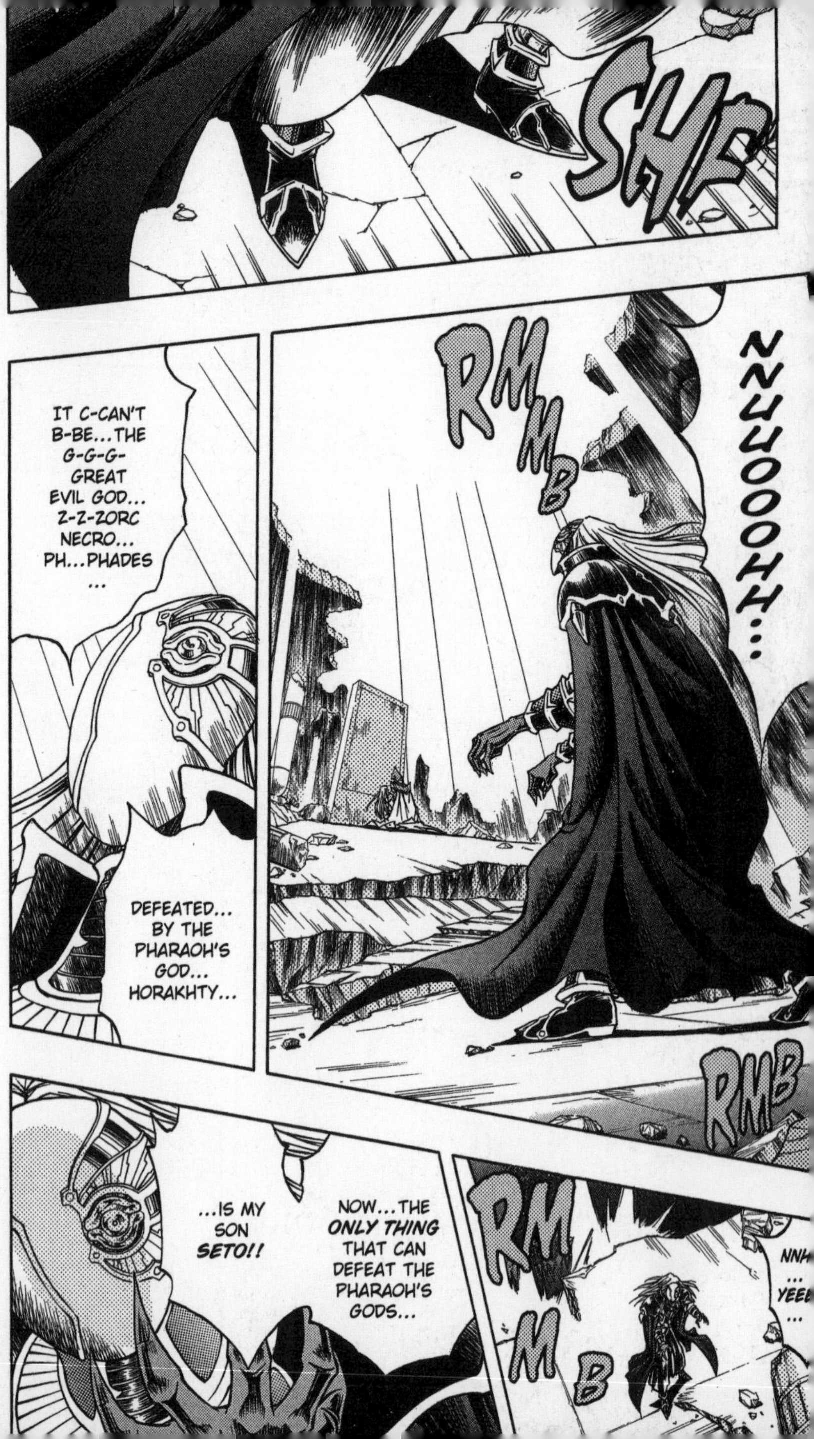
SHF
RMMB
NNUUOOOOHH...
IT C-CAN'T B-BE...THE G-G-G-GREAT EVIL GOD... Z-Z-ZORC NECRO... PH...PHADES ...
DEFEATED... BY THE PHARAOH'S GOD... HORAKHTY...
RMB
NNH ... YEE ...
RMMB
NOW...THE ONLY THING THAT CAN DEFEAT THE PHARAOH'S GODS...
...IS MY SON SETO!!

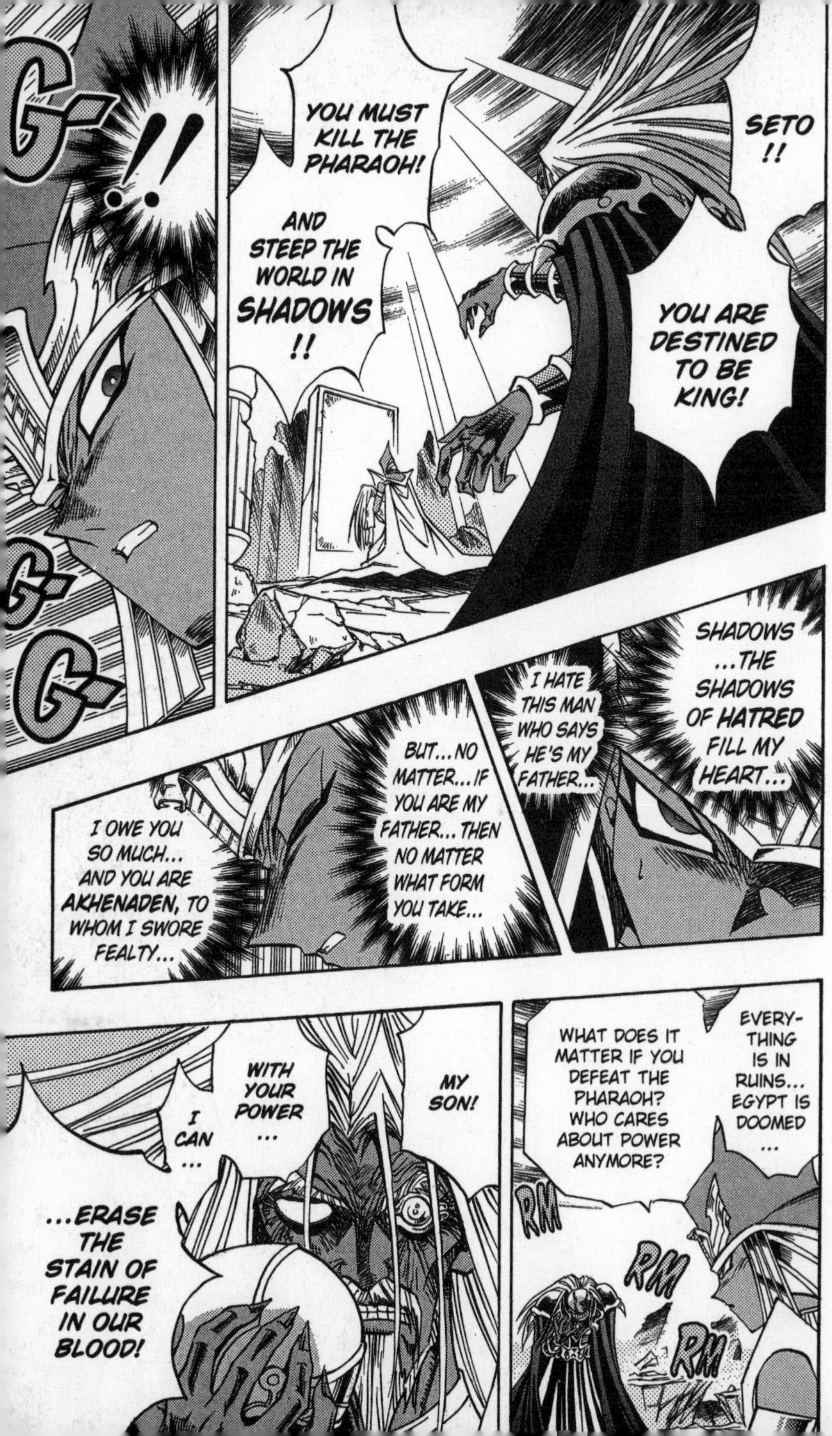
SETO !!
YOU ARE DESTINED TO BE KING!
YOU MUST KILL THE PHARAOH!
AND STEEP THE WORLD IN SHADOWS !!
G!!
G
G
SHADOWS ...THE SHADOWS OF HATRED FILL MY HEART...
I HATE THIS MAN WHO SAYS HE'S MY FATHER...
BUT... NO MATTER... IF YOU ARE MY FATHER... THEN NO MATTER WHAT FORM YOU TAKE...
I OWE YOU SO MUCH... AND YOU ARE AKHENADEN, TO WHOM I SWORE FEALTY...
EVERY-THING IS IN RUINS... EGYPT IS DOOMED ...
WHAT DOES IT MATTER IF YOU DEFEAT THE PHARAOH? WHO CARES ABOUT POWER ANYMORE?
RM
RM
RM
MY SON!
WITH YOUR POWER ...
I CAN ...
...ERASE THE STAIN OF FAILURE IN OUR BLOOD!

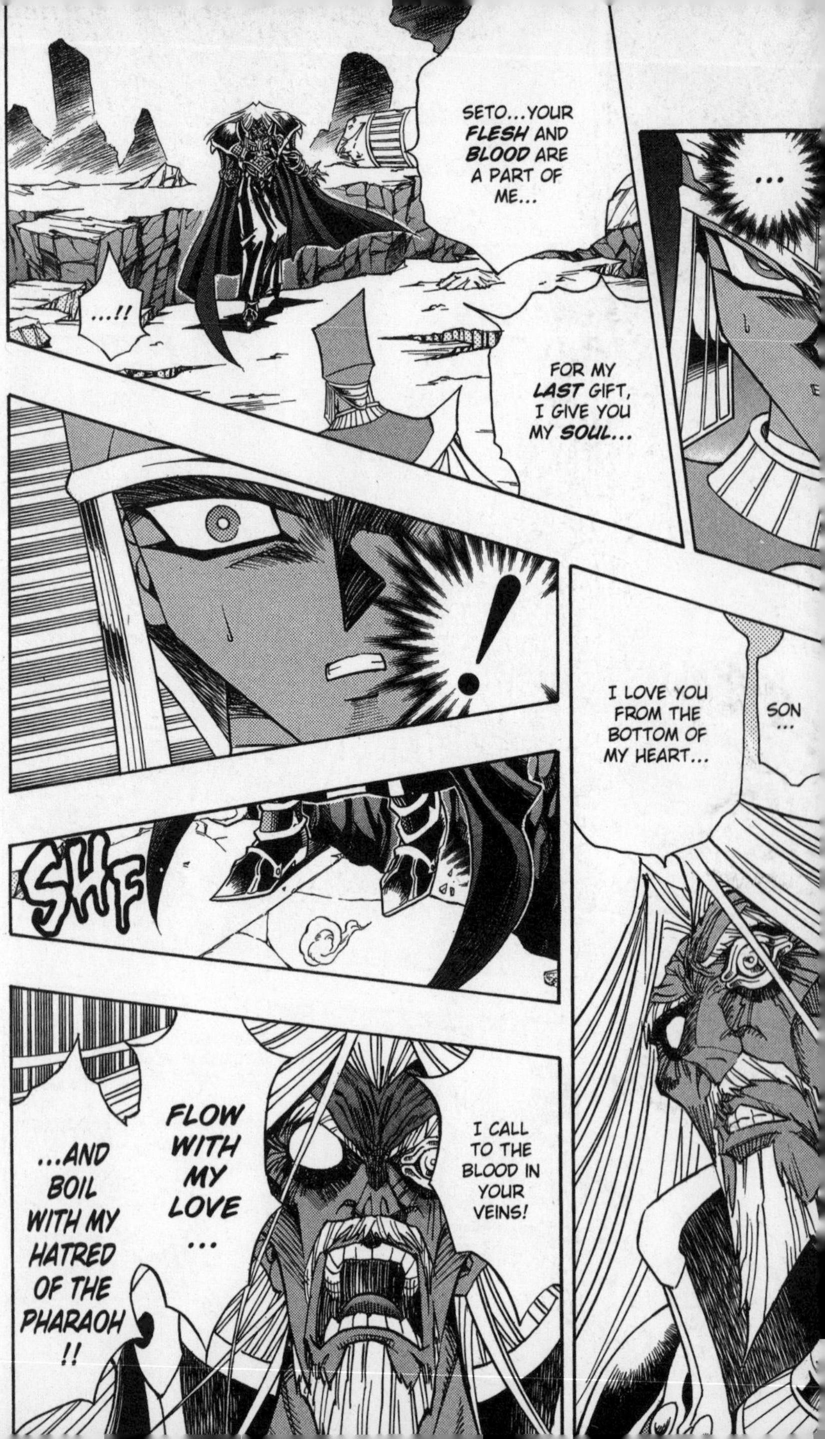
...
SETO...YOUR FLESH AND BLOOD ARE A PART OF ME...
...!!
FOR MY LAST GIFT, I GIVE YOU MY SOUL...
SON...
I LOVE YOU FROM THE BOTTOM OF MY HEART...
!
SHF
I CALL TO THE BLOOD IN YOUR VEINS!
FLOW WITH MY LOVE...
...AND BOIL WITH MY HATRED OF THE PHARAOH!!

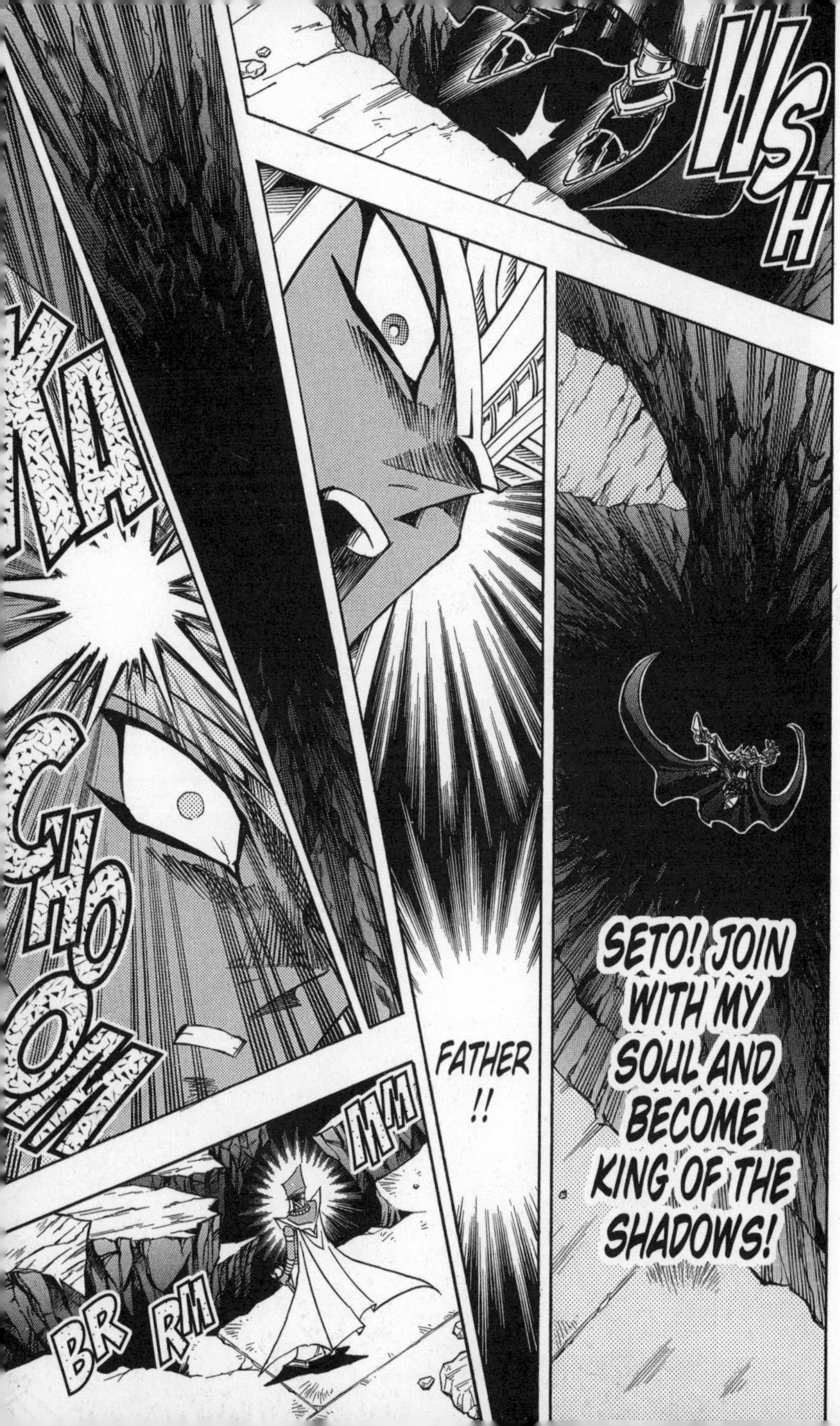
WHSH
SETO! JOIN WITH MY SOUL AND BECOME KING OF THE SHADOWS!
FATHER !!
KACHOOM
BRRMMM

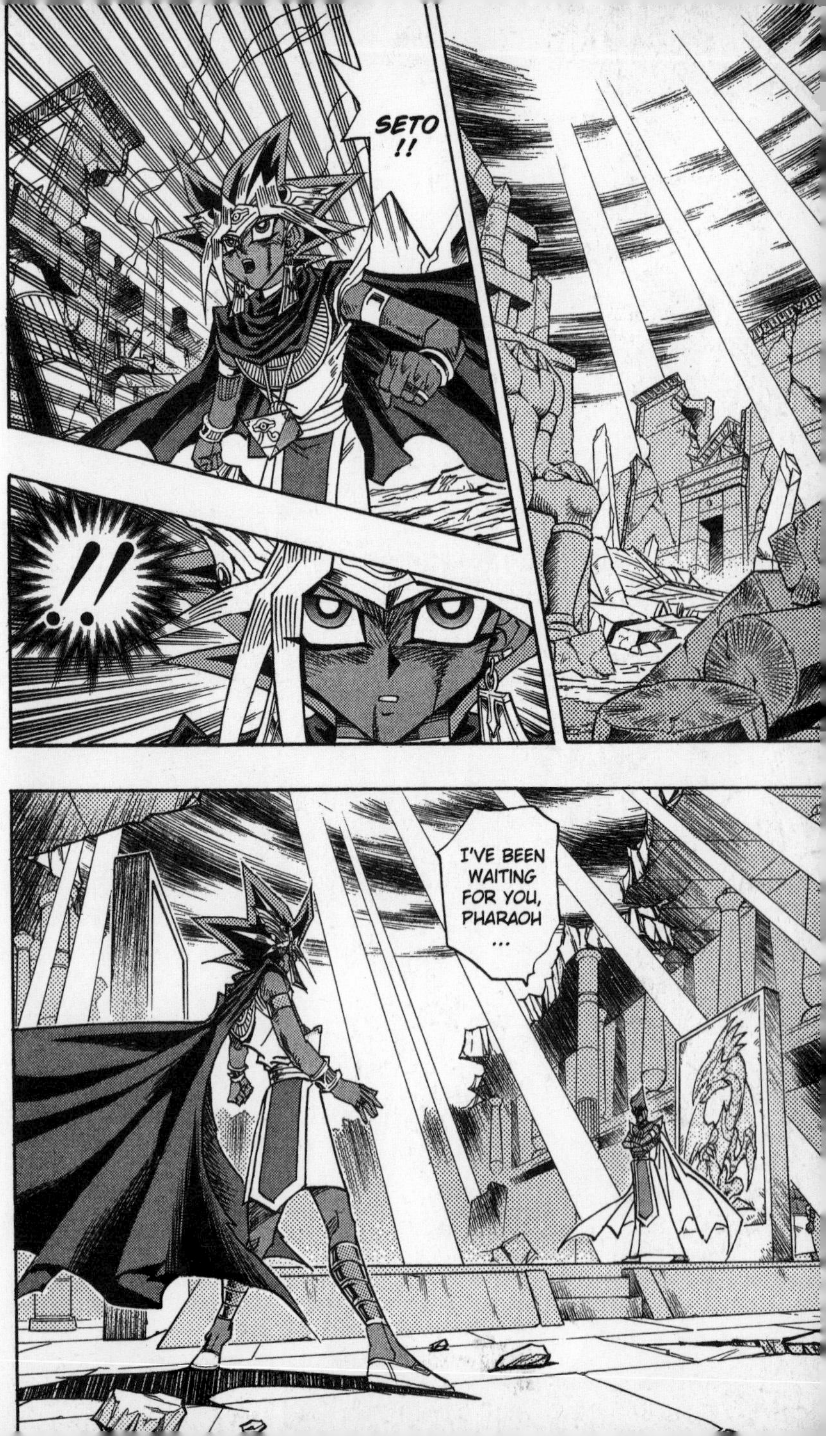
SETO !!
!!
I'VE BEEN WAITING FOR YOU, PHARAOH ...

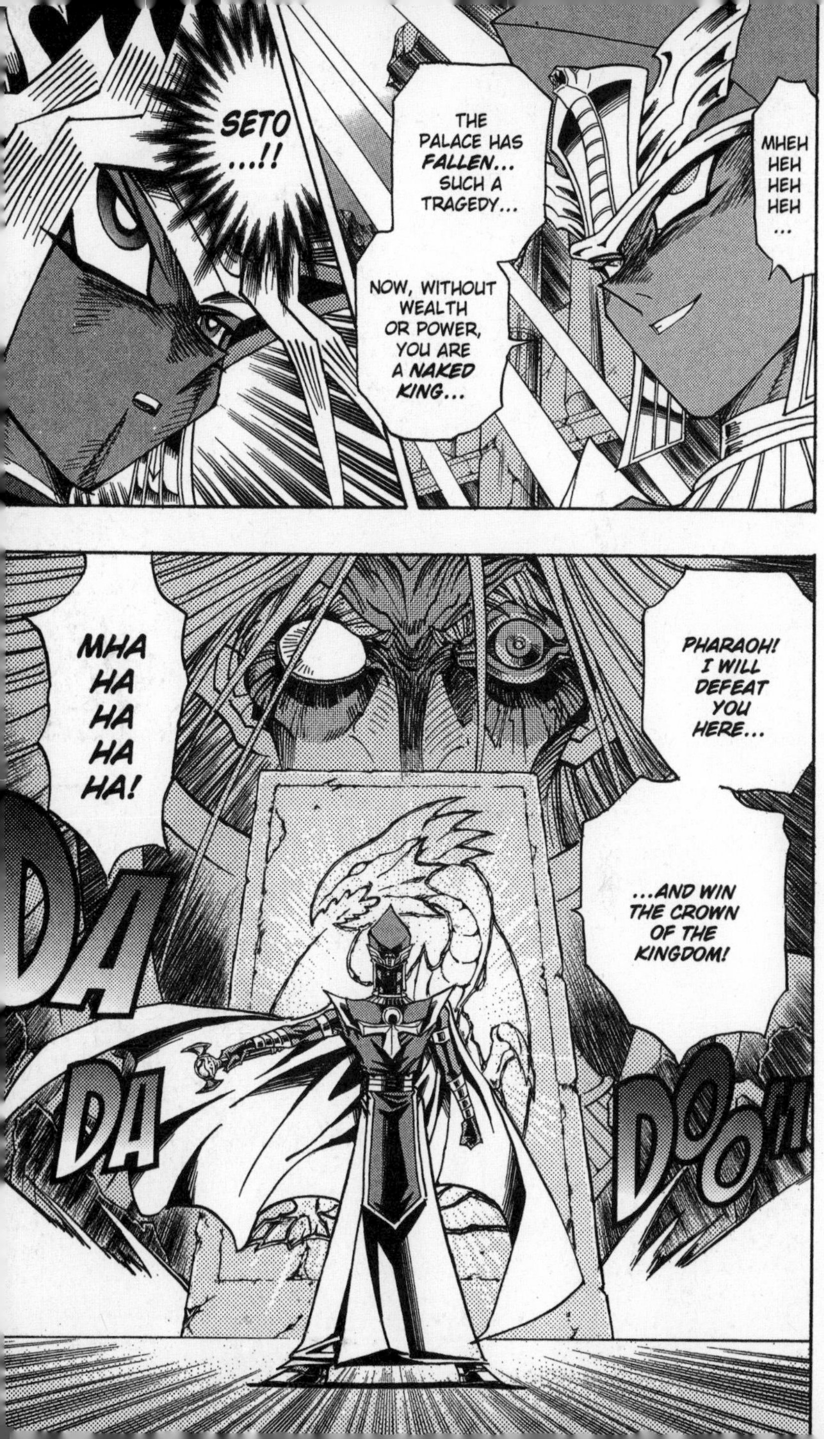
MHEH HEH HEH HEH...
THE PALACE HAS FALLEN... SUCH A TRAGEDY...
NOW, WITHOUT WEALTH OR POWER, YOU ARE A NAKED KING...
SETO ...!!
PHARAOH! I WILL DEFEAT YOU HERE...
...AND WIN THE CROWN OF THE KINGDOM!
MHA HA HA HA HA!
DOO
DA
DA

Duel 57: White Dragon, Black Magician

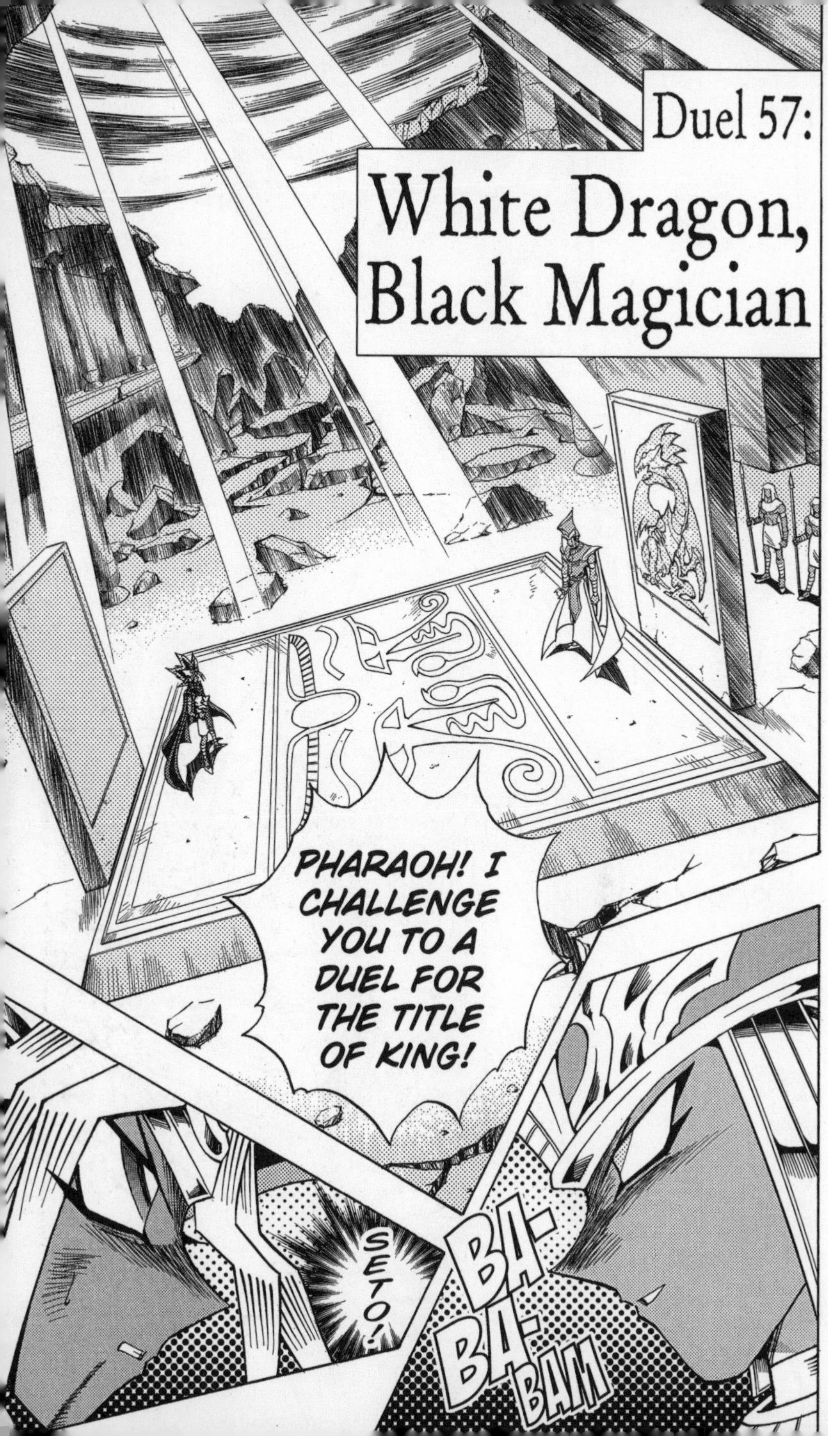
PHARAOH! I CHALLENGE YOU TO A DUEL FOR THE TITLE OF KING!
BA-BA-BAM
SETO!

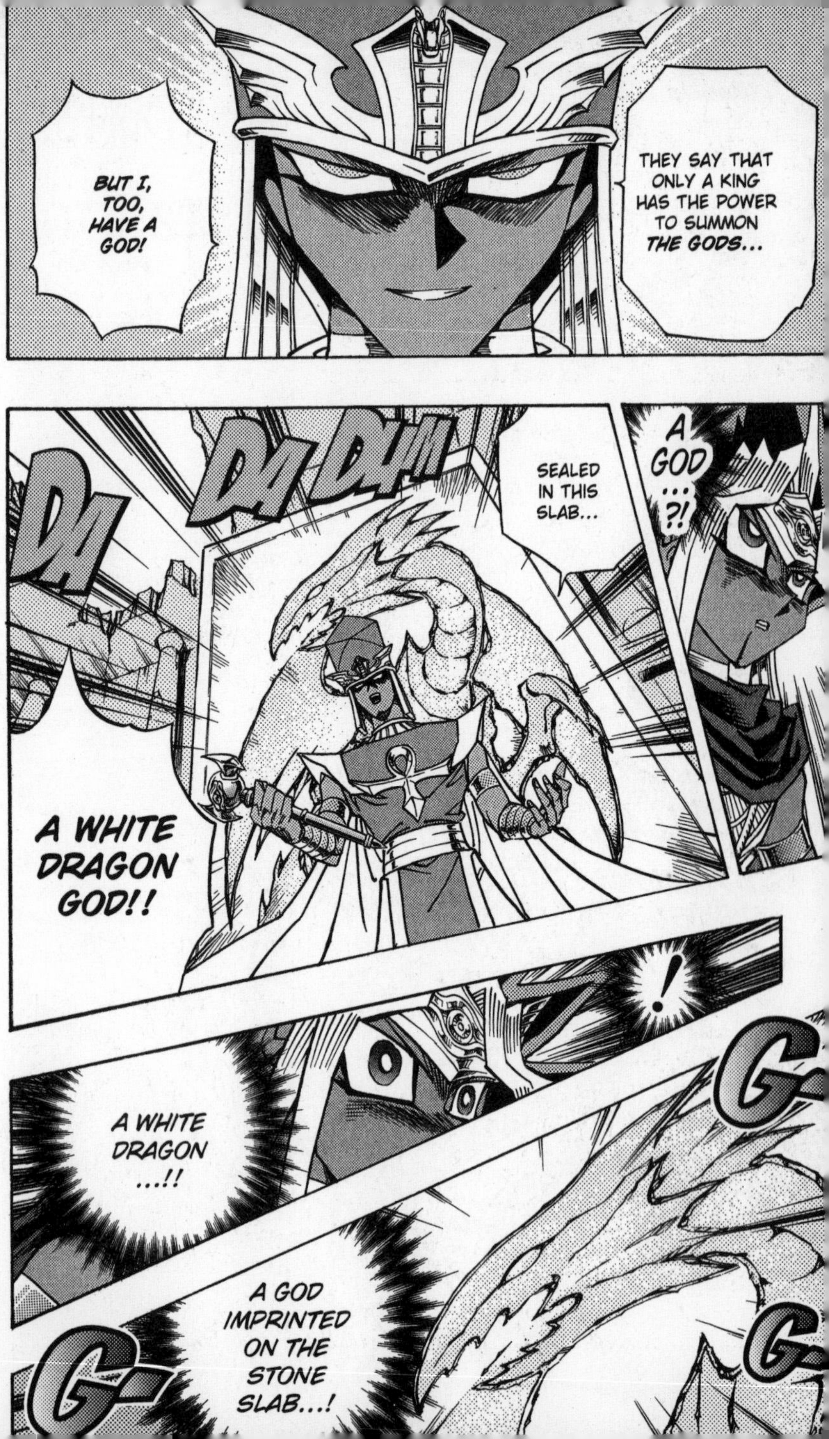
THEY SAY THAT ONLY A KING HAS THE POWER TO SUMMON THE GODS...
BUT I, TOO, HAVE A GOD!
A GOD ...?!
SEALED IN THIS SLAB...
DA DA DUM
A WHITE DRAGON GOD!!
!
G-
A WHITE DRAGON ...!!
A GOD IMPRINTED ON THE STONE SLAB...!
G-
G-

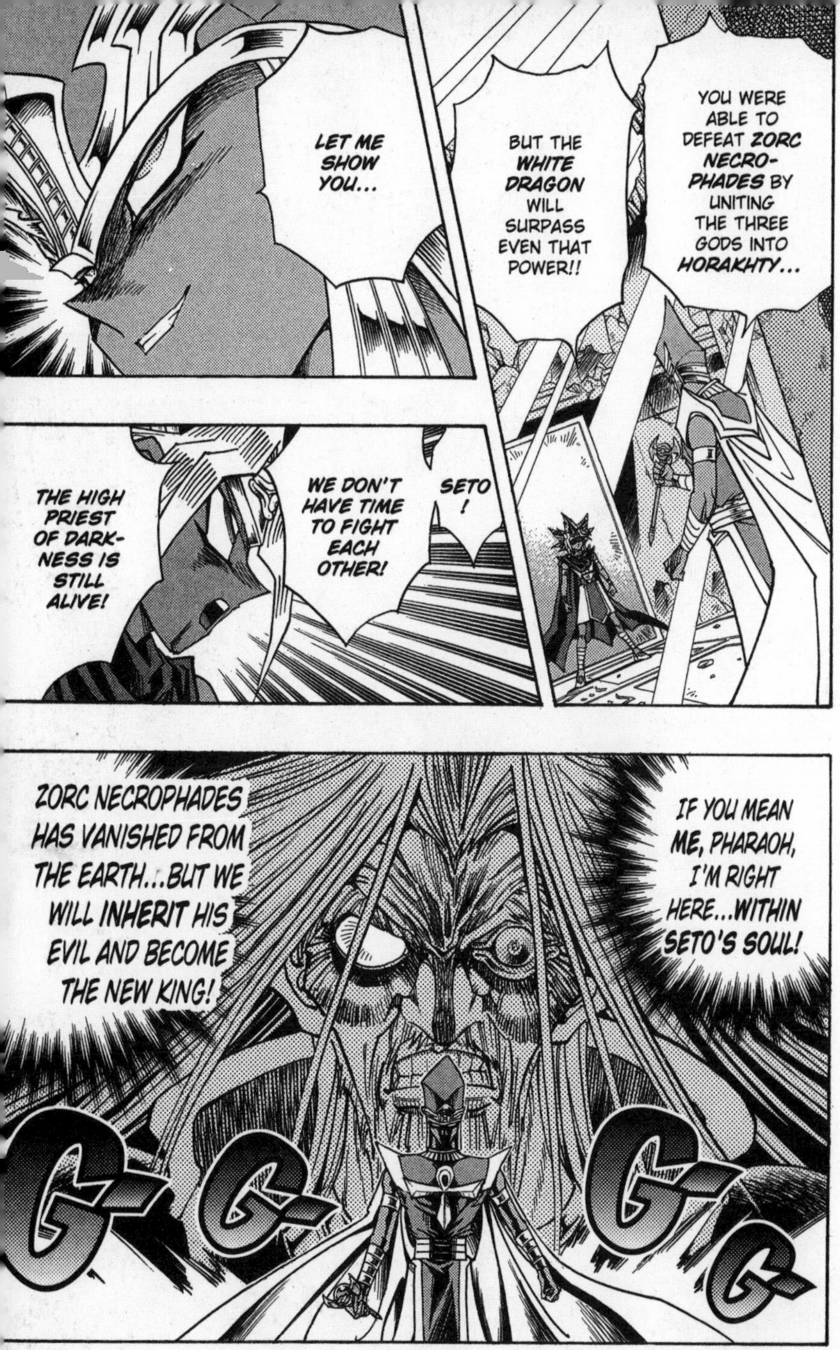
YOU WERE ABLE TO DEFEAT ZORC NECROPHADES BY UNITING THE THREE GODS INTO HORAKHTY...
BUT THE WHITE DRAGON WILL SURPASS EVEN THAT POWER!!
LET ME SHOW YOU...
SETO!
WE DON'T HAVE TIME TO FIGHT EACH OTHER!
THE HIGH PRIEST OF DARKNESS IS STILL ALIVE!
IF YOU MEAN ME, PHARAOH, I'M RIGHT HERE...WITHIN SETO'S SOUL!
ZORC NECROPHADES HAS VANISHED FROM THE EARTH...BUT WE WILL INHERIT HIS EVIL AND BECOME THE NEW KING!
G G G G G

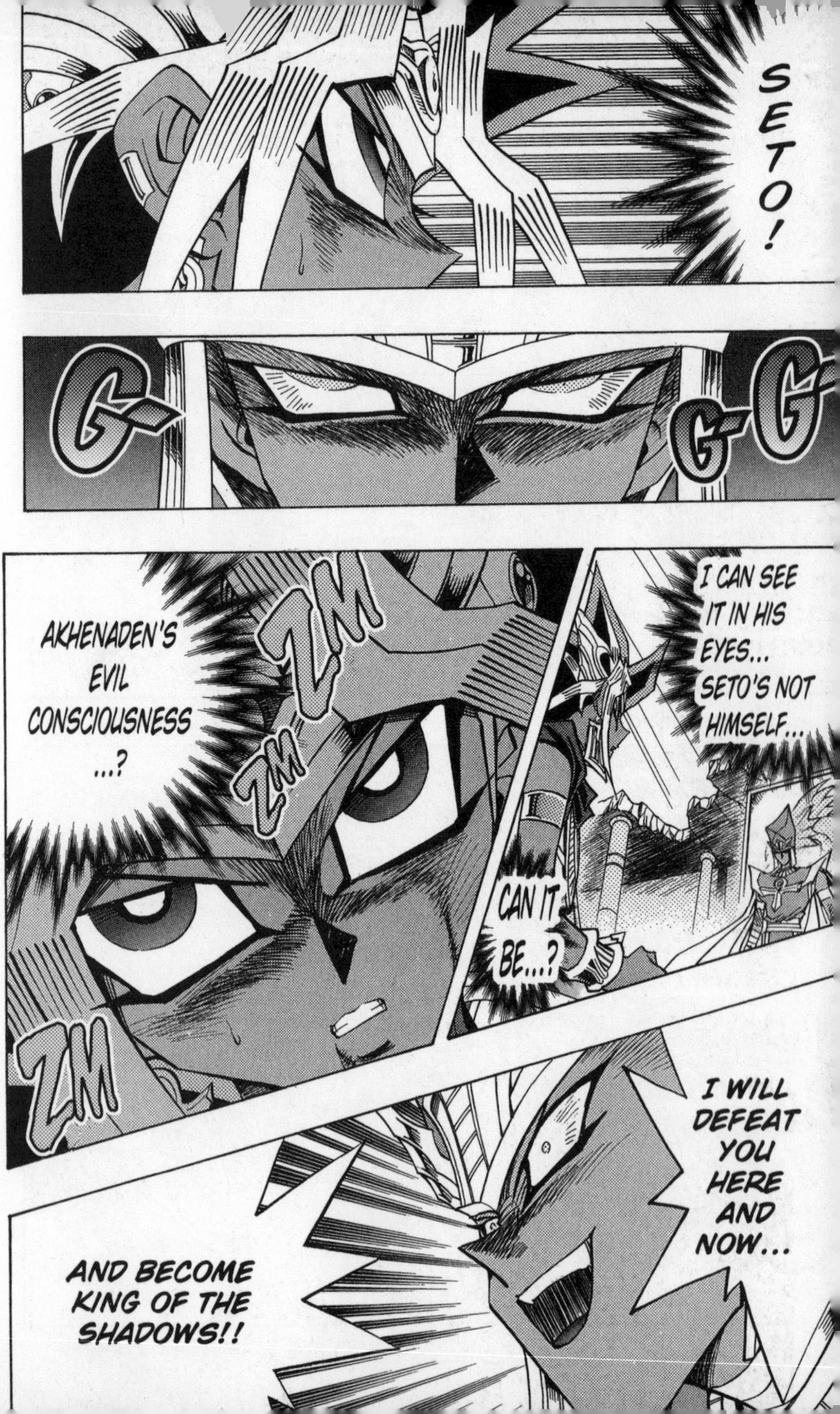
SETO!
GG
G
I CAN SEE IT IN HIS EYES... SETO'S NOT HIMSELF...
CAN IT BE...?
ZM ZM
AKHENADEN'S EVIL CONSCIOUSNESS ...?
ZM
ZM
I WILL DEFEAT YOU HERE AND NOW...
AND BECOME KING OF THE SHADOWS!!

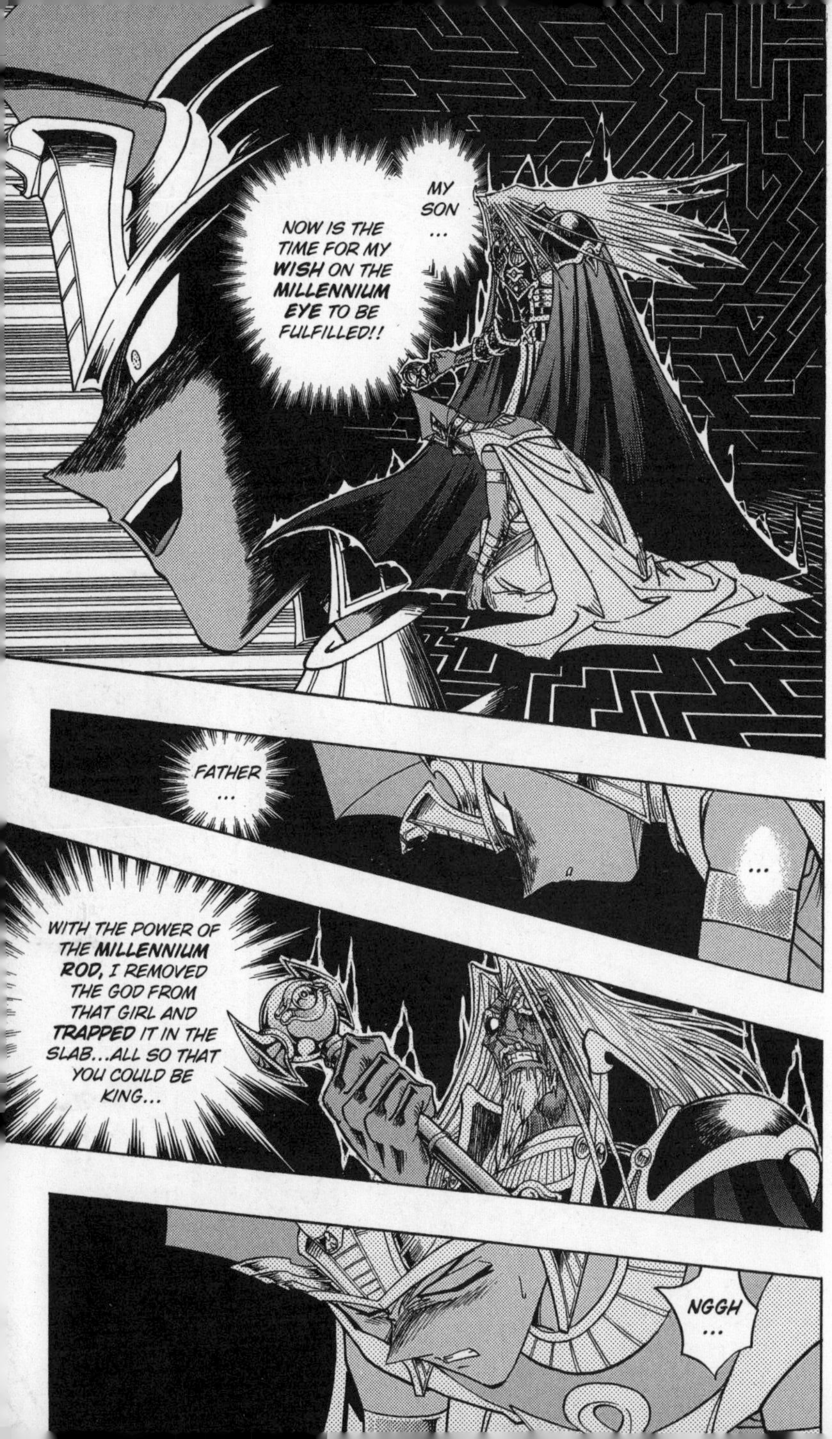
MY SON ...
NOW IS THE TIME FOR MY **WISH** ON THE **MILLENNIUM EYE** TO BE FULFILLED!!
...
FATHER ...
WITH THE POWER OF THE **MILLENNIUM ROD,** I REMOVED THE GOD FROM THAT GIRL AND **TRAPPED** IT IN THE SLAB...ALL SO THAT YOU COULD BE KING...
NGGH ...

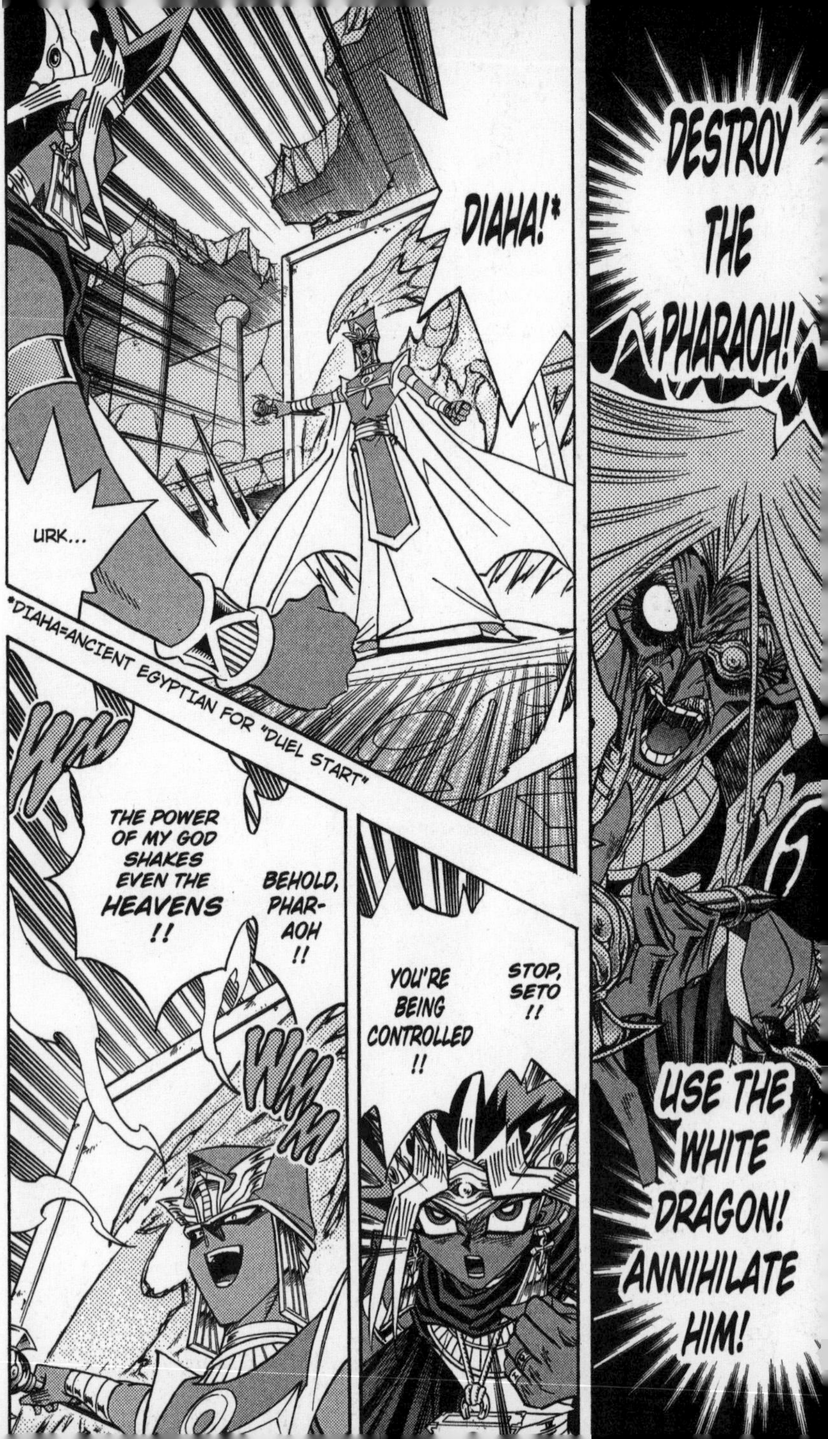
DESTROY THE PHARAOH!
USE THE WHITE DRAGON! ANNIHILATE HIM!
DIAHA!*
URK...
*DIAHA=ANCIENT EGYPTIAN FOR "DUEL START"
STOP, SETO!!
YOU'RE BEING CONTROLLED!!
BEHOLD, PHARAOH!!
THE POWER OF MY GOD SHAKES EVEN THE HEAVENS!!

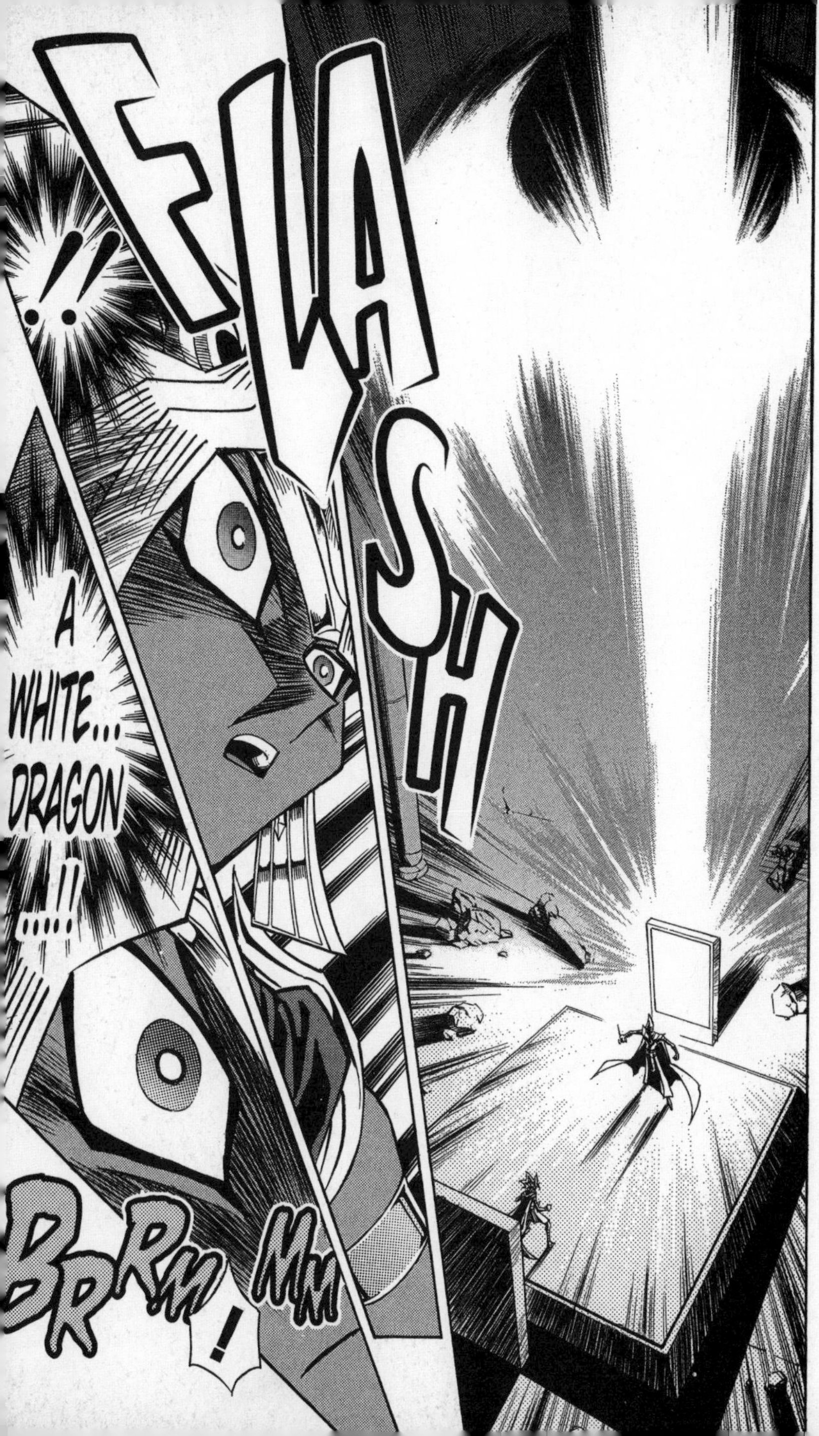
FLASH
!!
A WHITE... DRAGON ...!!
BRRMMM!

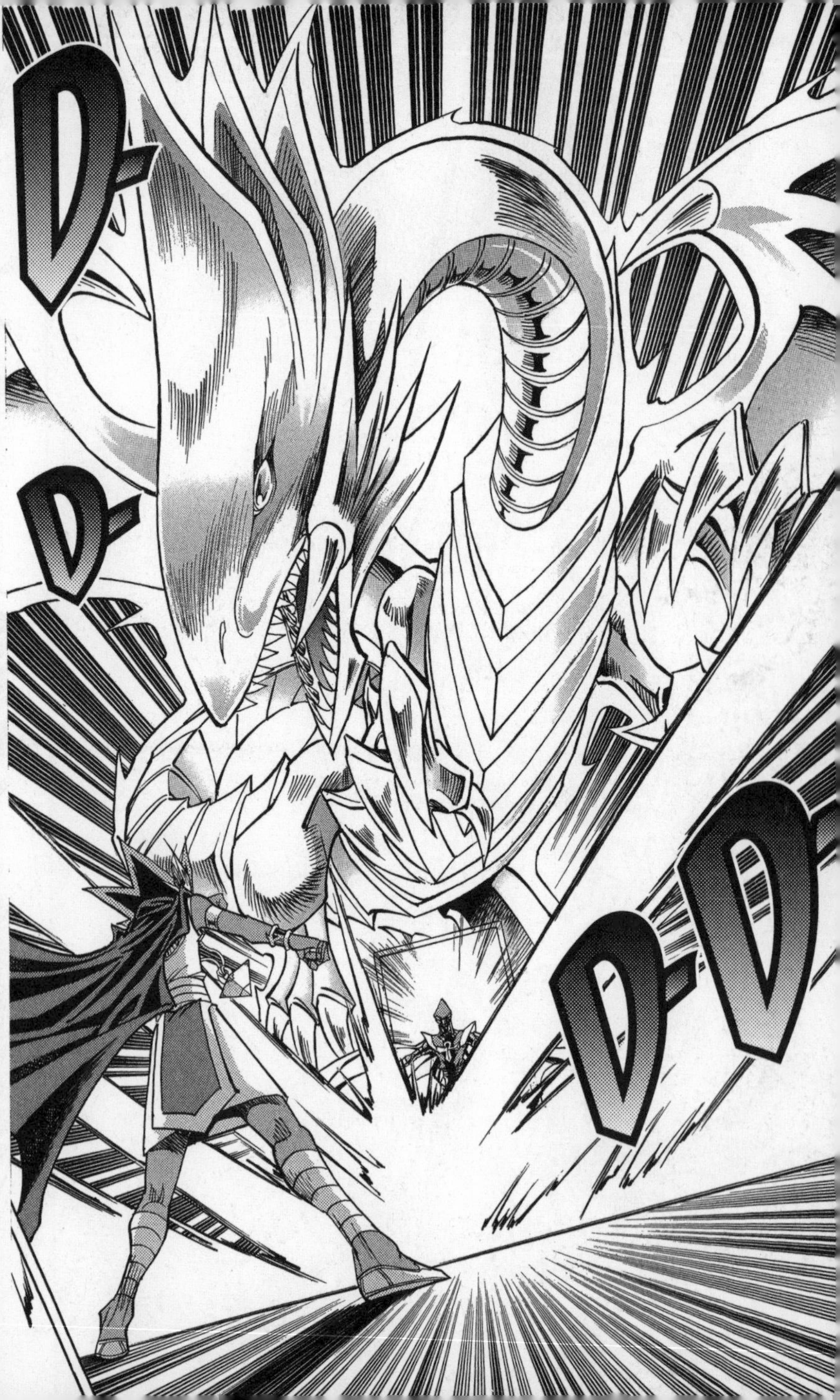
D-
D-
D-D-

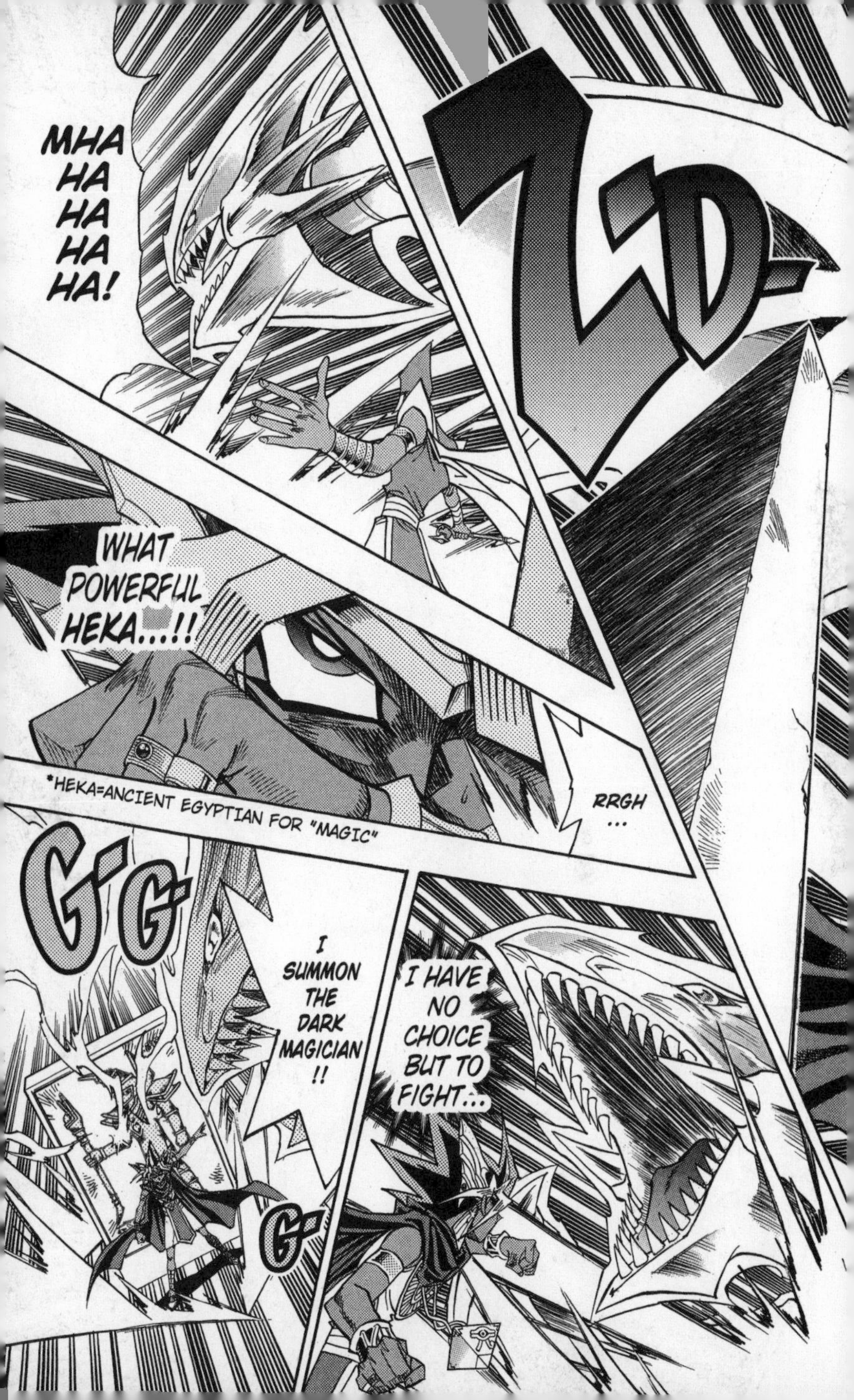
ZD
MHA HA HA HA HA!
WHAT POWERFUL HEKA...!!
*HEKA=ANCIENT EGYPTIAN FOR "MAGIC"
RRGH ...
I HAVE NO CHOICE BUT TO FIGHT...
I SUMMON THE DARK MAGICIAN !!
GG
G

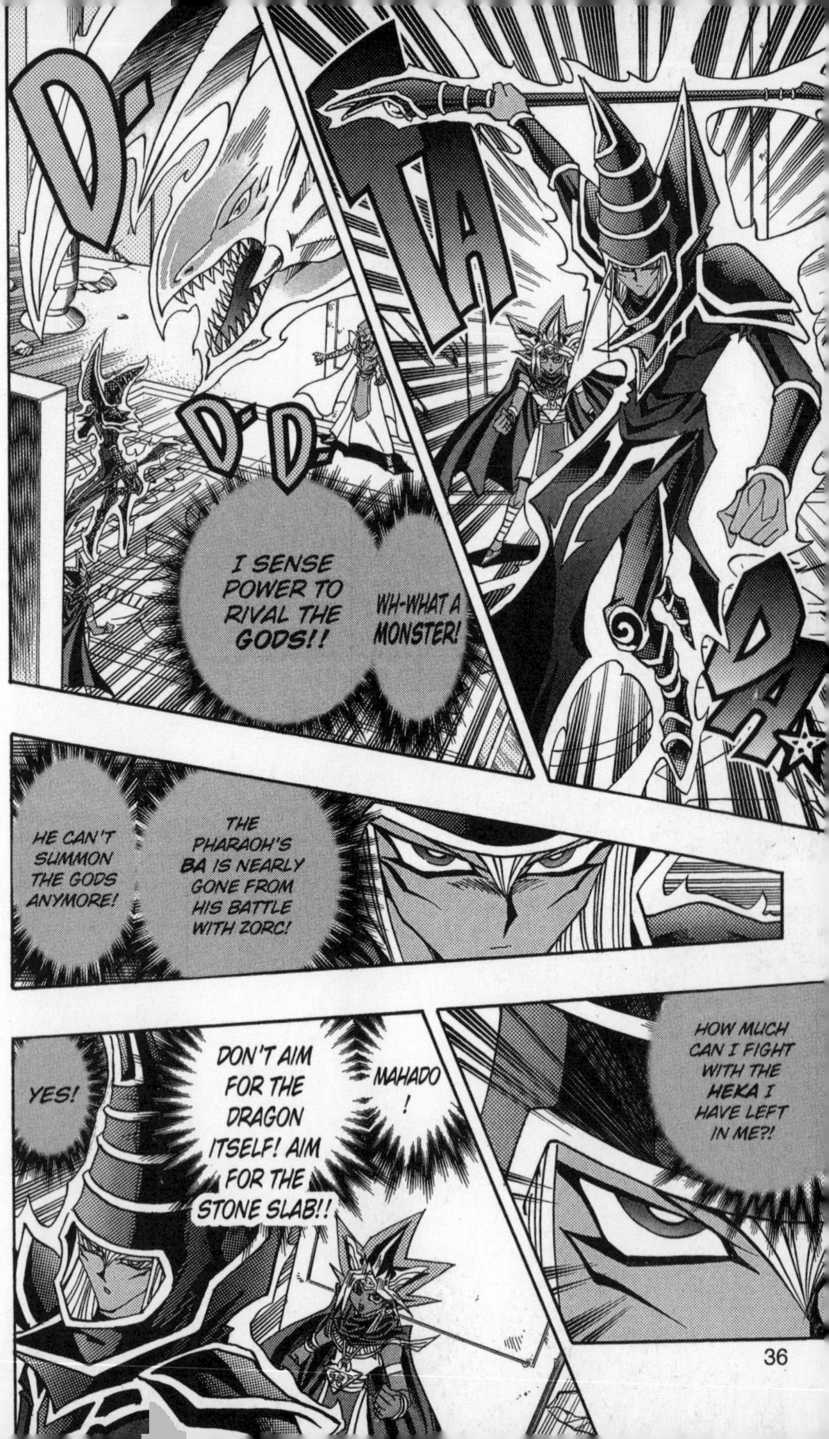
TA
DA☆
D-
D-D
WH-WHAT A MONSTER!
I SENSE POWER TO RIVAL THE GODS!!
THE PHARAOH'S BA IS NEARLY GONE FROM HIS BATTLE WITH ZORC!
HE CAN'T SUMMON THE GODS ANYMORE!
HOW MUCH CAN I FIGHT WITH THE HEKA I HAVE LEFT IN ME?!
MAHADO!
DON'T AIM FOR THE DRAGON ITSELF! AIM FOR THE STONE SLAB!!
YES!

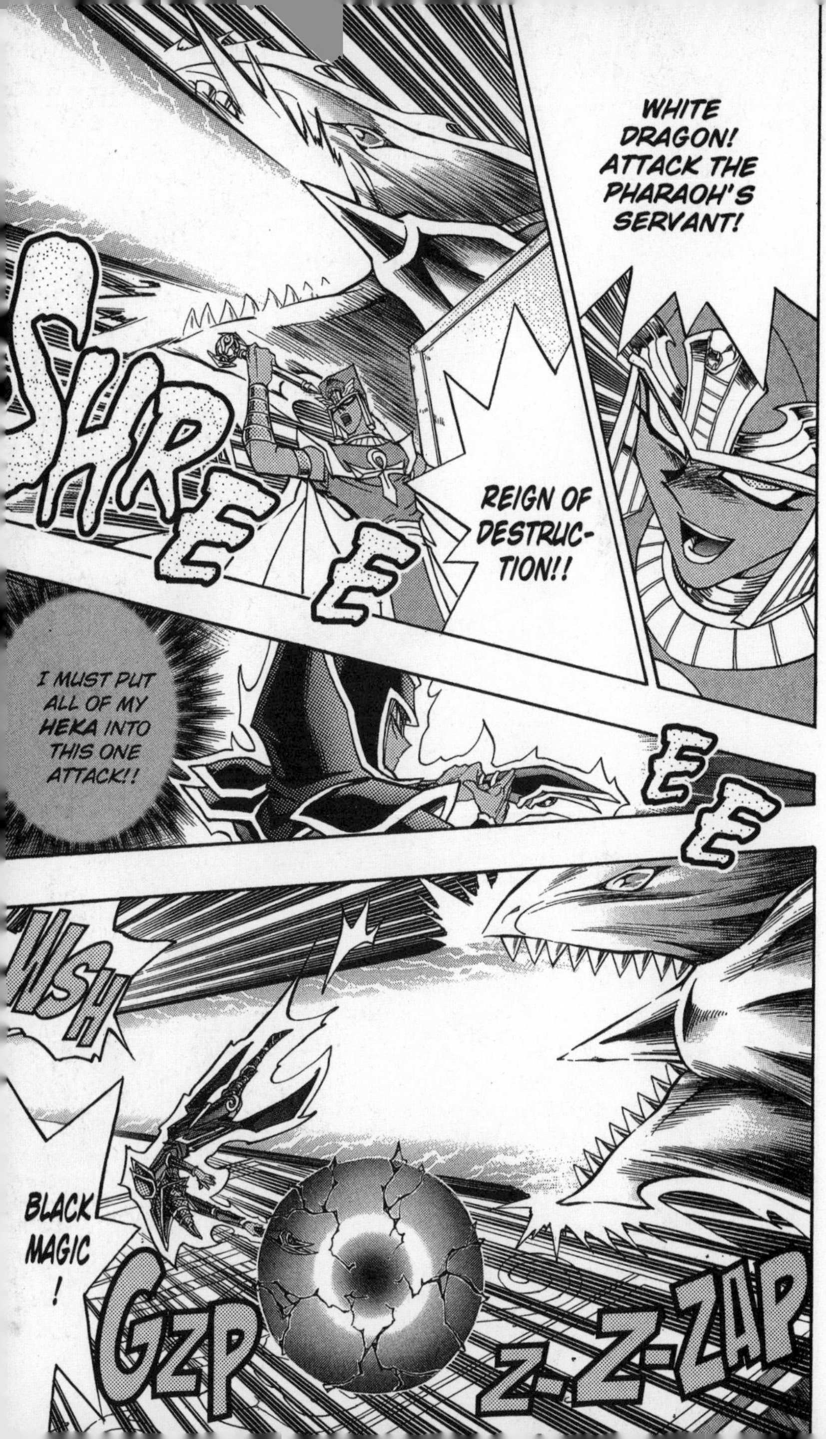
WHITE DRAGON! ATTACK THE PHARAOH'S SERVANT!
REIGN OF DESTRUCTION!!
SHREE
EE
I MUST PUT ALL OF MY HEKA INTO THIS ONE ATTACK!!
WUSH
BLACK MAGIC!
GZP
Z-Z-ZAP

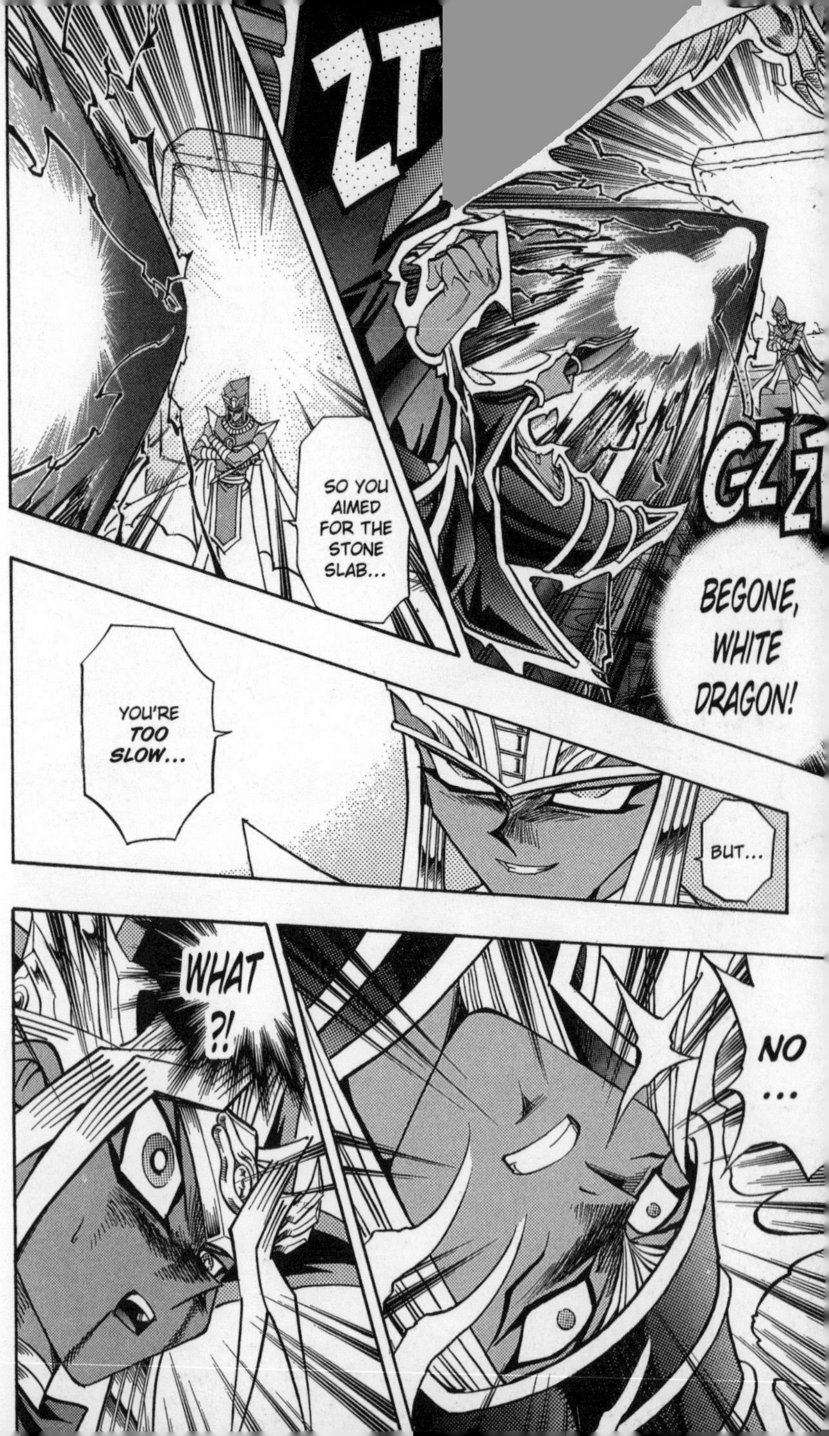
ZT
GZZ
BEGONE, WHITE DRAGON!
SO YOU AIMED FOR THE STONE SLAB...
BUT...
YOU'RE *TOO SLOW*...
NO...
WHAT?!

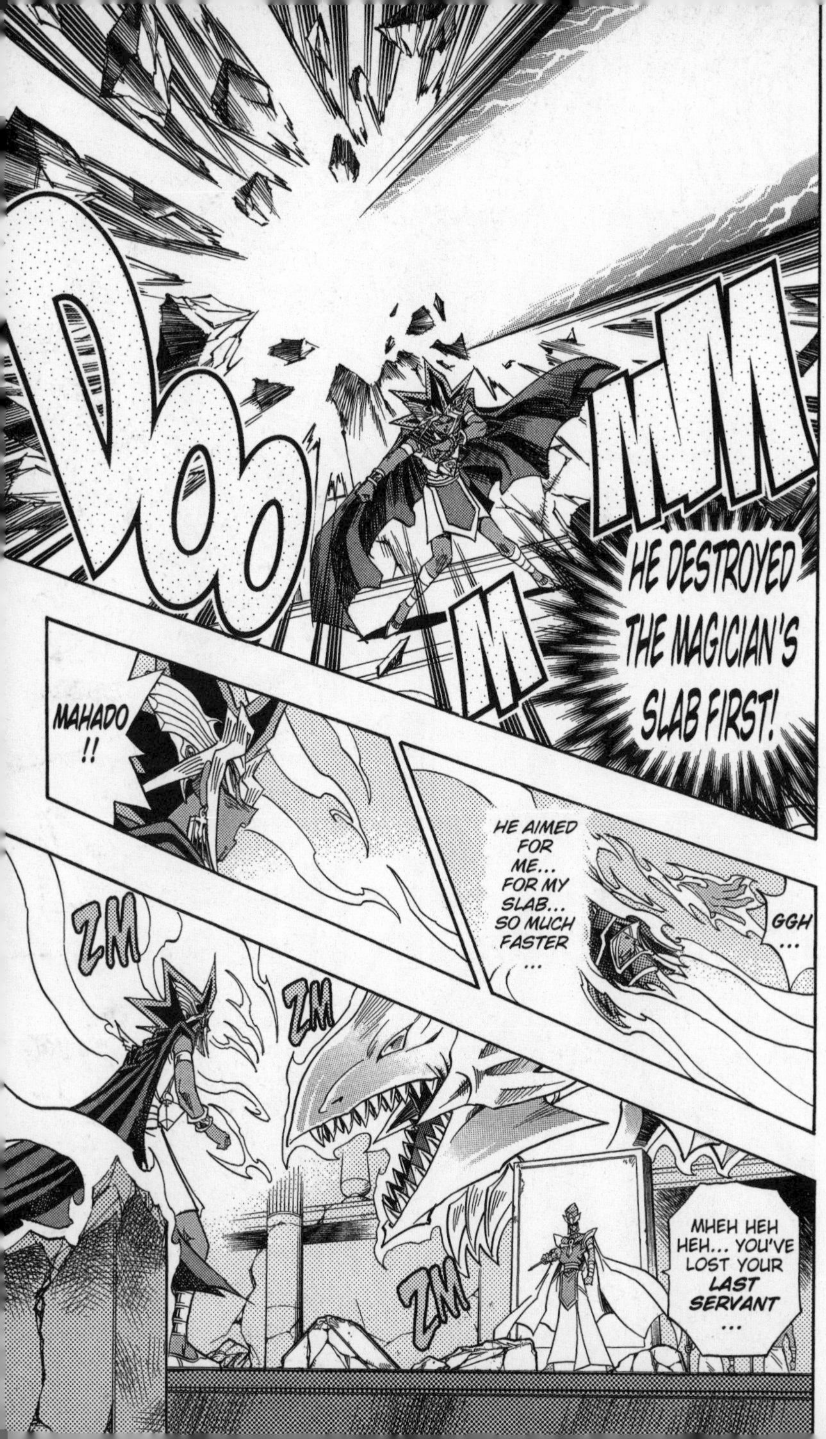
HE DESTROYED THE MAGICIAN'S SLAB FIRST!
DOOOMMM
GGH ...
HE AIMED FOR ME... FOR MY SLAB... SO MUCH FASTER ...
MAHADO !!
MHEH HEH HEH... YOU'VE LOST YOUR *LAST SERVANT* ...
ZM
ZM
ZM

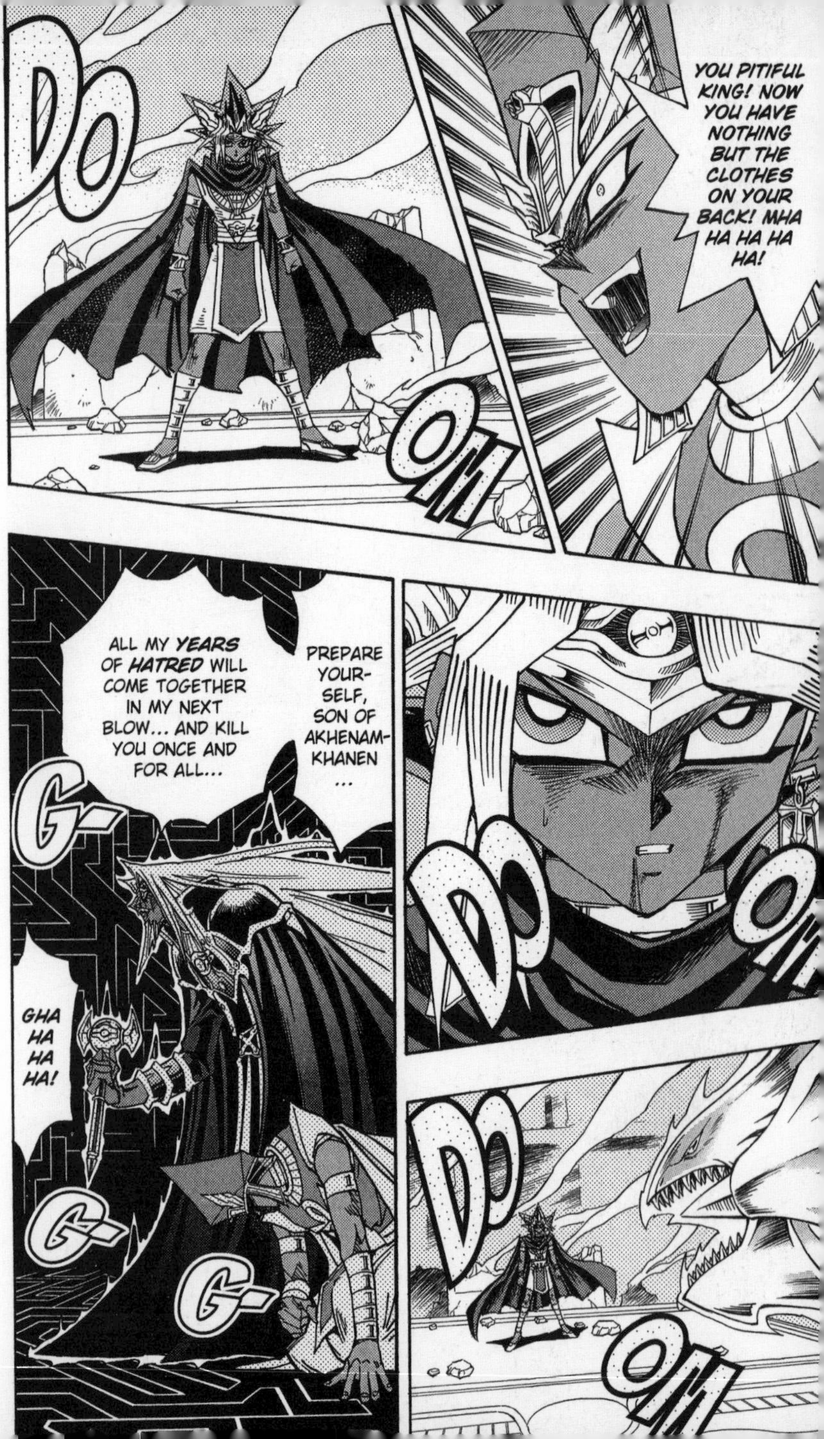

YOU PITIFUL KING! NOW YOU HAVE NOTHING BUT THE CLOTHES ON YOUR BACK! MHA HA HA HA HA!
DO
OM
DO
OM
DO
OM
PREPARE YOURSELF, SON OF AKHENAMKHANEN...
ALL MY *YEARS* OF *HATRED* WILL COME TOGETHER IN MY NEXT BLOW... AND KILL YOU ONCE AND FOR ALL...
G-
GHA HA HA HA!
G-
G-

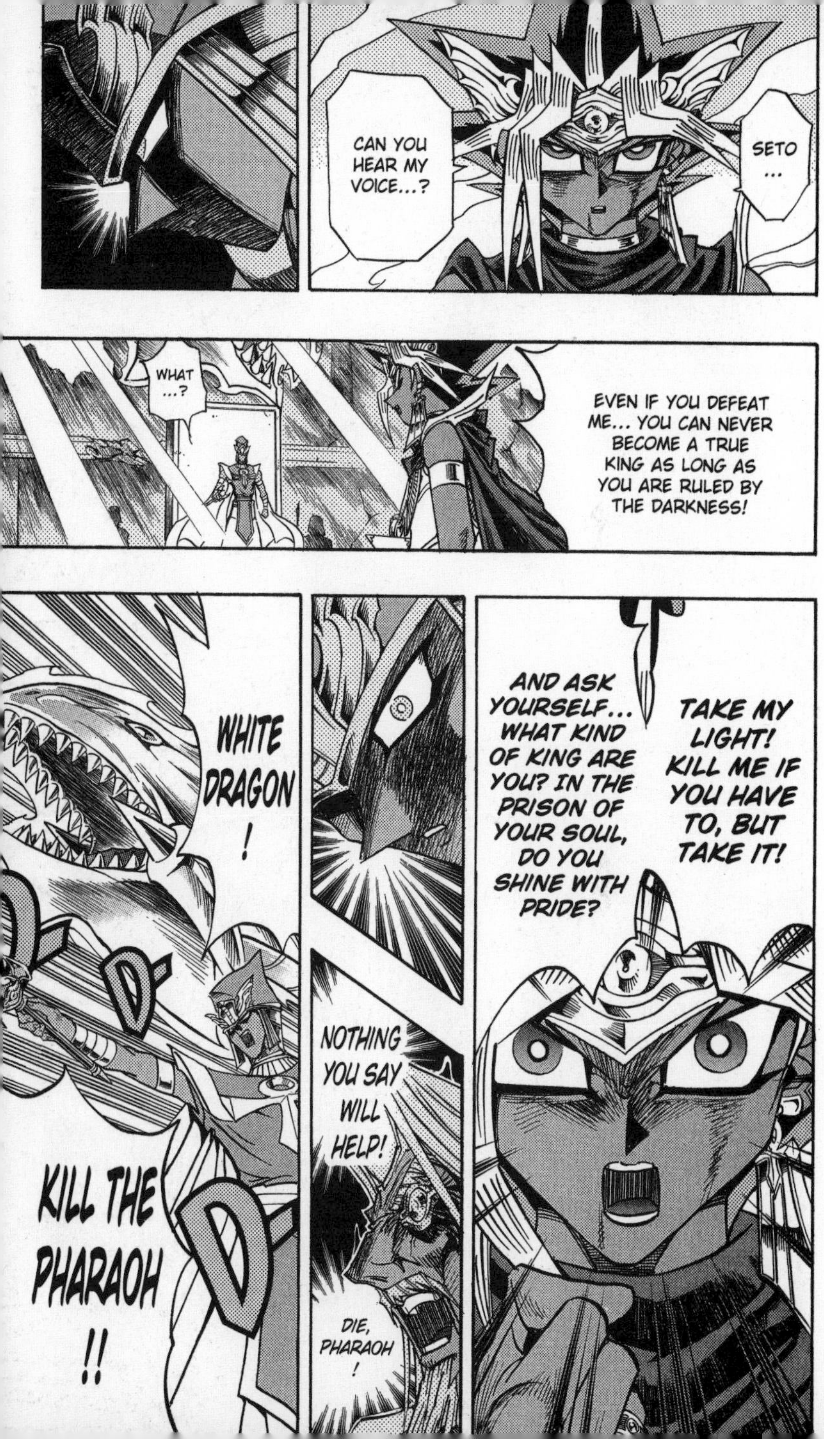
SETO ...
CAN YOU HEAR MY VOICE...?
EVEN IF YOU DEFEAT ME... YOU CAN NEVER BECOME A TRUE KING AS LONG AS YOU ARE RULED BY THE DARKNESS!
WHAT ...?
TAKE MY LIGHT! KILL ME IF YOU HAVE TO, BUT TAKE IT!
AND ASK YOURSELF... WHAT KIND OF KING ARE YOU? IN THE PRISON OF YOUR SOUL, DO YOU SHINE WITH PRIDE?
NOTHING YOU SAY WILL HELP!
DIE, PHARAOH!
WHITE DRAGON!
KILL THE PHARAOH!!

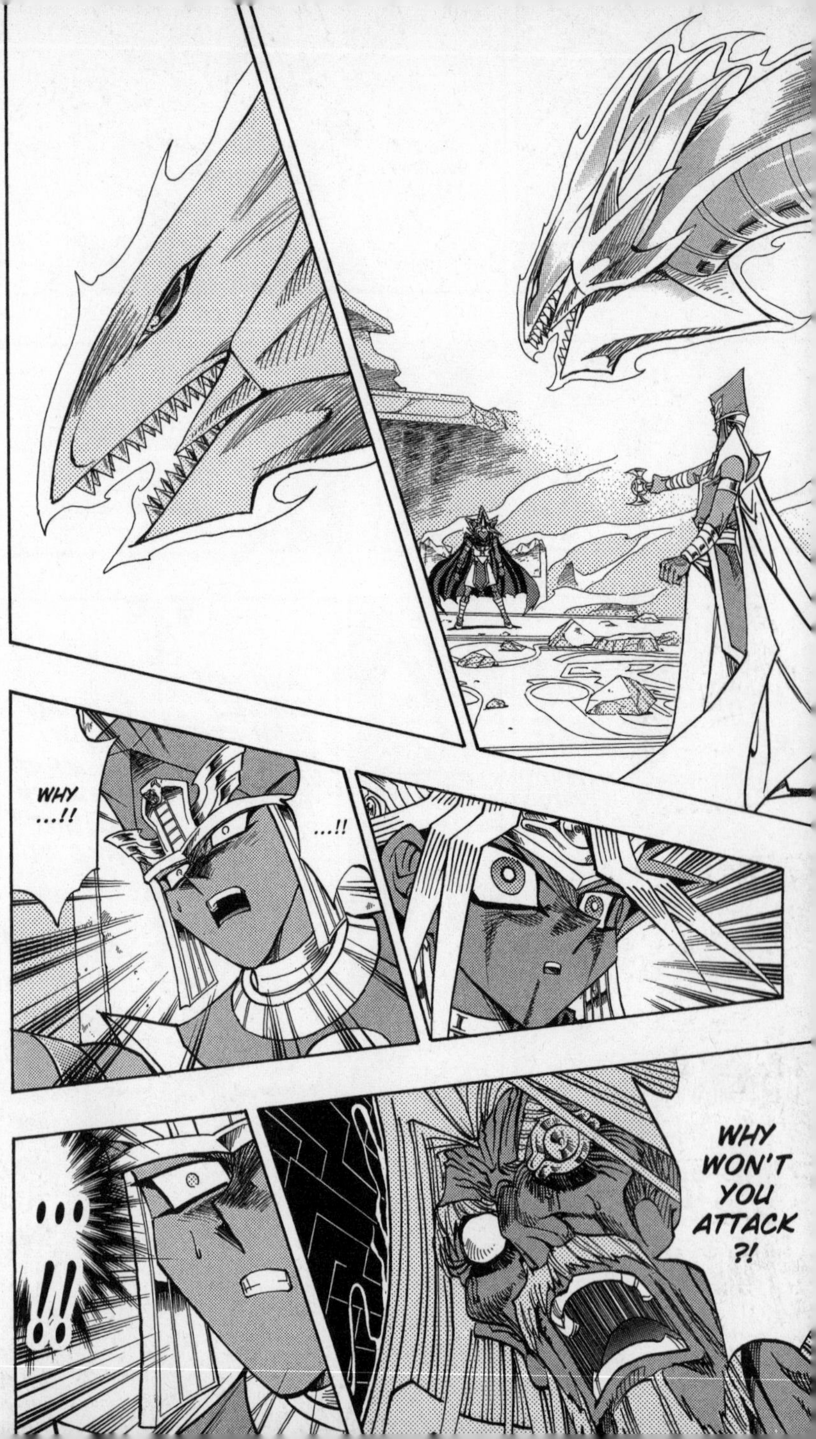
...!!
WHY ...!!
WHY WON'T YOU ATTACK ?!
...!!

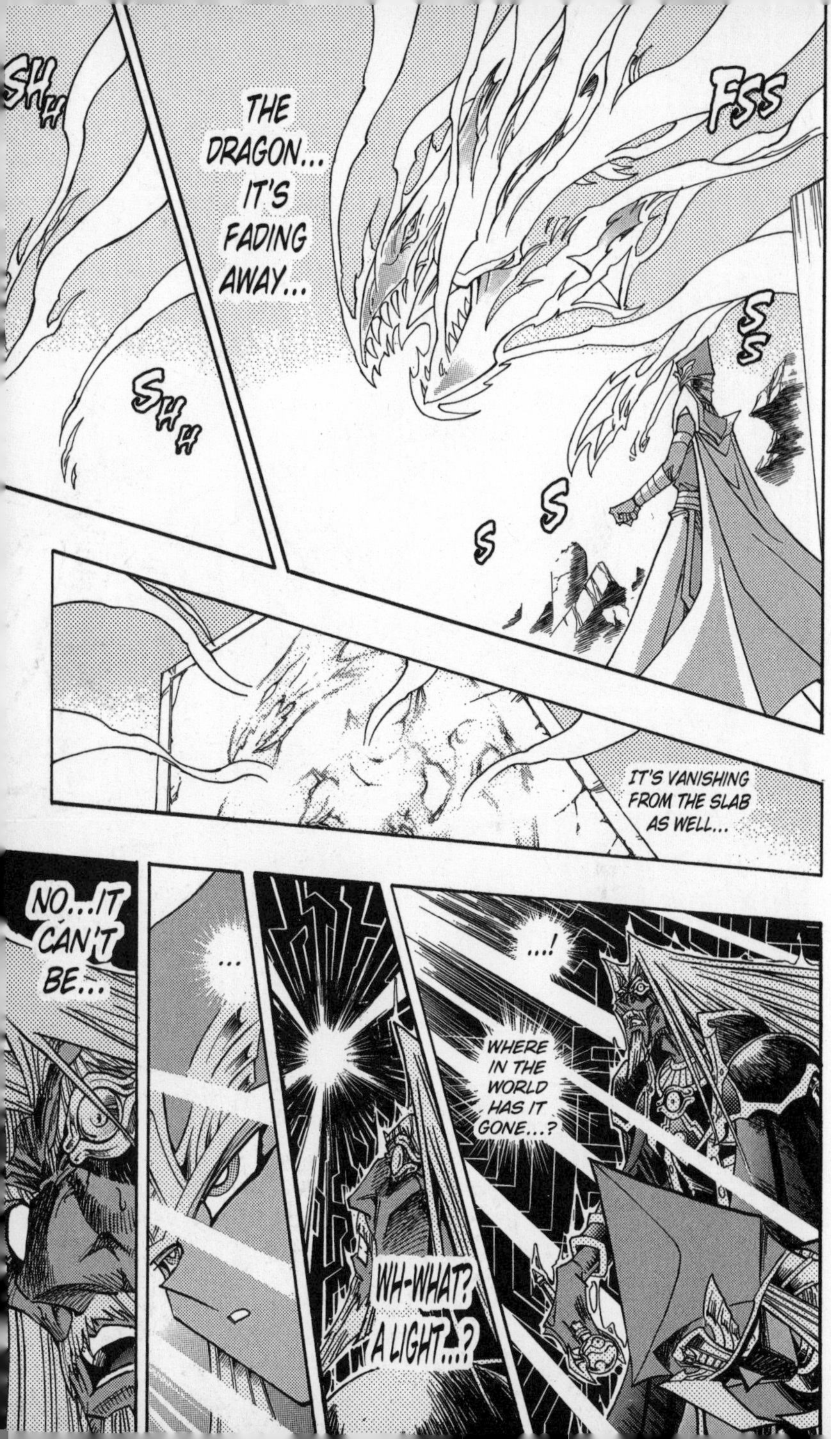
FSS
THE DRAGON... IT'S FADING AWAY...
SS
S
S
SHH
SHH
IT'S VANISHING FROM THE SLAB AS WELL...
...!
WHERE IN THE WORLD HAS IT GONE...?
WH-WHAT? A LIGHT...?
...
NO...IT CAN'T BE...

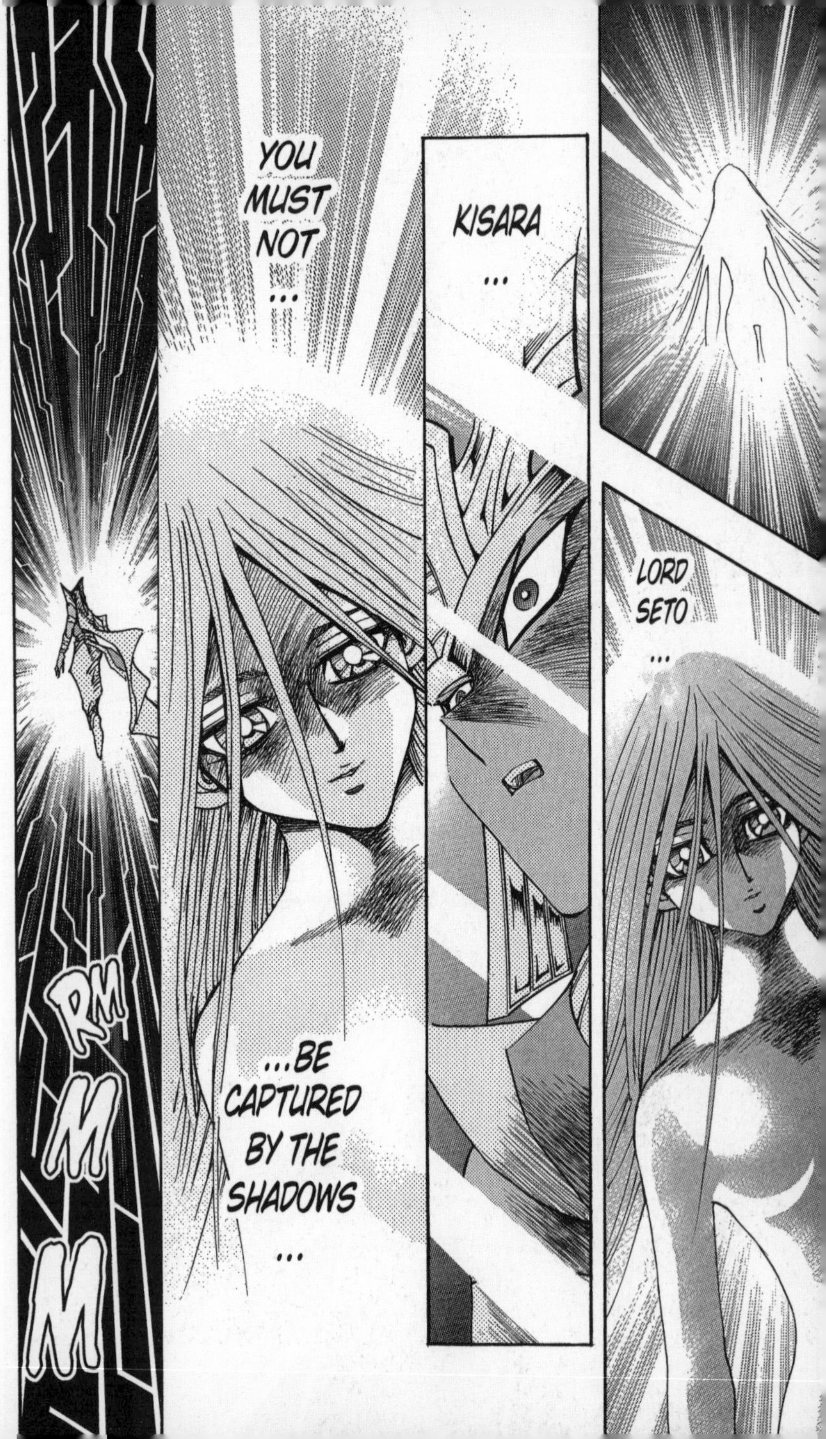
LORD SETO ...
KISARA ...
YOU MUST NOT ...
...BE CAPTURED BY THE SHADOWS ...
RMMM

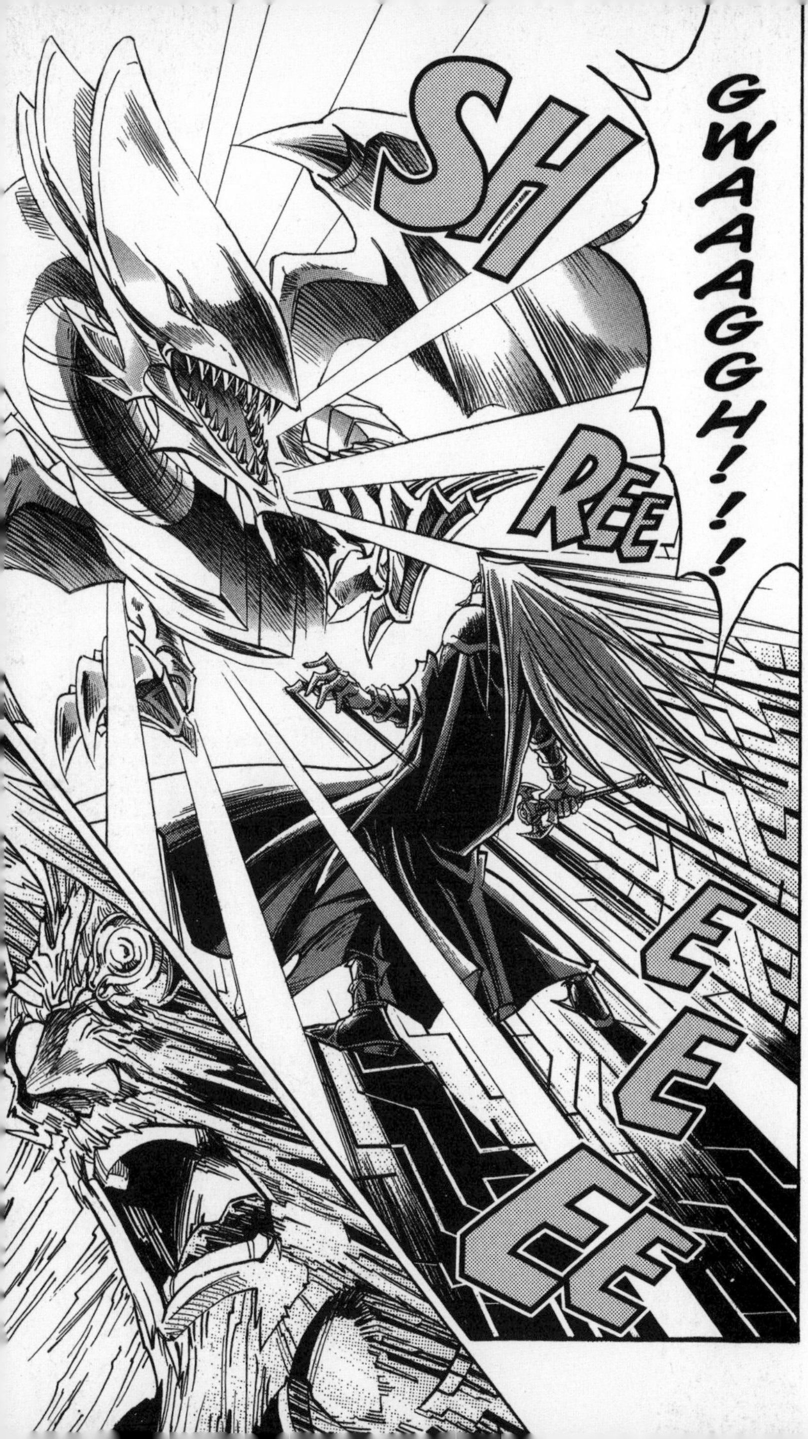
GWAAAGGH!!!
SHREEEEEEE

Duel 58: He Who Inherits the Light

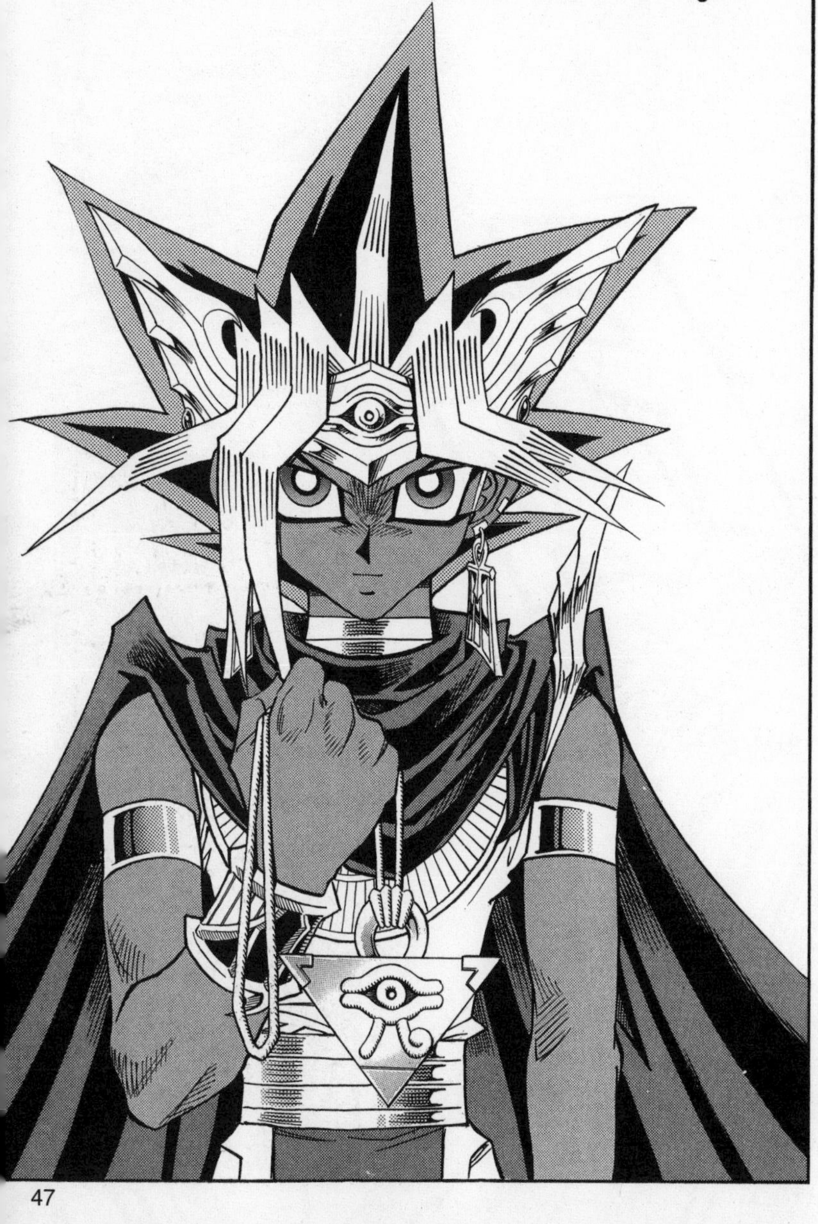

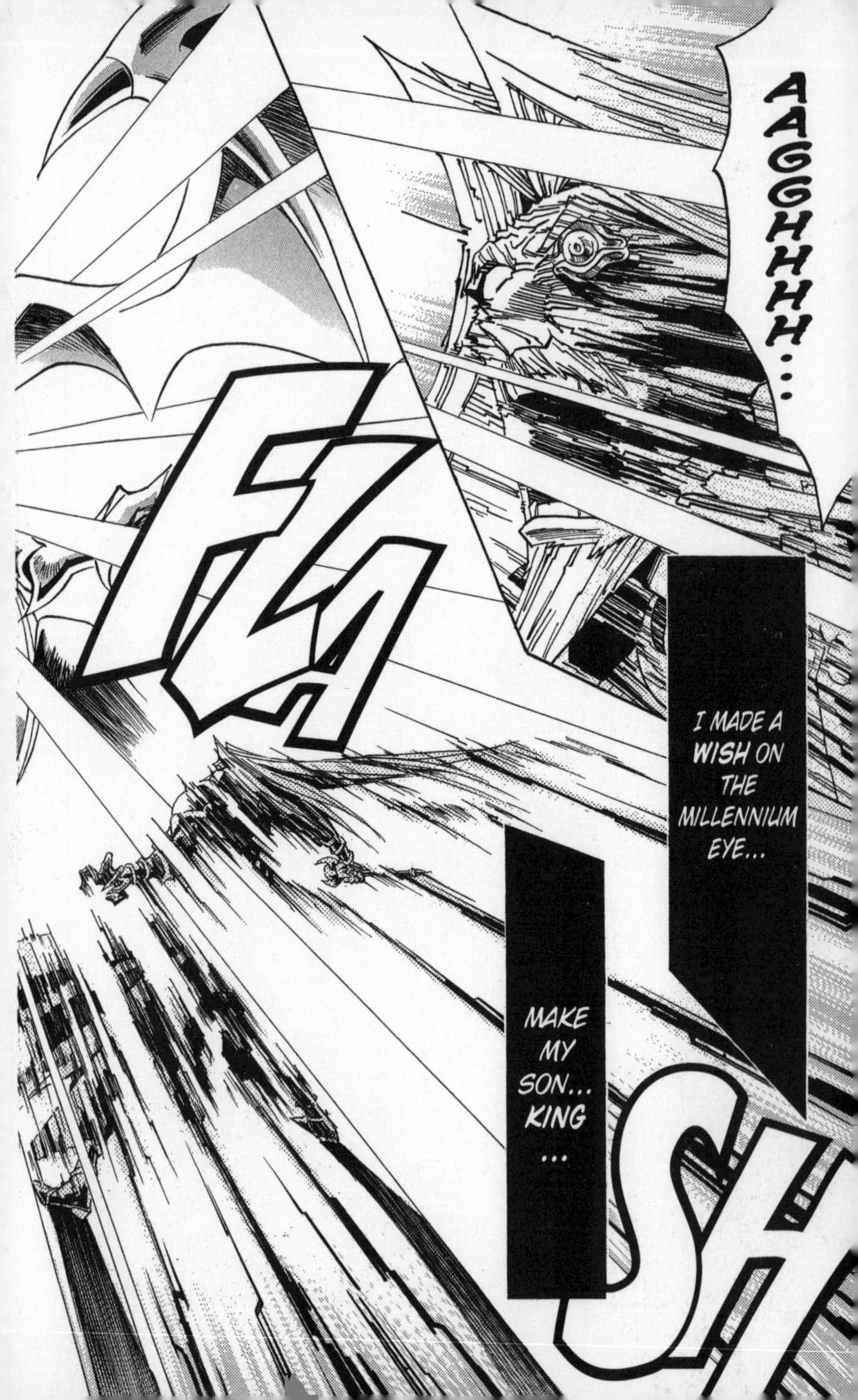
AAGGHHHH...
I MADE A WISH ON THE MILLENNIUM EYE...
MAKE MY SON... KING ...
FLA
SH

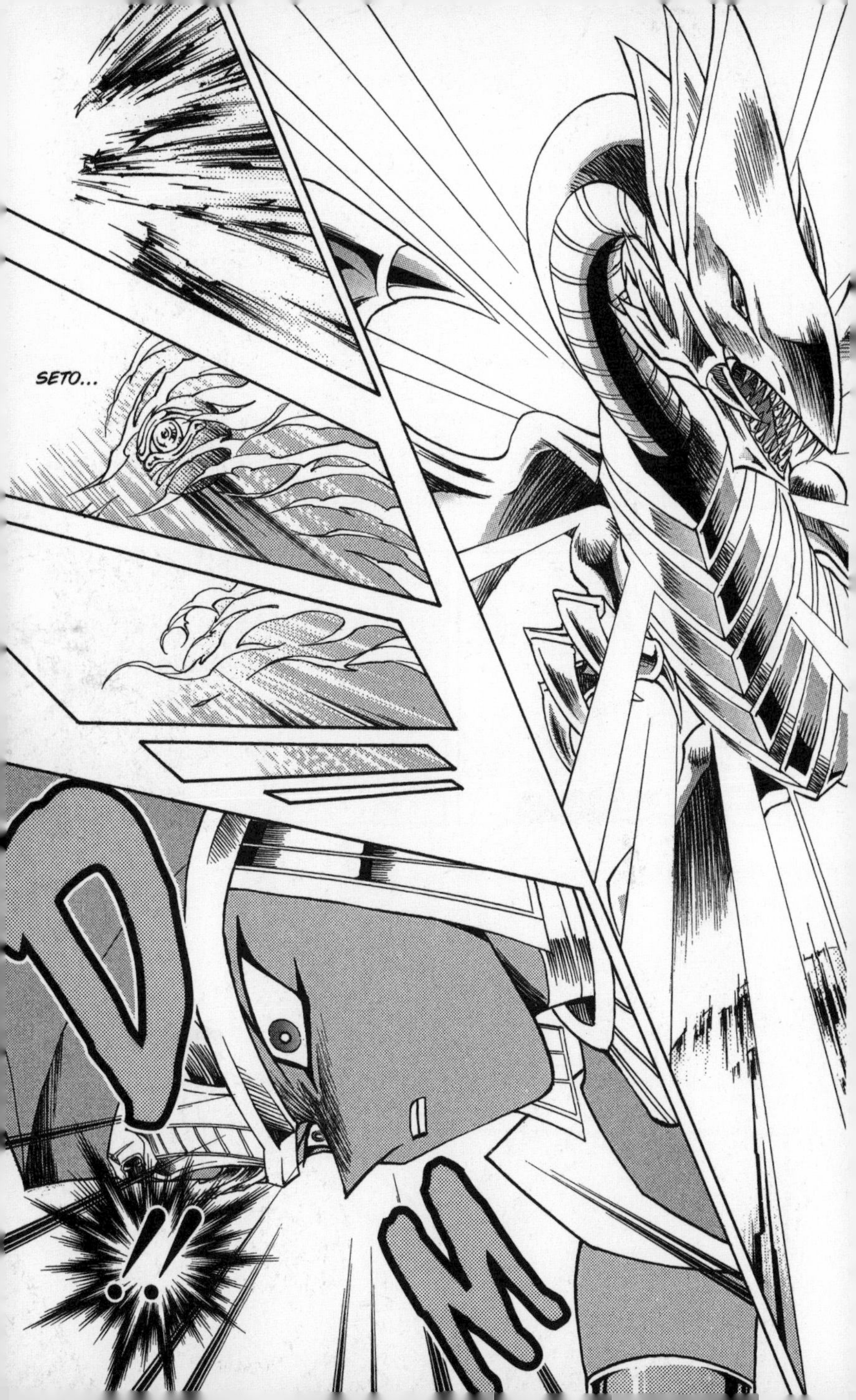
SETO...
!!

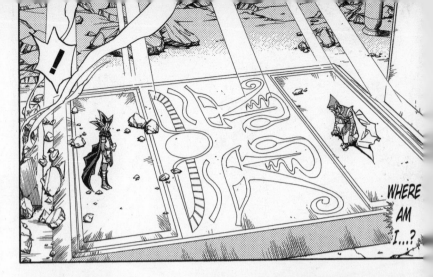

WHERE AM I...?

THAT'S RIGHT... MY FATHER CHOSE TO DIE...

AND DRAGGED MY SOUL WITH HIM INTO THE SHADOWS...

...!

THE PHAR-AOH...

SETO!

KISARA...

AND YOU SAVED ME FROM THOSE SHADOWS...

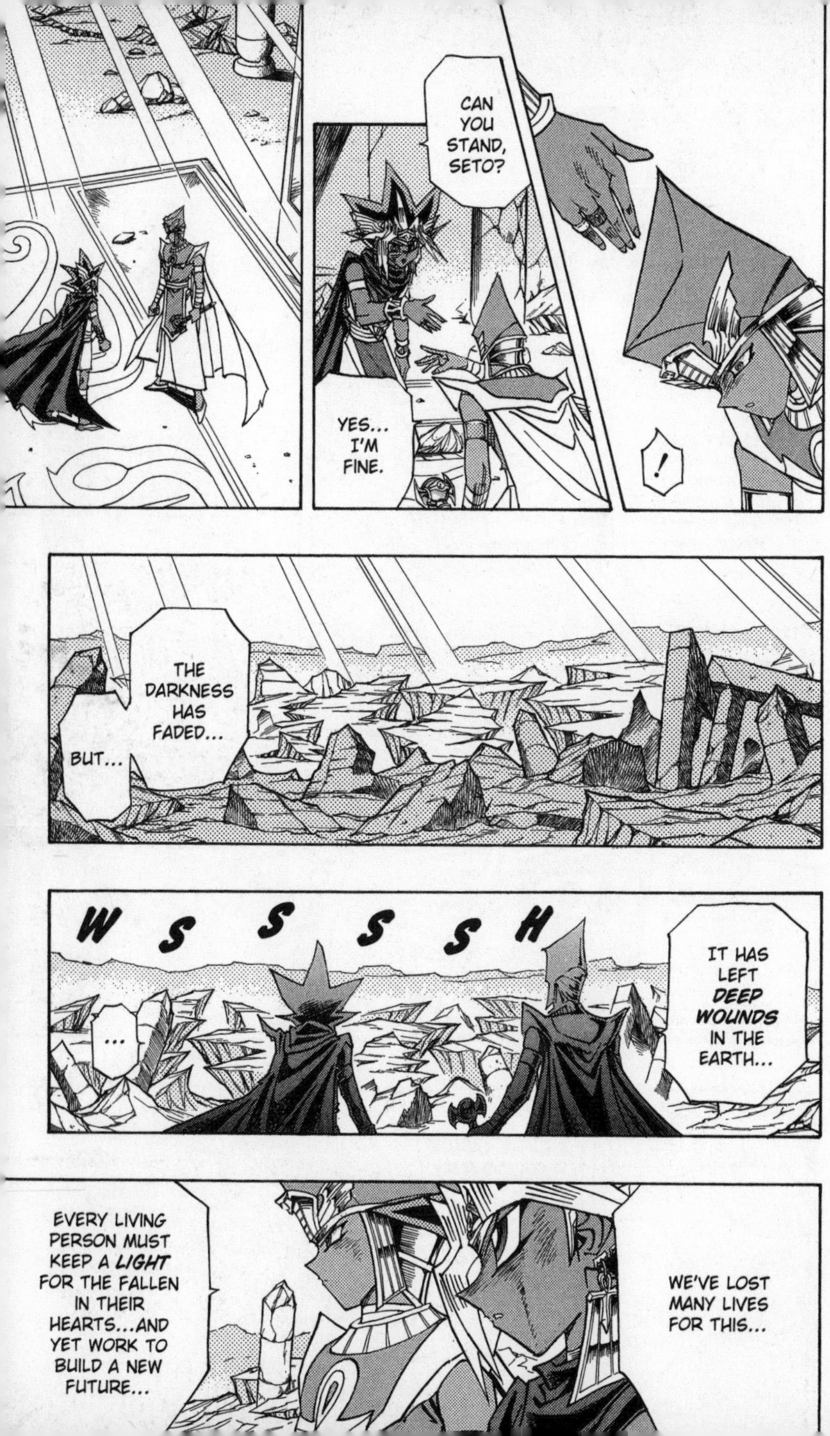
!
CAN YOU STAND, SETO?
YES... I'M FINE.
THE DARKNESS HAS FADED...
BUT...
W S S S S H
IT HAS LEFT *DEEP WOUNDS* IN THE EARTH...
...
WE'VE LOST MANY LIVES FOR THIS...
EVERY LIVING PERSON MUST KEEP A *LIGHT* FOR THE FALLEN IN THEIR HEARTS...AND YET WORK TO BUILD A NEW FUTURE...

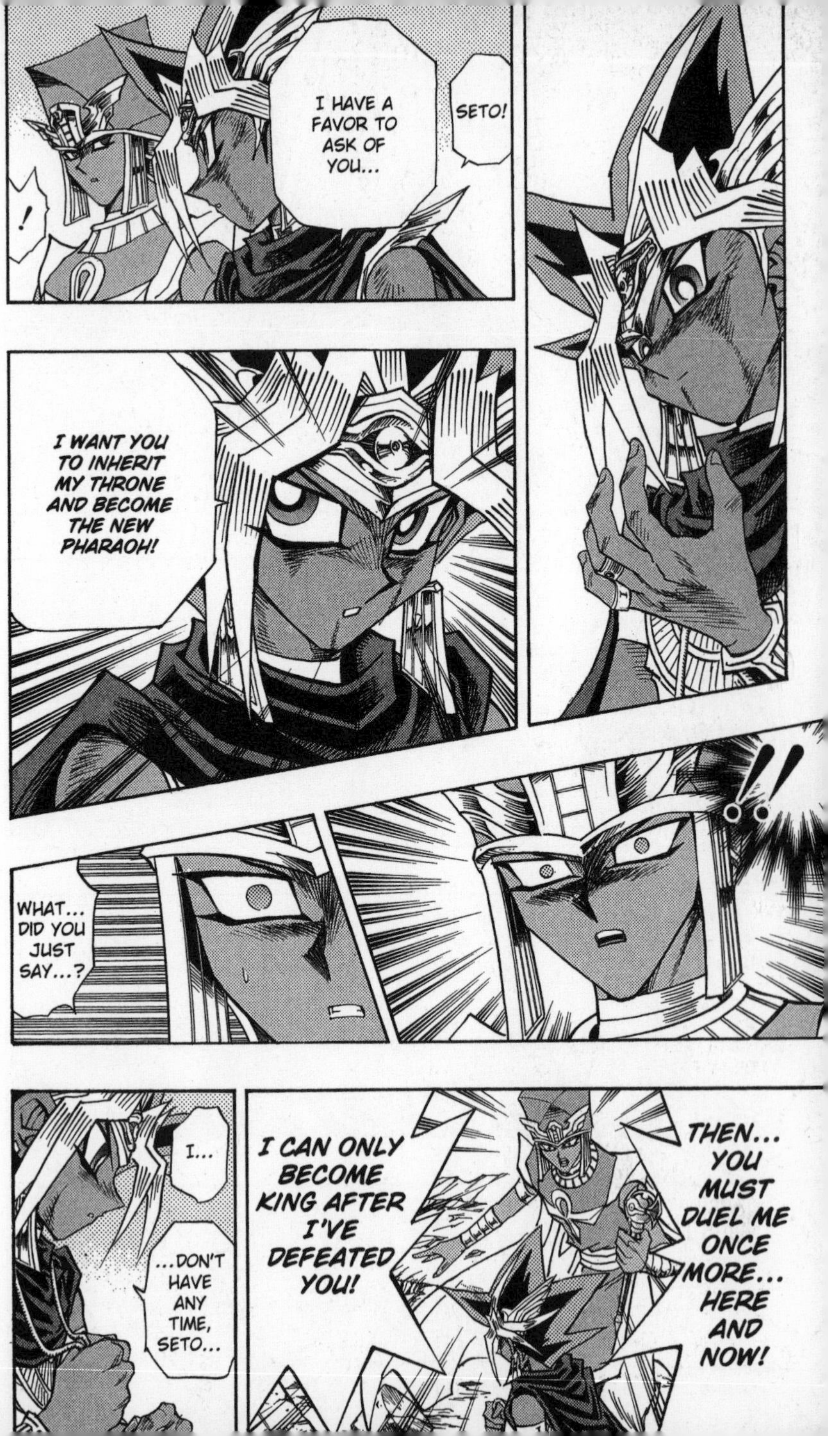
SETO!
I HAVE A FAVOR TO ASK OF YOU...
!
I WANT YOU TO INHERIT MY THRONE AND BECOME THE NEW PHARAOH!
!!
WHAT... DID YOU JUST SAY...?
THEN... YOU MUST DUEL ME ONCE MORE... HERE AND NOW!
I CAN ONLY BECOME KING AFTER I'VE DEFEATED YOU!
I...
...DON'T HAVE ANY TIME, SETO...

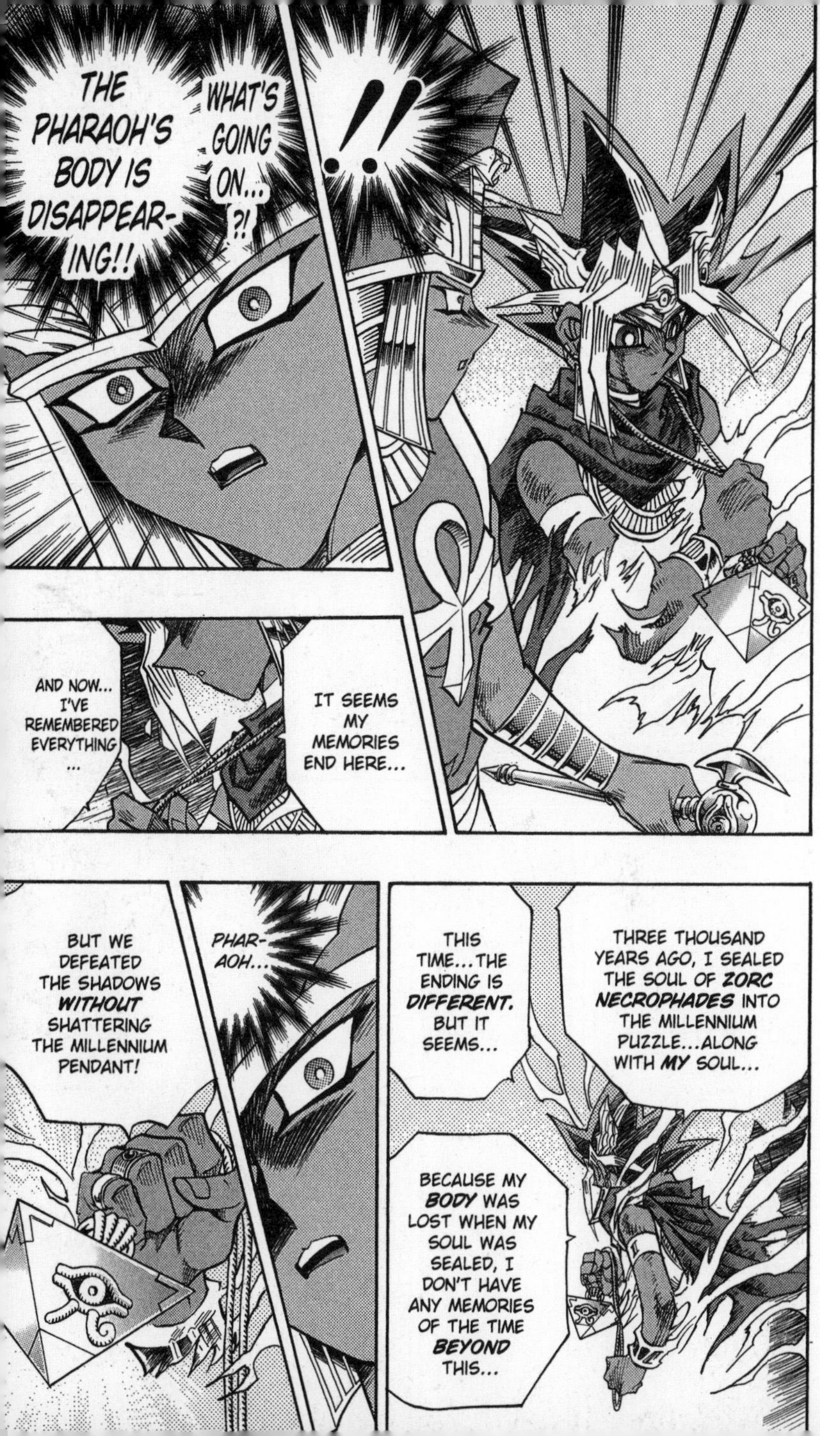
!!
WHAT'S GOING ON... ?!
THE PHARAOH'S BODY IS DISAPPEARING!!
IT SEEMS MY MEMORIES END HERE...
AND NOW... I'VE REMEMBERED EVERYTHING...
THREE THOUSAND YEARS AGO, I SEALED THE SOUL OF ***ZORC NECROPHADES*** INTO THE MILLENNIUM PUZZLE...ALONG WITH ***MY*** SOUL...
THIS TIME...THE ENDING IS ***DIFFERENT.*** BUT IT SEEMS...
BECAUSE MY ***BODY*** WAS LOST WHEN MY SOUL WAS SEALED, I DON'T HAVE ANY MEMORIES OF THE TIME ***BEYOND*** THIS...
PHARAOH...
BUT WE DEFEATED THE SHADOWS ***WITHOUT*** SHATTERING THE MILLENNIUM PENDANT!

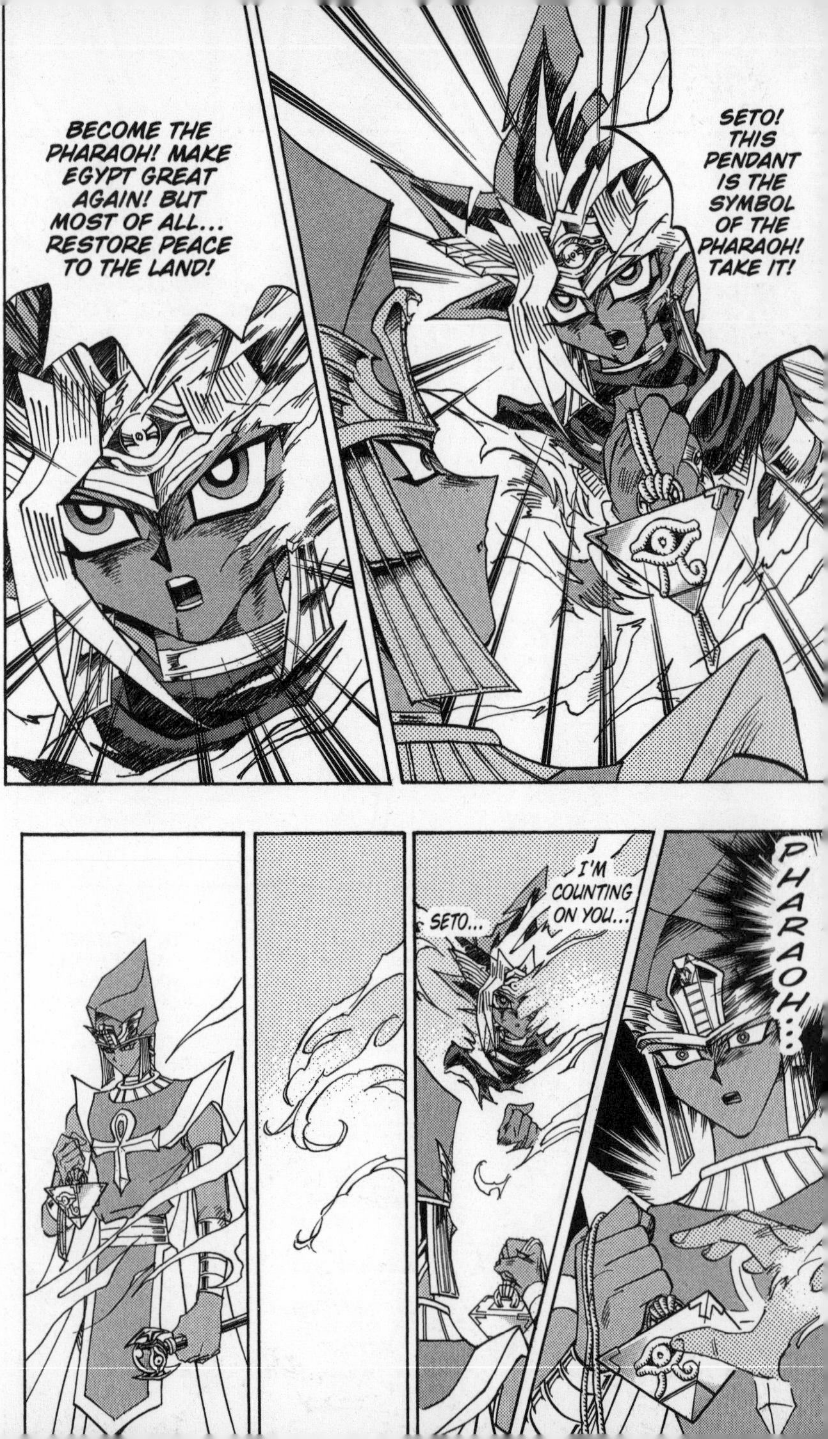
SETO! THIS PENDANT IS THE SYMBOL OF THE PHARAOH! TAKE IT!
BECOME THE PHARAOH! MAKE EGYPT GREAT AGAIN! BUT MOST OF ALL... RESTORE PEACE TO THE LAND!
PHARAOH...
I'M COUNTING ON YOU...
SETO...

READ THIS WAY

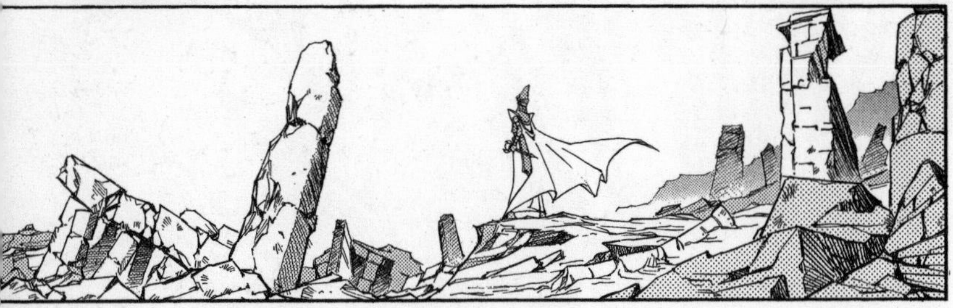

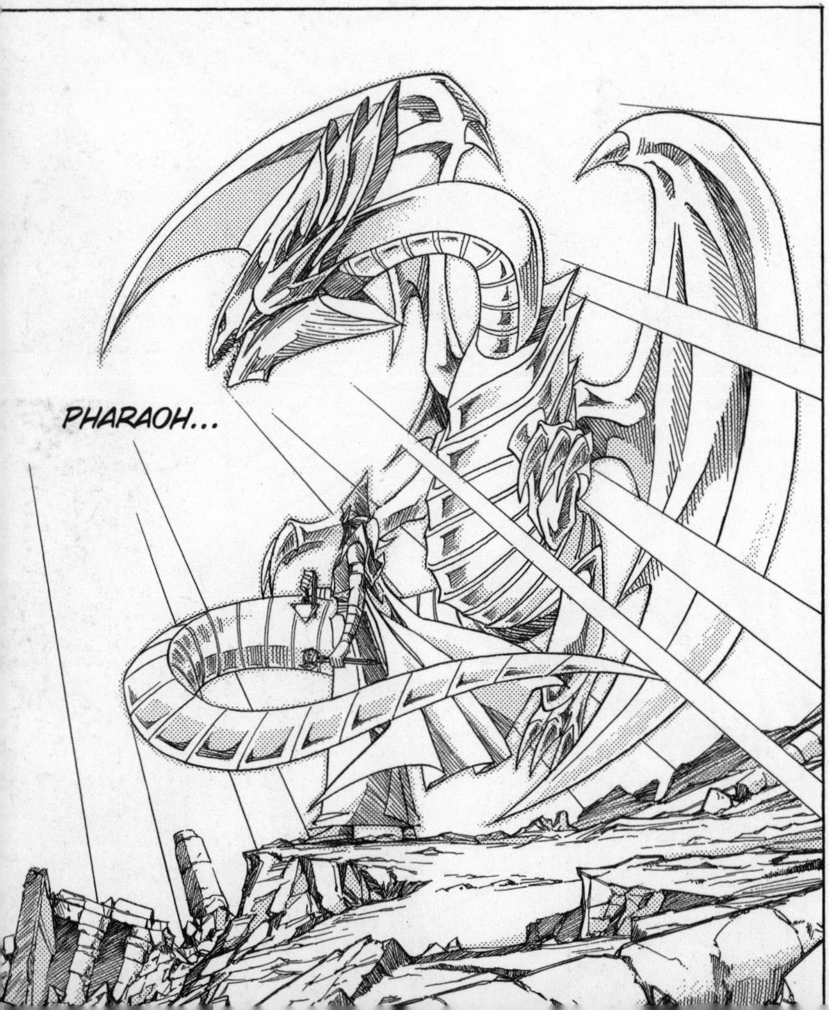
PHARAOH...

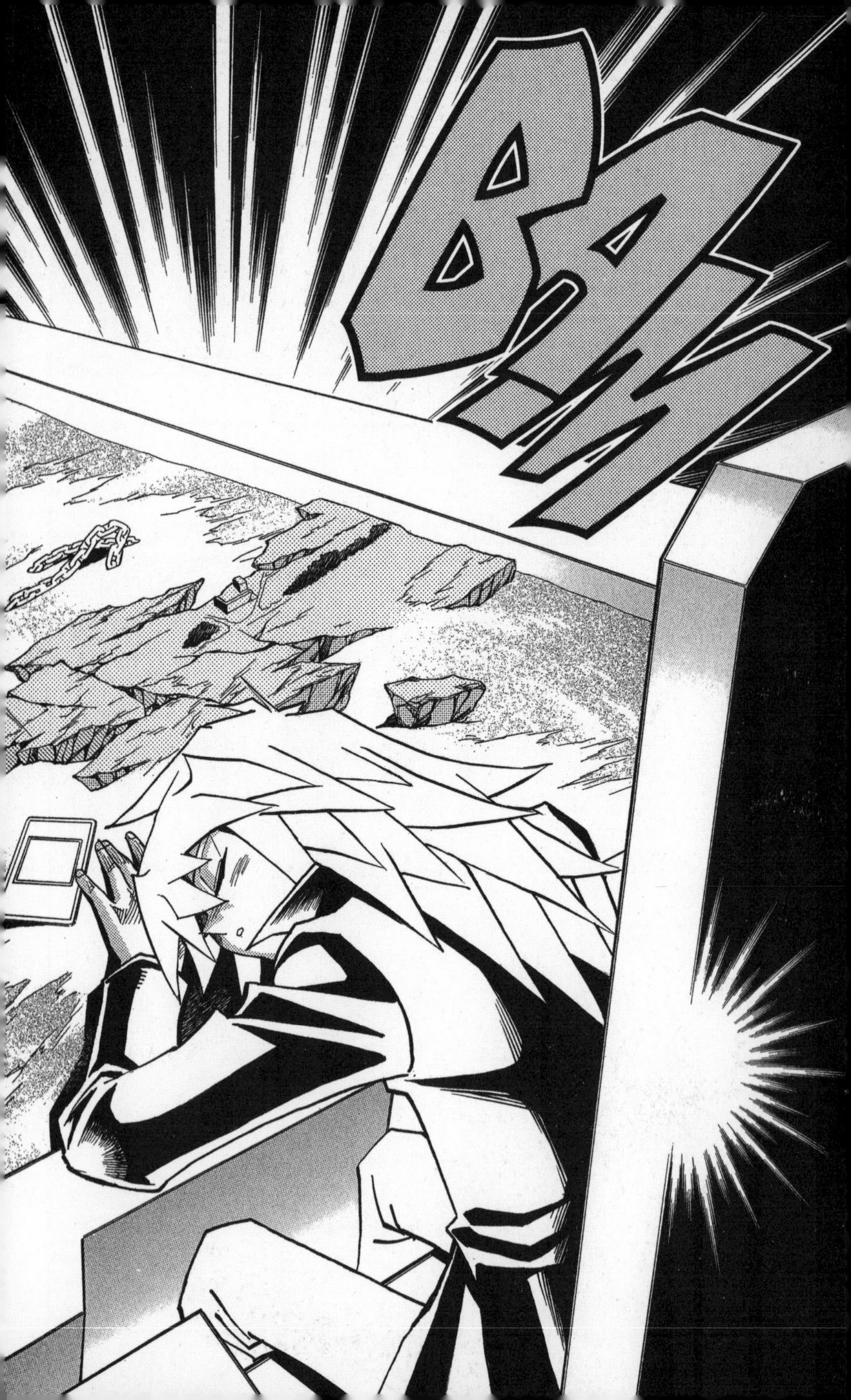
BAM

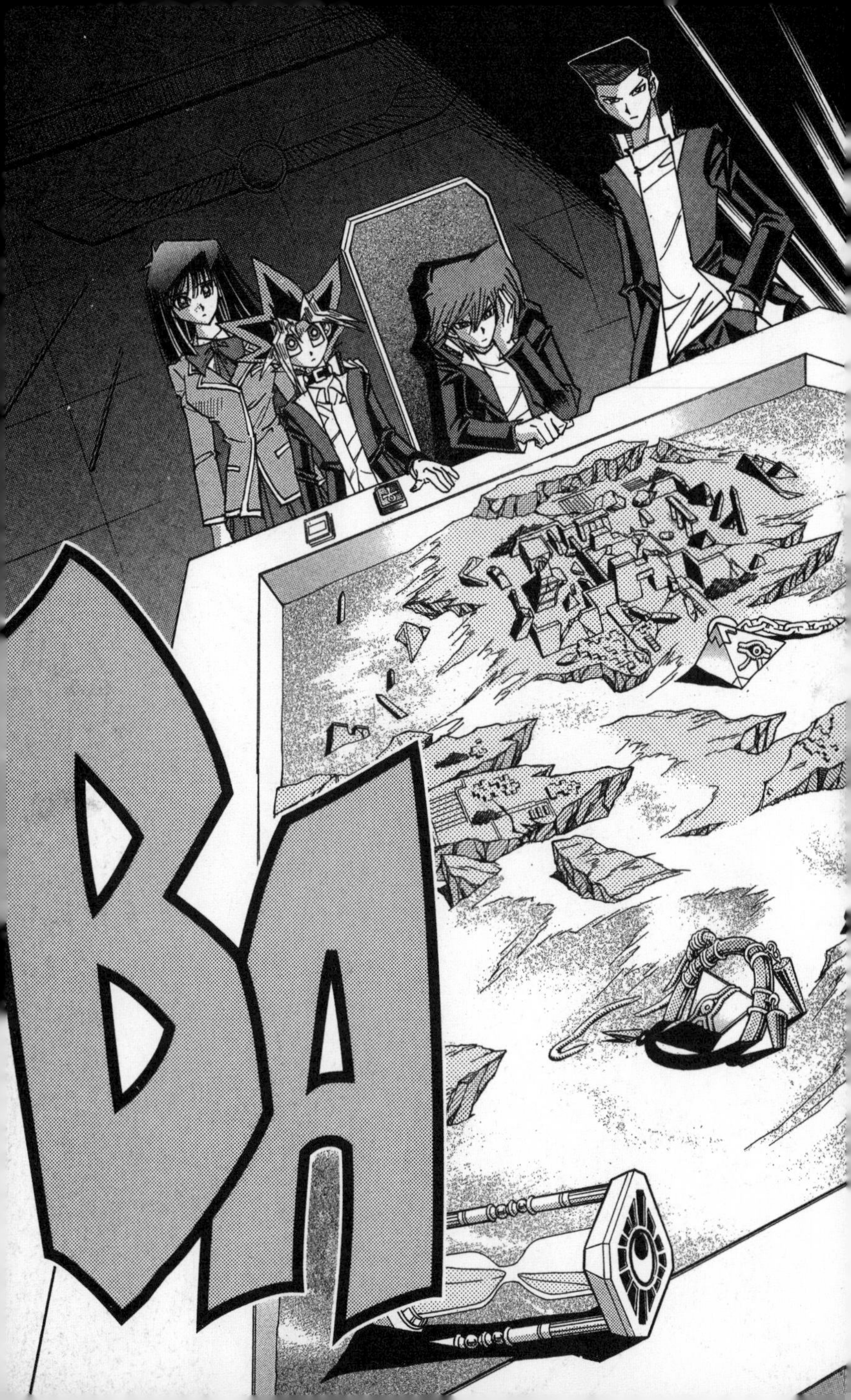
BA

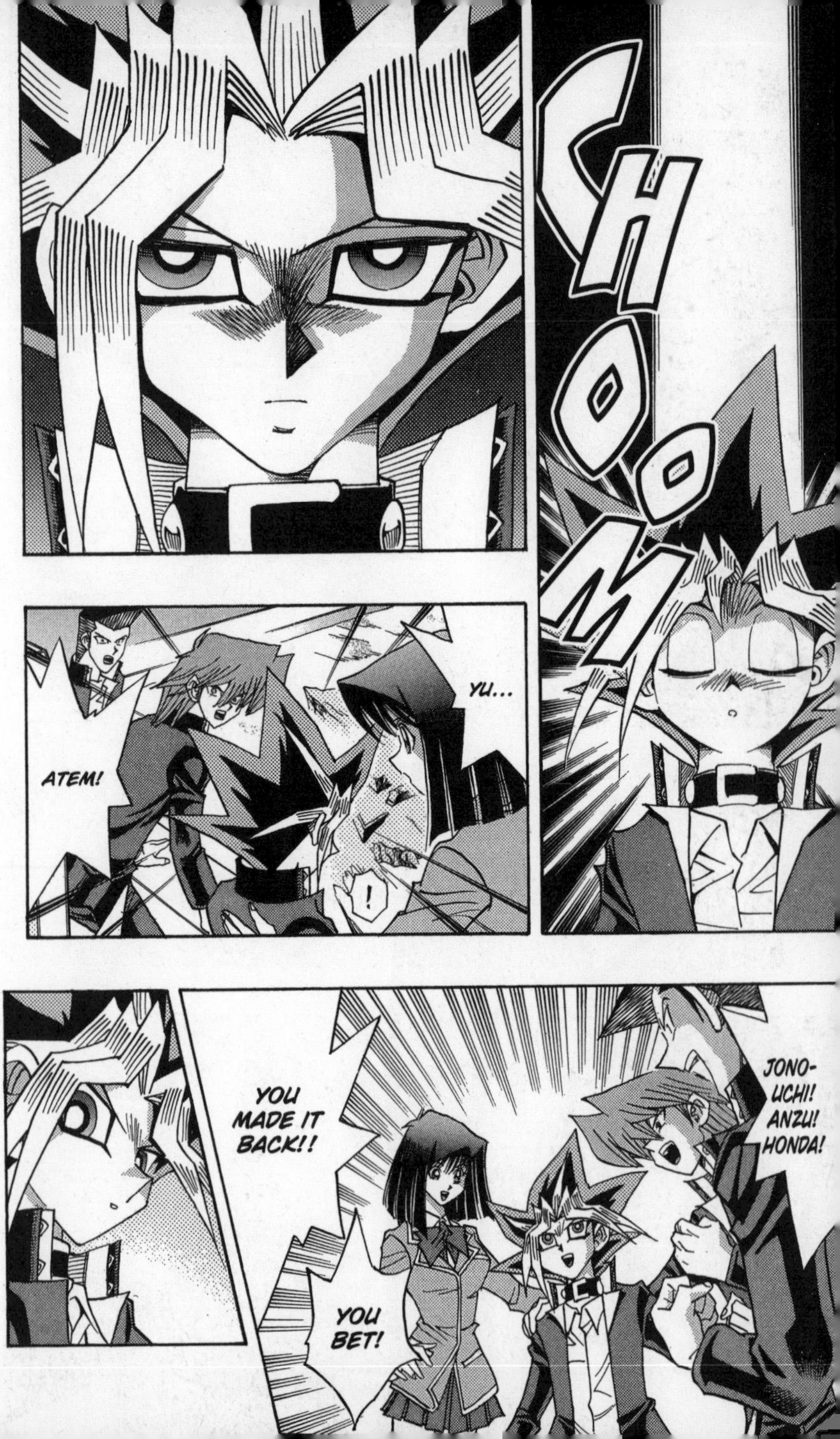
CHOOOM
YU...
ATEM!
!
JONO-UCHI! ANZU! HONDA!
YOU MADE IT BACK!!
YOU BET!

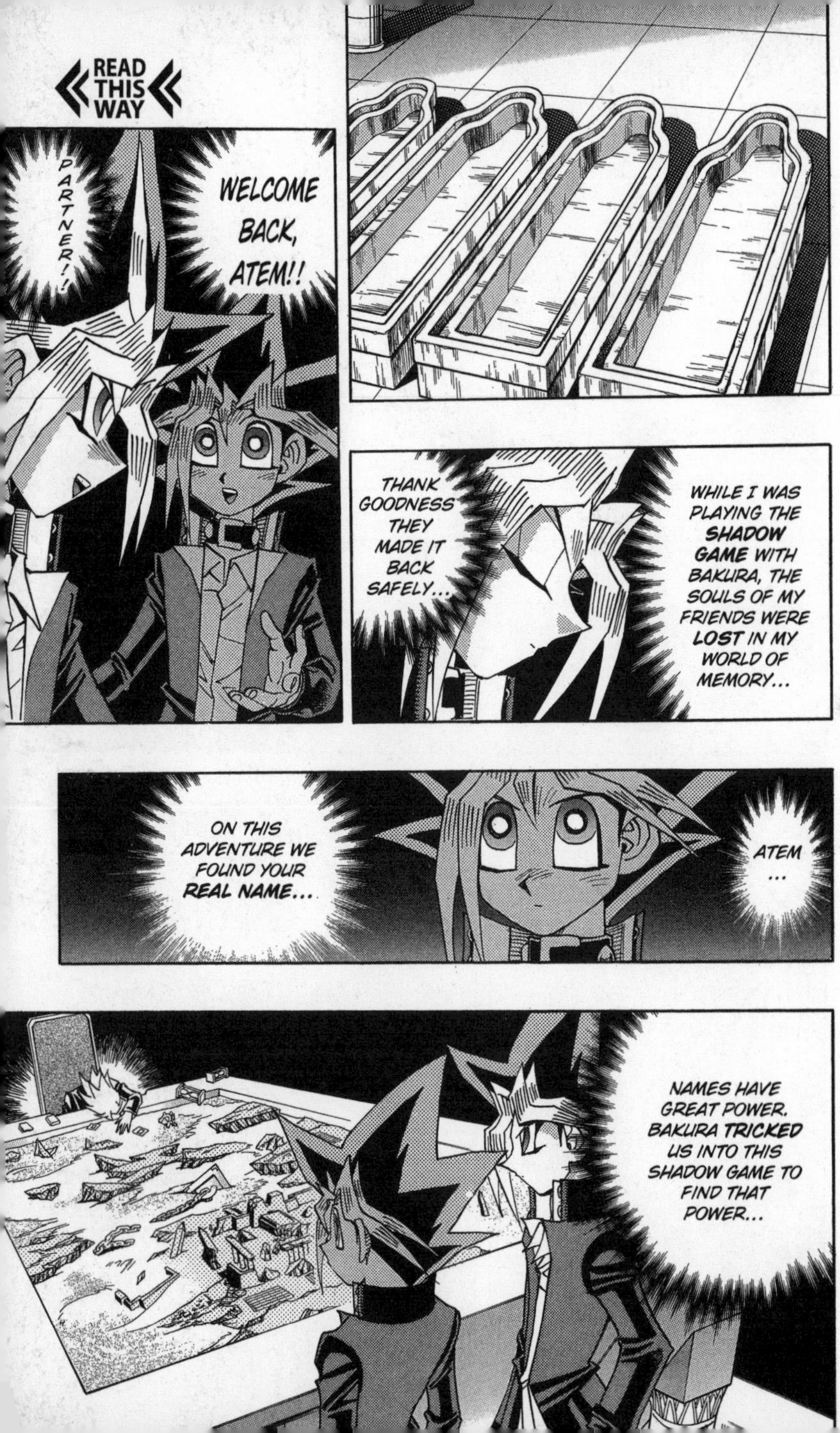
READ THIS WAY
WHILE I WAS PLAYING THE SHADOW GAME WITH BAKURA, THE SOULS OF MY FRIENDS WERE LOST IN MY WORLD OF MEMORY...
THANK GOODNESS THEY MADE IT BACK SAFELY...
WELCOME BACK, ATEM!!
PARTNER!!
ATEM ...
ON THIS ADVENTURE WE FOUND YOUR REAL NAME...
NAMES HAVE GREAT POWER. BAKURA TRICKED US INTO THIS SHADOW GAME TO FIND THAT POWER...

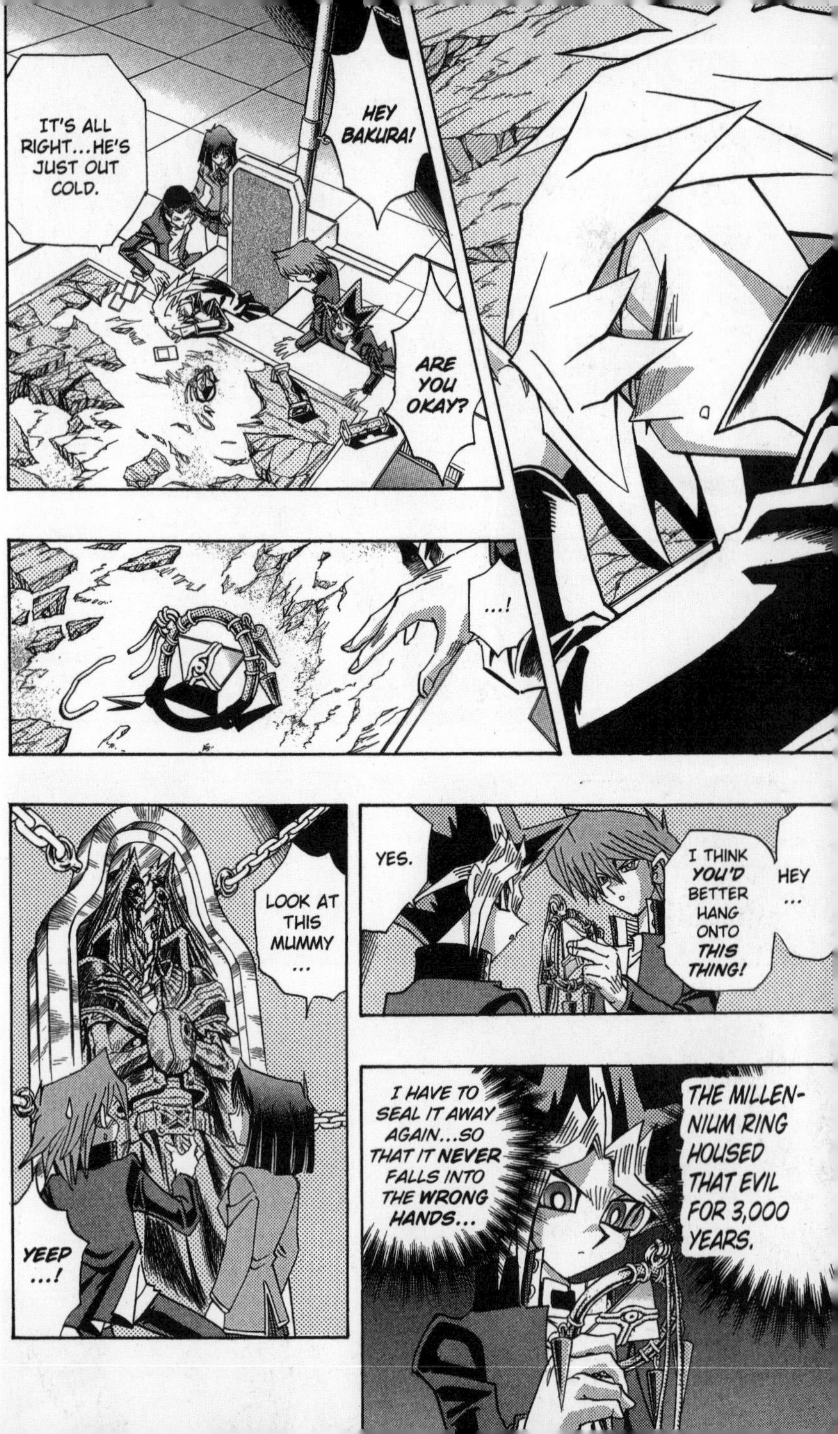
HEY BAKURA!
ARE YOU OKAY?
IT'S ALL RIGHT...HE'S JUST OUT COLD.
...!
HEY...
I THINK YOU'D BETTER HANG ONTO THIS THING!
YES.
THE MILLEN-NIUM RING HOUSED THAT EVIL FOR 3,000 YEARS.
I HAVE TO SEAL IT AWAY AGAIN...SO THAT IT NEVER FALLS INTO THE WRONG HANDS...
LOOK AT THIS MUMMY...
YEEP...!

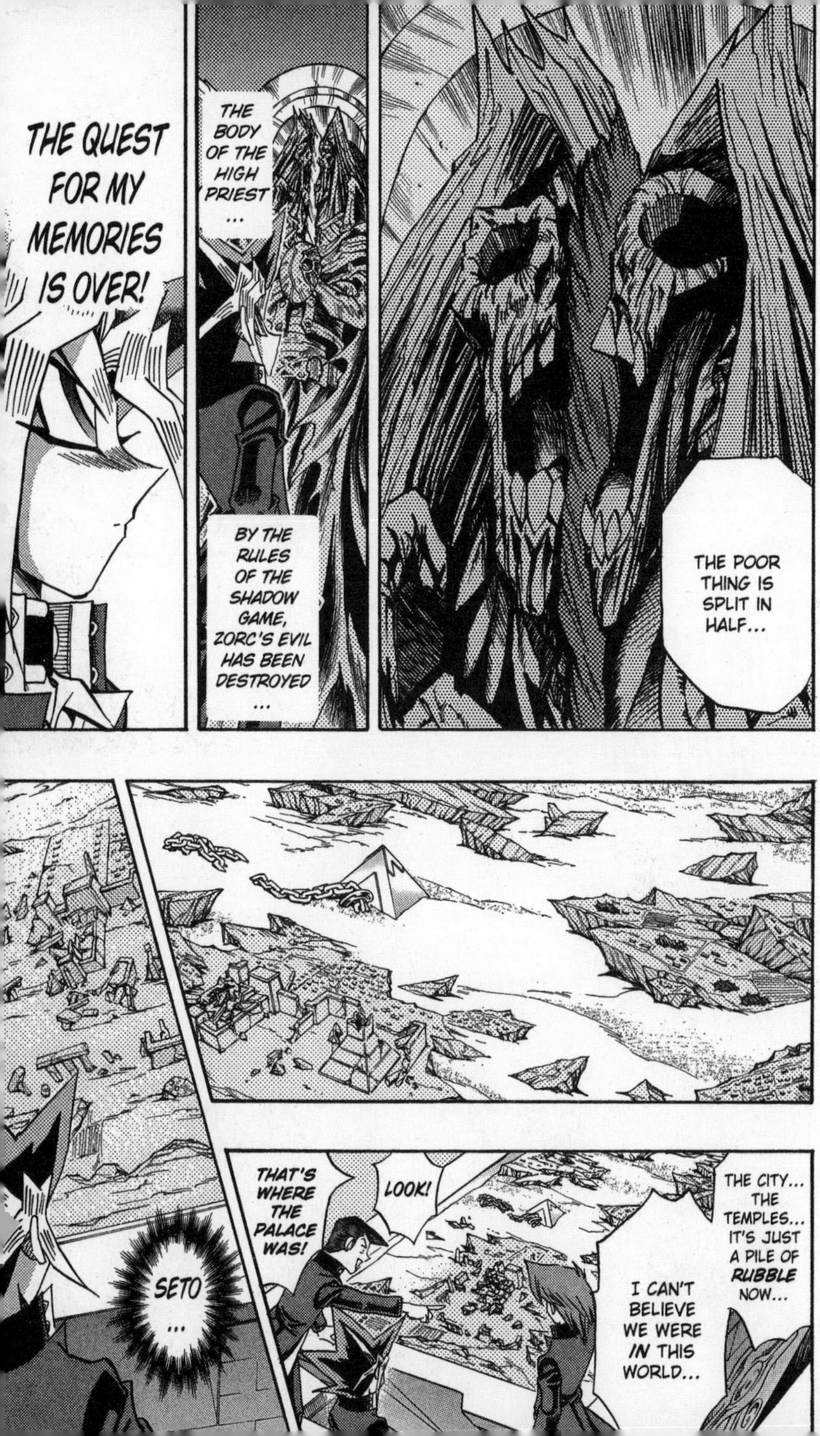
THE POOR THING IS SPLIT IN HALF...
THE BODY OF THE HIGH PRIEST...
BY THE RULES OF THE SHADOW GAME, ZORC'S EVIL HAS BEEN DESTROYED...
THE QUEST FOR MY MEMORIES IS OVER!
THE CITY... THE TEMPLES... IT'S JUST A PILE OF *RUBBLE* NOW...
I CAN'T BELIEVE WE WERE *IN* THIS WORLD...
LOOK!
THAT'S WHERE THE PALACE WAS!
SETO...

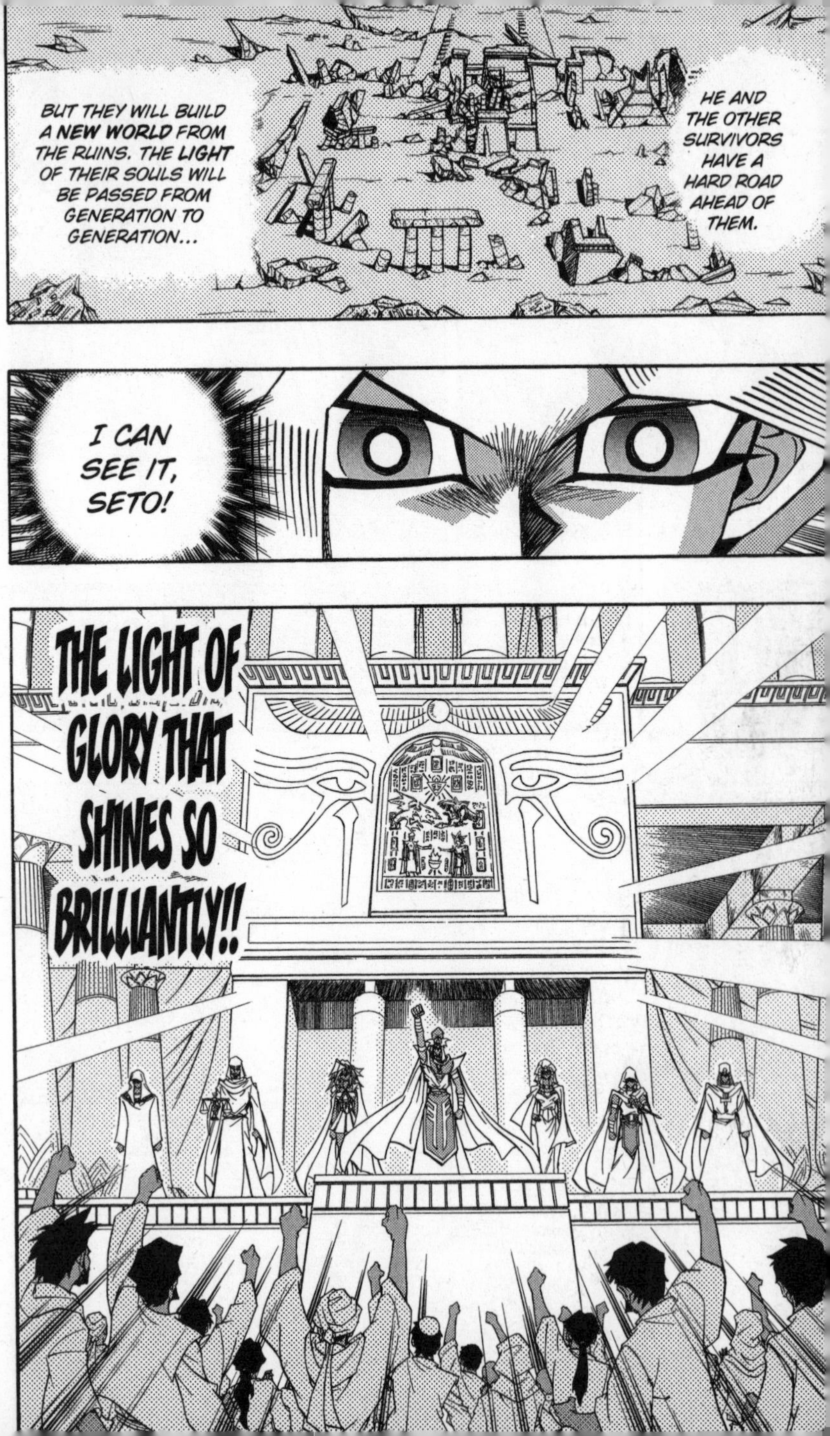
HE AND THE OTHER SURVIVORS HAVE A HARD ROAD AHEAD OF THEM.
BUT THEY WILL BUILD A NEW WORLD FROM THE RUINS. THE LIGHT OF THEIR SOULS WILL BE PASSED FROM GENERATION TO GENERATION...
I CAN SEE IT, SETO!
THE LIGHT OF GLORY THAT SHINES SO BRILLIANTLY!!

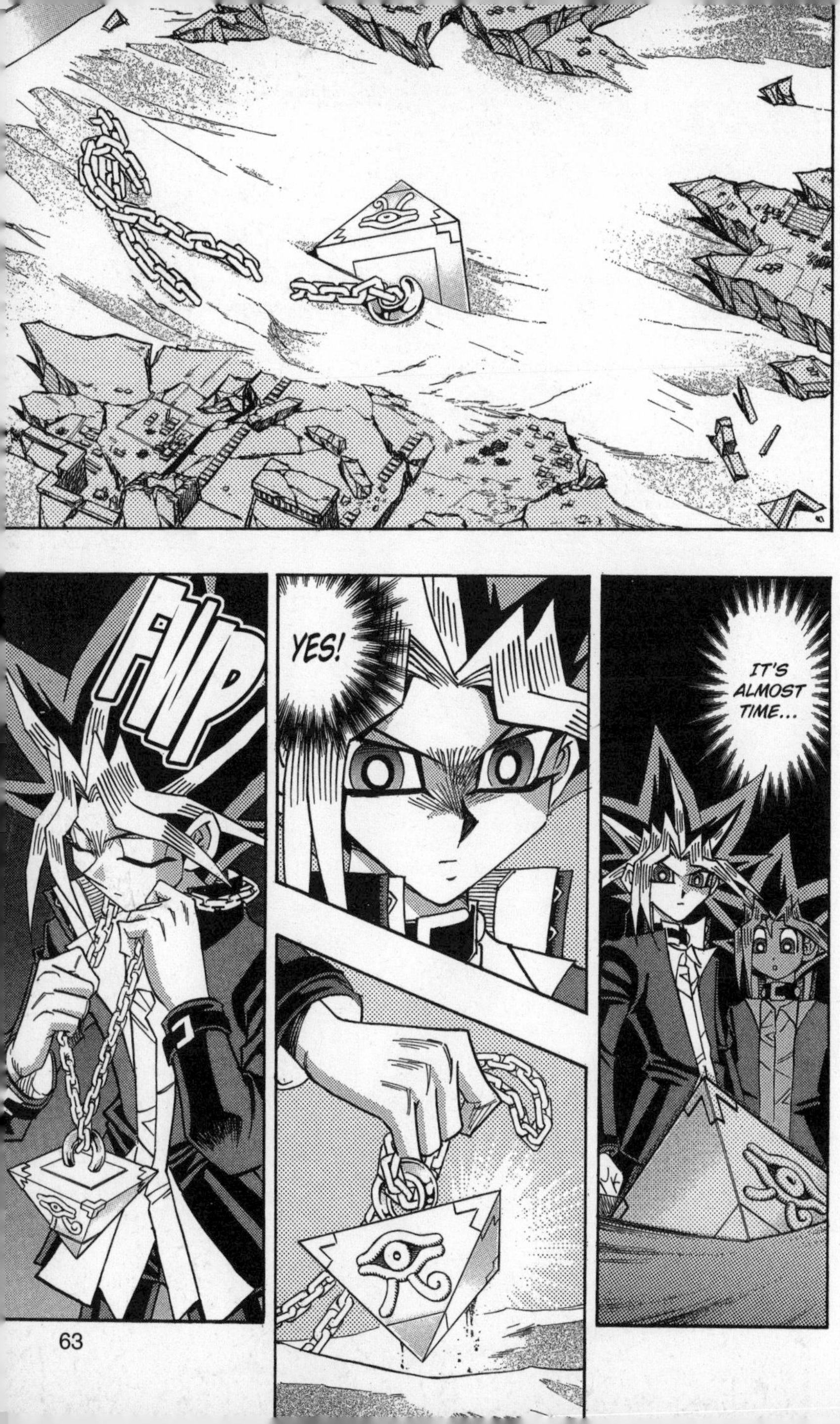
IT'S ALMOST TIME...
YES!
FWIP

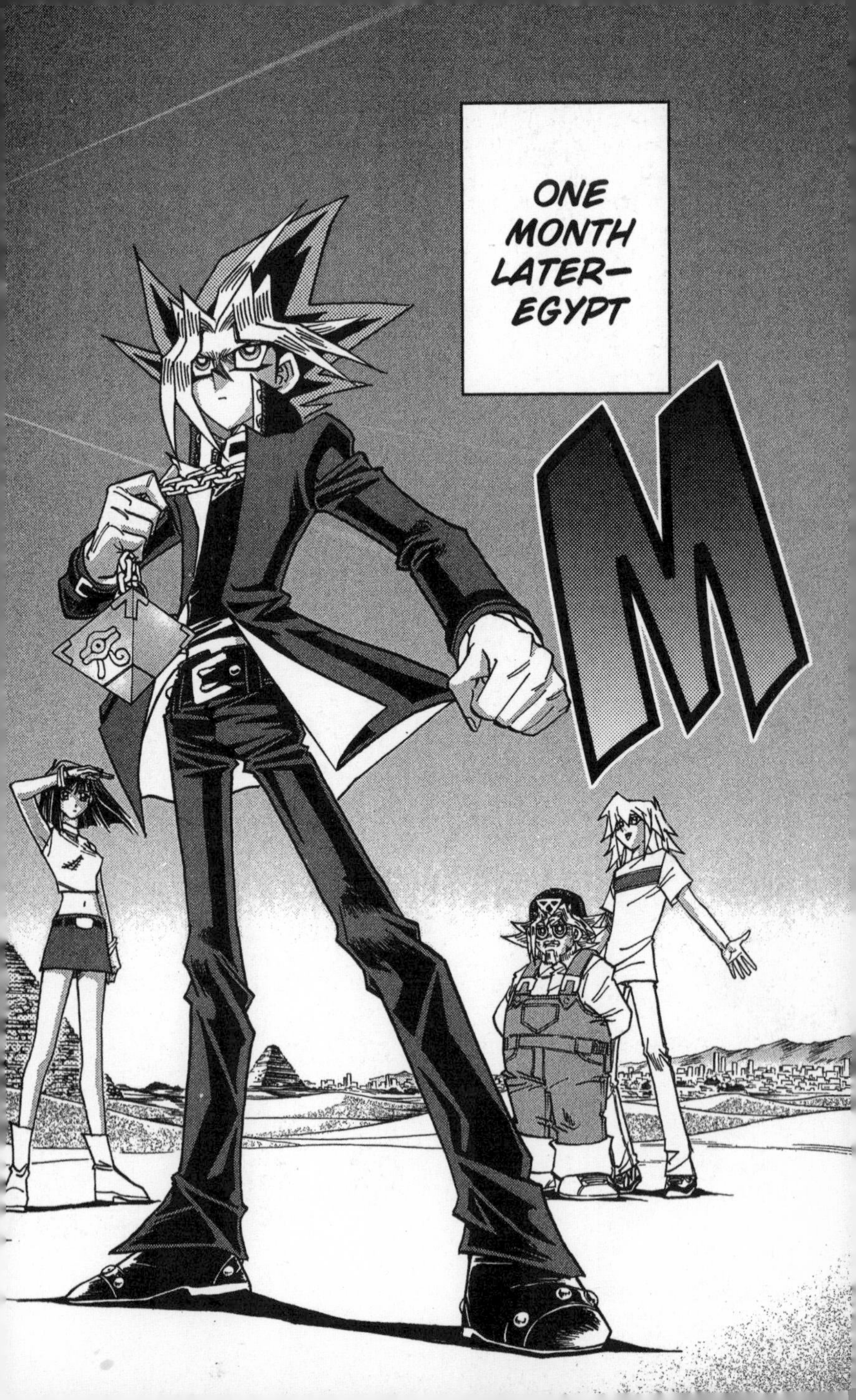
ONE MONTH LATER—EGYPT
M

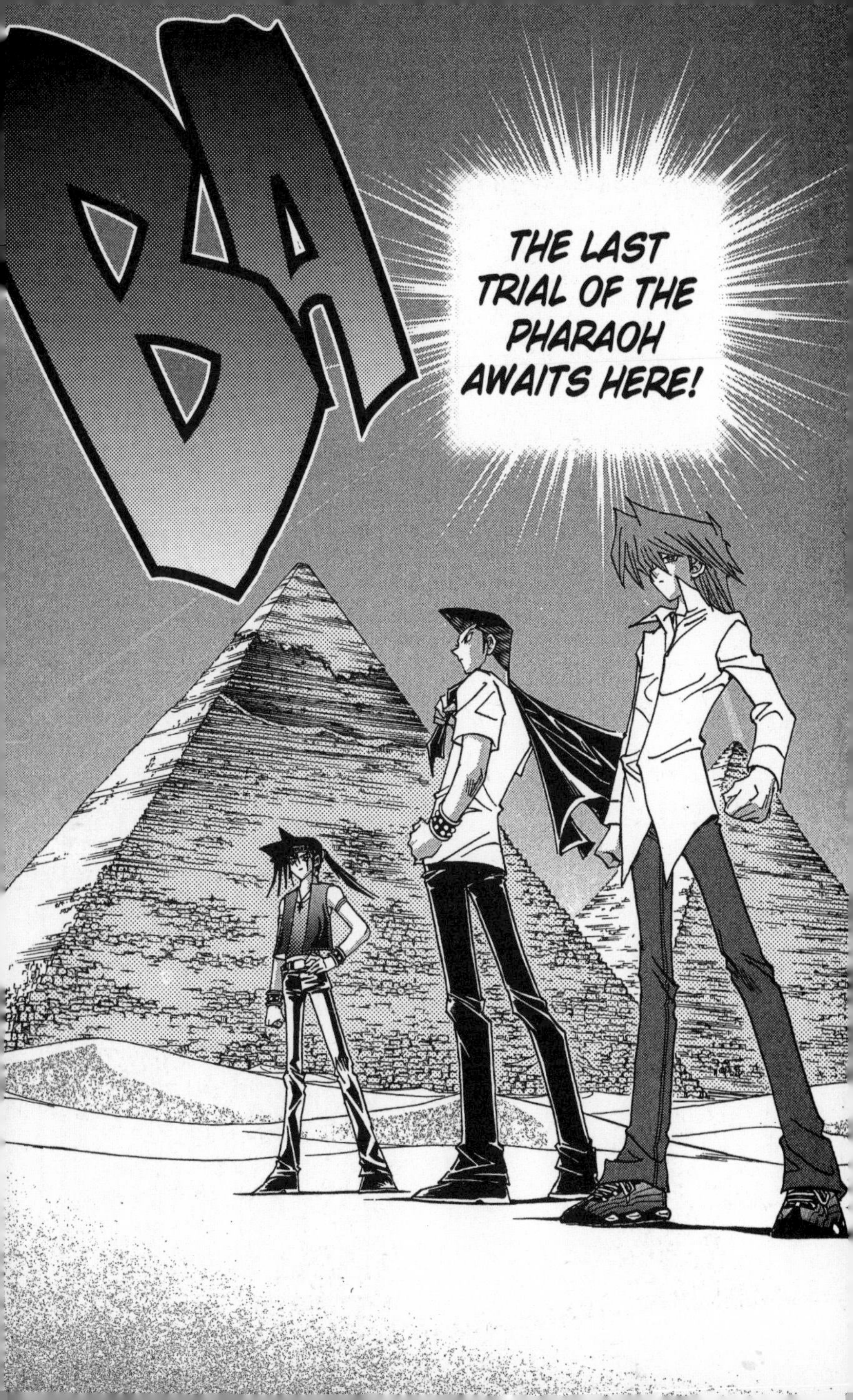
BA
THE LAST TRIAL OF THE PHARAOH AWAITS HERE!

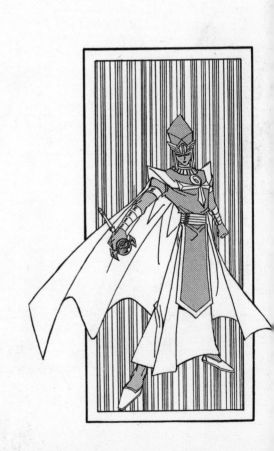

Duel 59: Over the Nile!!

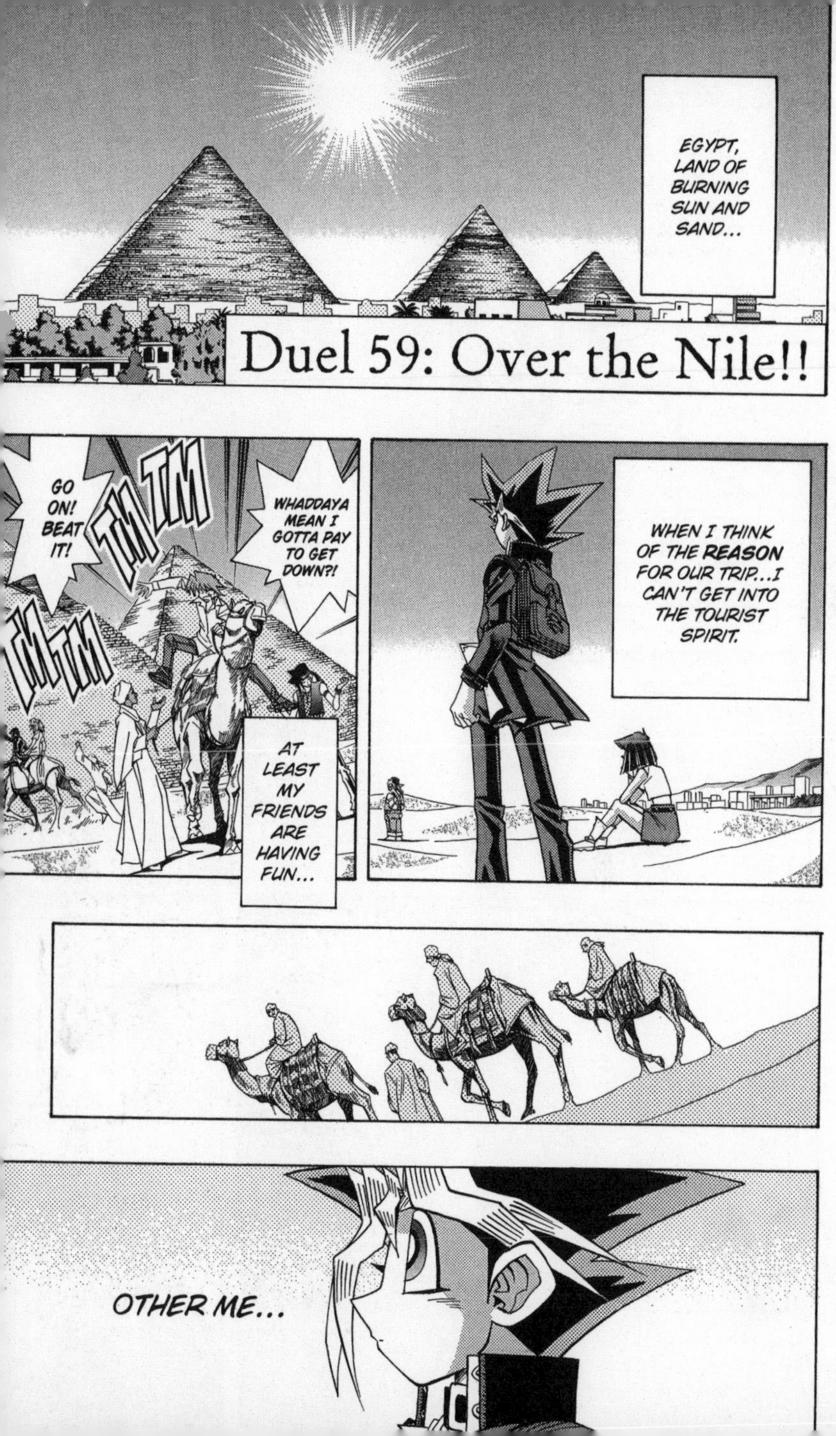
EGYPT, LAND OF BURNING SUN AND SAND...
WHEN I THINK OF THE **REASON** FOR OUR TRIP...I CAN'T GET INTO THE TOURIST SPIRIT.
WHADDAYA MEAN I GOTTA PAY TO GET DOWN?!
TM TM
GO ON! BEAT IT!
TM TM
AT LEAST MY FRIENDS ARE HAVING FUN...
OTHER ME...

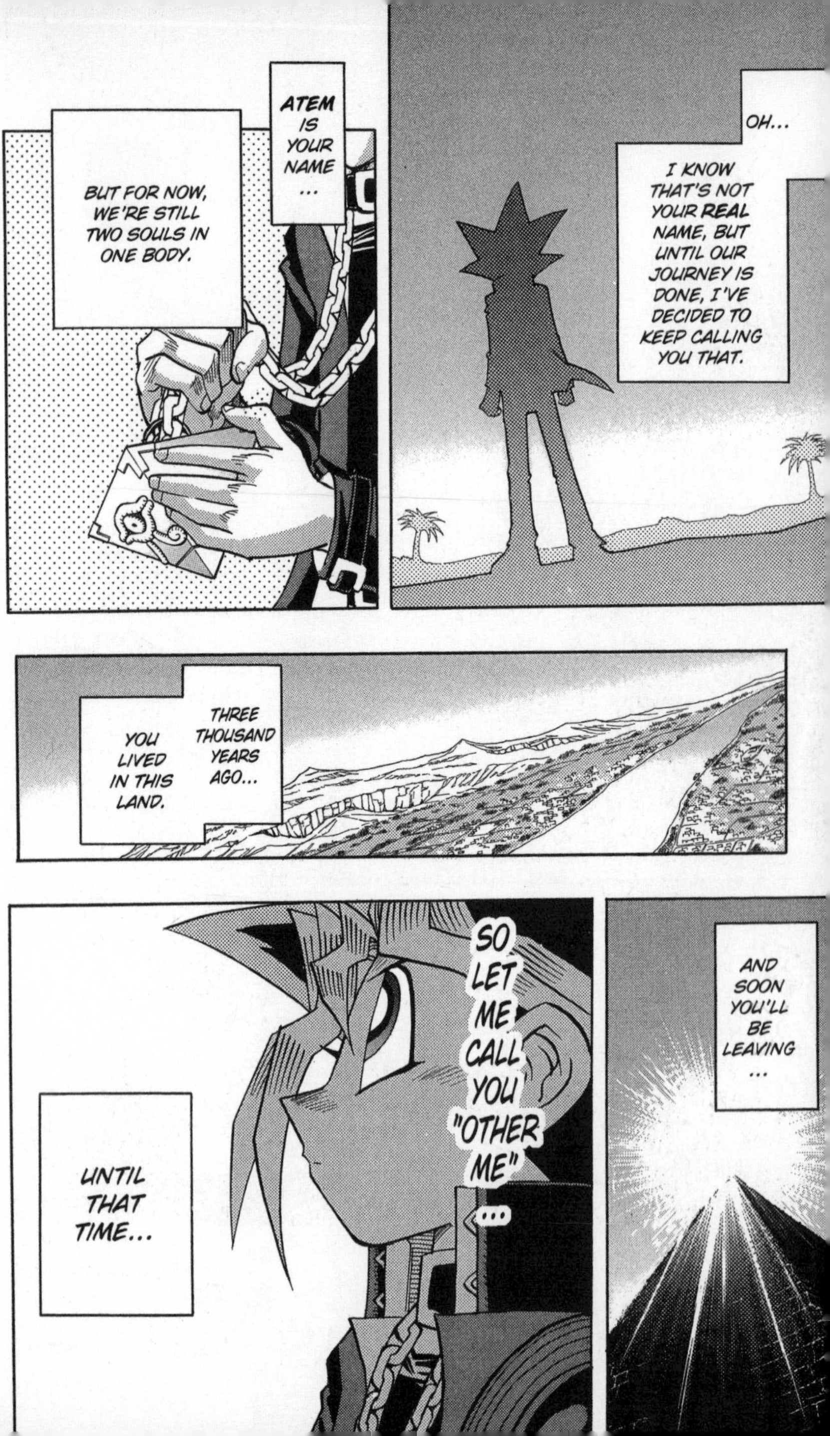
OH...
I KNOW THAT'S NOT YOUR **REAL** NAME, BUT UNTIL OUR JOURNEY IS DONE, I'VE DECIDED TO KEEP CALLING YOU THAT.
ATEM IS YOUR NAME ...
BUT FOR NOW, WE'RE STILL TWO SOULS IN ONE BODY.
THREE THOUSAND YEARS AGO...
YOU LIVED IN THIS LAND.
AND SOON YOU'LL BE LEAVING ...
SO LET ME CALL YOU "OTHER ME" ...
UNTIL THAT TIME...

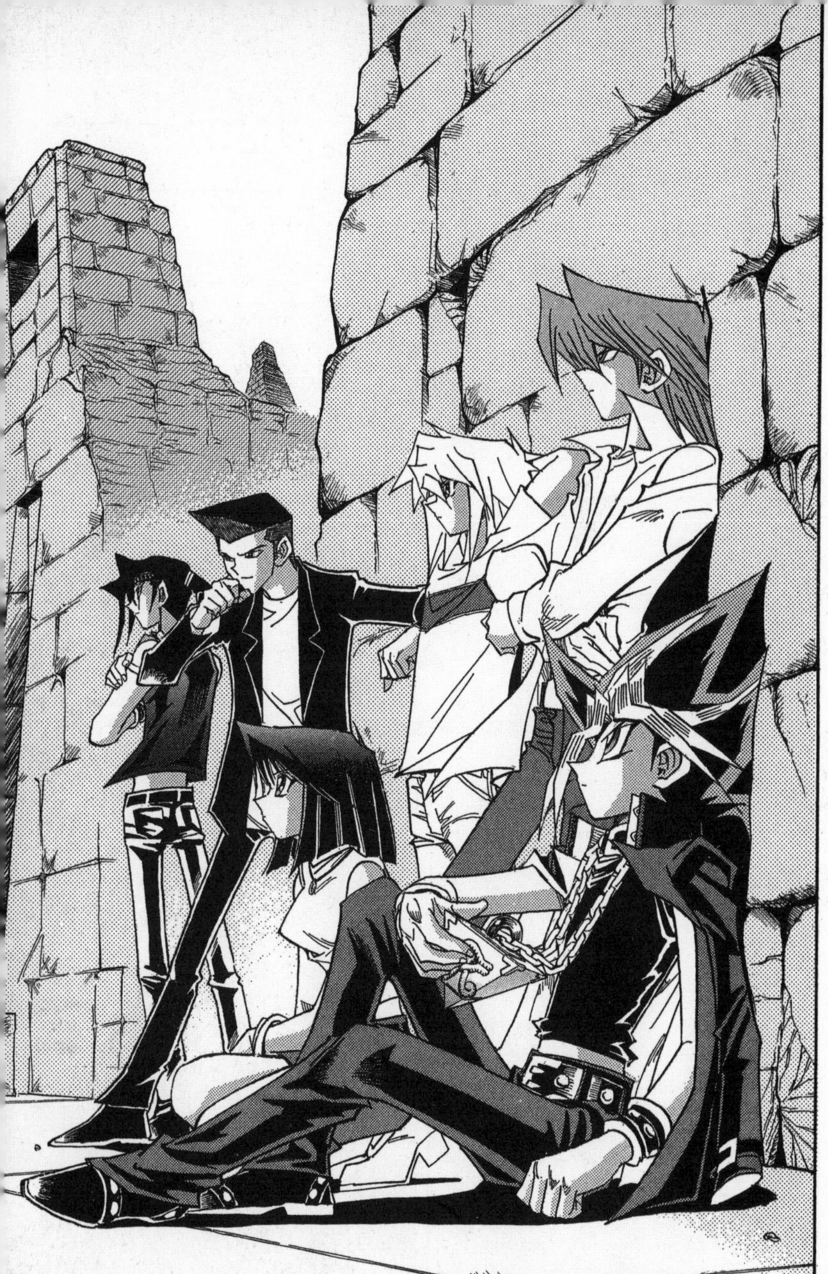

Duel 59: Over the Nile!!

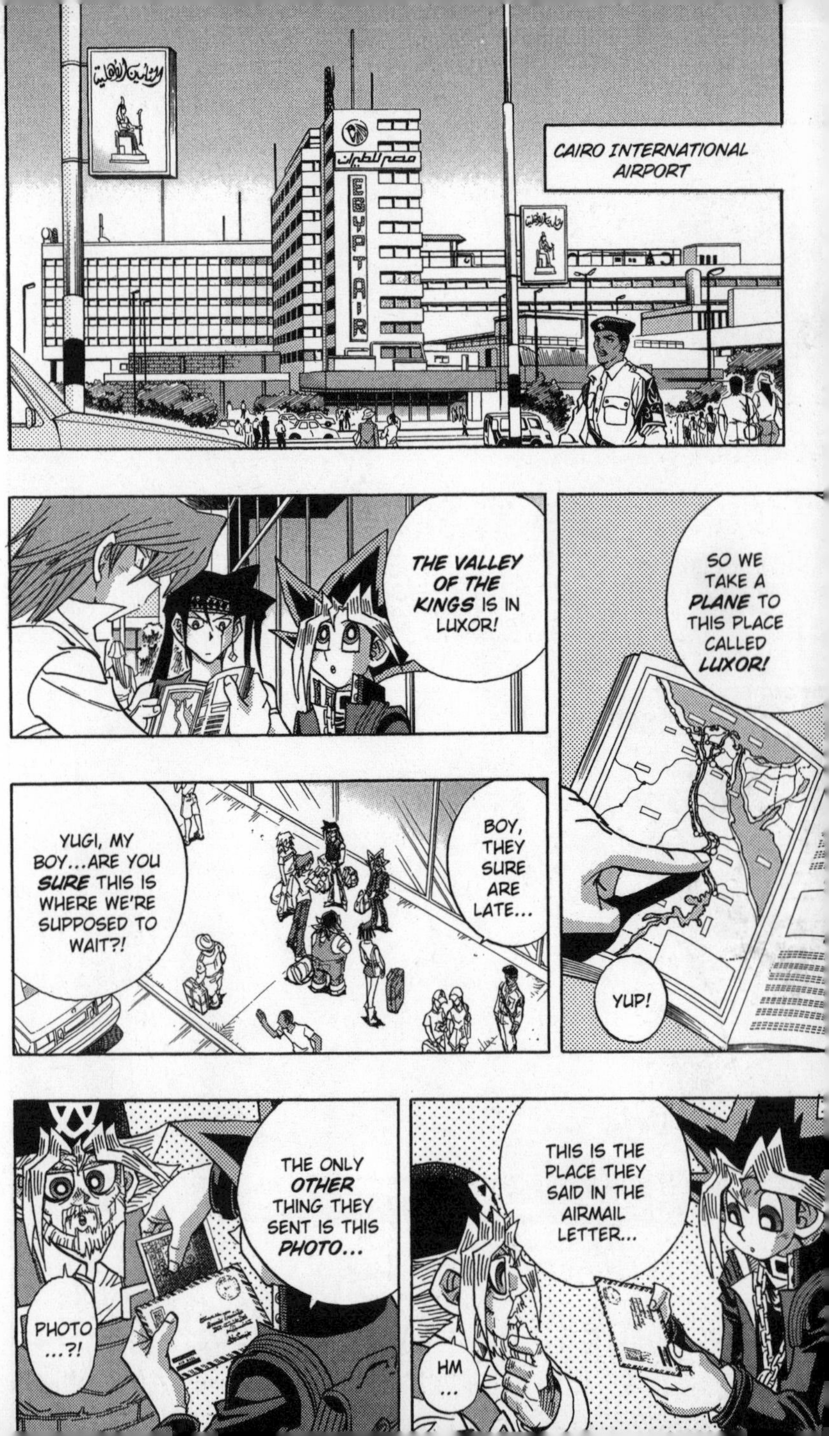
CAIRO INTERNATIONAL AIRPORT
EGYPT AIR
SO WE TAKE A *PLANE* TO THIS PLACE CALLED *LUXOR!*
YUP!
THE VALLEY OF THE KINGS IS IN LUXOR!
BOY, THEY SURE ARE LATE...
YUGI, MY BOY...ARE YOU *SURE* THIS IS WHERE WE'RE SUPPOSED TO WAIT?!
THIS IS THE PLACE THEY SAID IN THE AIRMAIL LETTER...
HM...
THE ONLY *OTHER* THING THEY SENT IS THIS *PHOTO...*
PHOTO...?!

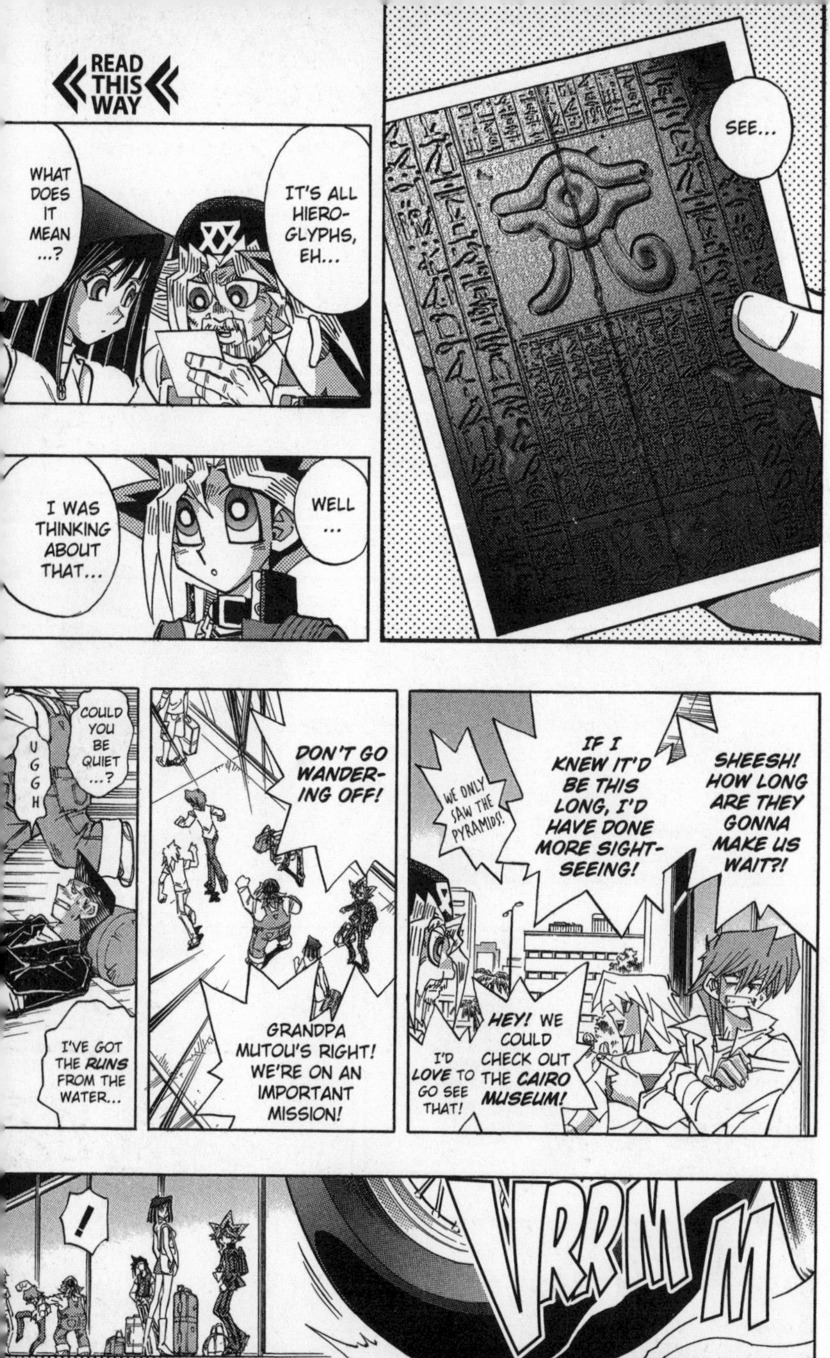
READ THIS WAY
SEE...
IT'S ALL HIERO-GLYPHS, EH...
WHAT DOES IT MEAN ...?
WELL ...
I WAS THINKING ABOUT THAT...
SHEESH! HOW LONG ARE THEY GONNA MAKE US WAIT?!
IF I KNEW IT'D BE THIS LONG, I'D HAVE DONE MORE SIGHT-SEEING!
WE ONLY SAW THE PYRAMIDS!
HEY! WE COULD CHECK OUT THE CAIRO MUSEUM!
I'D LOVE TO GO SEE THAT!
DON'T GO WANDER-ING OFF!
GRANDPA MUTOU'S RIGHT! WE'RE ON AN IMPORTANT MISSION!
COULD YOU BE QUIET ...?
UGGH
I'VE GOT THE RUNS FROM THE WATER...
VRRM M
!

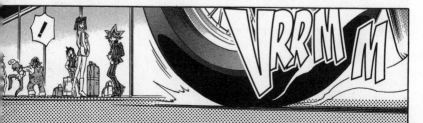

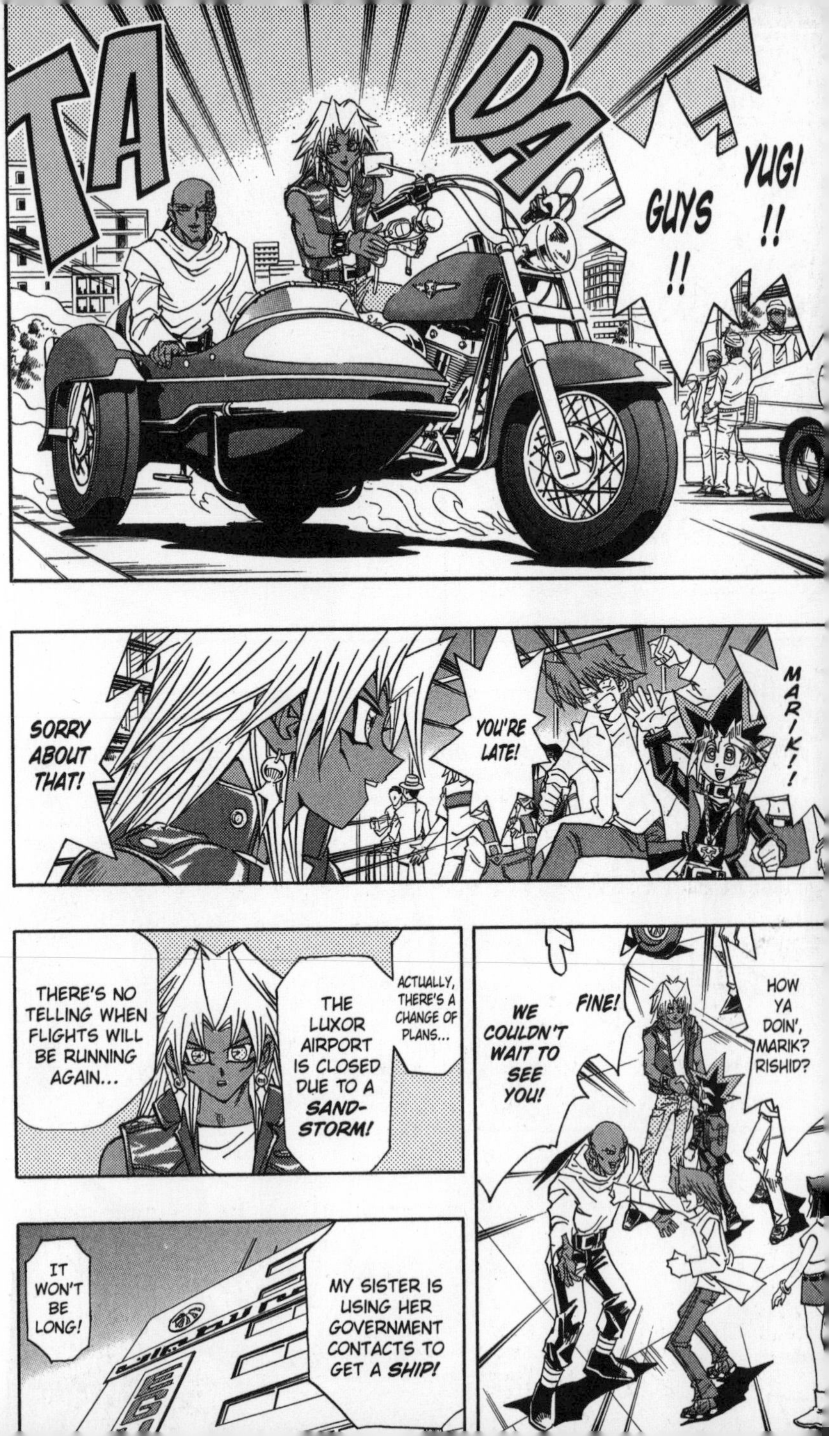
YUGI!!
GUYS!!
TA DA
MARIK!!
YOU'RE LATE!
SORRY ABOUT THAT!
HOW YA DOIN', MARIK? RISHID?
FINE!
WE COULDN'T WAIT TO SEE YOU!
ACTUALLY, THERE'S A CHANGE OF PLANS...
THE LUXOR AIRPORT IS CLOSED DUE TO A SANDSTORM!
THERE'S NO TELLING WHEN FLIGHTS WILL BE RUNNING AGAIN...
MY SISTER IS USING HER GOVERNMENT CONTACTS TO GET A SHIP!
IT WON'T BE LONG!

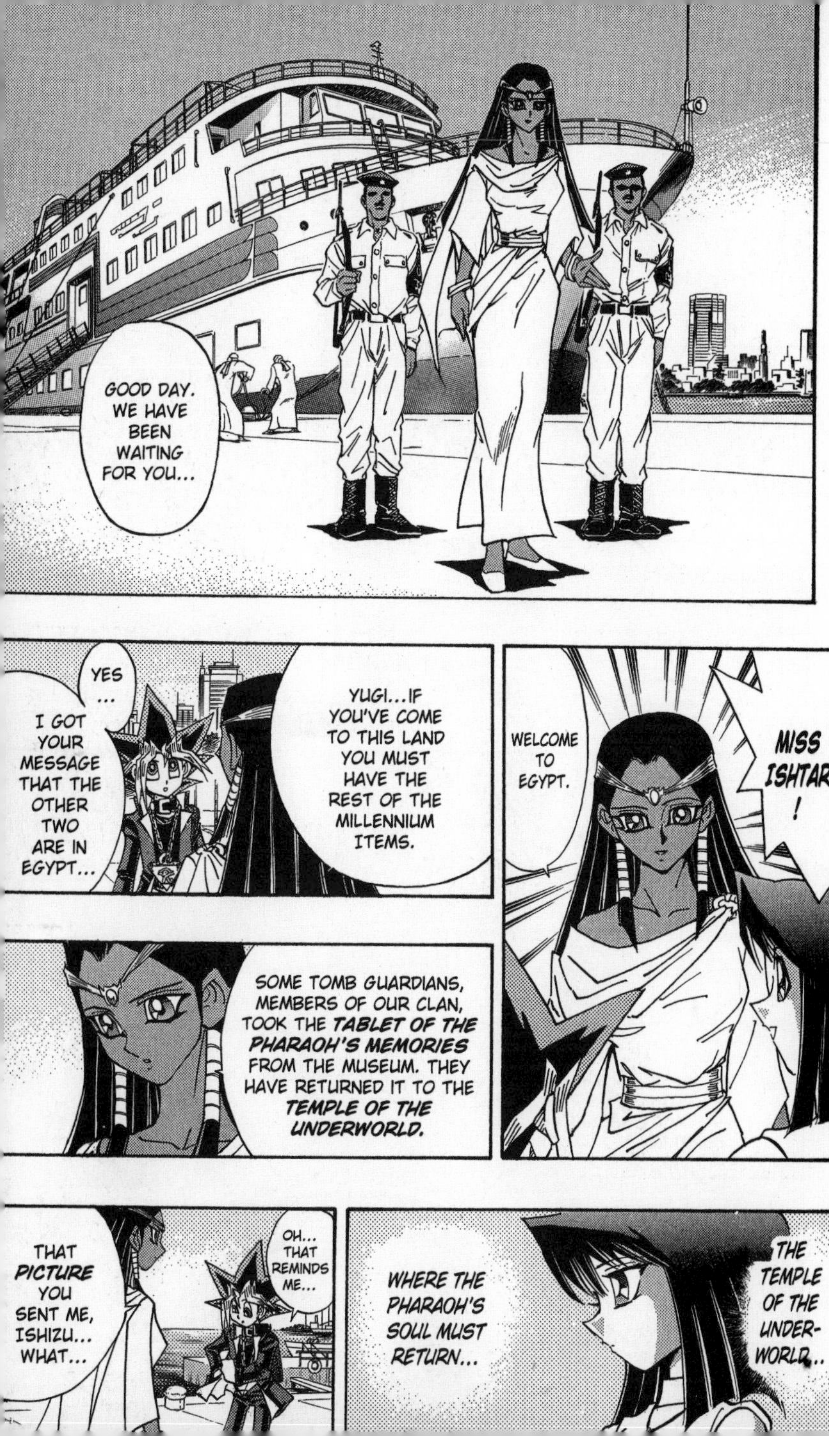
GOOD DAY. WE HAVE BEEN WAITING FOR YOU...
MISS ISHTAR!
WELCOME TO EGYPT.
YUGI...IF YOU'VE COME TO THIS LAND YOU MUST HAVE THE REST OF THE MILLENNIUM ITEMS.
YES...
I GOT YOUR MESSAGE THAT THE OTHER TWO ARE IN EGYPT...
SOME TOMB GUARDIANS, MEMBERS OF OUR CLAN, TOOK THE TABLET OF THE PHARAOH'S MEMORIES FROM THE MUSEUM. THEY HAVE RETURNED IT TO THE TEMPLE OF THE UNDERWORLD.
THE TEMPLE OF THE UNDERWORLD...
WHERE THE PHARAOH'S SOUL MUST RETURN...
OH... THAT REMINDS ME...
THAT PICTURE YOU SENT ME, ISHIZU... WHAT...

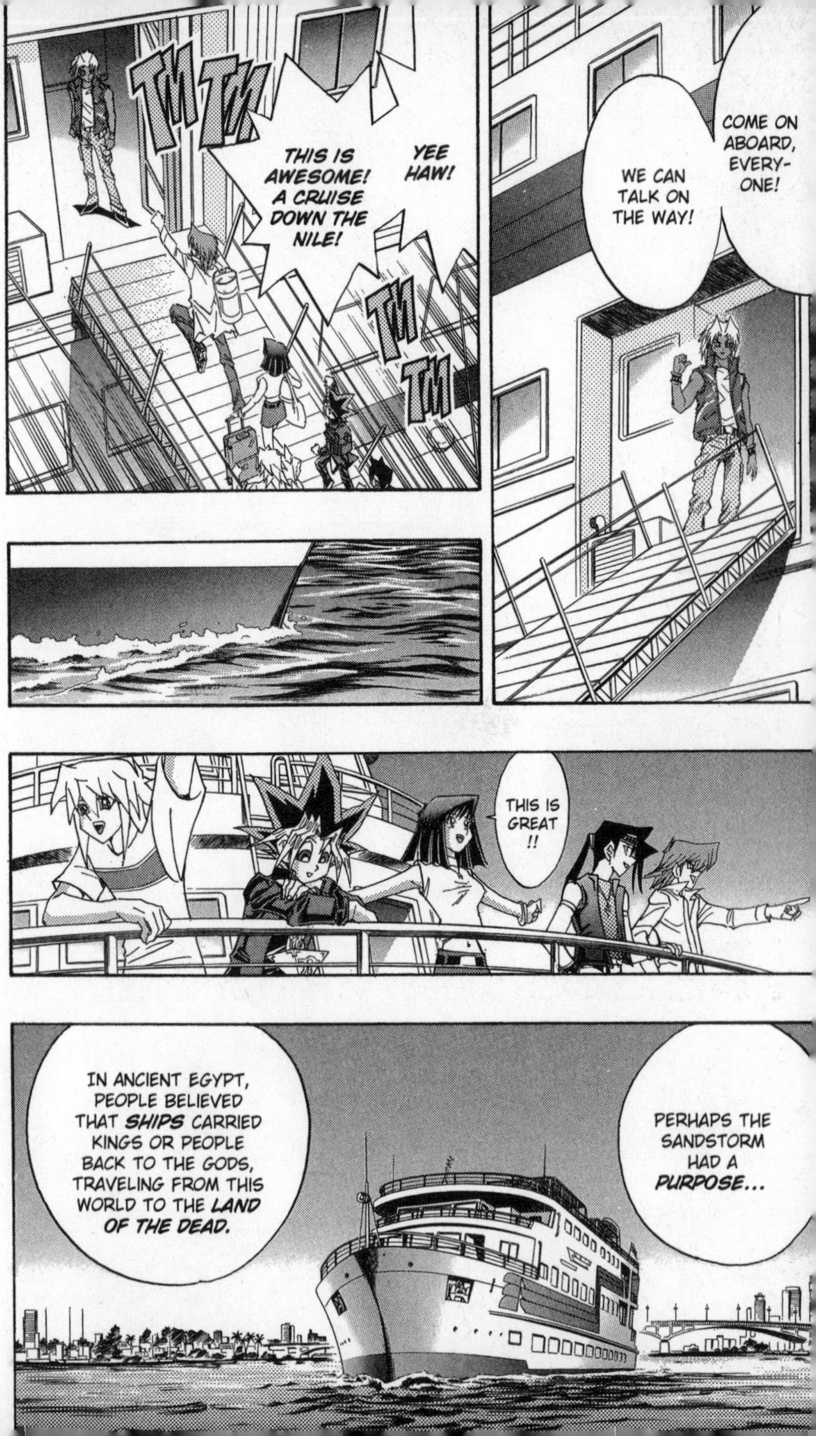
COME ON ABOARD, EVERYONE!
WE CAN TALK ON THE WAY!
TMTM
YEE HAW!
THIS IS AWESOME! A CRUISE DOWN THE NILE!
TM
TM
THIS IS GREAT!!
PERHAPS THE SANDSTORM HAD A PURPOSE...
IN ANCIENT EGYPT, PEOPLE BELIEVED THAT SHIPS CARRIED KINGS OR PEOPLE BACK TO THE GODS, TRAVELING FROM THIS WORLD TO THE LAND OF THE DEAD.

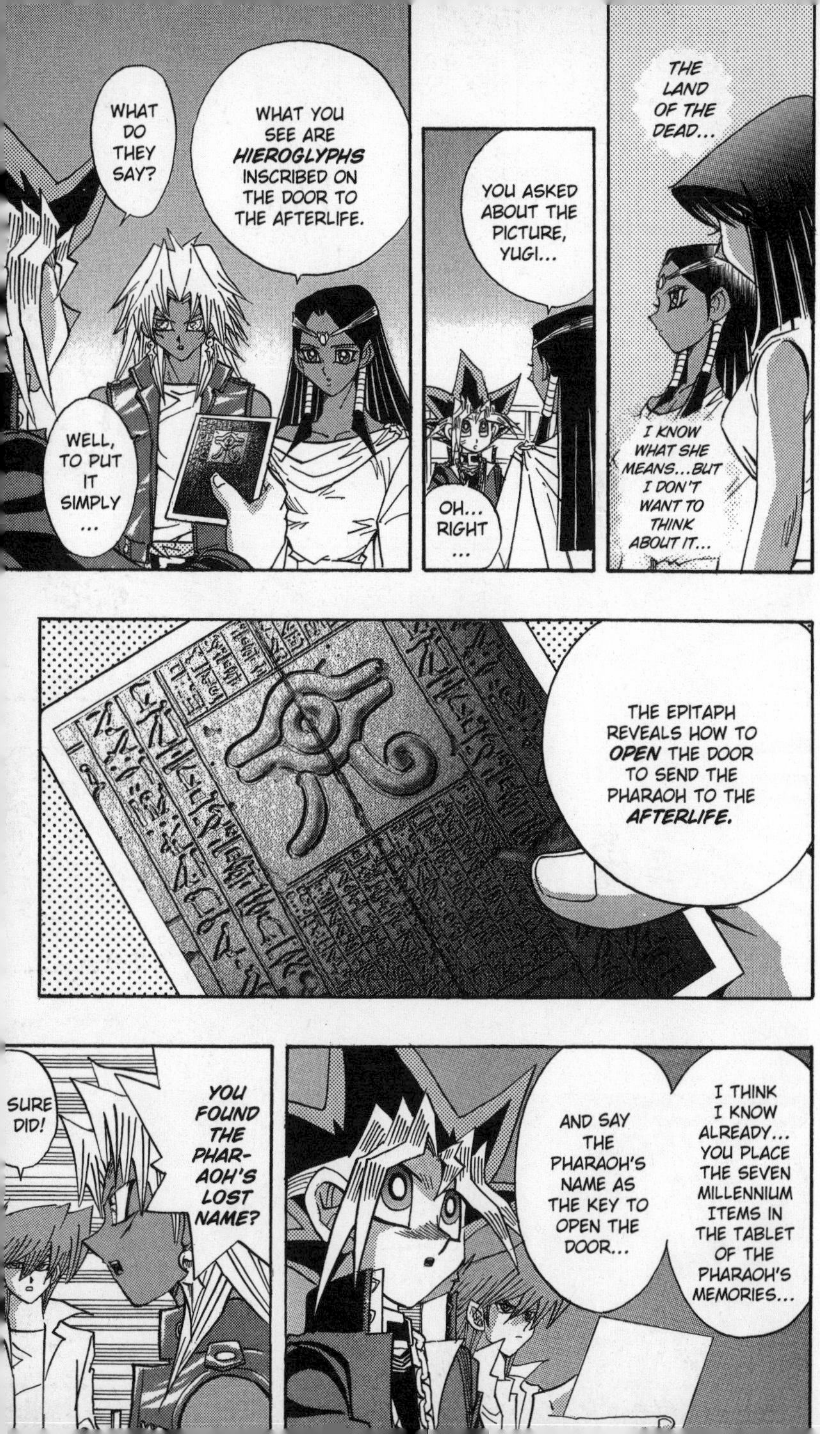
THE LAND OF THE DEAD...
I KNOW WHAT SHE MEANS...BUT I DON'T WANT TO THINK ABOUT IT...
YOU ASKED ABOUT THE PICTURE, YUGI...
OH... RIGHT ...
WHAT YOU SEE ARE HIEROGLYPHS INSCRIBED ON THE DOOR TO THE AFTERLIFE.
WHAT DO THEY SAY?
WELL, TO PUT IT SIMPLY ...
THE EPITAPH REVEALS HOW TO OPEN THE DOOR TO SEND THE PHARAOH TO THE AFTERLIFE.
I THINK I KNOW ALREADY... YOU PLACE THE SEVEN MILLENNIUM ITEMS IN THE TABLET OF THE PHARAOH'S MEMORIES...
AND SAY THE PHARAOH'S NAME AS THE KEY TO OPEN THE DOOR...
YOU FOUND THE PHAR-AOH'S LOST NAME?
SURE DID!

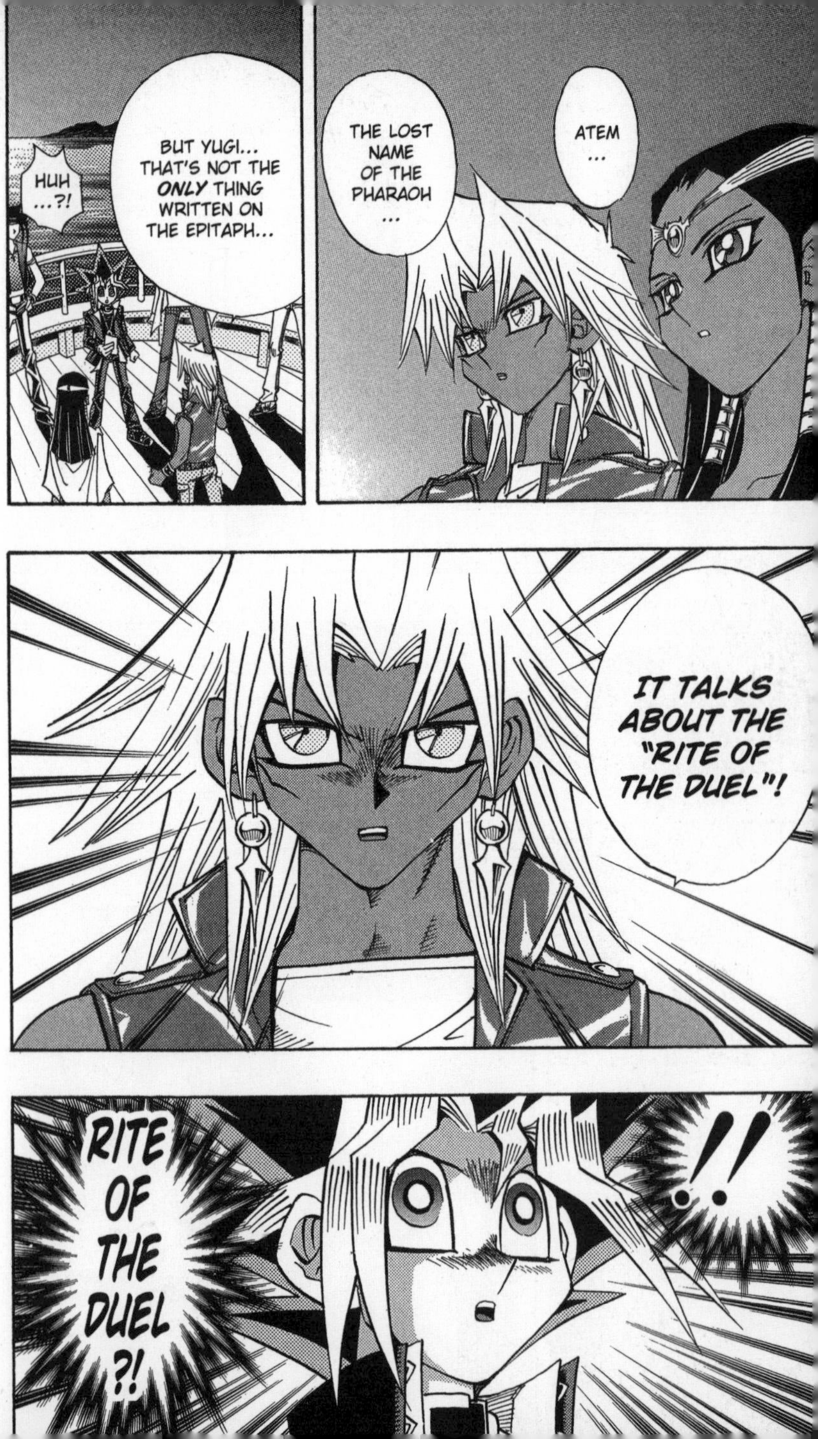
ATEM ...
THE LOST NAME OF THE PHARAOH ...
BUT YUGI... THAT'S NOT THE ONLY THING WRITTEN ON THE EPITAPH...
HUH ...?!
IT TALKS ABOUT THE "RITE OF THE DUEL"!
!!
RITE OF THE DUEL ?!

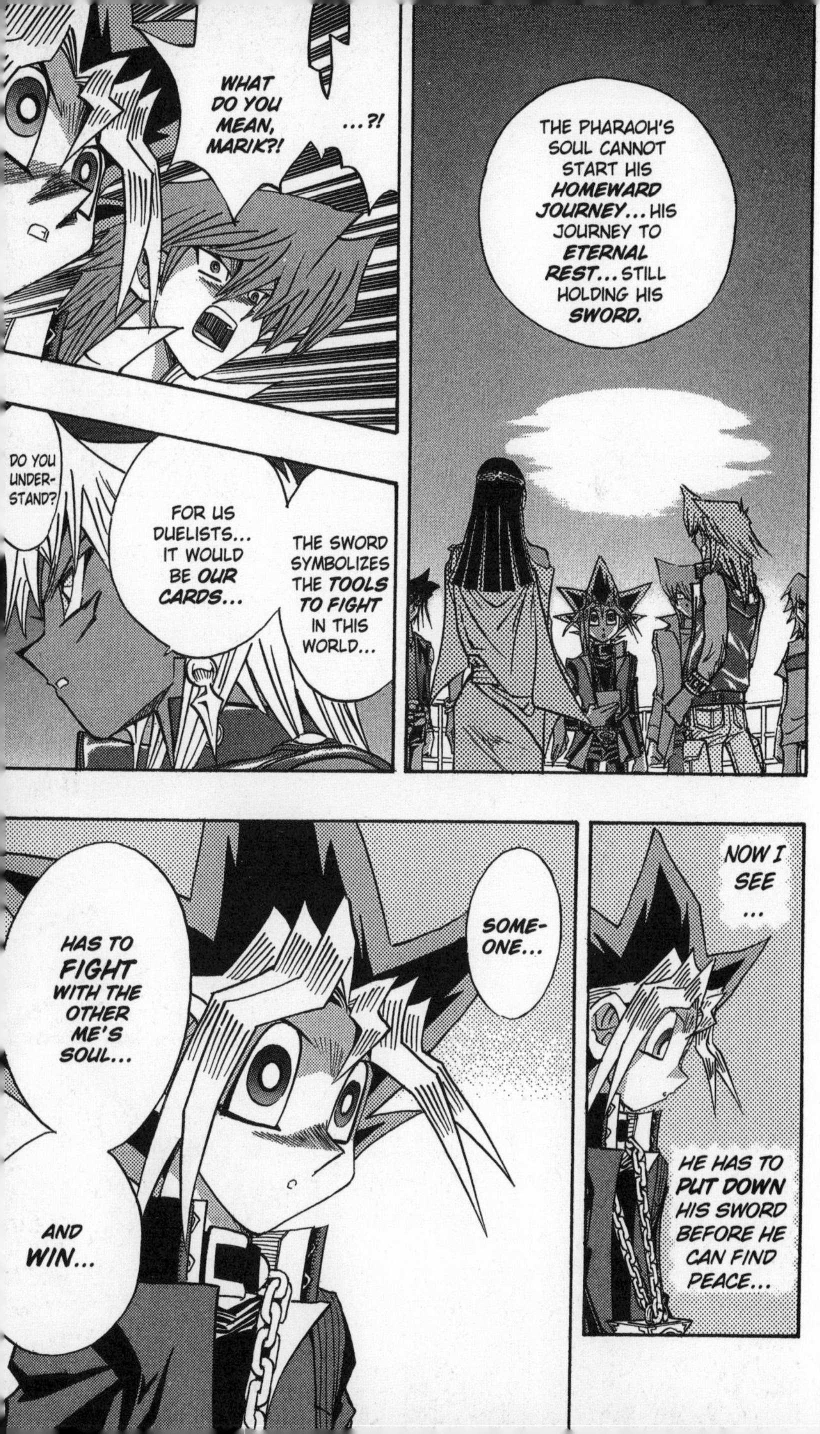
THE PHARAOH'S SOUL CANNOT START HIS **HOMEWARD JOURNEY...** HIS JOURNEY TO **ETERNAL REST...** STILL HOLDING HIS **SWORD.**
...?!
WHAT DO YOU MEAN, MARIK?!
THE SWORD SYMBOLIZES THE **TOOLS TO FIGHT** IN THIS WORLD...
FOR US DUELISTS... IT WOULD BE **OUR CARDS...**
DO YOU UNDER-STAND?
NOW I SEE ...
HE HAS TO **PUT DOWN** HIS SWORD BEFORE HE CAN FIND PEACE...
SOME-ONE...
HAS TO **FIGHT** WITH THE OTHER ME'S SOUL...
AND **WIN...**

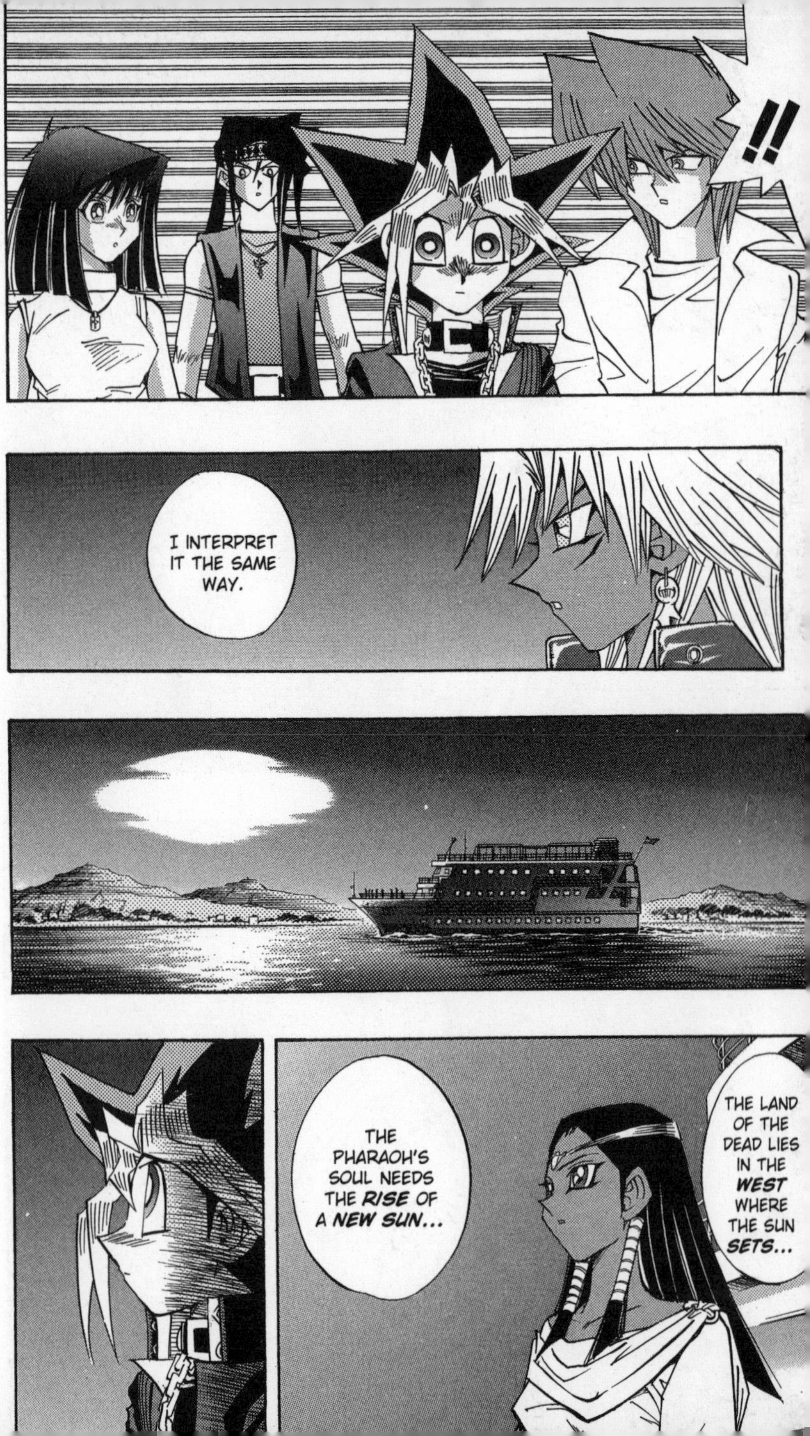
!!
I INTERPRET IT THE SAME WAY.
THE LAND OF THE DEAD LIES IN THE WEST WHERE THE SUN SETS...
THE PHARAOH'S SOUL NEEDS THE RISE OF A NEW SUN...

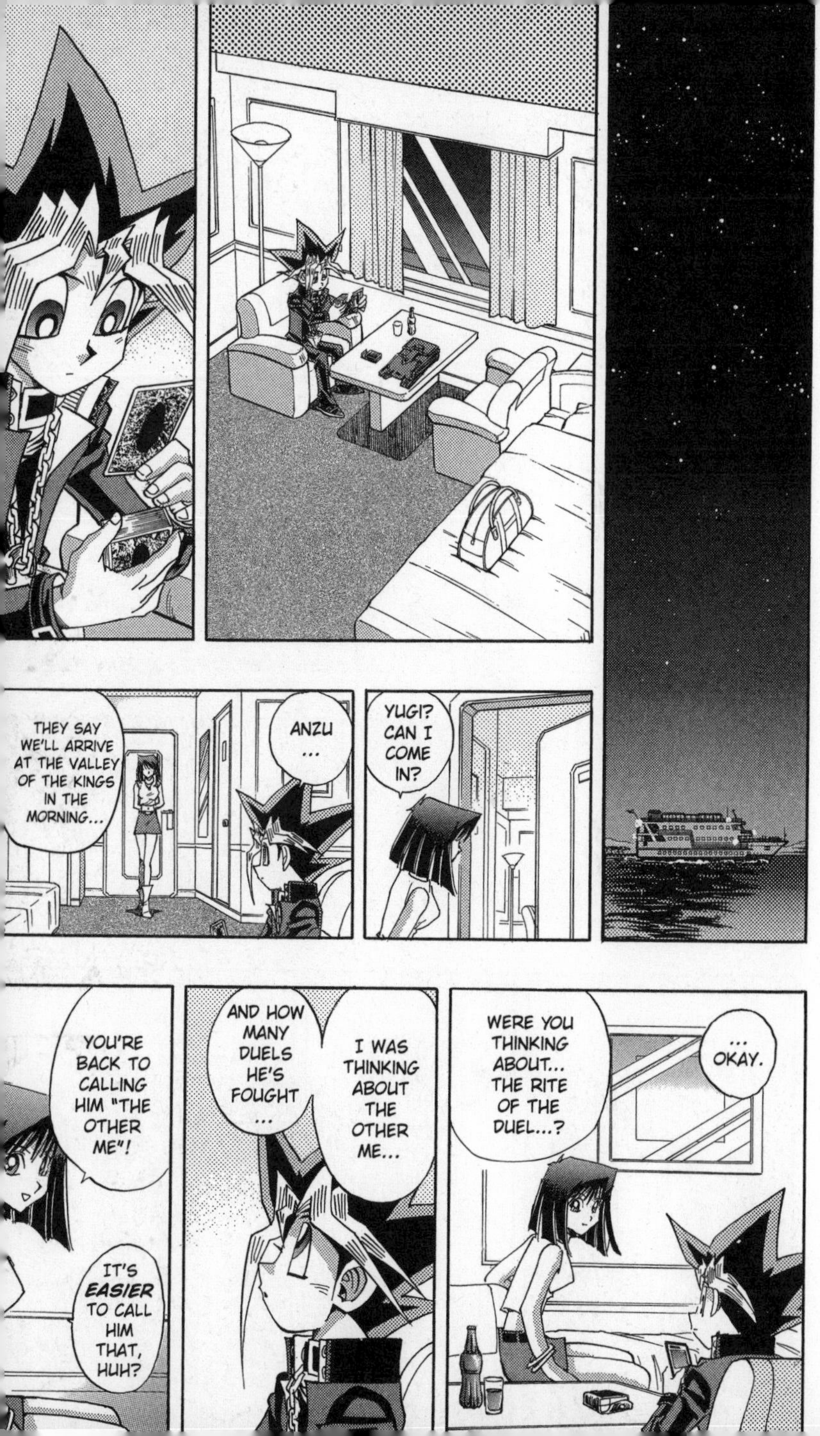
YUGI? CAN I COME IN?
ANZU...
THEY SAY WE'LL ARRIVE AT THE VALLEY OF THE KINGS IN THE MORNING...
...OKAY.
WERE YOU THINKING ABOUT... THE RITE OF THE DUEL...?
I WAS THINKING ABOUT THE OTHER ME...
AND HOW MANY DUELS HE'S FOUGHT...
YOU'RE BACK TO CALLING HIM "THE OTHER ME"!
IT'S *EASIER* TO CALL HIM THAT, HUH?

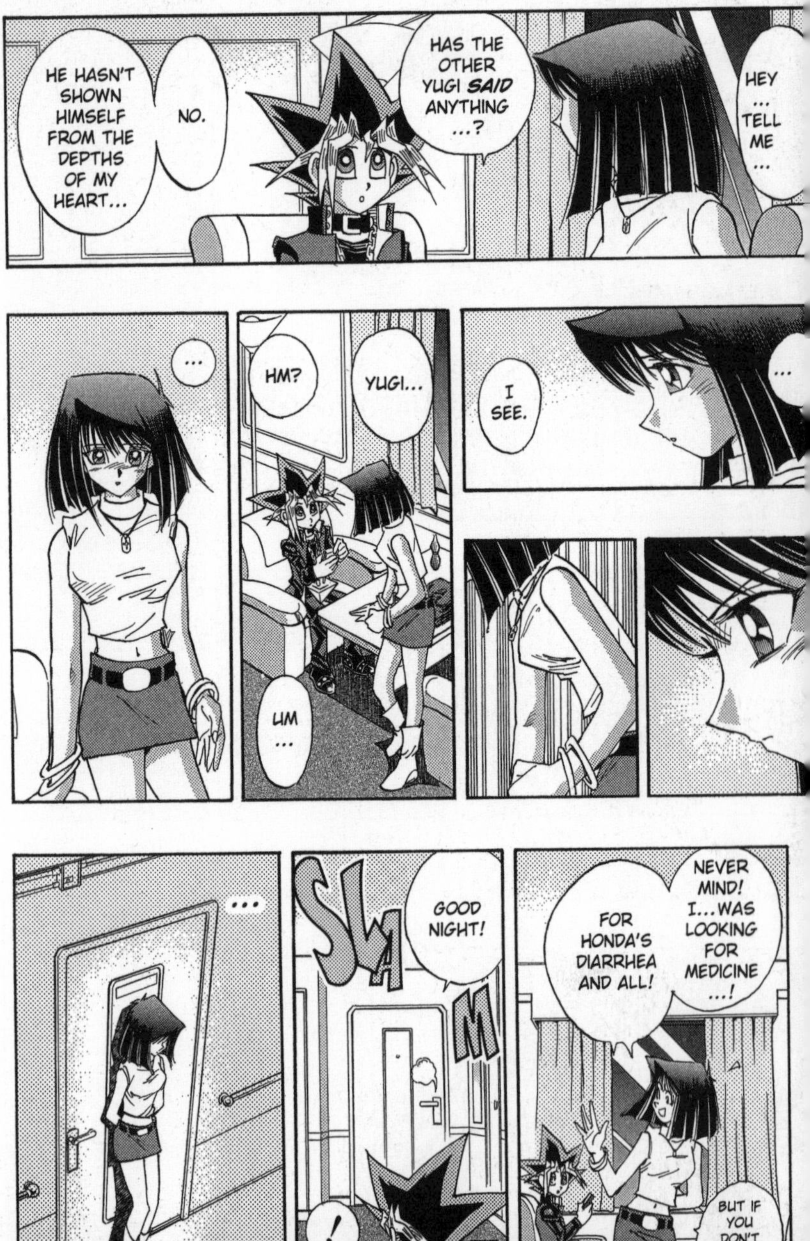
HEY ... TELL ME ...
HAS THE OTHER YUGI SAID ANYTHING ...?
NO.
HE HASN'T SHOWN HIMSELF FROM THE DEPTHS OF MY HEART...
...
I SEE.
YUGI...
HM?
UM ...
...
NEVER MIND! I...WAS LOOKING FOR MEDICINE ...!
FOR HONDA'S DIARRHEA AND ALL!
BUT IF YOU DON'T HAVE ANY...
GOOD NIGHT!
SLAM
!
...

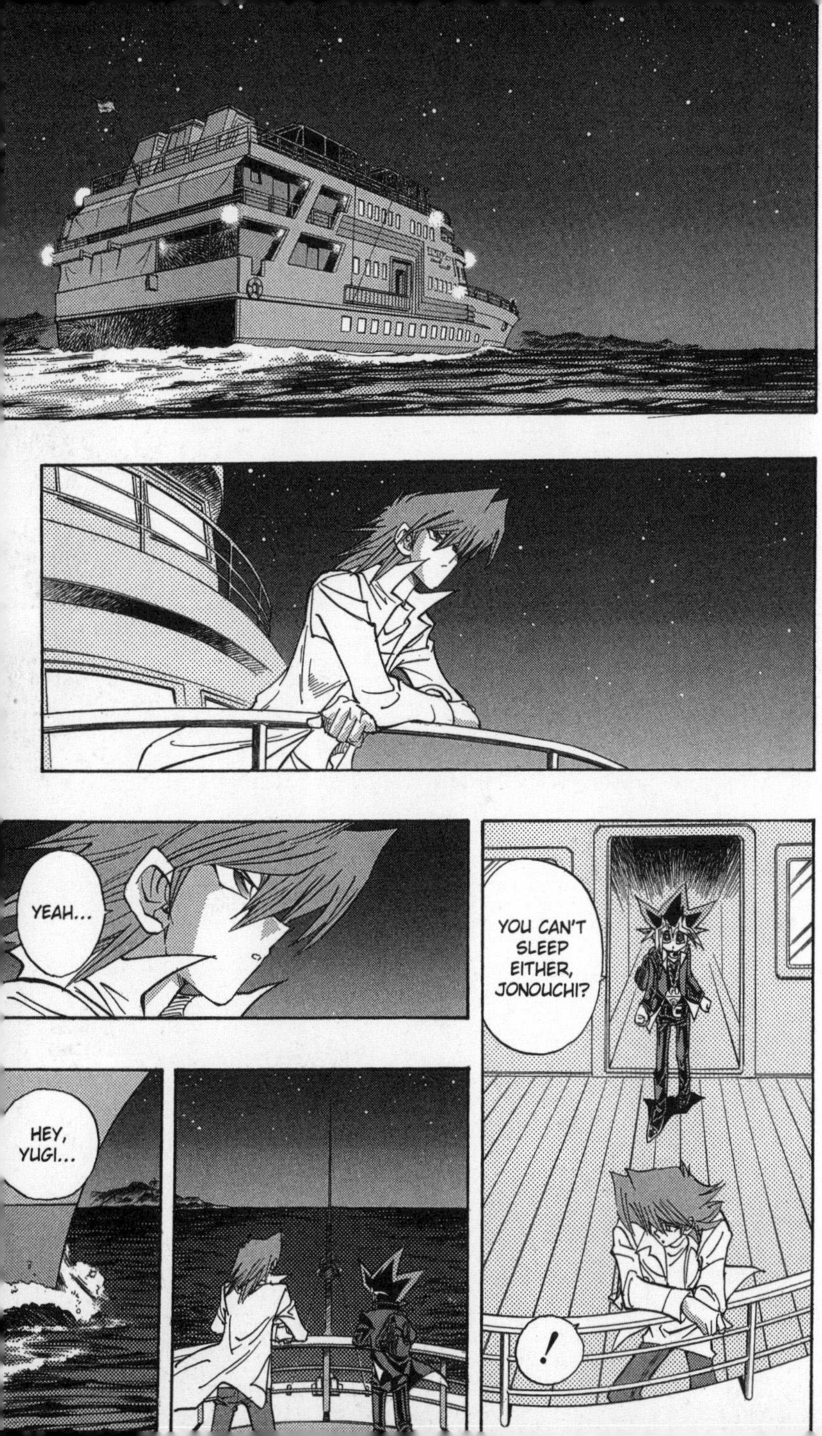
YOU CAN'T SLEEP EITHER, JONOUCHI?
!
YEAH...
HEY, YUGI...

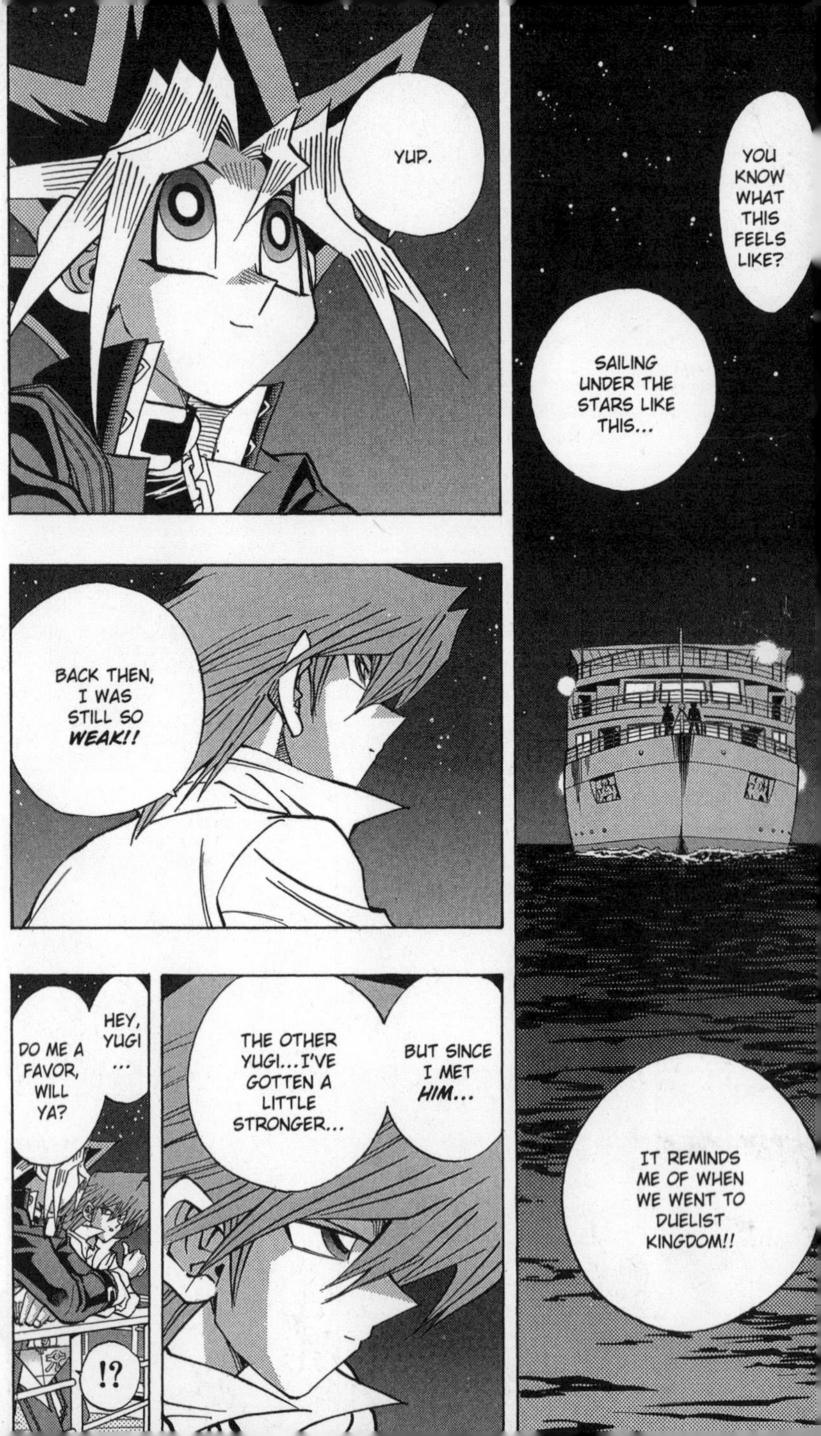
YOU KNOW WHAT THIS FEELS LIKE?
SAILING UNDER THE STARS LIKE THIS...
IT REMINDS ME OF WHEN WE WENT TO DUELIST KINGDOM!!
YUP.
BACK THEN, I WAS STILL SO *WEAK!!*
BUT SINCE I MET *HIM...*
THE OTHER YUGI...I'VE GOTTEN A LITTLE STRONGER...
HEY, YUGI ...
DO ME A FAVOR, WILL YA?
!?

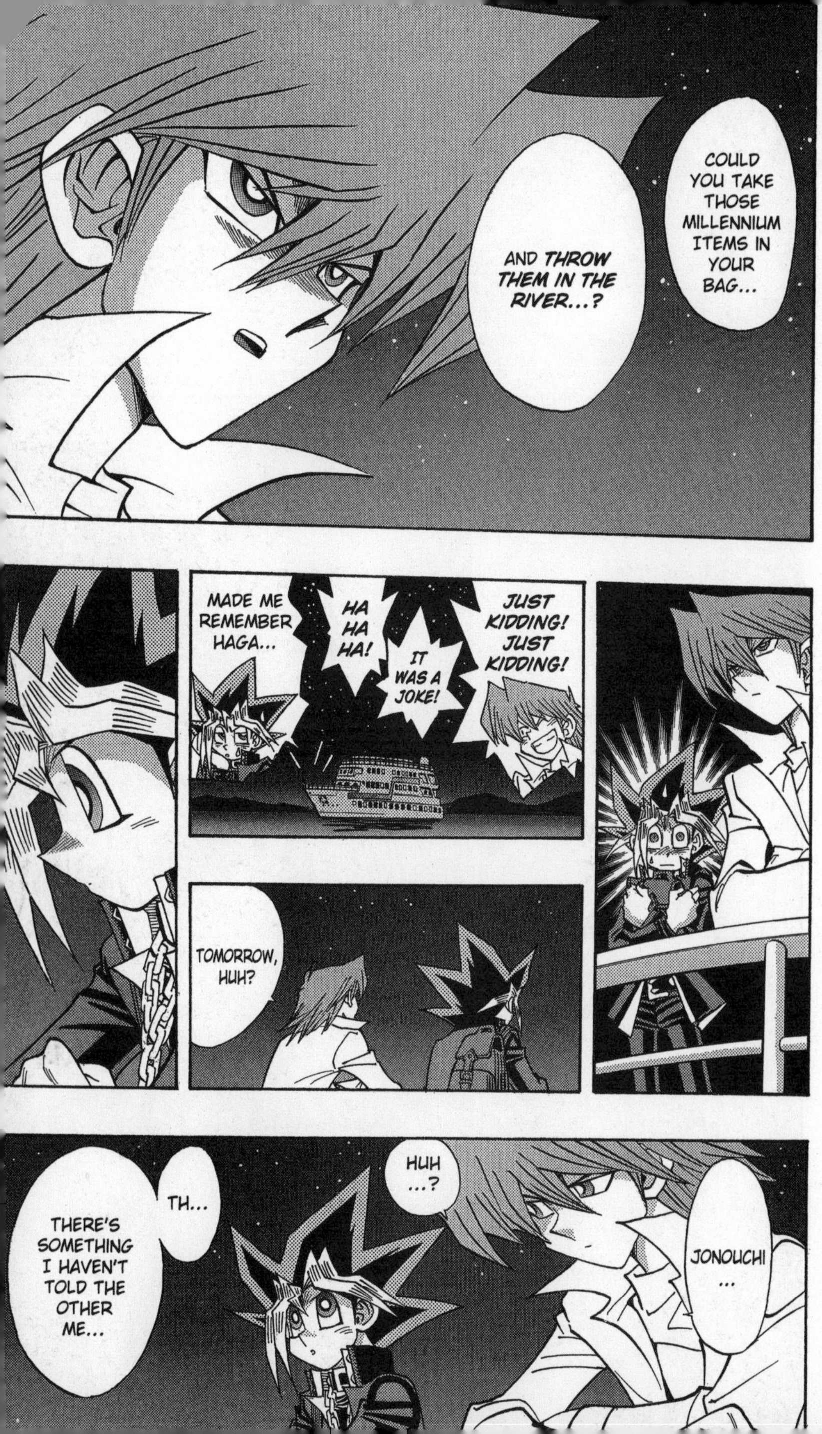
COULD YOU TAKE THOSE MILLENNIUM ITEMS IN YOUR BAG...
AND THROW THEM IN THE RIVER...?
JUST KIDDING! JUST KIDDING!
IT WAS A JOKE!
HA HA HA!
MADE ME REMEMBER HAGA...
TOMORROW, HUH?
JONOUCHI ...
HUH ...?
TH...
THERE'S SOMETHING I HAVEN'T TOLD THE OTHER ME...

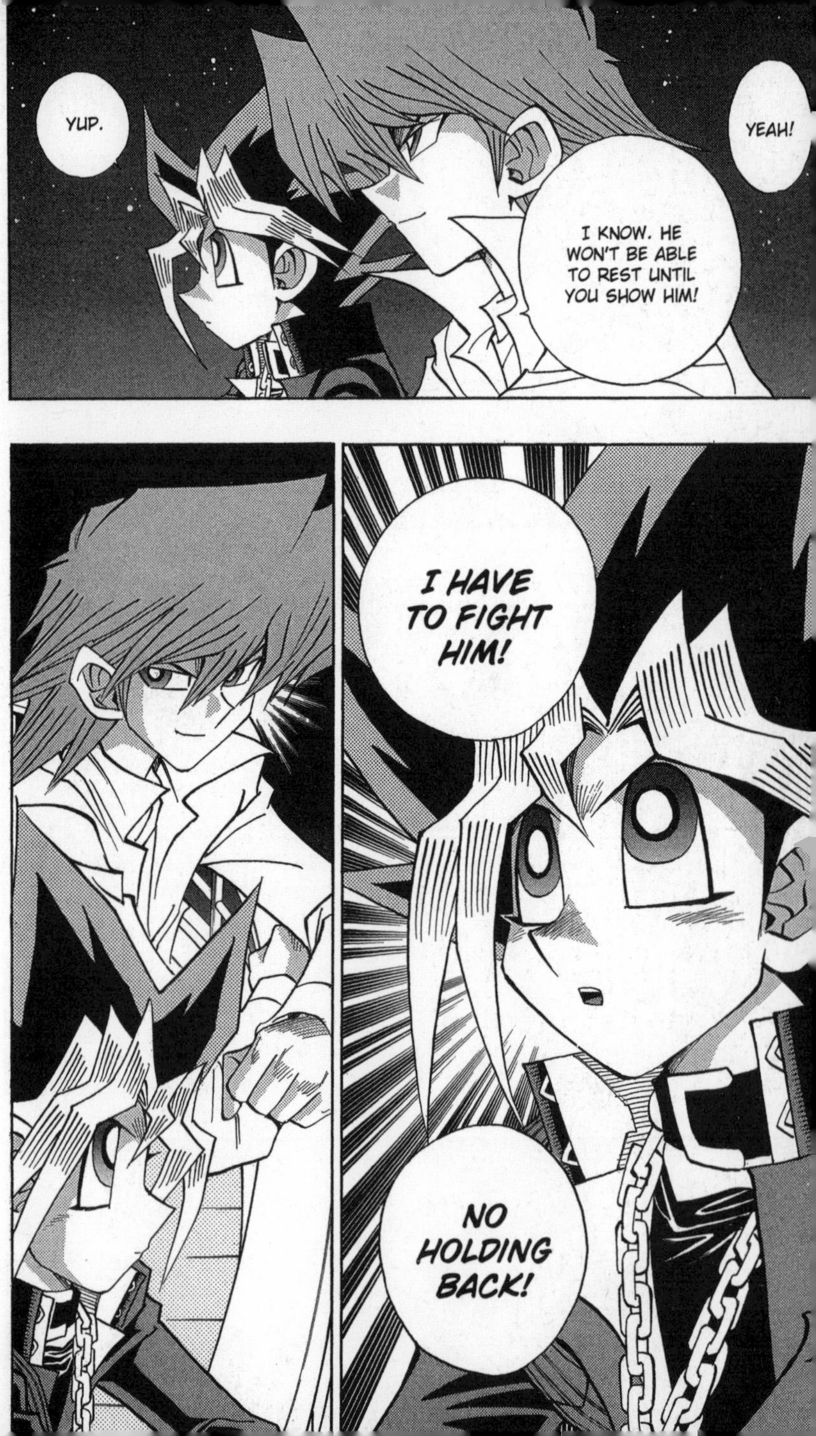
YEAH!
I KNOW. HE WON'T BE ABLE TO REST UNTIL YOU SHOW HIM!
YUP.
I HAVE TO FIGHT HIM!
NO HOLDING BACK!

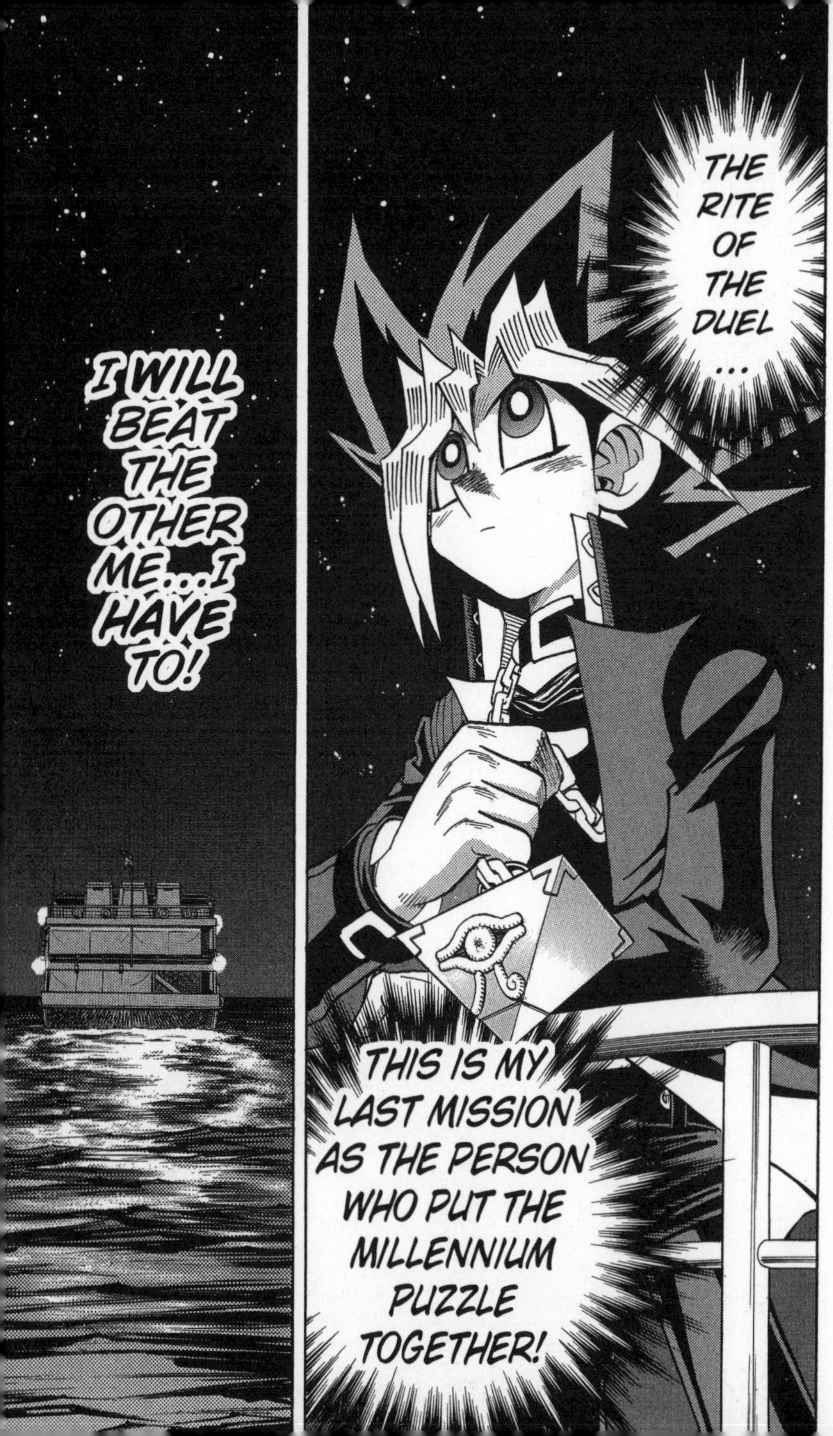
THE RITE OF THE DUEL...
THIS IS MY LAST MISSION AS THE PERSON WHO PUT THE MILLENNIUM PUZZLE TOGETHER!
I WILL BEAT THE OTHER ME...I HAVE TO!

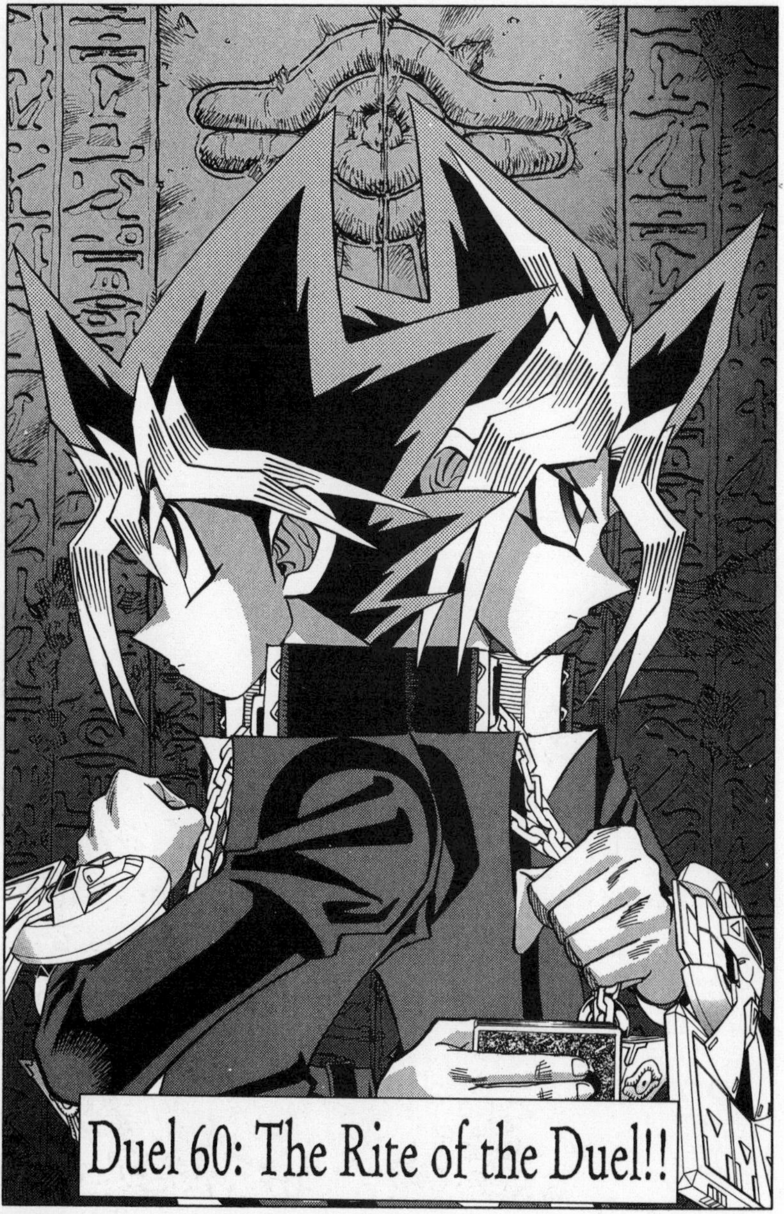
Duel 60: The Rite of the Duel!!

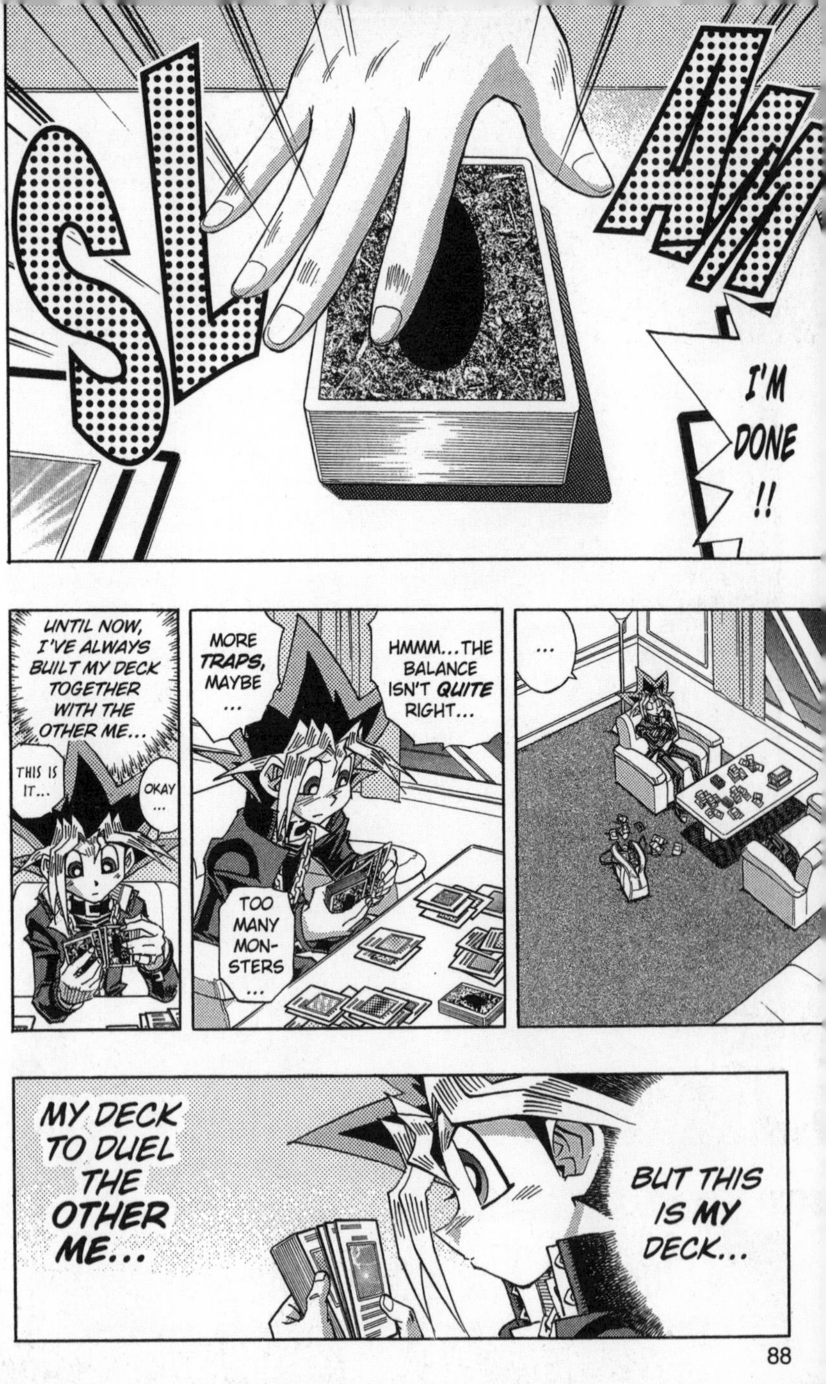
SLAM
I'M DONE!!
...
HMMM...THE BALANCE ISN'T QUITE RIGHT...
MORE TRAPS, MAYBE...
TOO MANY MONSTERS...
UNTIL NOW, I'VE ALWAYS BUILT MY DECK TOGETHER WITH THE OTHER ME...
OKAY...
THIS IS IT...
BUT THIS IS MY DECK...
MY DECK TO DUEL THE OTHER ME...

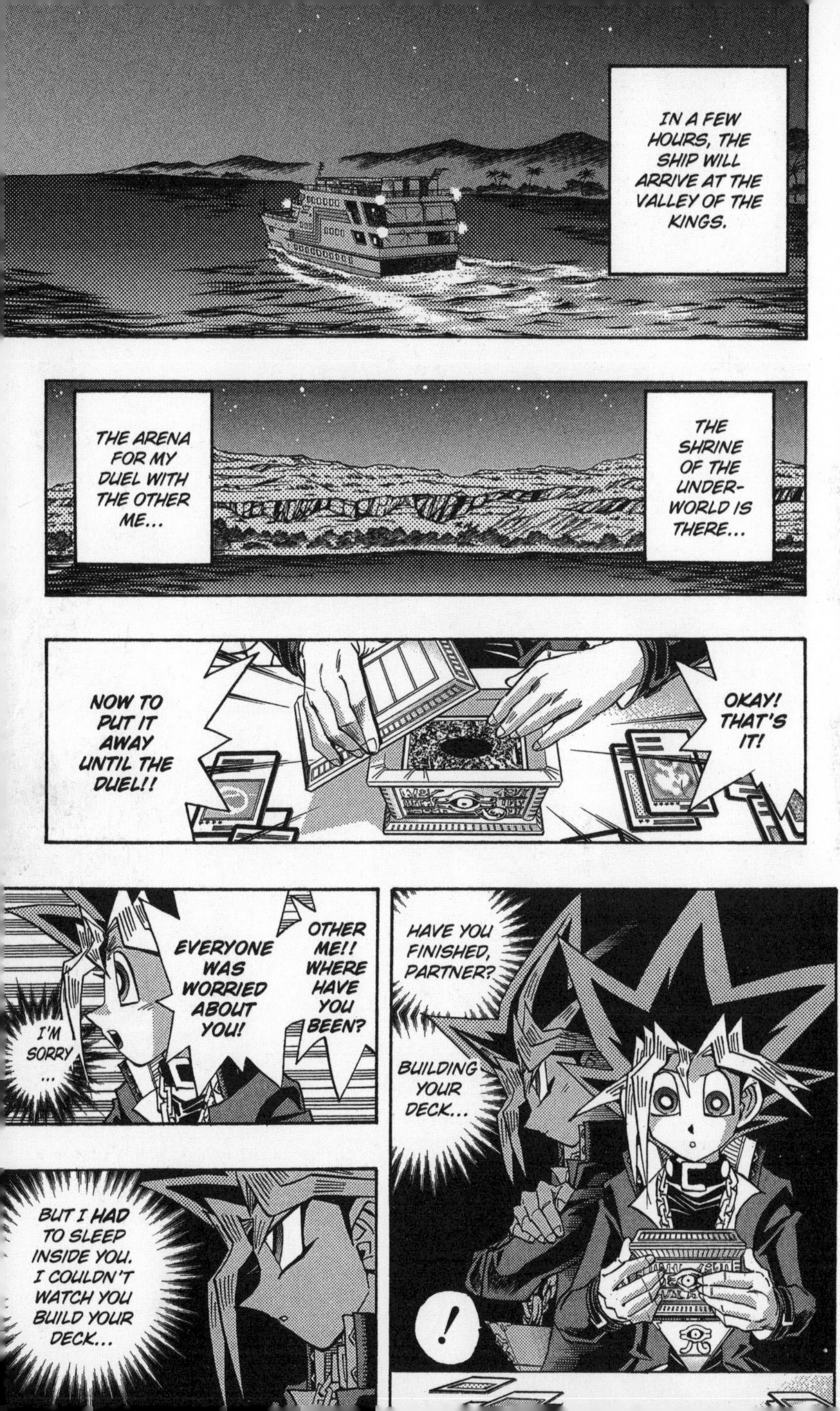
IN A FEW HOURS, THE SHIP WILL ARRIVE AT THE VALLEY OF THE KINGS.
THE SHRINE OF THE UNDER-WORLD IS THERE...
THE ARENA FOR MY DUEL WITH THE OTHER ME...
OKAY! THAT'S IT!
NOW TO PUT IT AWAY UNTIL THE DUEL!!
HAVE YOU FINISHED, PARTNER?
BUILDING YOUR DECK...
!
OTHER ME!! WHERE HAVE YOU BEEN?
EVERYONE WAS WORRIED ABOUT YOU!
I'M SORRY...
BUT I HAD TO SLEEP INSIDE YOU. I COULDN'T WATCH YOU BUILD YOUR DECK...

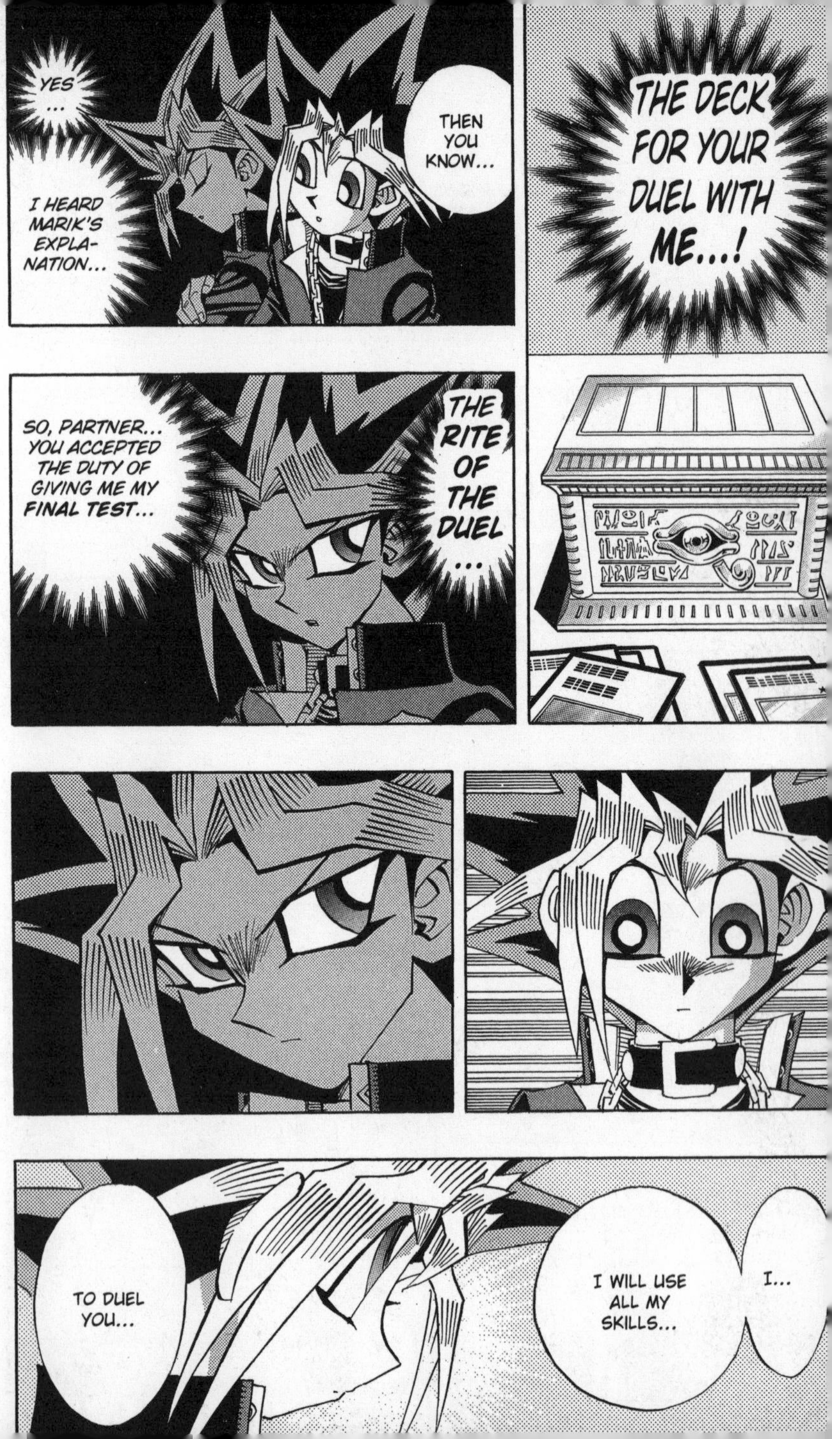
THE DECK FOR YOUR DUEL WITH ME...!
THEN YOU KNOW...
YES ...
I HEARD MARIK'S EXPLA- NATION...
THE RITE OF THE DUEL ...
SO, PARTNER... YOU ACCEPTED THE DUTY OF GIVING ME MY FINAL TEST...
I...
I WILL USE ALL MY SKILLS...
TO DUEL YOU...

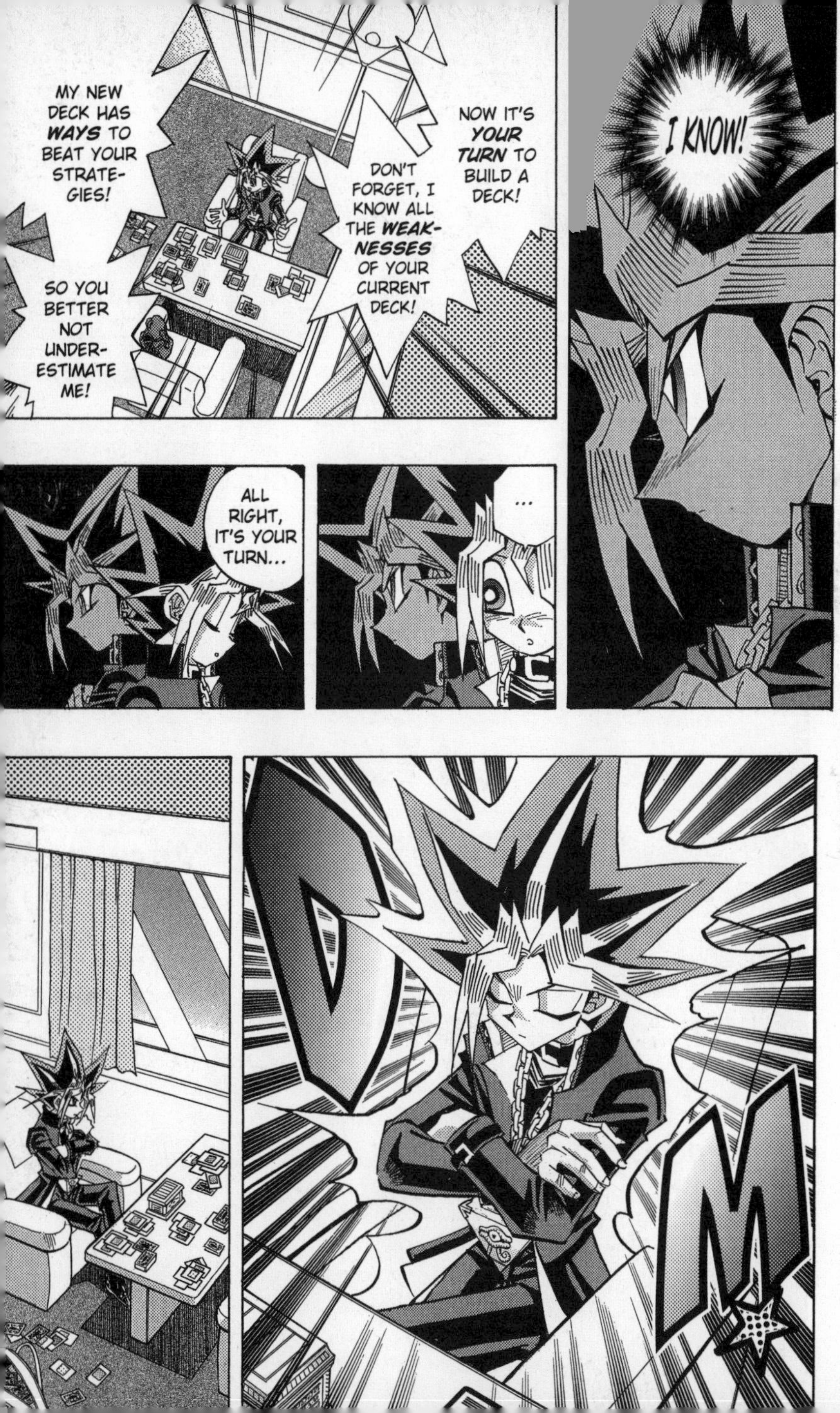
I KNOW!
NOW IT'S YOUR TURN TO BUILD A DECK!
DON'T FORGET, I KNOW ALL THE WEAKNESSES OF YOUR CURRENT DECK!
MY NEW DECK HAS WAYS TO BEAT YOUR STRATEGIES!
SO YOU BETTER NOT UNDERESTIMATE ME!
...
ALL RIGHT, IT'S YOUR TURN...
M

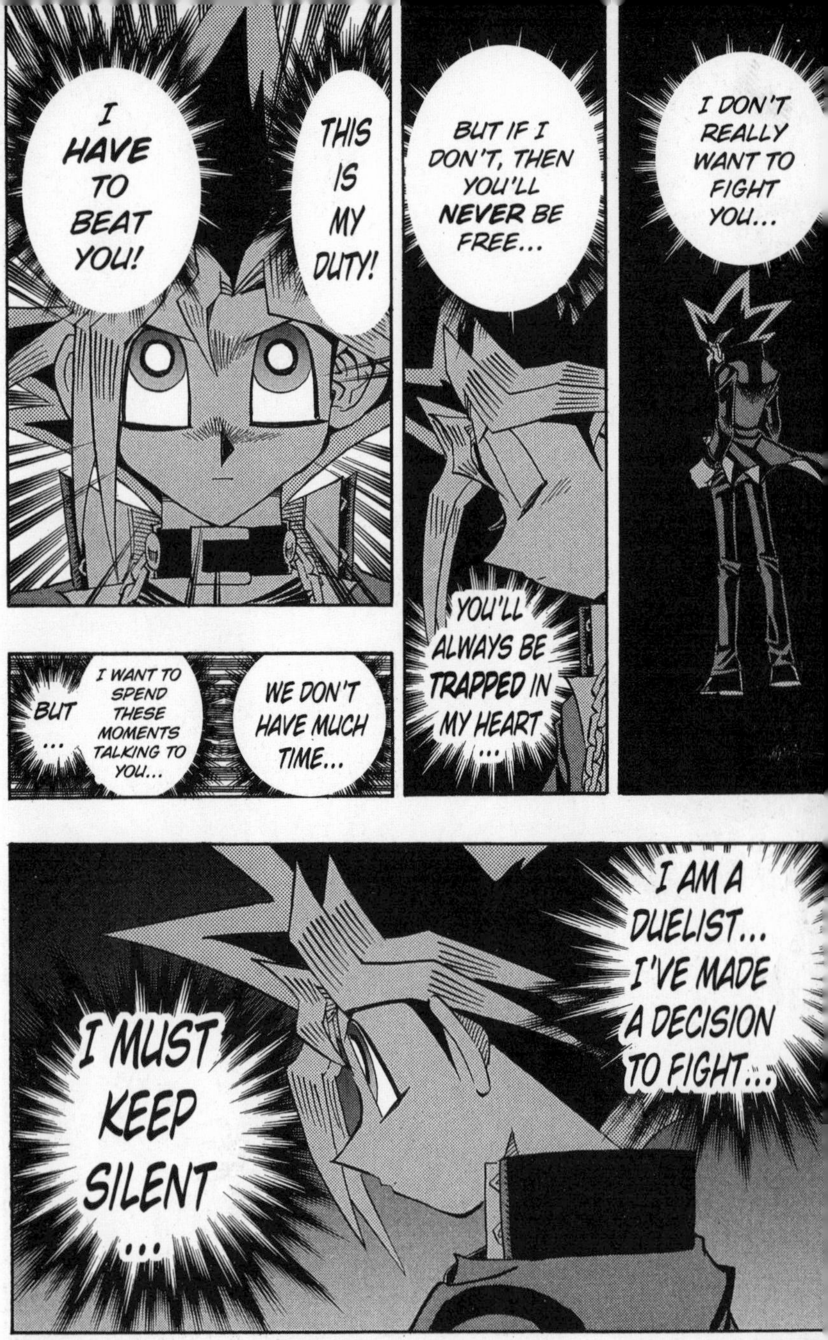
I DON'T REALLY WANT TO FIGHT YOU...
BUT IF I DON'T, THEN YOU'LL NEVER BE FREE...
YOU'LL ALWAYS BE TRAPPED IN MY HEART...
THIS IS MY DUTY!
I HAVE TO BEAT YOU!
WE DON'T HAVE MUCH TIME...
I WANT TO SPEND THESE MOMENTS TALKING TO YOU...
BUT...
I AM A DUELIST... I'VE MADE A DECISION TO FIGHT...
I MUST KEEP SILENT...

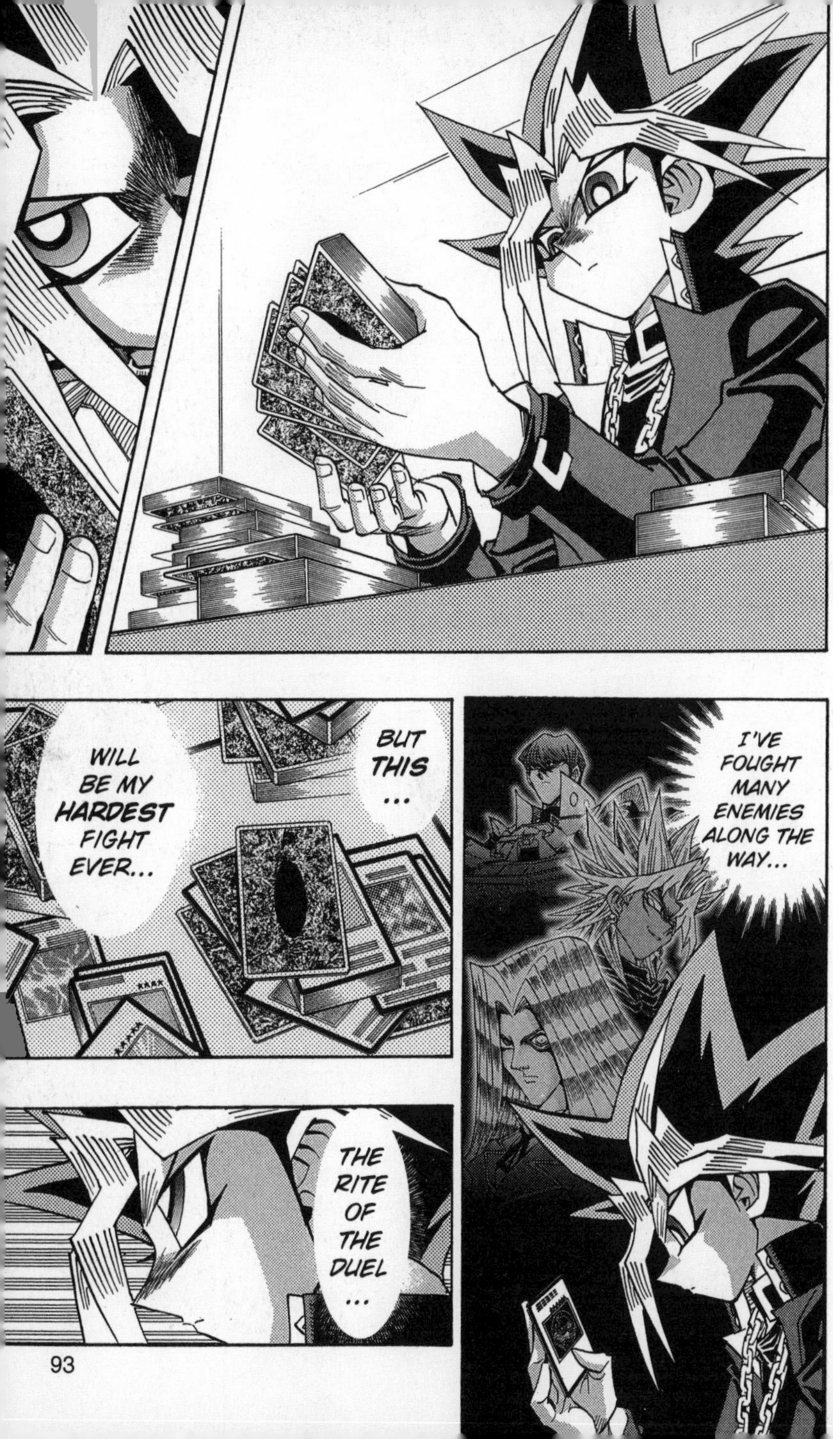
I'VE FOUGHT MANY ENEMIES ALONG THE WAY...
BUT THIS...
WILL BE MY HARDEST FIGHT EVER...
THE RITE OF THE DUEL...

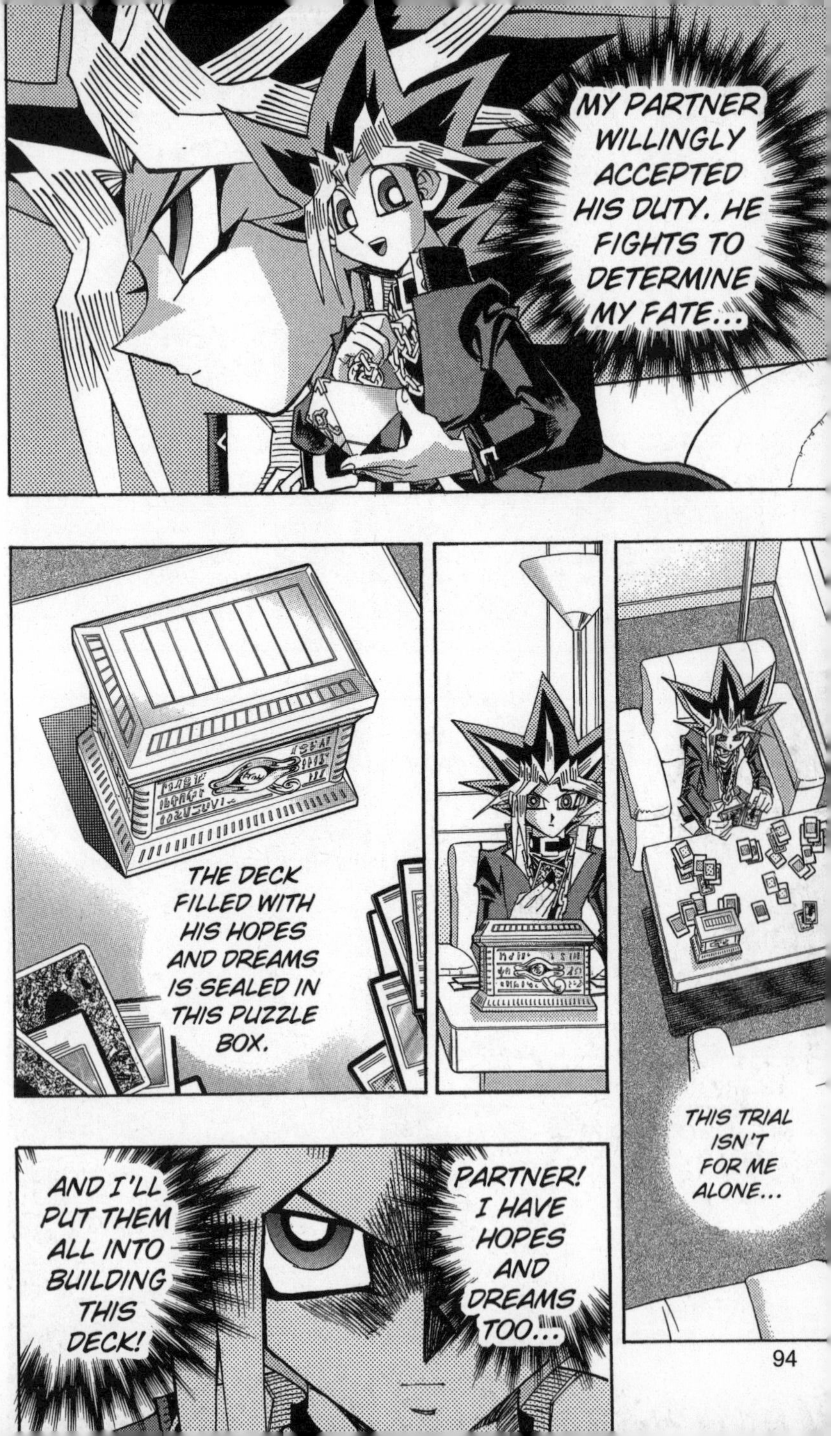
MY PARTNER WILLINGLY ACCEPTED HIS DUTY. HE FIGHTS TO DETERMINE MY FATE...
THIS TRIAL ISN'T FOR ME ALONE...
THE DECK FILLED WITH HIS HOPES AND DREAMS IS SEALED IN THIS PUZZLE BOX.
PARTNER! I HAVE HOPES AND DREAMS TOO...
AND I'LL PUT THEM ALL INTO BUILDING THIS DECK!

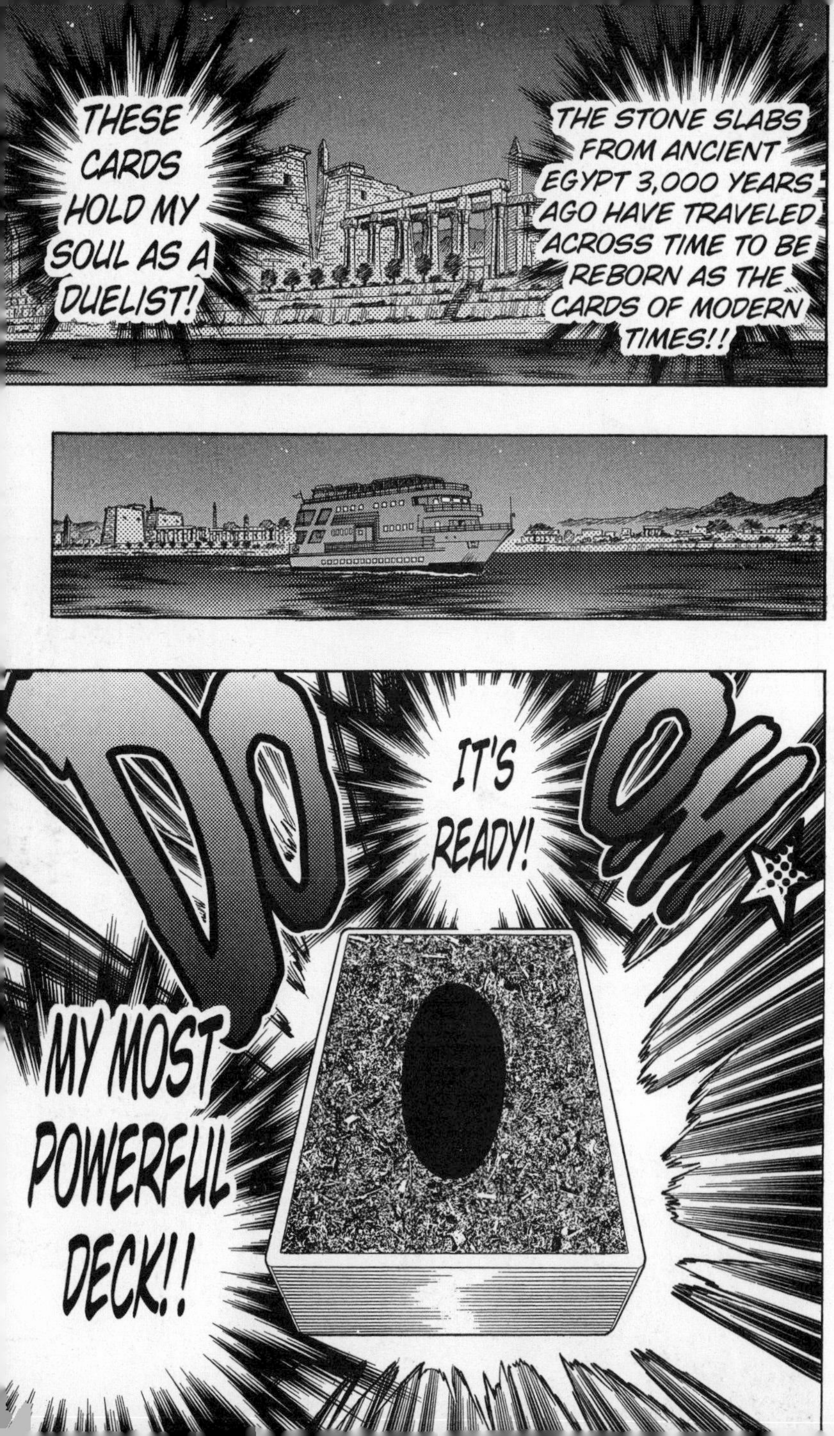
THE STONE SLABS FROM ANCIENT EGYPT 3,000 YEARS AGO HAVE TRAVELED ACROSS TIME TO BE REBORN AS THE CARDS OF MODERN TIMES!!
THESE CARDS HOLD MY SOUL AS A DUELIST!
IT'S READY!
MY MOST POWERFUL DECK!!

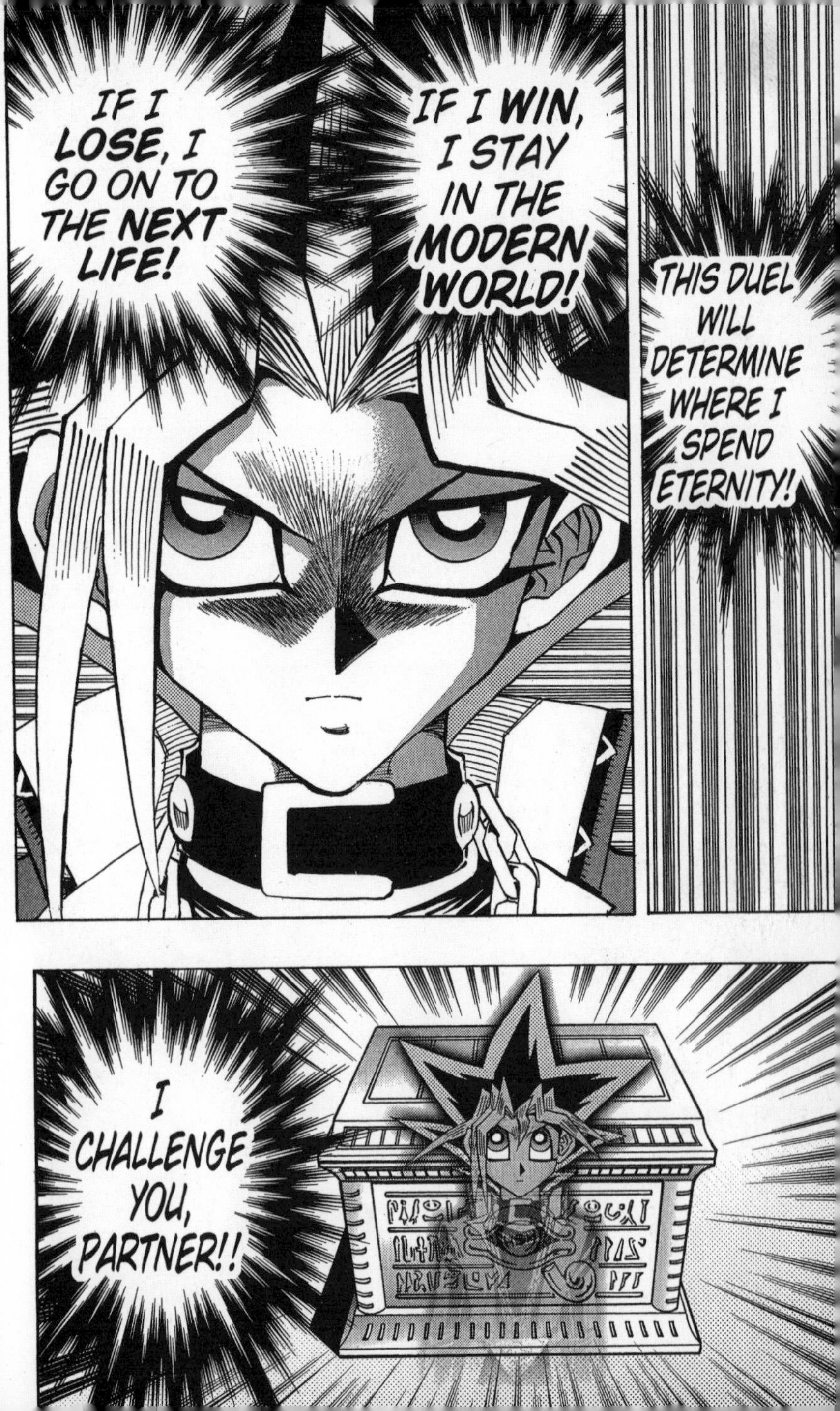
THIS DUEL WILL DETERMINE WHERE I SPEND ETERNITY!
IF I WIN, I STAY IN THE MODERN WORLD!
IF I LOSE, I GO ON TO THE NEXT LIFE!
I CHALLENGE YOU, PARTNER!!

READ THIS WAY

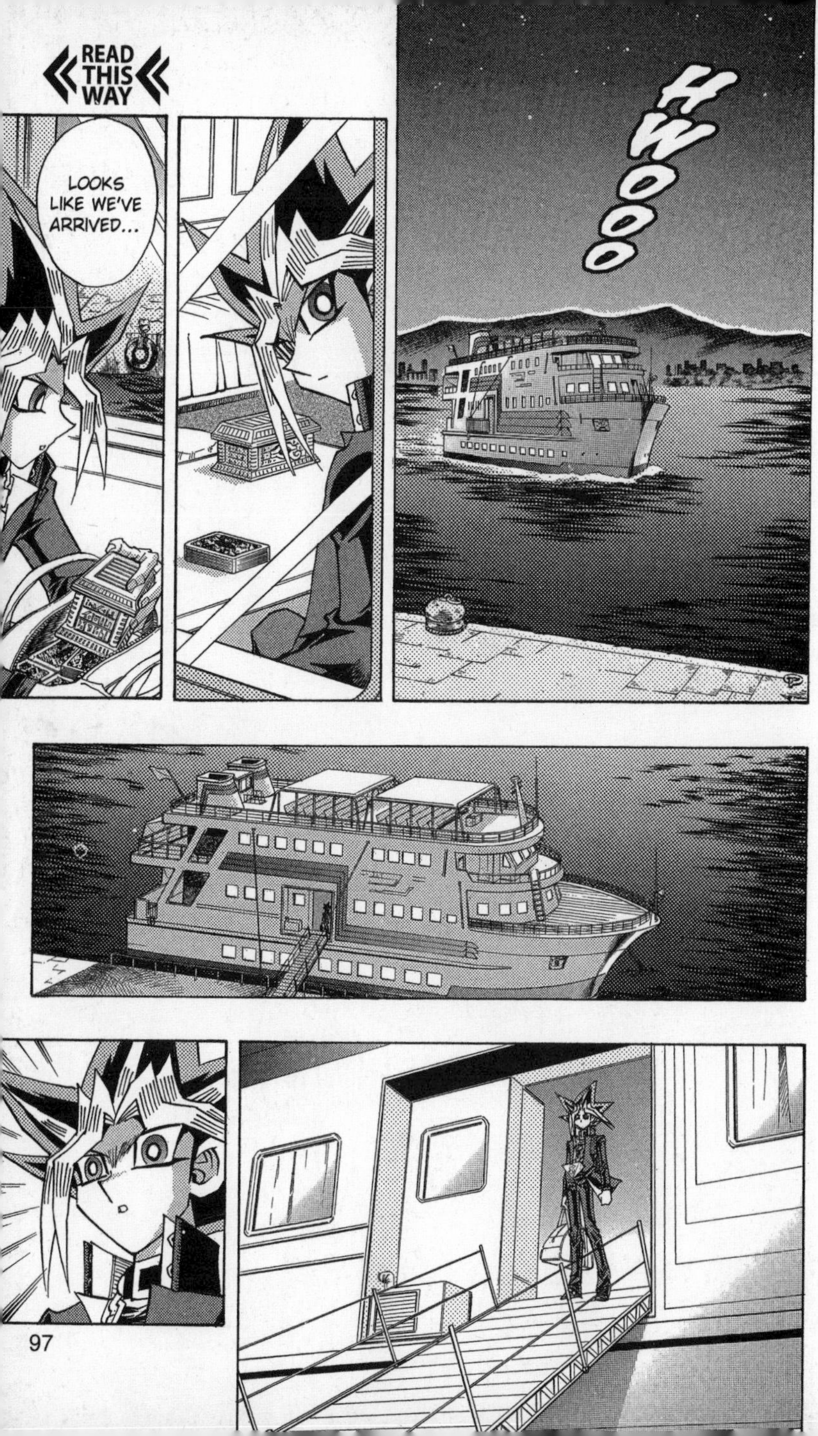

HWOOOO
LOOKS LIKE WE'VE ARRIVED...

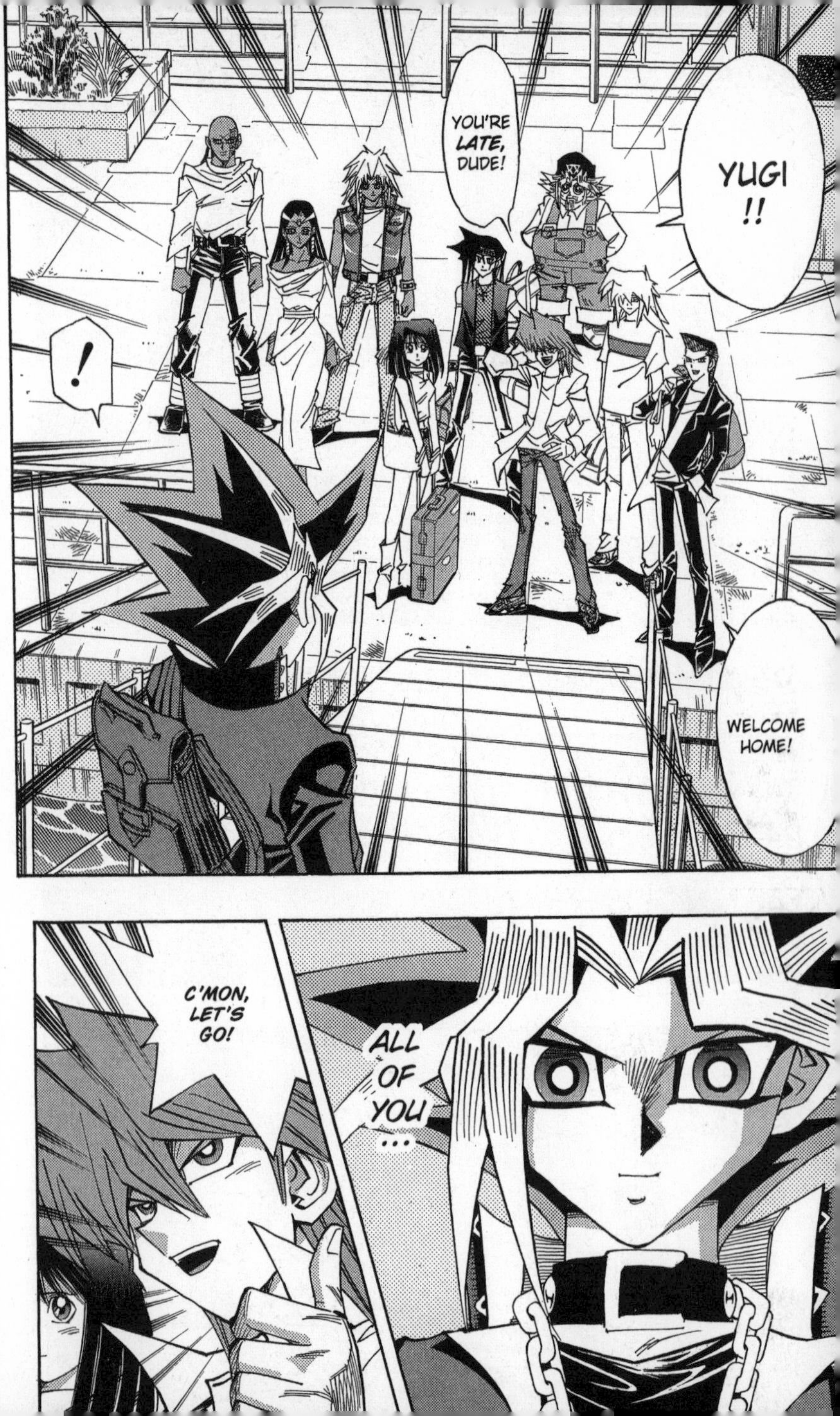
YUGI !!
YOU'RE LATE, DUDE!
WELCOME HOME!
!
ALL OF YOU ...
C'MON, LET'S GO!

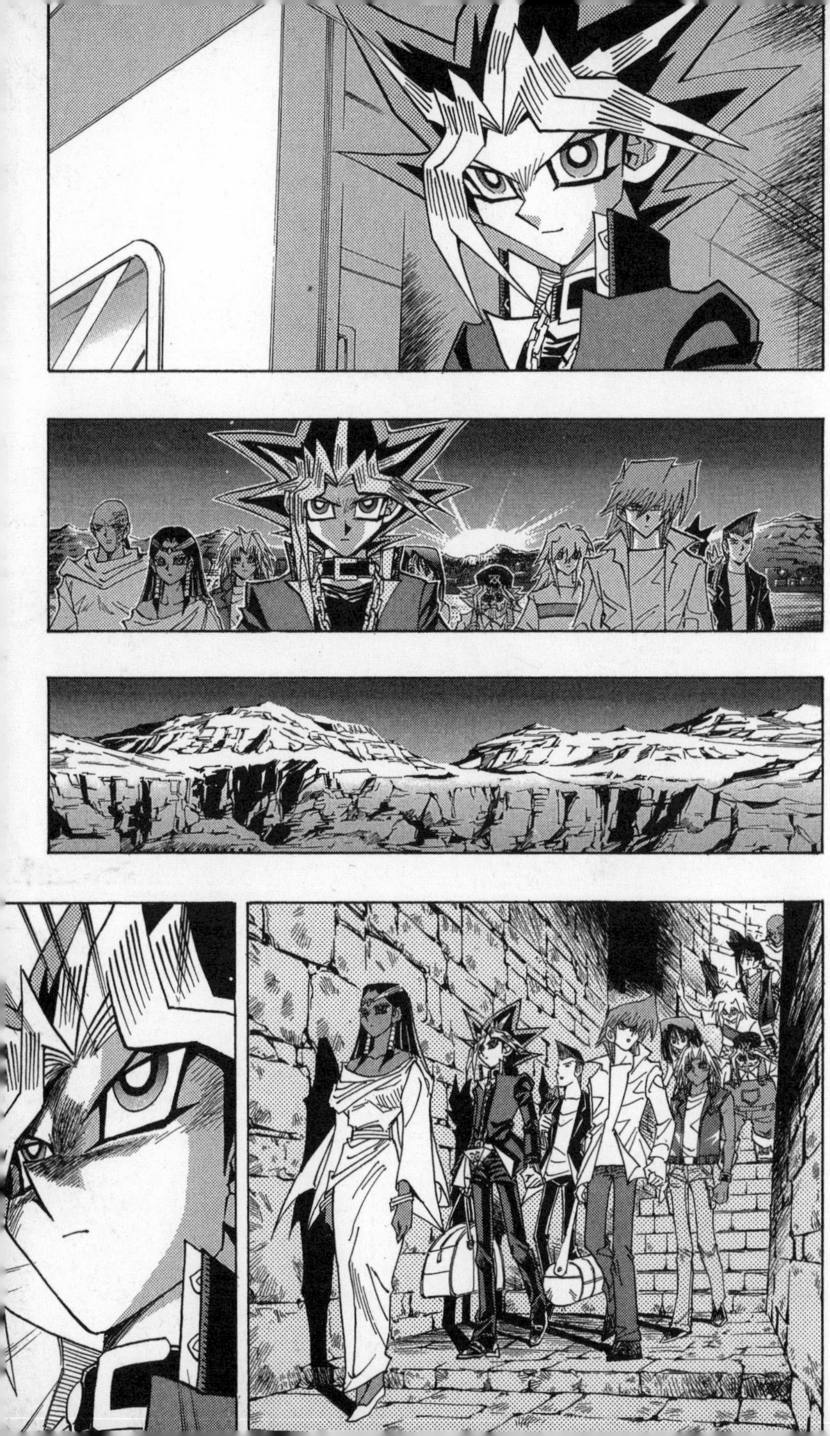

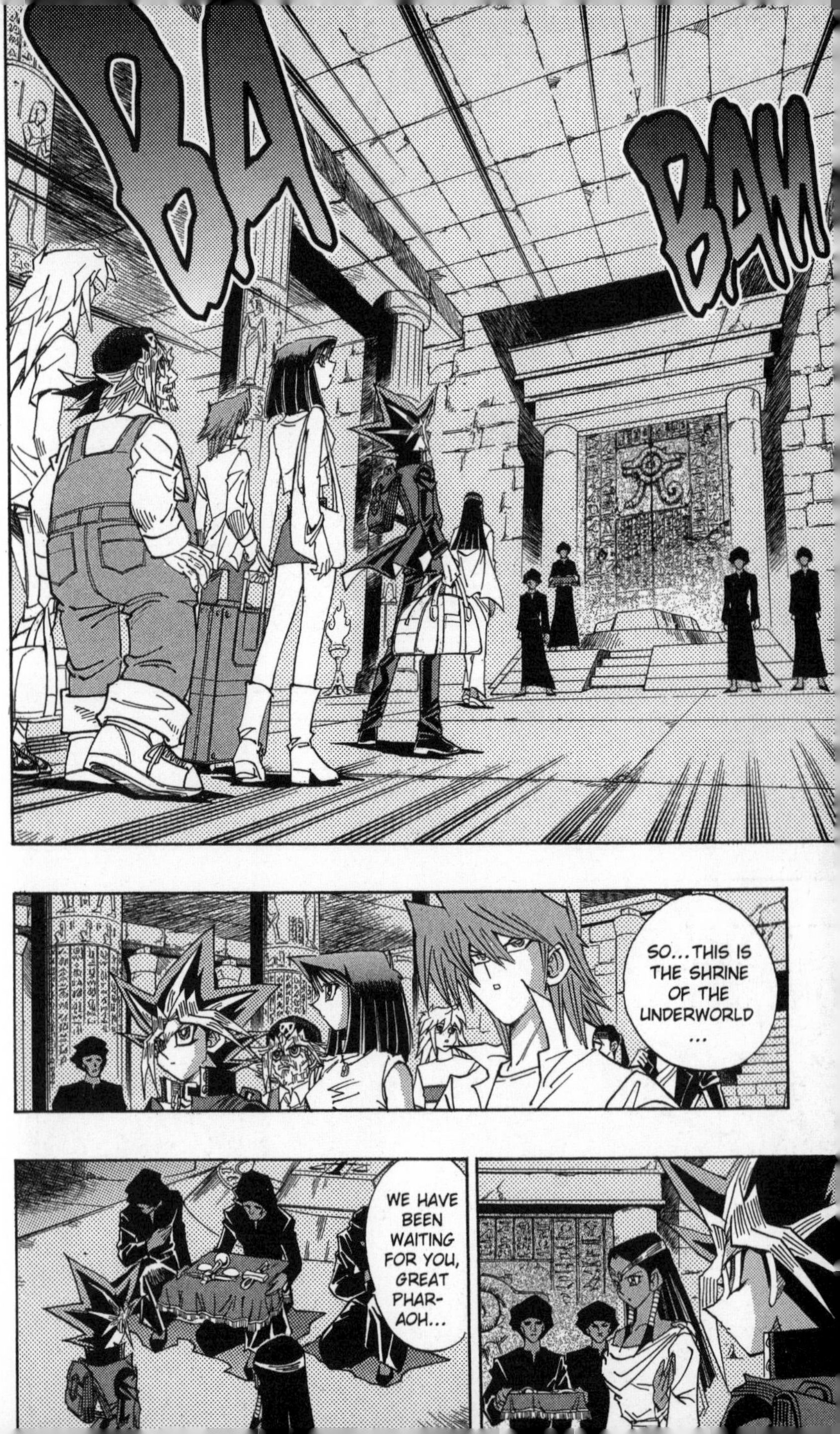
BAM
BA
SO...THIS IS THE SHRINE OF THE UNDERWORLD ...
WE HAVE BEEN WAITING FOR YOU, GREAT PHAR-AOH...

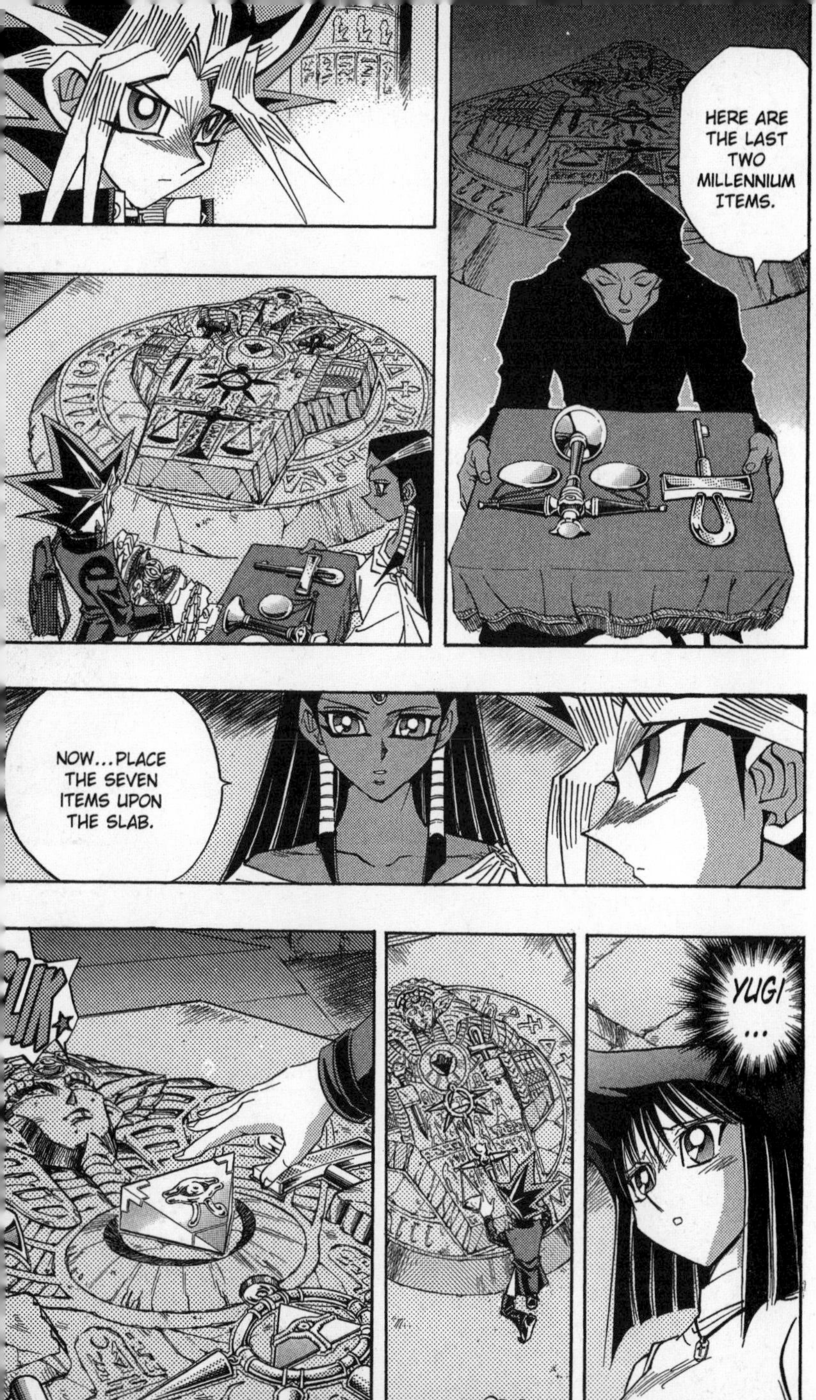
HERE ARE THE LAST TWO MILLENNIUM ITEMS.
NOW...PLACE THE SEVEN ITEMS UPON THE SLAB.
YUGI ...

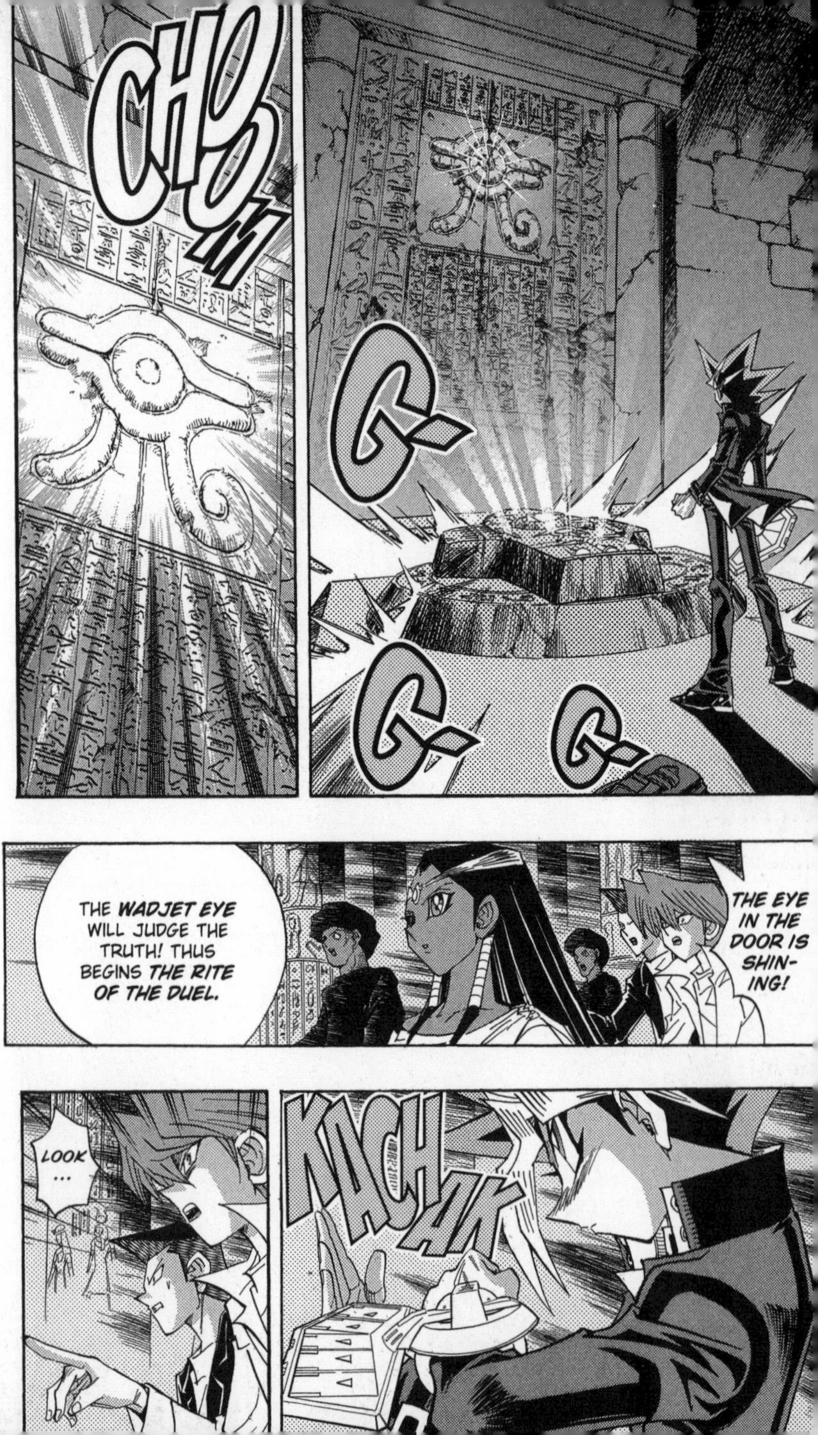
G-
G-
G
CHOOM
THE EYE IN THE DOOR IS SHINING!
THE WADJET EYE WILL JUDGE THE TRUTH! THUS BEGINS THE RITE OF THE DUEL.
KACHAK
LOOK ...

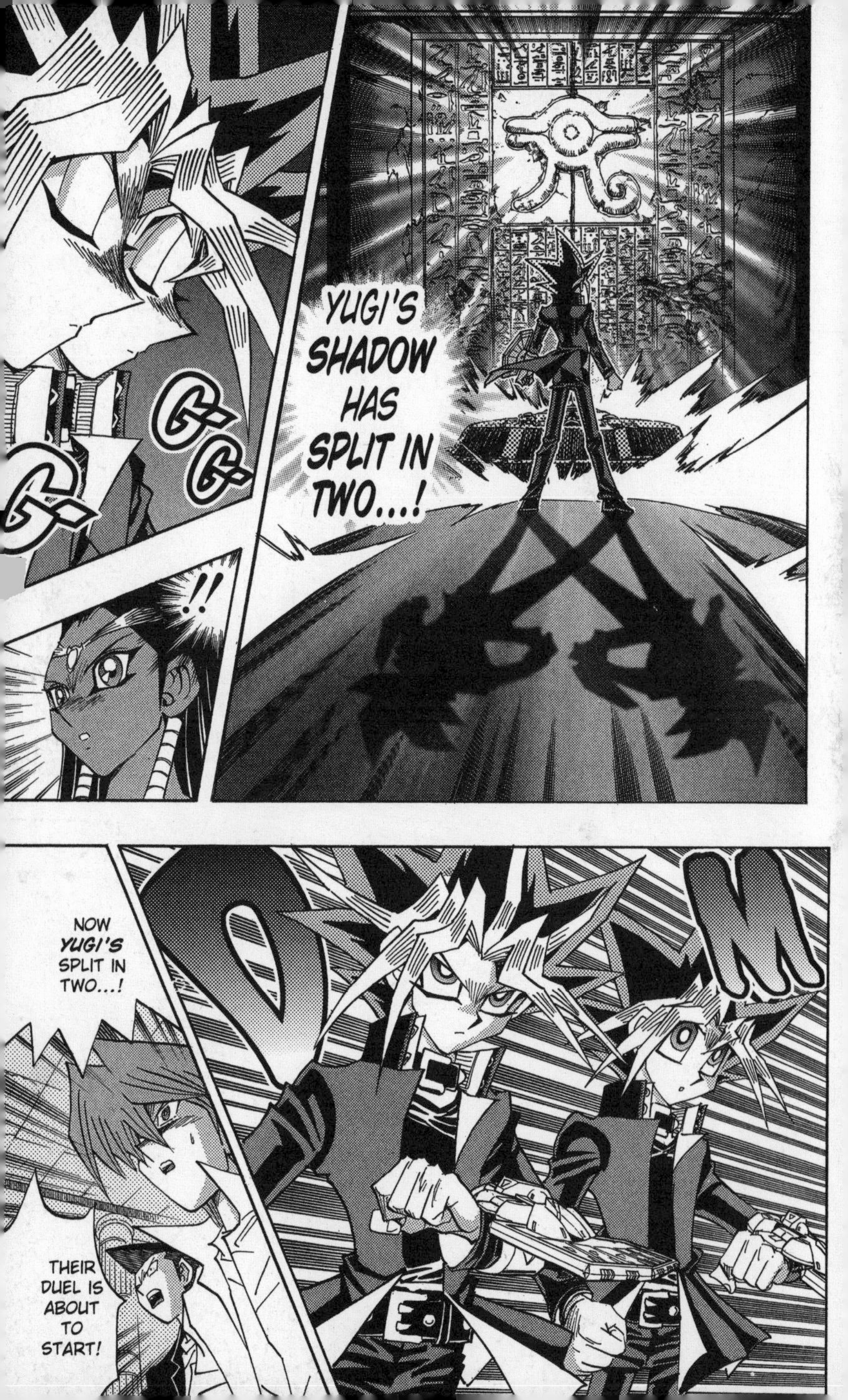
YUGI'S SHADOW HAS SPLIT IN TWO...!
GGG
!!
M
NOW YUGI'S SPLIT IN TWO...!
THEIR DUEL IS ABOUT TO START!

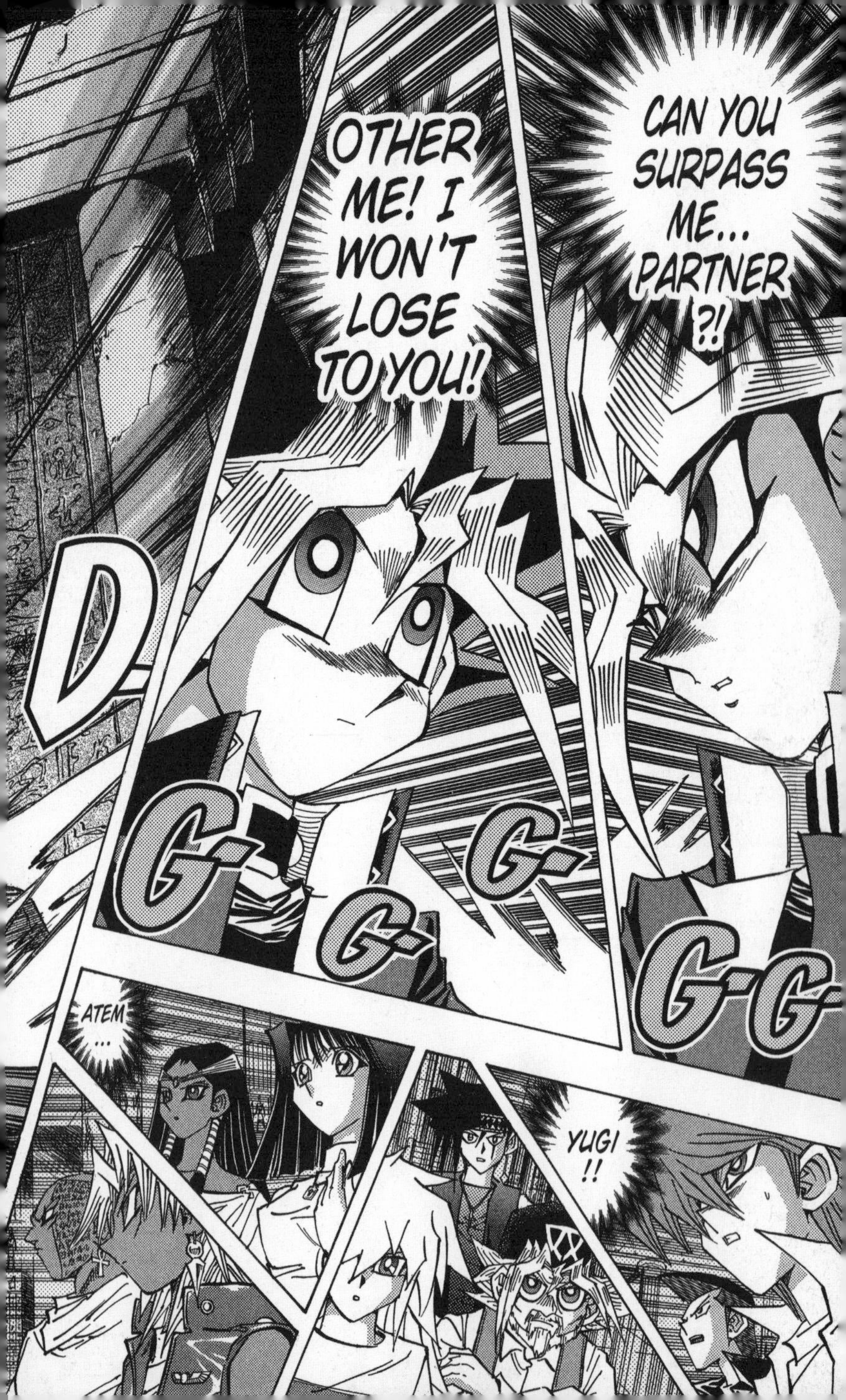
CAN YOU SURPASS ME... PARTNER ?!
OTHER ME! I WON'T LOSE TO YOU!
D
G-
G-
G-
G-G
YUGI !!
ATEM ...

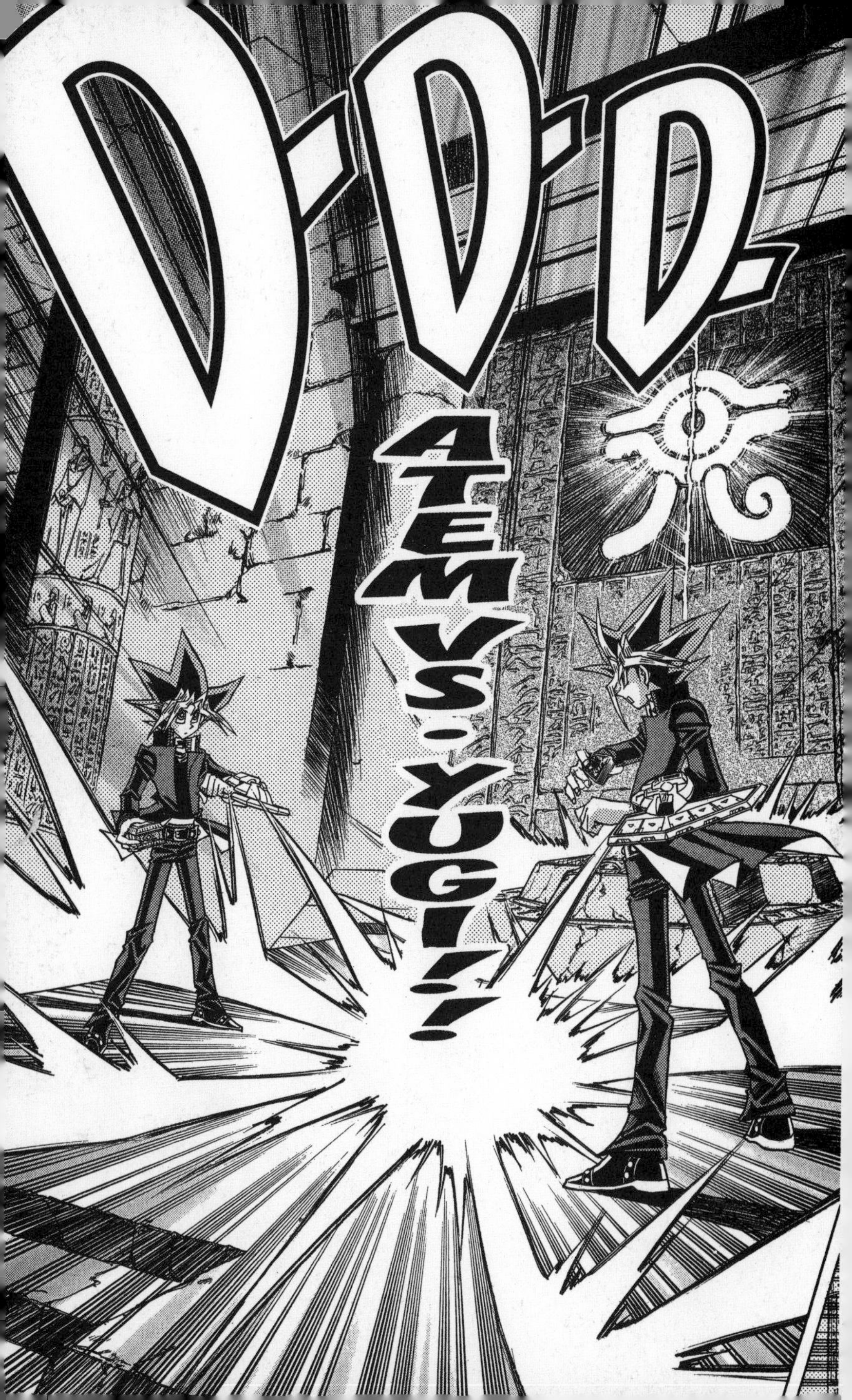

D-D-D
ATEM VS. YUGI!!

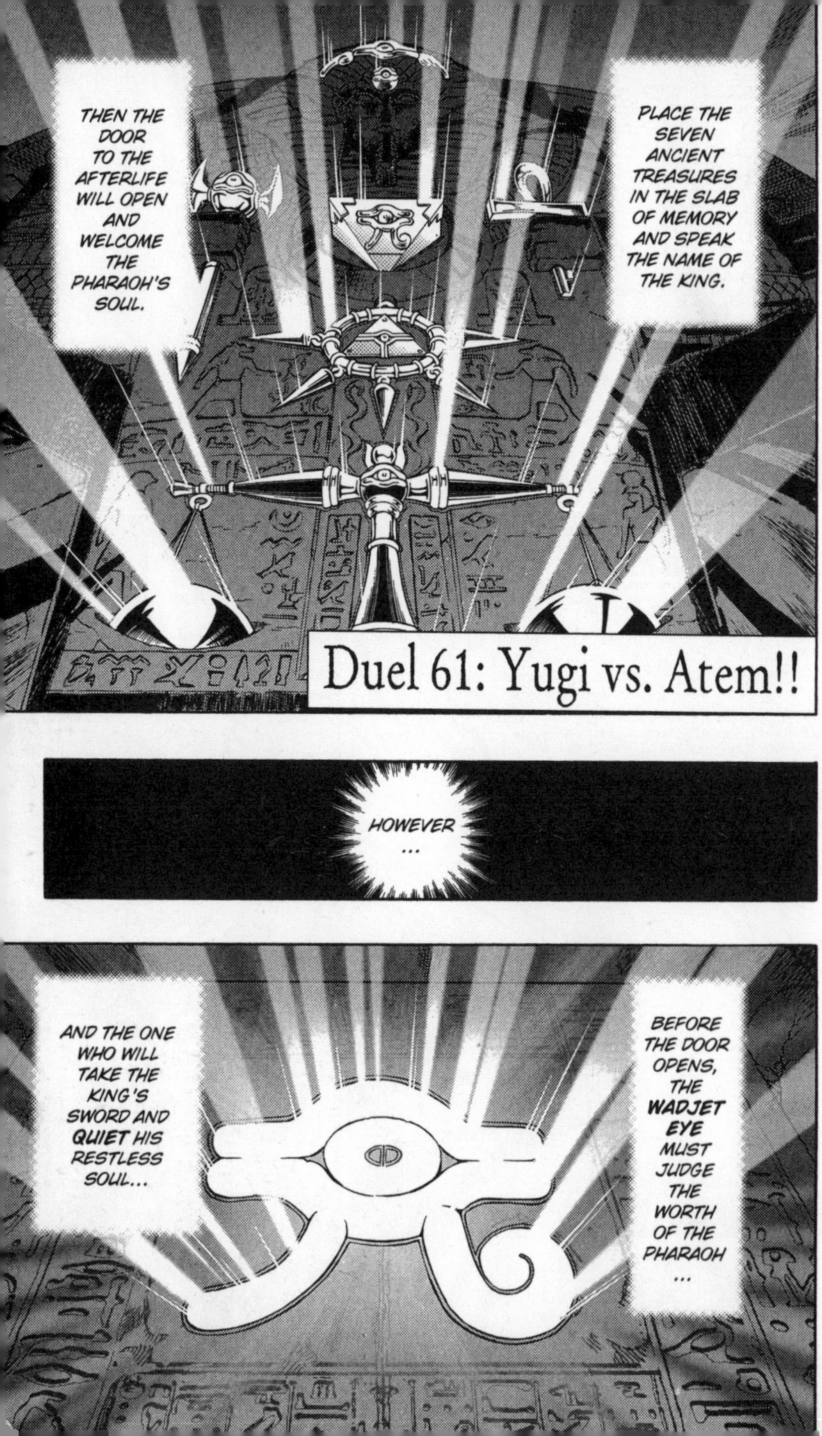
PLACE THE SEVEN ANCIENT TREASURES IN THE SLAB OF MEMORY AND SPEAK THE NAME OF THE KING.
THEN THE DOOR TO THE AFTERLIFE WILL OPEN AND WELCOME THE PHARAOH'S SOUL.
Duel 61: Yugi vs. Atem!!
HOWEVER ...
BEFORE THE DOOR OPENS, THE **WADJET EYE** MUST JUDGE THE WORTH OF THE PHARAOH ...
AND THE ONE WHO WILL TAKE THE KING'S SWORD AND **QUIET** HIS RESTLESS SOUL...

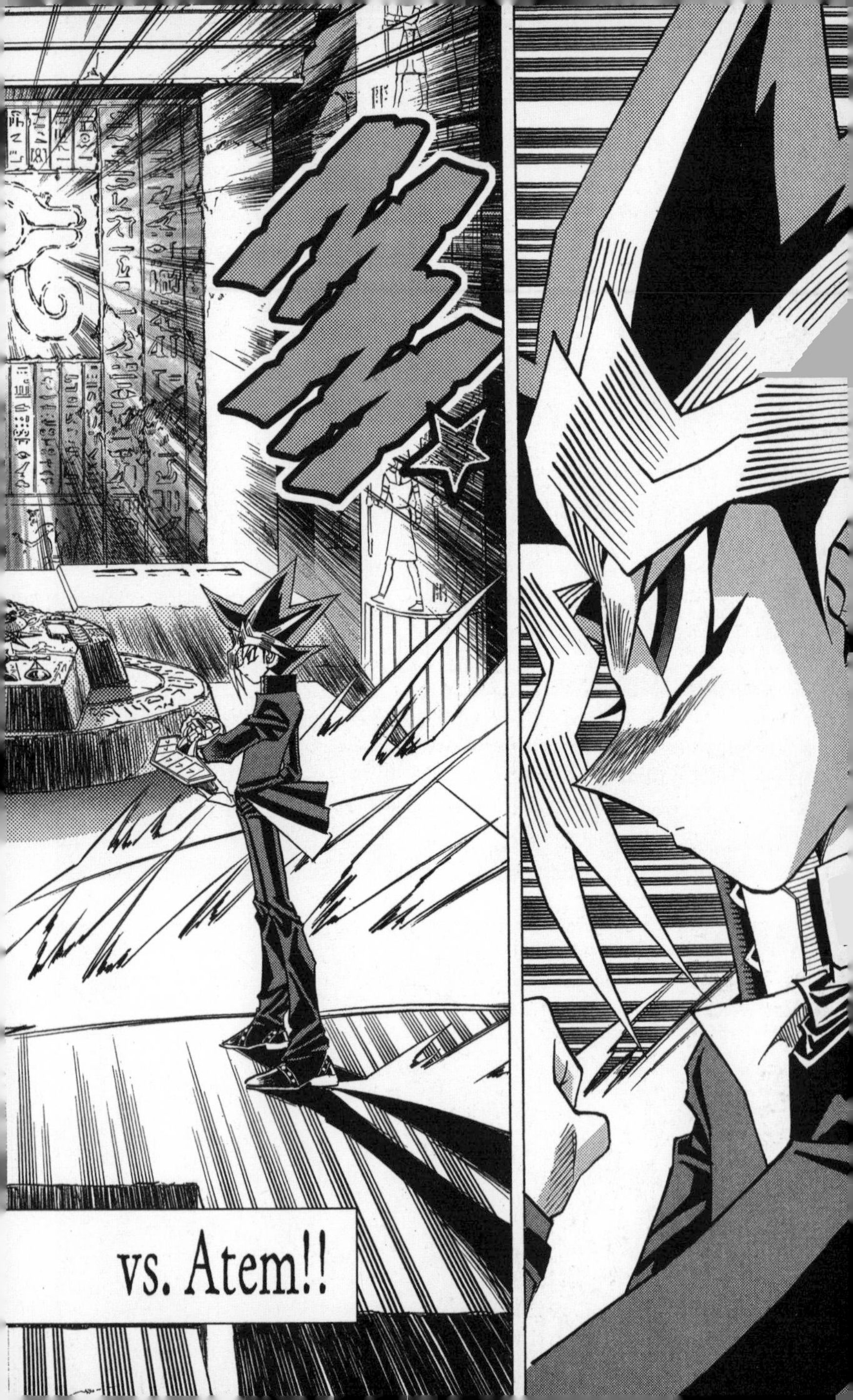
vs. Atem!!

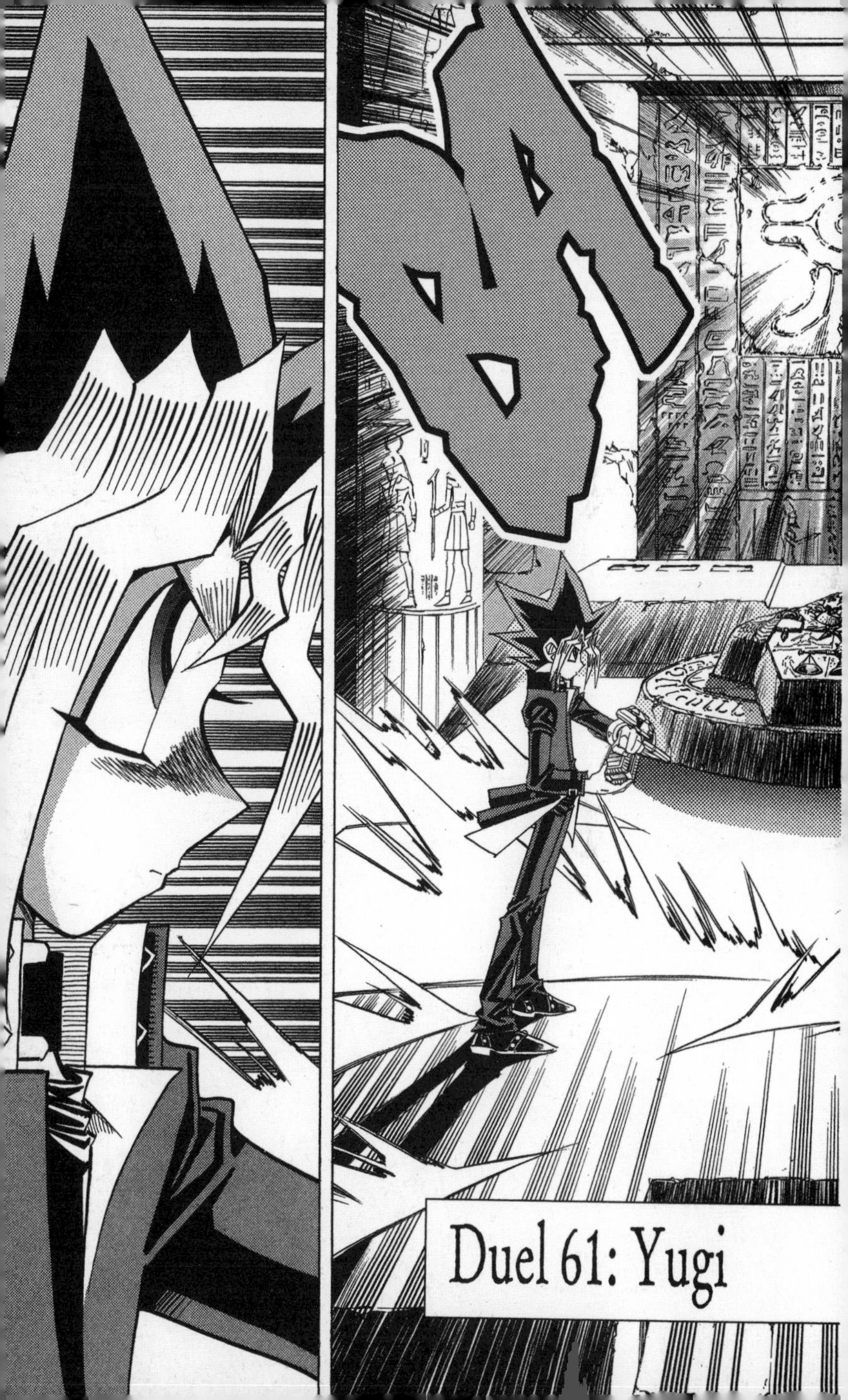

Duel 61: Yugi

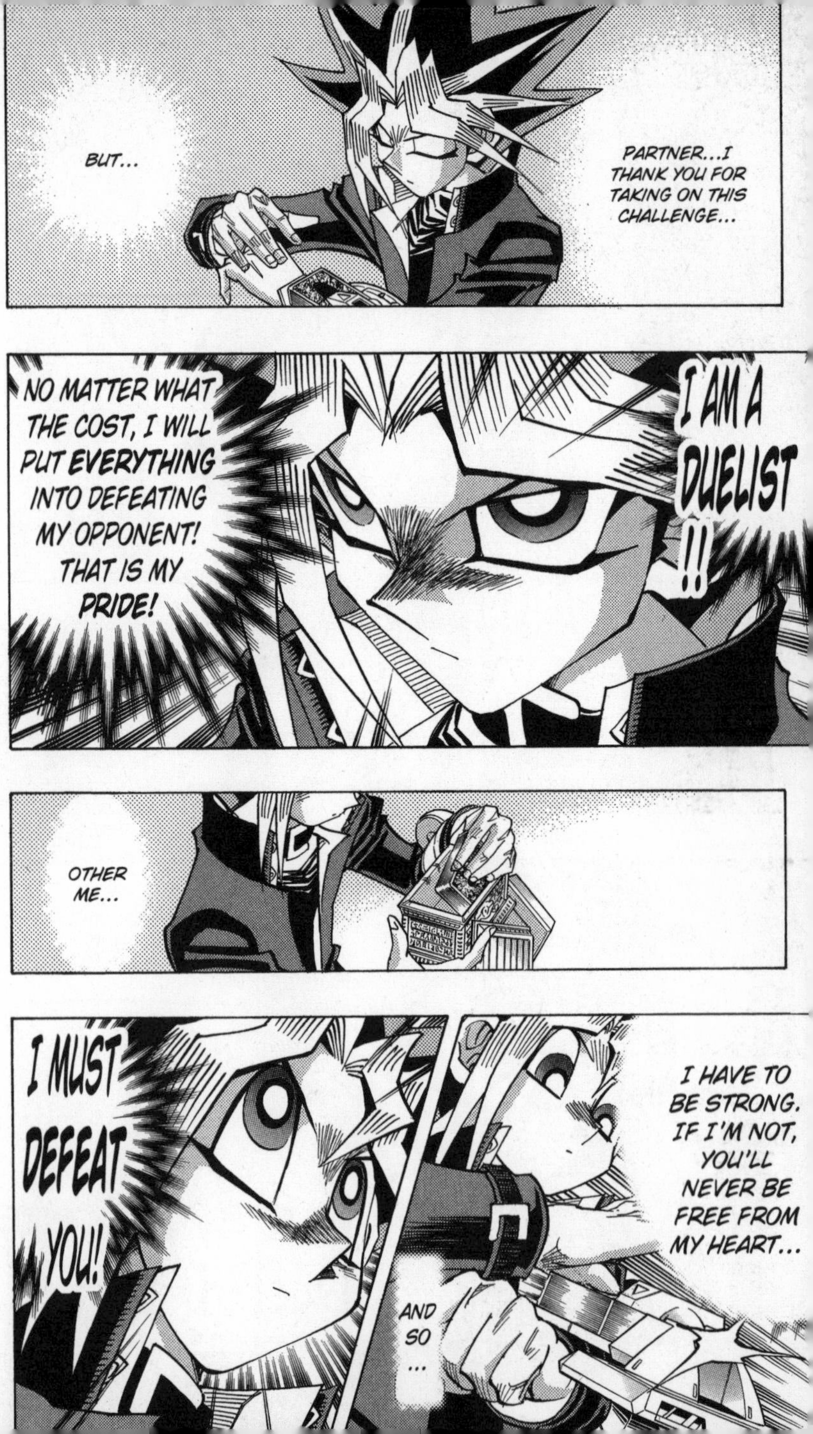
PARTNER...I THANK YOU FOR TAKING ON THIS CHALLENGE...
BUT...
I AM A DUELIST!!
NO MATTER WHAT THE COST, I WILL PUT **EVERYTHING** INTO DEFEATING MY OPPONENT! THAT IS MY **PRIDE!**
OTHER ME...
I HAVE TO BE STRONG. IF I'M NOT, YOU'LL NEVER BE FREE FROM MY HEART...
AND SO...
I MUST DEFEAT YOU!

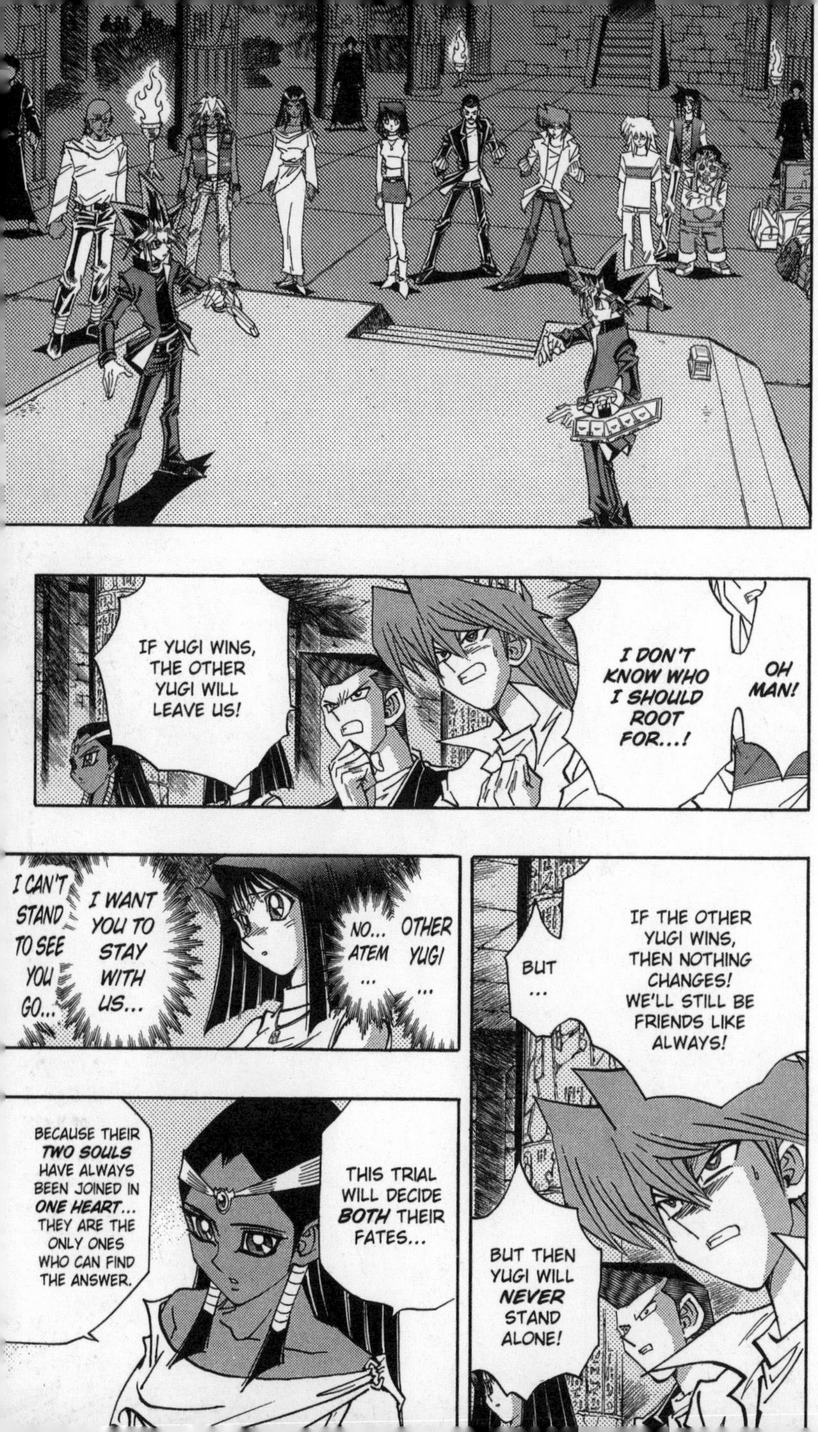

OH MAN!
I DON'T KNOW WHO I SHOULD ROOT FOR...!
IF YUGI WINS, THE OTHER YUGI WILL LEAVE US!
IF THE OTHER YUGI WINS, THEN NOTHING CHANGES! WE'LL STILL BE FRIENDS LIKE ALWAYS!
BUT...
BUT THEN YUGI WILL NEVER STAND ALONE!
OTHER YUGI...
NO... ATEM...
I WANT YOU TO STAY WITH US...
I CAN'T STAND TO SEE YOU GO...
THIS TRIAL WILL DECIDE BOTH THEIR FATES...
BECAUSE THEIR TWO SOULS HAVE ALWAYS BEEN JOINED IN ONE HEART... THEY ARE THE ONLY ONES WHO CAN FIND THE ANSWER.

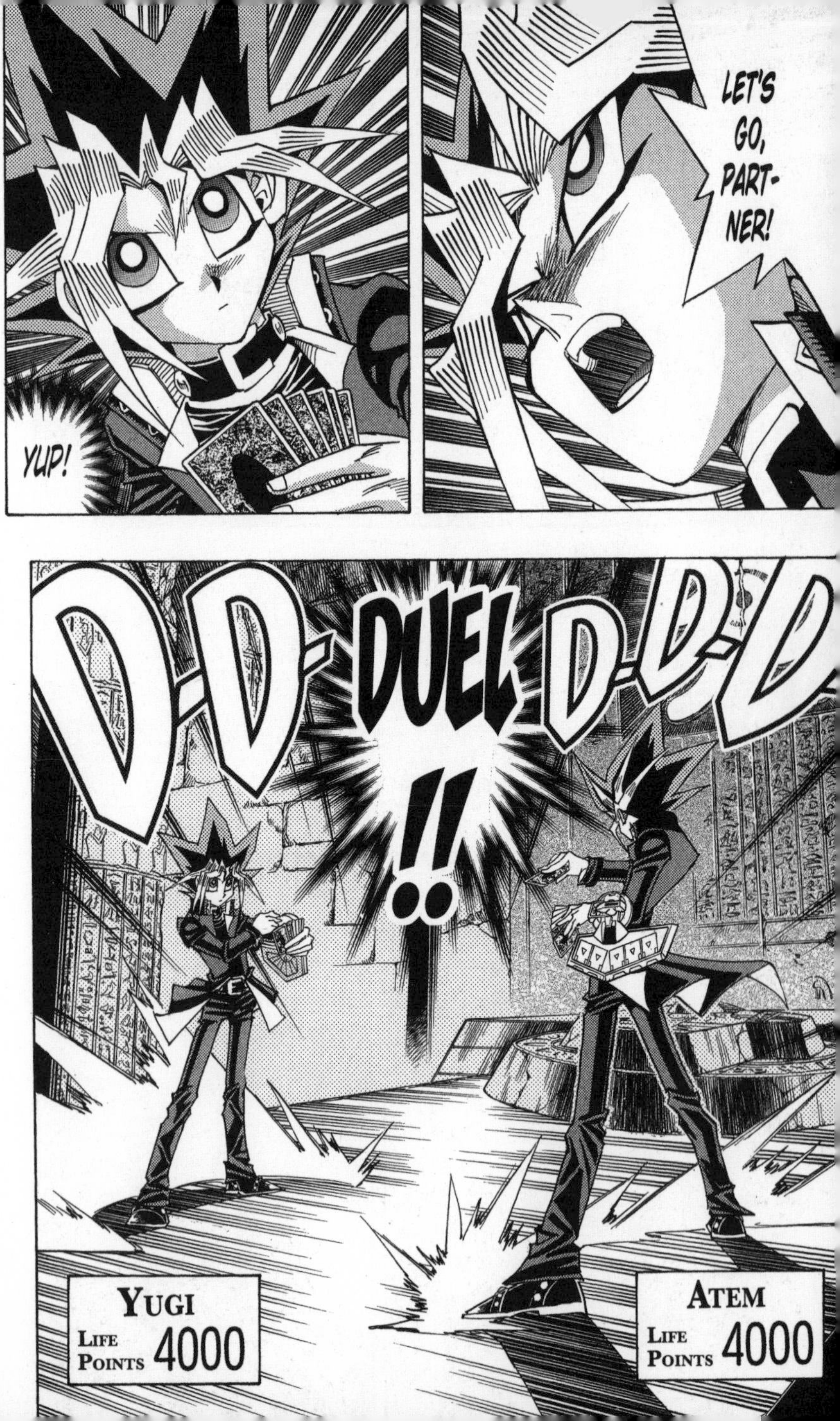
LET'S GO, PART-NER!
YUP!
D-D-DUEL D-D-D!!
ATEM LIFE POINTS 4000
YUGI LIFE POINTS 4000

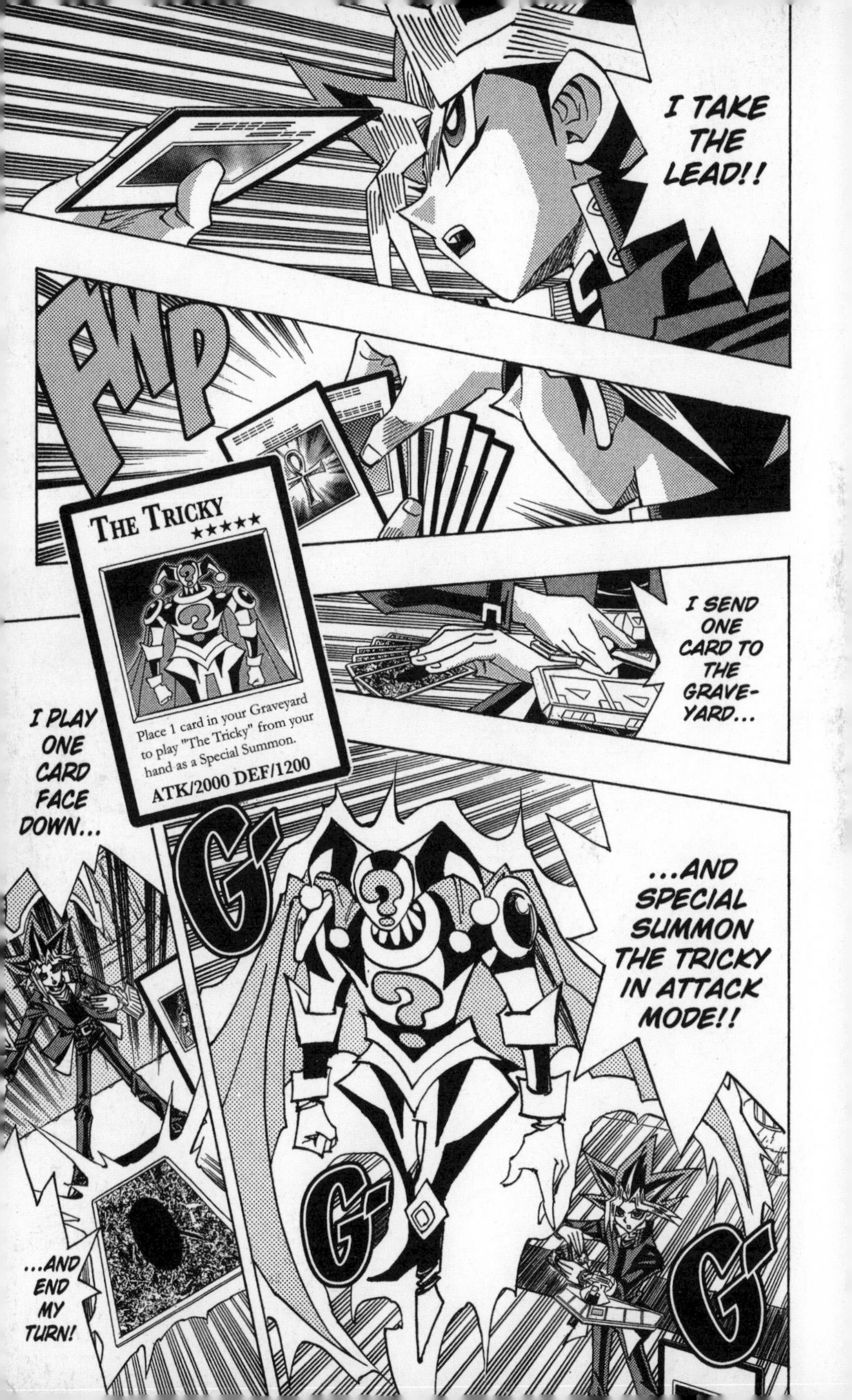
I TAKE THE LEAD!!
I SEND ONE CARD TO THE GRAVE-YARD...
THE TRICKY ★★★★★
Place 1 card in your Graveyard to play "The Tricky" from your hand as a Special Summon.
ATK/2000 DEF/1200
...AND SPECIAL SUMMON THE TRICKY IN ATTACK MODE!!
G
G
G
I PLAY ONE CARD FACE DOWN...
...AND END MY TURN!

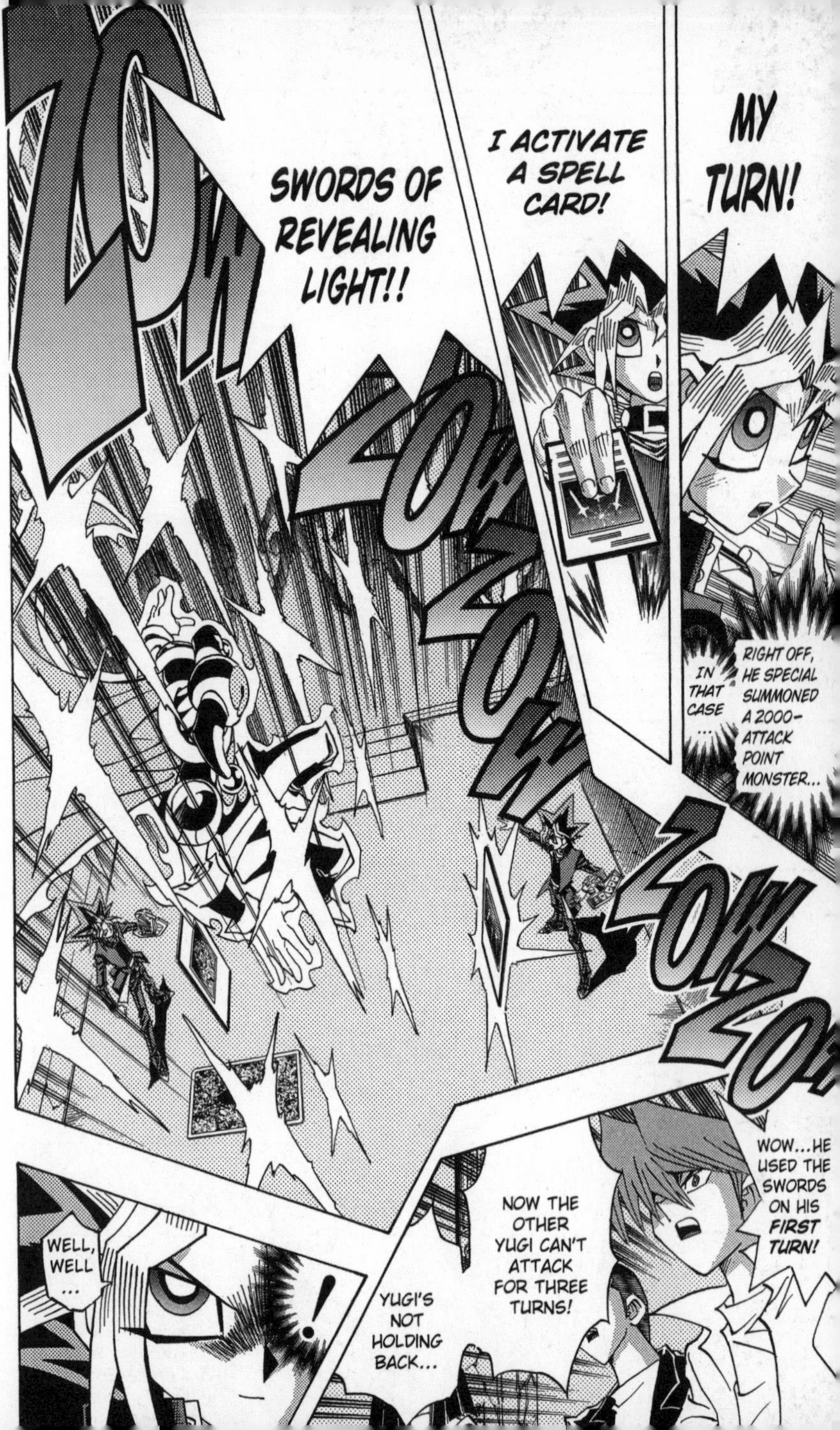
MY TURN!
RIGHT OFF, HE SPECIAL SUMMONED A 2000-ATTACK POINT MONSTER...
IN THAT CASE...
I ACTIVATE A SPELL CARD!
SWORDS OF REVEALING LIGHT!!
WOW...HE USED THE SWORDS ON HIS FIRST TURN!
NOW THE OTHER YUGI CAN'T ATTACK FOR THREE TURNS!
YUGI'S NOT HOLDING BACK...
!
WELL, WELL...

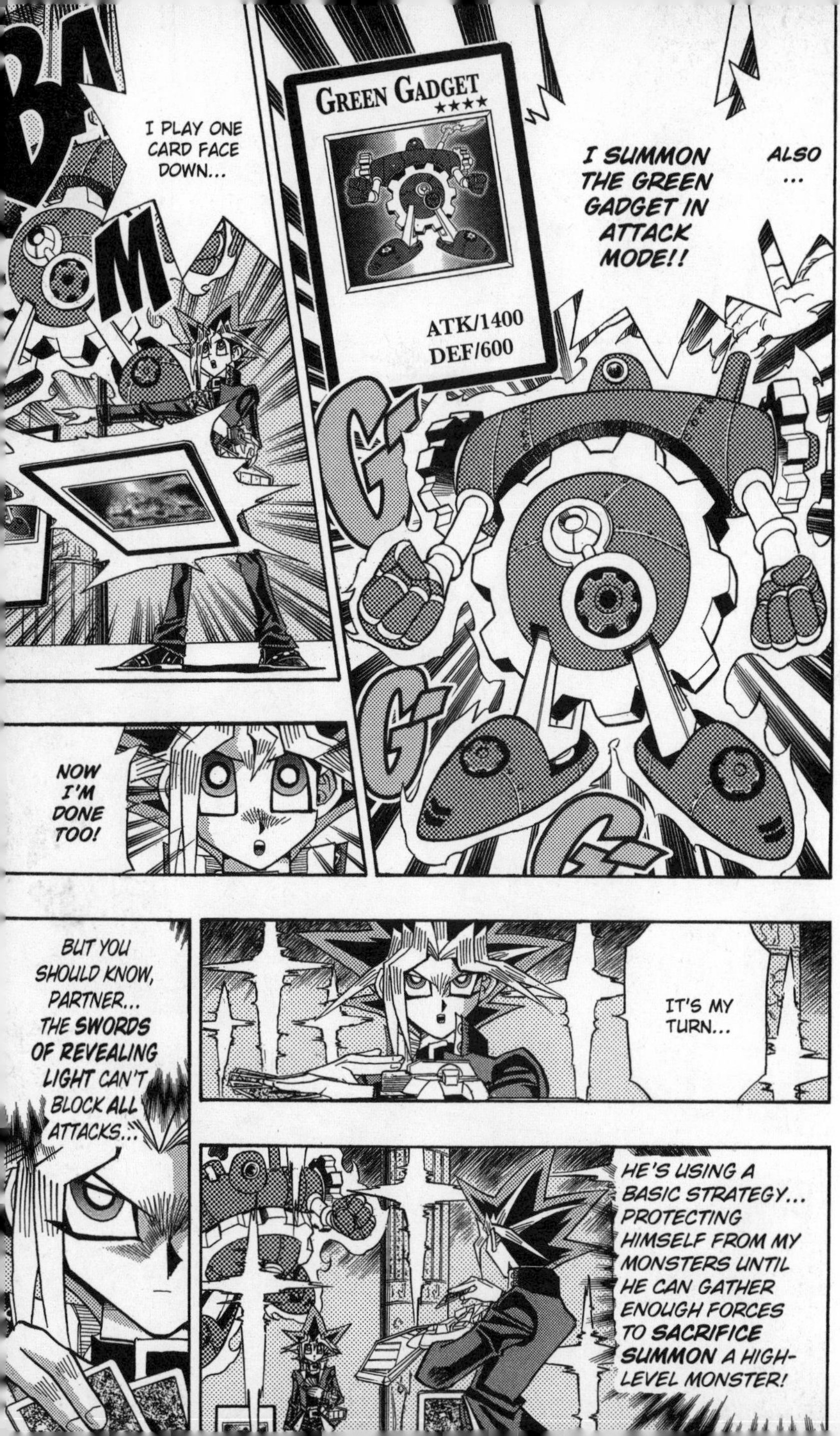
ALSO ...
I SUMMON THE GREEN GADGET IN ATTACK MODE!!
GREEN GADGET ★★★★
ATK/1400 DEF/600
I PLAY ONE CARD FACE DOWN...
NOW I'M DONE TOO!
IT'S MY TURN...
HE'S USING A BASIC STRATEGY... PROTECTING HIMSELF FROM MY MONSTERS UNTIL HE CAN GATHER ENOUGH FORCES TO **SACRIFICE SUMMON** A HIGH-LEVEL MONSTER!
BUT YOU SHOULD KNOW, PARTNER... THE **SWORDS OF REVEALING LIGHT** CAN'T BLOCK ALL ATTACKS...

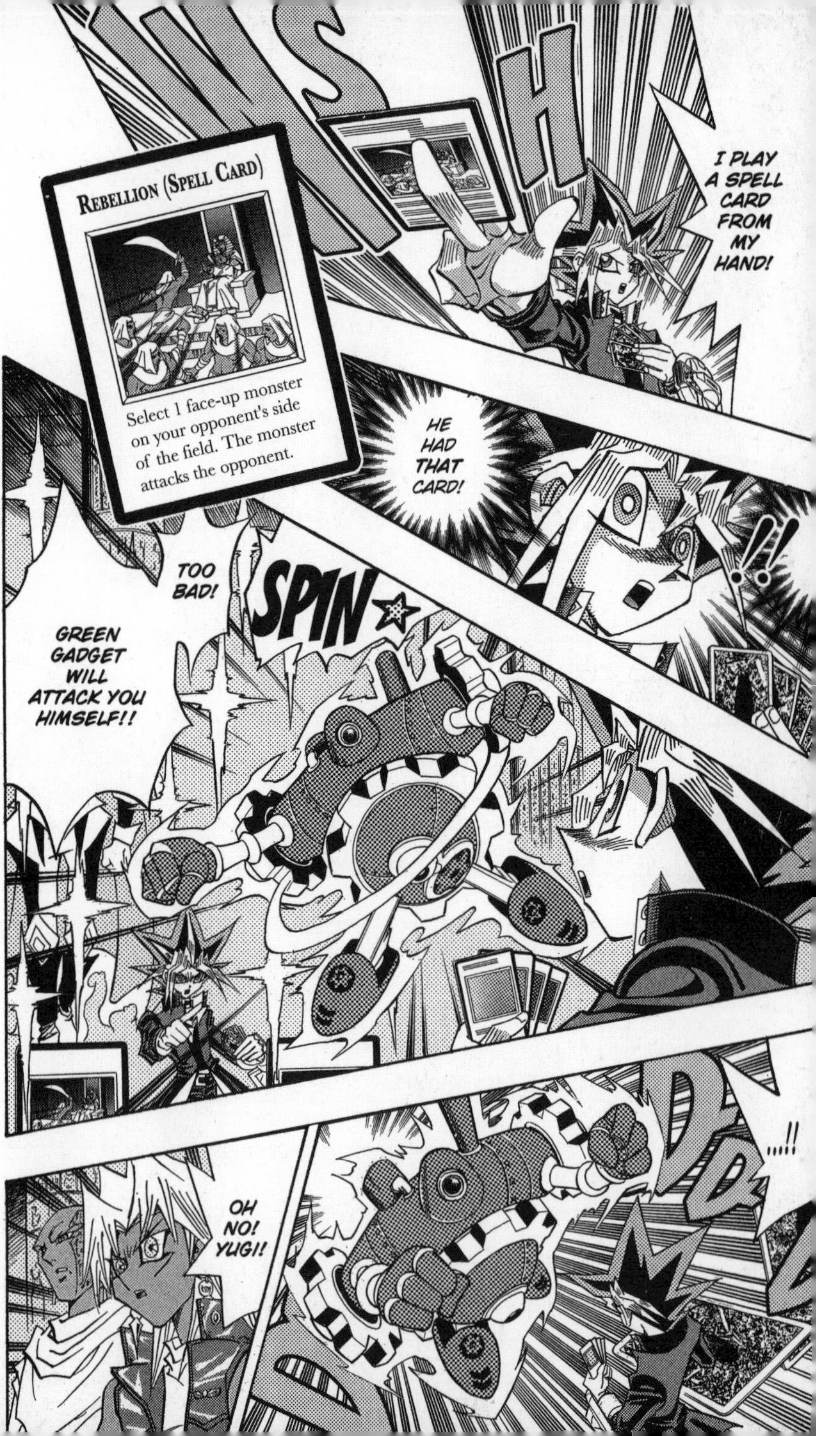
WHSH
I PLAY A SPELL CARD FROM MY HAND!
REBELLION (SPELL CARD)
Select 1 face-up monster on your opponent's side of the field. The monster attacks the opponent.
HE HAD THAT CARD!
!!
TOO BAD!
SPIN
GREEN GADGET WILL ATTACK YOU HIMSELF!!
...!!
OH NO! YUGI!

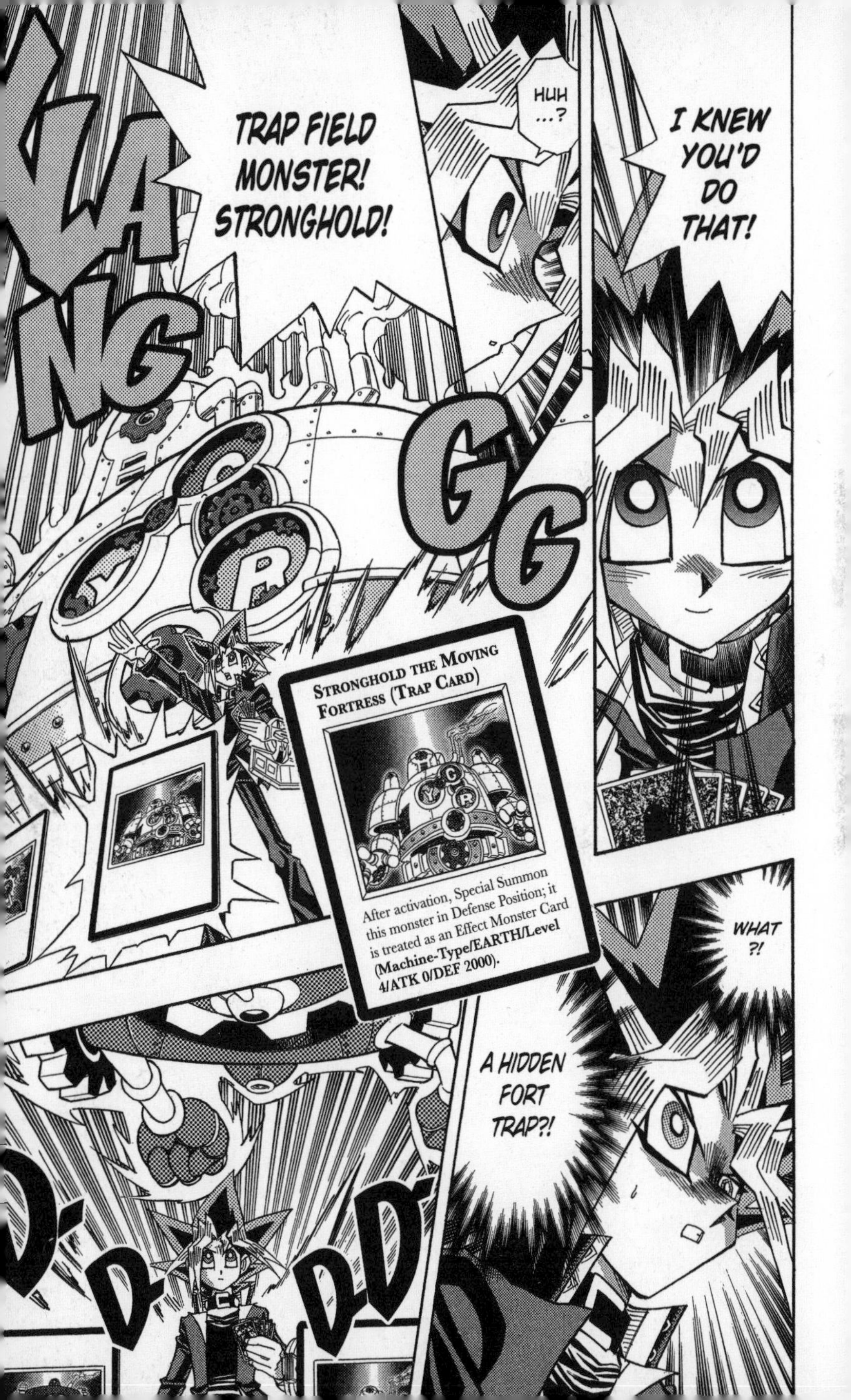
I KNEW YOU'D DO THAT!
HUH ...?
TRAP FIELD MONSTER! STRONGHOLD!
GG
STRONGHOLD THE MOVING FORTRESS (TRAP CARD)
After activation, Special Summon this monster in Defense Position; it is treated as an Effect Monster Card (Machine-Type/EARTH/Level 4/ATK 0/DEF 2000).
WHAT ?!
A HIDDEN FORT TRAP?!

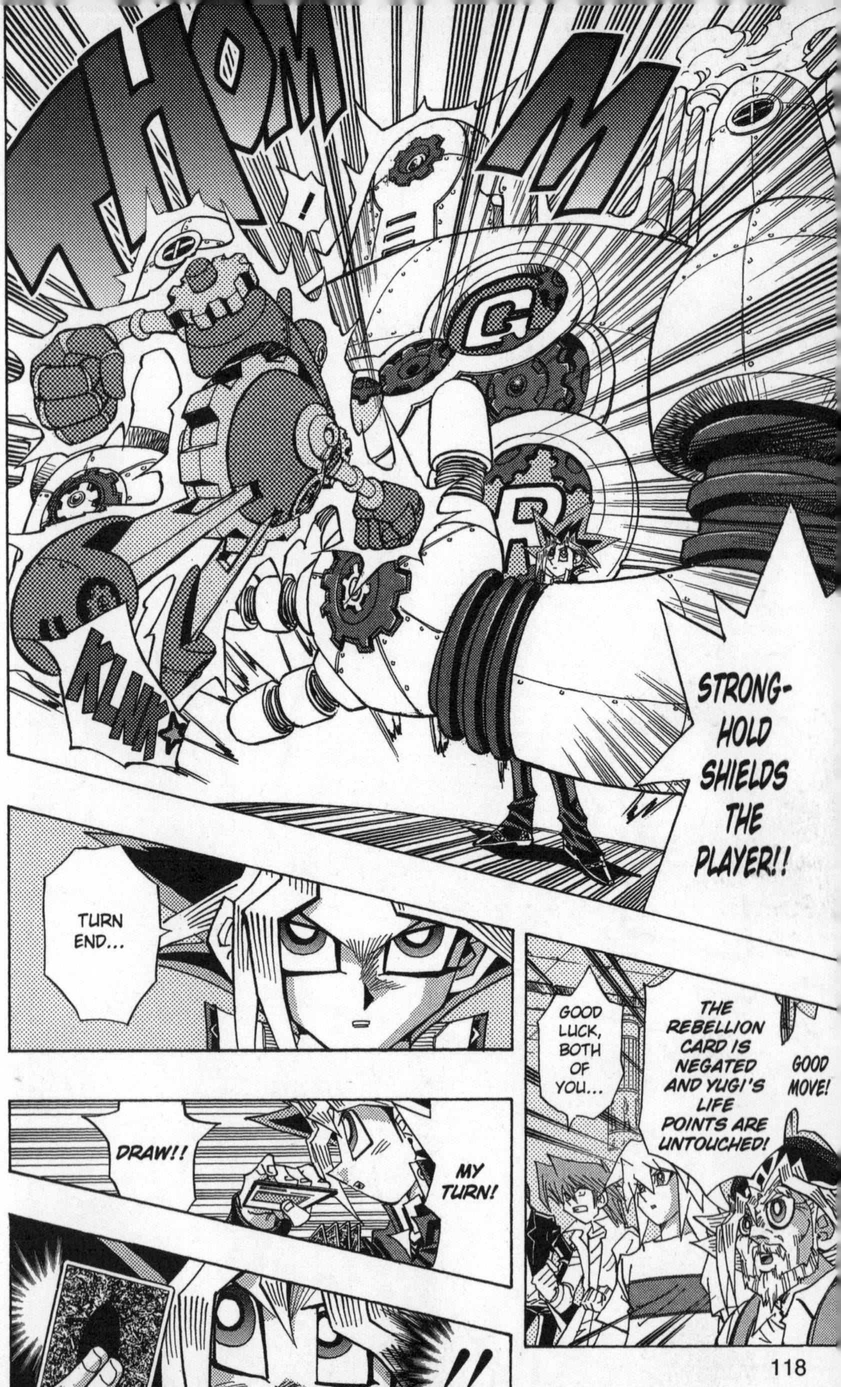
WHOMM
STRONG-HOLD SHIELDS THE PLAYER!!
KLINK
GOOD MOVE!
THE REBELLION CARD IS NEGATED AND YUGI'S LIFE POINTS ARE UNTOUCHED!
GOOD LUCK, BOTH OF YOU...
TURN END...
MY TURN!
DRAW!!
!!

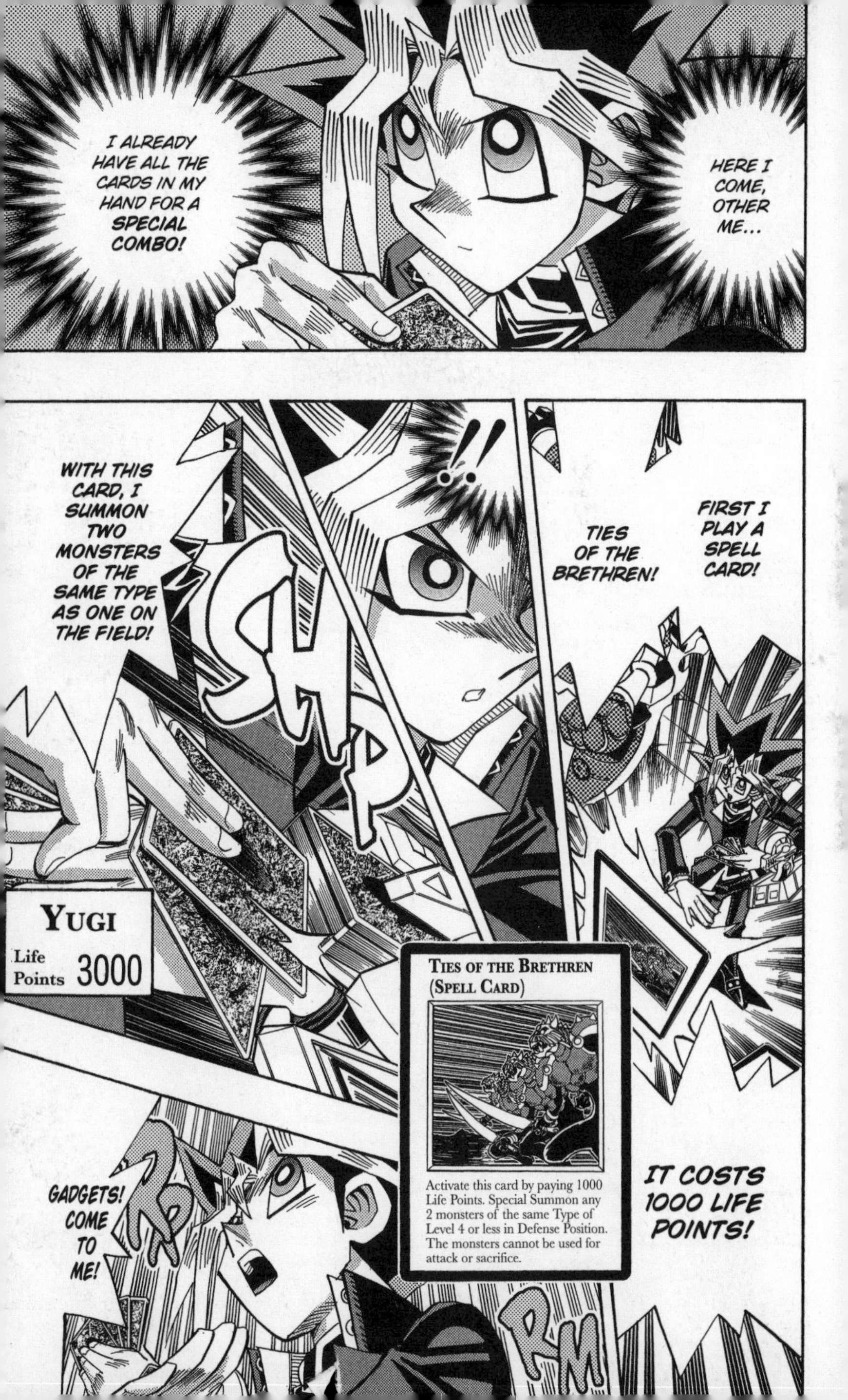
HERE I COME, OTHER ME...
I ALREADY HAVE ALL THE CARDS IN MY HAND FOR A SPECIAL COMBO!
FIRST I PLAY A SPELL CARD!
TIES OF THE BRETHREN!
!!
WITH THIS CARD, I SUMMON TWO MONSTERS OF THE SAME TYPE AS ONE ON THE FIELD!
YUGI
Life Points 3000
IT COSTS 1000 LIFE POINTS!
TIES OF THE BRETHREN
(SPELL CARD)
Activate this card by paying 1000 Life Points. Special Summon any 2 monsters of the same Type of Level 4 or less in Defense Position. The monsters cannot be used for attack or sacrifice.
GADGETS! COME TO ME!

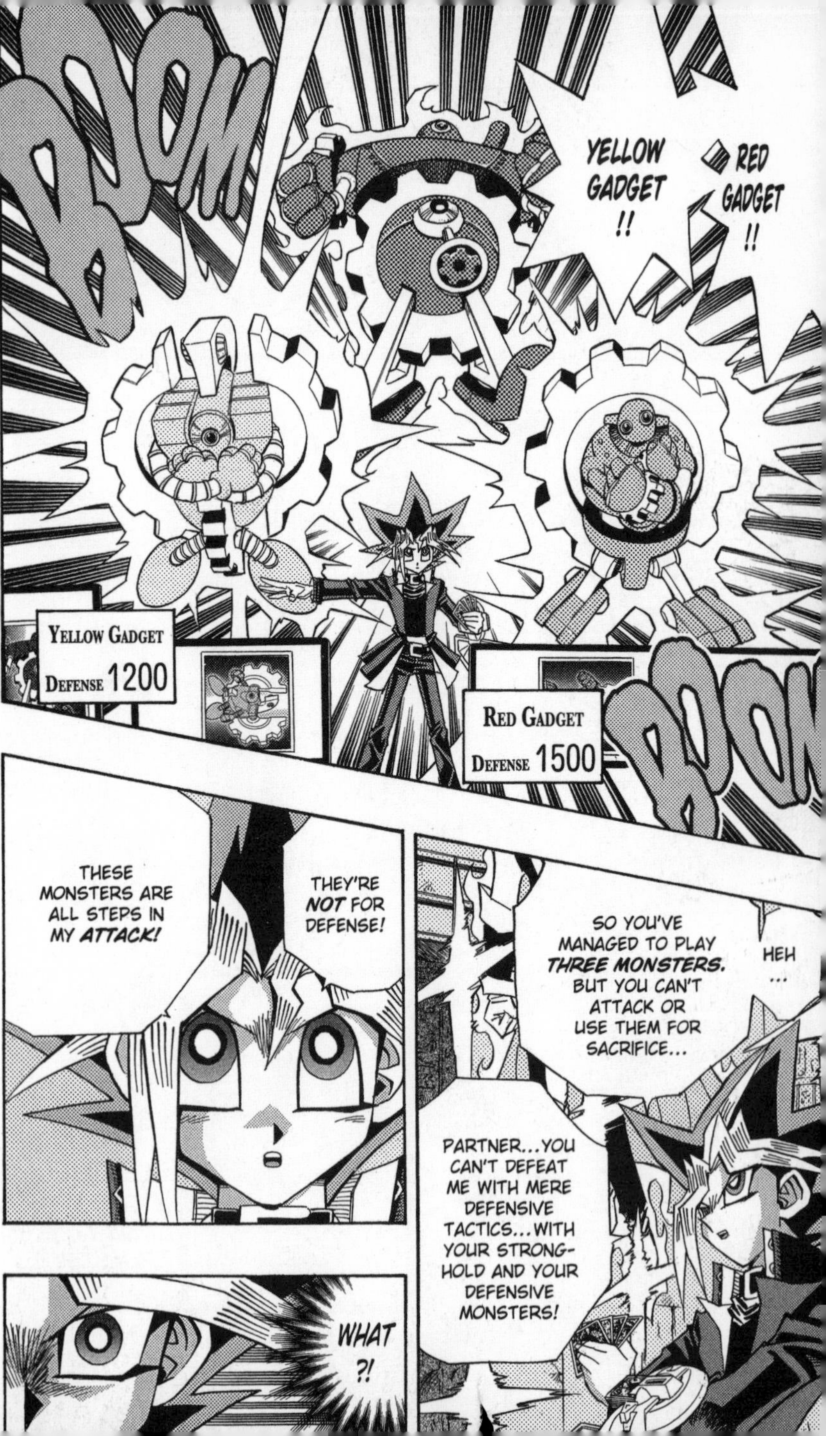
RED GADGET!!
YELLOW GADGET!!
BOOM
BOOM
YELLOW GADGET DEFENSE 1200
RED GADGET DEFENSE 1500
HEH...
SO YOU'VE MANAGED TO PLAY *THREE MONSTERS.* BUT YOU CAN'T ATTACK OR USE THEM FOR SACRIFICE...
PARTNER...YOU CAN'T DEFEAT ME WITH MERE DEFENSIVE TACTICS...WITH YOUR STRONG-HOLD AND YOUR DEFENSIVE MONSTERS!
THEY'RE *NOT* FOR DEFENSE!
THESE MONSTERS ARE ALL STEPS IN MY *ATTACK!*
WHAT?!

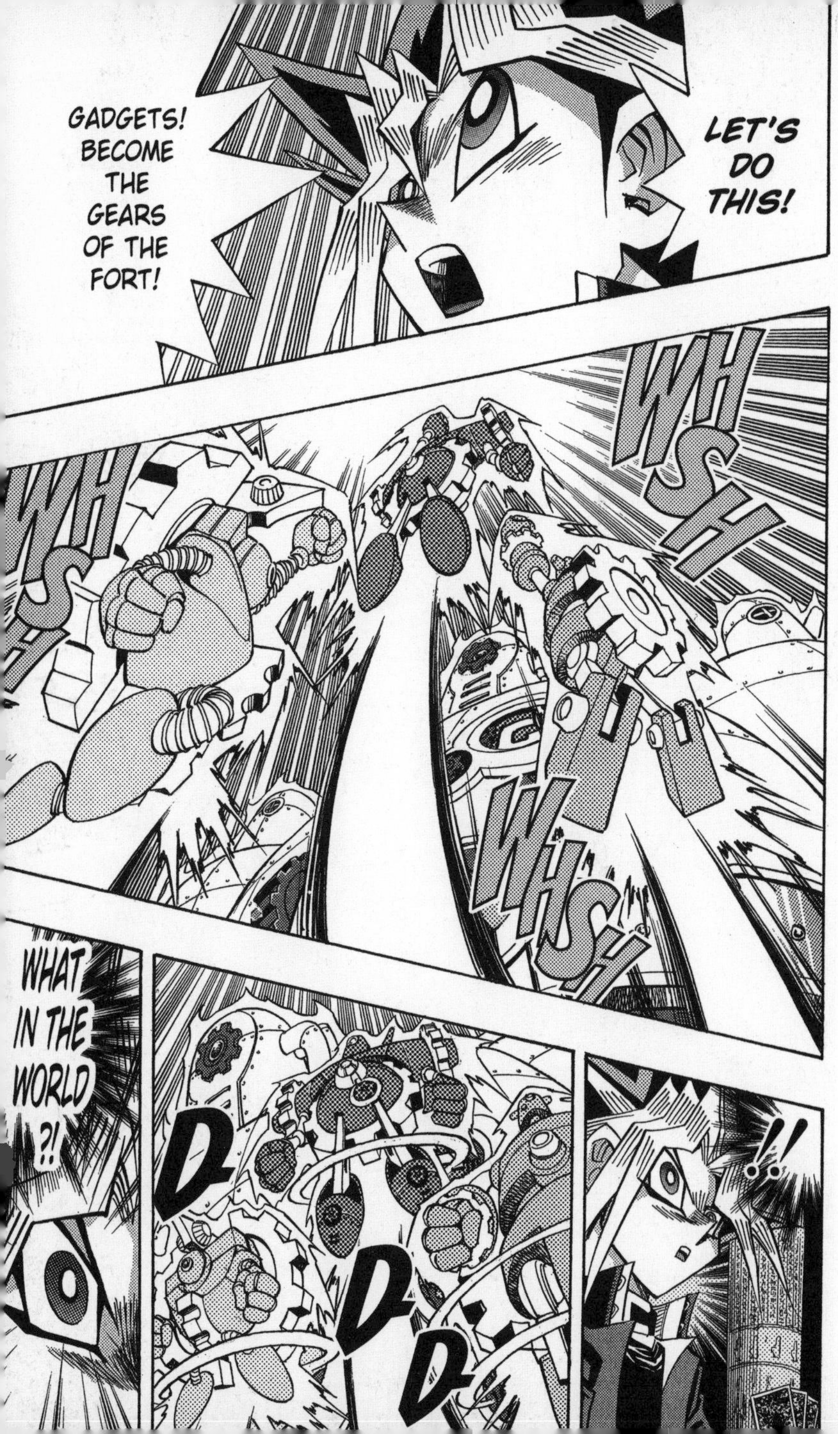
LET'S DO THIS!
GADGETS! BECOME THE GEARS OF THE FORT!
WHSH
WHSH
WHSH
!!
D
D
D
WHAT IN THE WORLD ?!

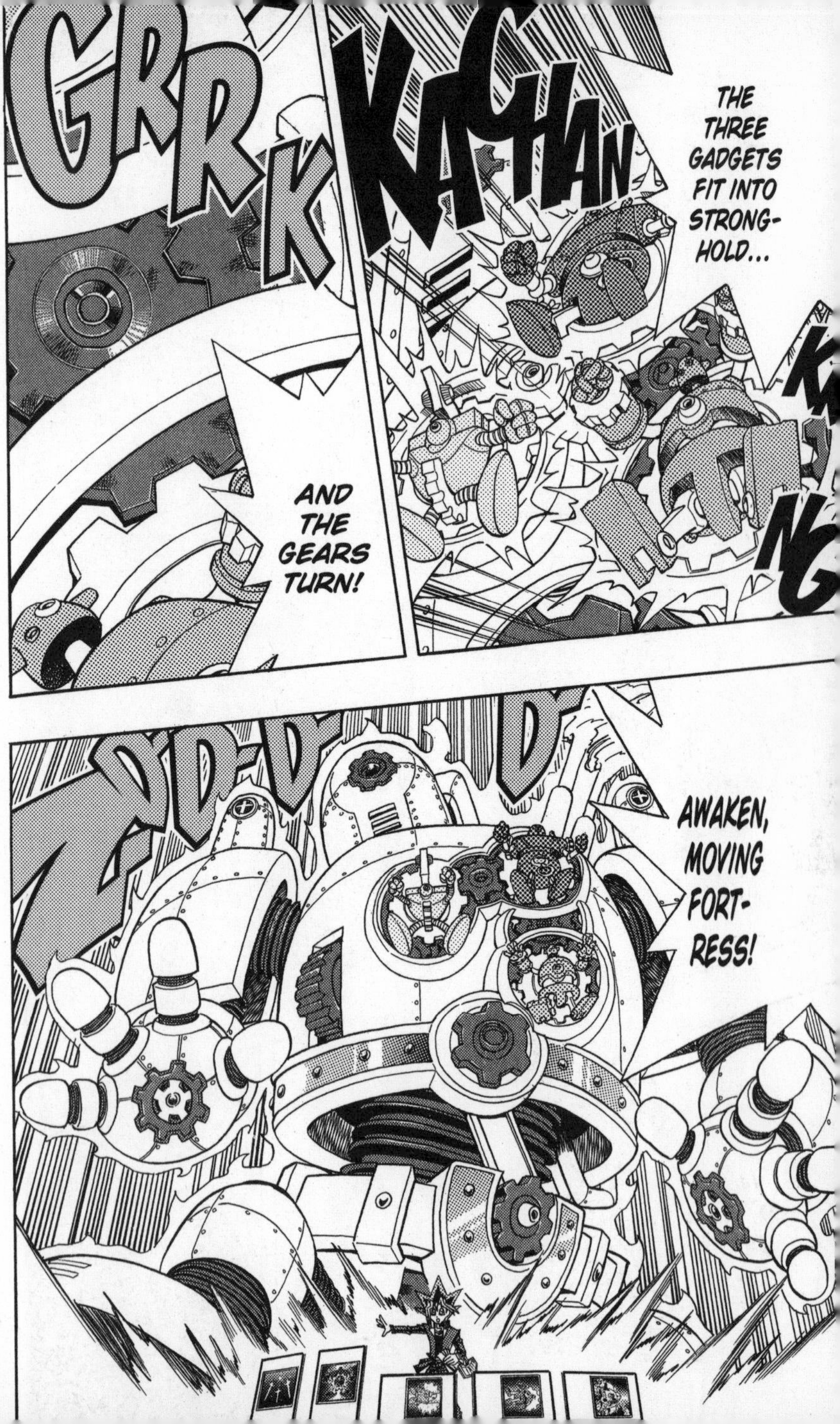
KACHAN
THE THREE GADGETS FIT INTO STRONGHOLD...
GRRK
AND THE GEARS TURN!
AWAKEN, MOVING FORTRESS!

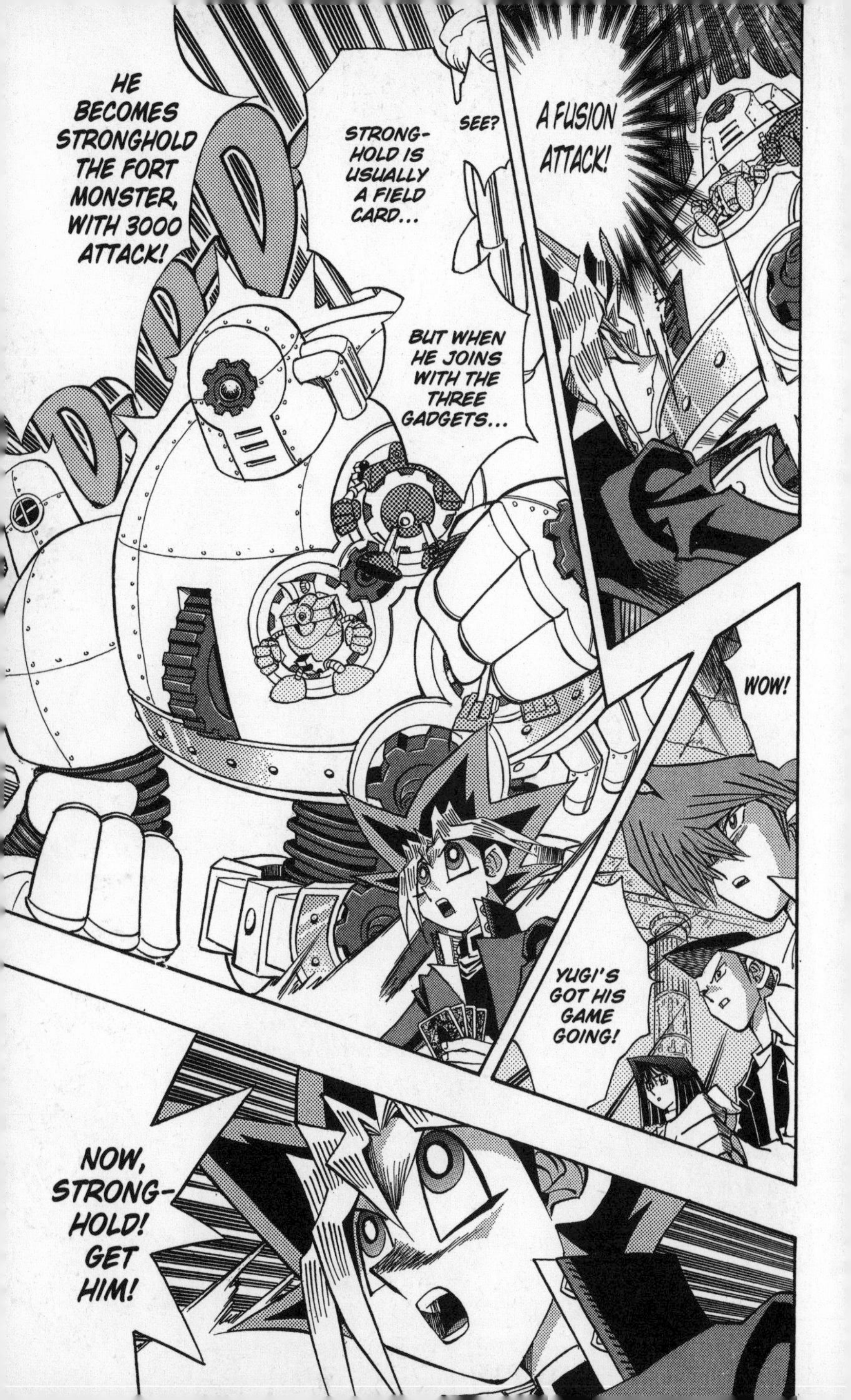
A FUSION ATTACK!
WOW!
YUGI'S GOT HIS GAME GOING!
SEE?
STRONG-HOLD IS USUALLY A FIELD CARD...
BUT WHEN HE JOINS WITH THE THREE GADGETS...
HE BECOMES STRONGHOLD THE FORT MONSTER, WITH 3000 ATTACK!
NOW, STRONG-HOLD! GET HIM!

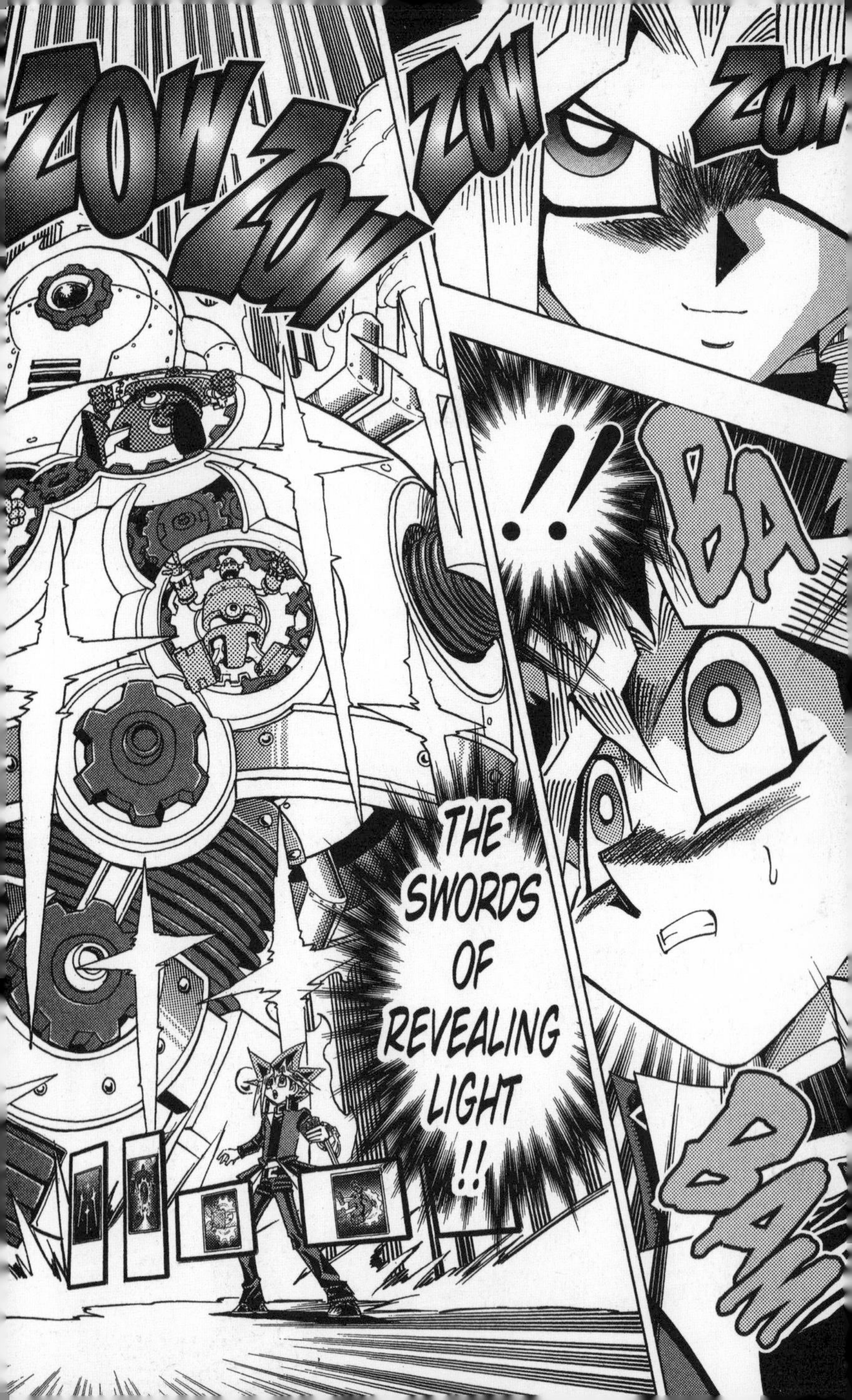
ZOW
ZOW
!!
BA
BAM
ZOW
ZOW
THE SWORDS OF REVEALING LIGHT!!

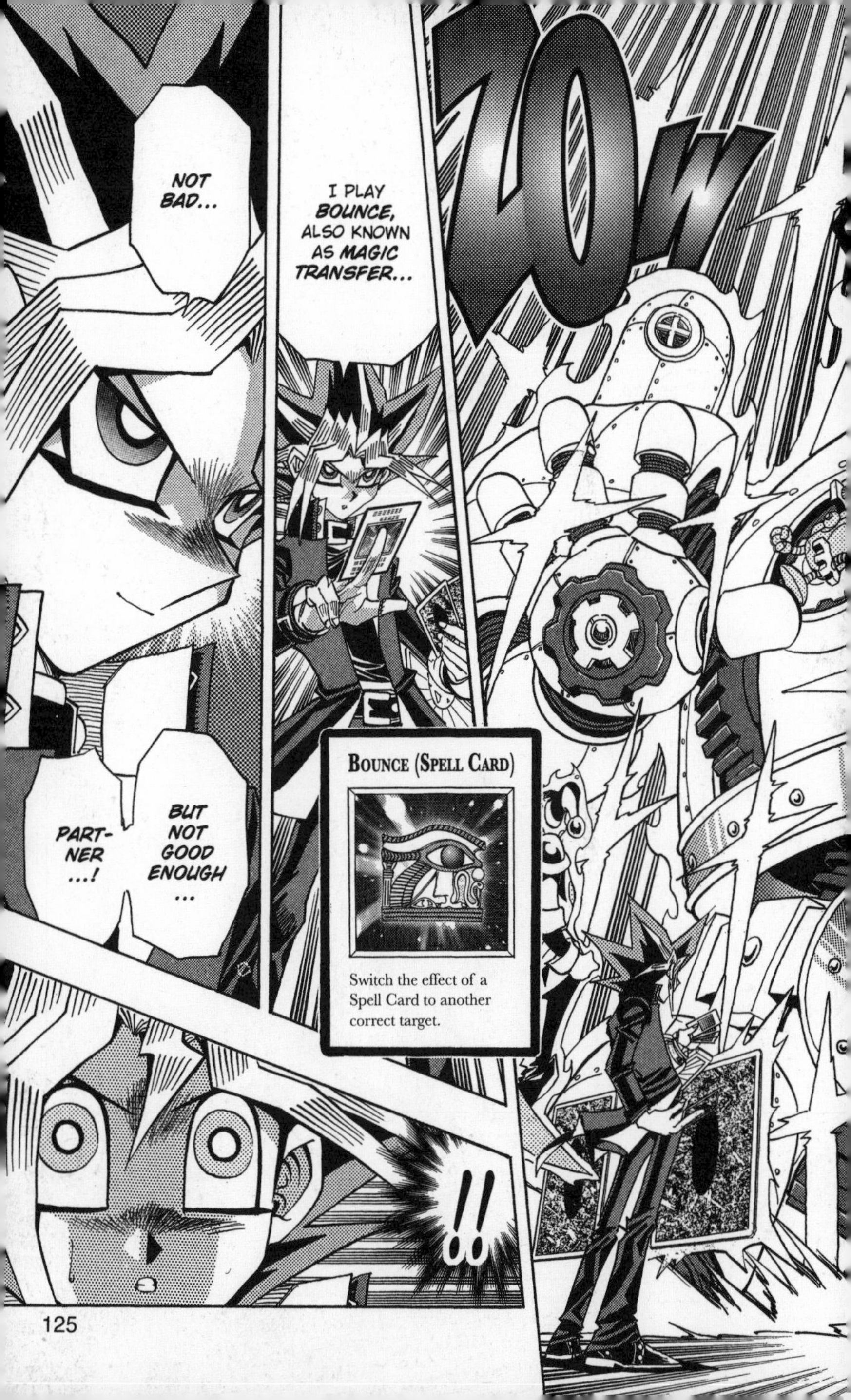
ZOW
BOUNCE (SPELL CARD)
Switch the effect of a Spell Card to another correct target.
I PLAY BOUNCE, ALSO KNOWN AS MAGIC TRANSFER...
NOT BAD...
BUT NOT GOOD ENOUGH...
PART-NER...!
!!

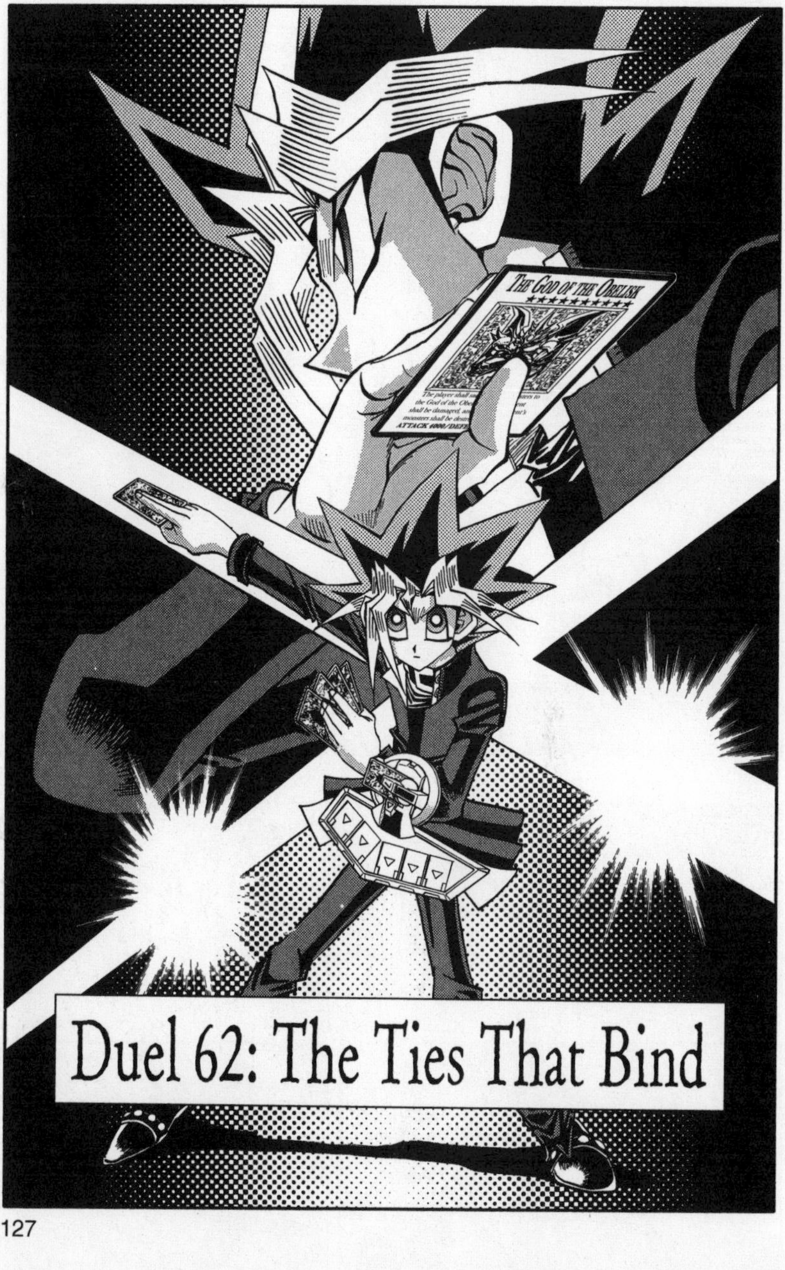
THE GOD OF THE OBELISK
Duel 62: The Ties That Bind

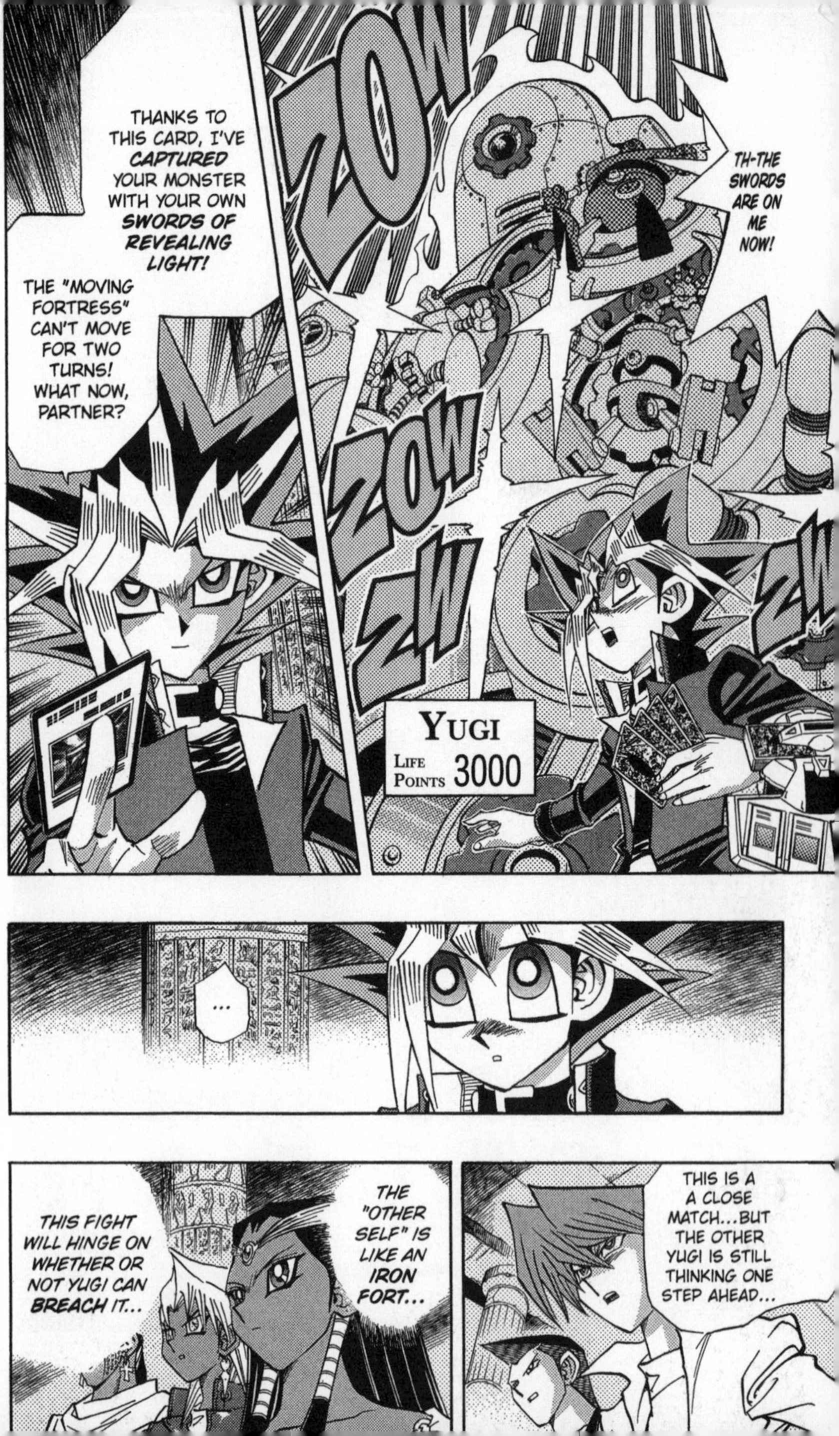
ZOW
TH-THE SWORDS ARE ON ME NOW!
ZOW
ZIN
YUGI
LIFE POINTS 3000
THANKS TO THIS CARD, I'VE CAPTURED YOUR MONSTER WITH YOUR OWN SWORDS OF REVEALING LIGHT!
THE "MOVING FORTRESS" CAN'T MOVE FOR TWO TURNS! WHAT NOW, PARTNER?
...
THIS IS A A CLOSE MATCH...BUT THE OTHER YUGI IS STILL THINKING ONE STEP AHEAD...
THE "OTHER SELF" IS LIKE AN IRON FORT...
THIS FIGHT WILL HINGE ON WHETHER OR NOT YUGI CAN BREACH IT...

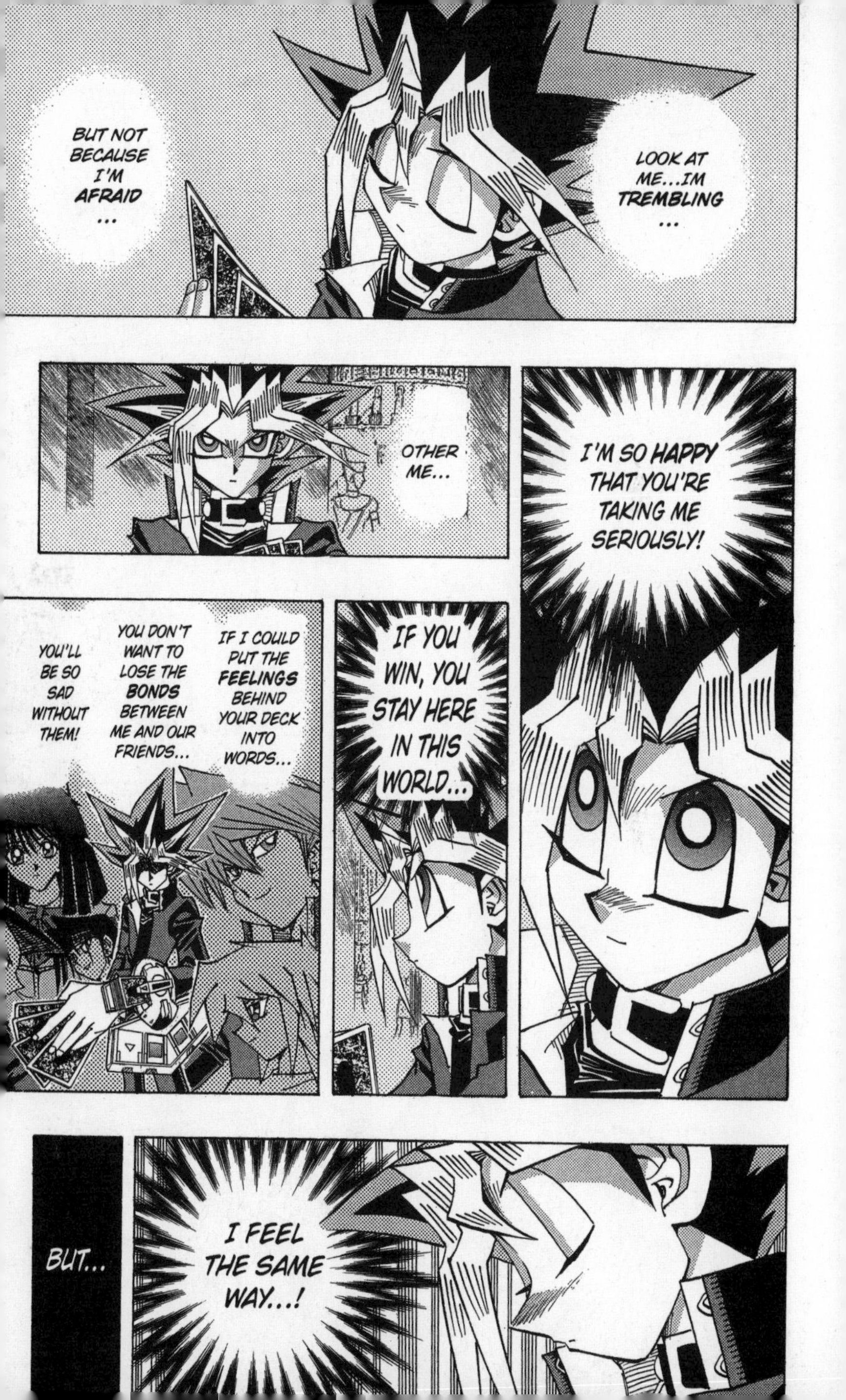
LOOK AT ME...IM TREMBLING...
BUT NOT BECAUSE I'M AFRAID...
I'M SO HAPPY THAT YOU'RE TAKING ME SERIOUSLY!
OTHER ME...
IF YOU WIN, YOU STAY HERE IN THIS WORLD...
IF I COULD PUT THE FEELINGS BEHIND YOUR DECK INTO WORDS...
YOU DON'T WANT TO LOSE THE BONDS BETWEEN ME AND OUR FRIENDS...
YOU'LL BE SO SAD WITHOUT THEM!
I FEEL THE SAME WAY...!
BUT...

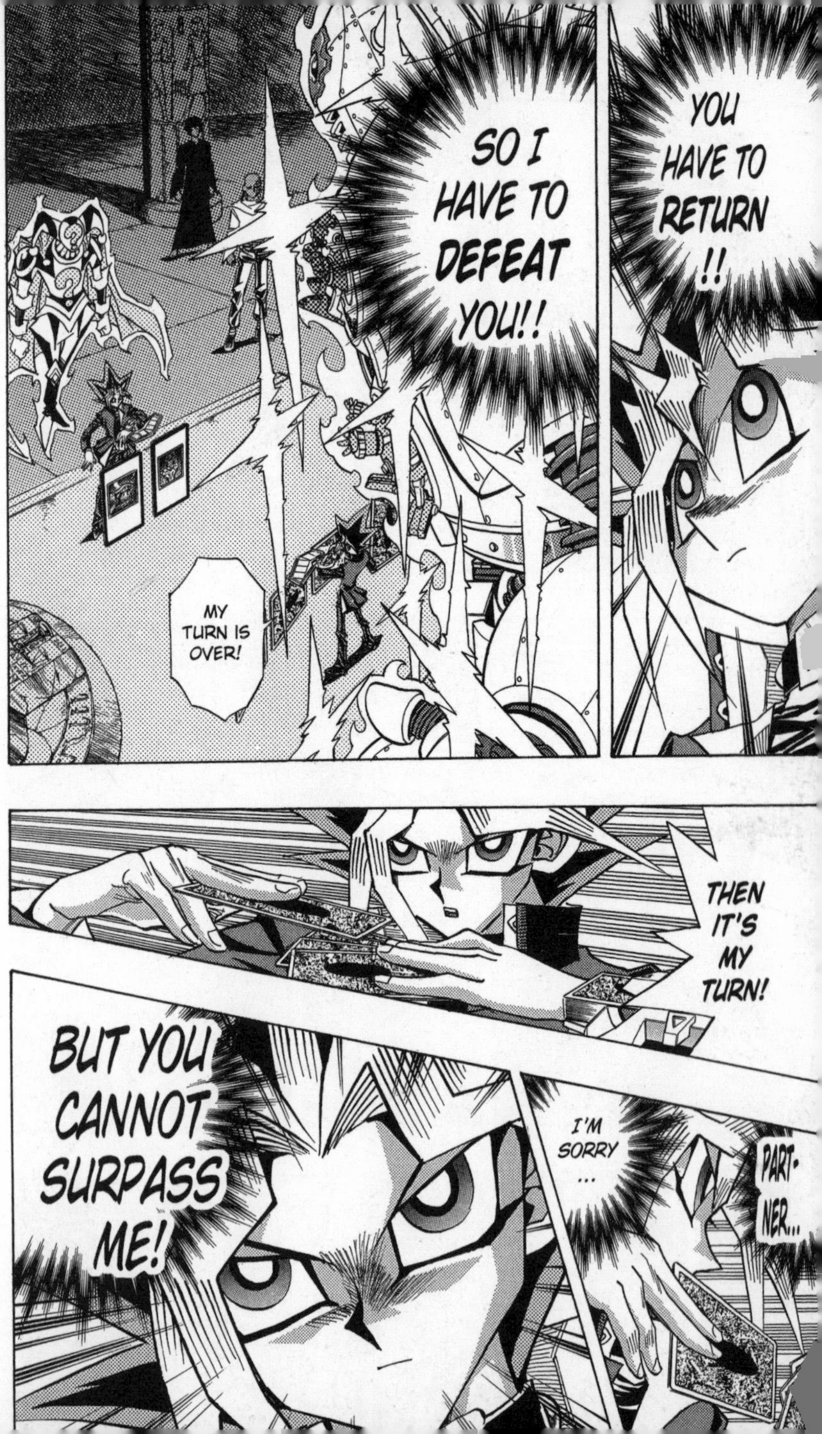
YOU HAVE TO RETURN!!
SO I HAVE TO DEFEAT YOU!!
MY TURN IS OVER!
THEN IT'S MY TURN!
I'M SORRY...
PART-NER...
BUT YOU CANNOT SURPASS ME!

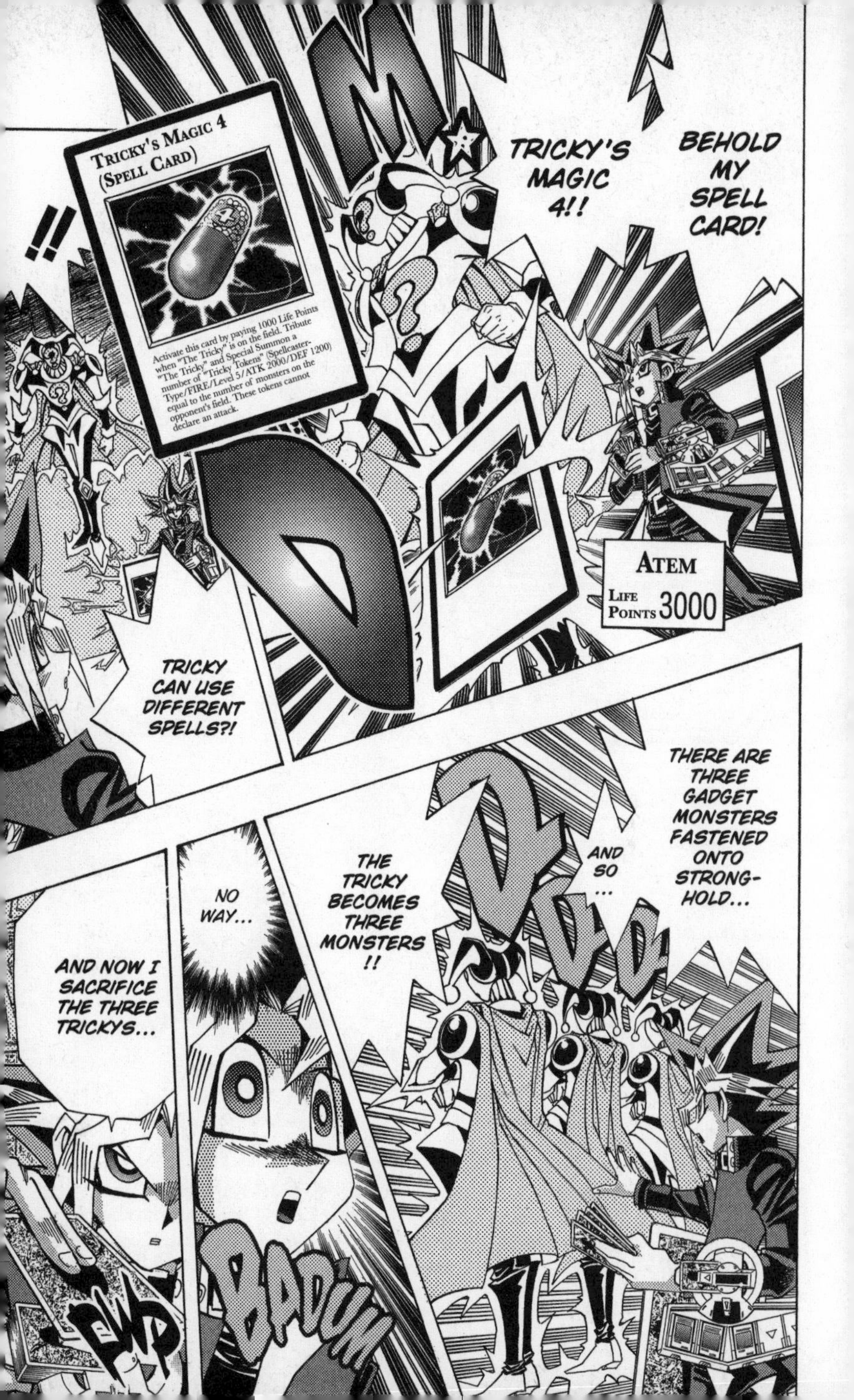
BEHOLD MY SPELL CARD!
TRICKY'S MAGIC 4!!
TRICKY'S MAGIC 4
(SPELL CARD)
Activate this card by paying 1000 Life Points when "The Tricky" is on the field. Tribute "The Tricky" and Special Summon a number of "Tricky Tokens" (Spellcaster-Type/FIRE/Level 5/ATK 2000/DEF 1200) equal to the number of monsters on the opponent's field. These tokens cannot declare an attack.
!!
ATEM
LIFE POINTS 3000
TRICKY CAN USE DIFFERENT SPELLS?!
THERE ARE THREE GADGET MONSTERS FASTENED ONTO STRONG-HOLD...
AND SO...
THE TRICKY BECOMES THREE MONSTERS!!
NO WAY...
BADUM
AND NOW I SACRIFICE THE THREE TRICKYS...

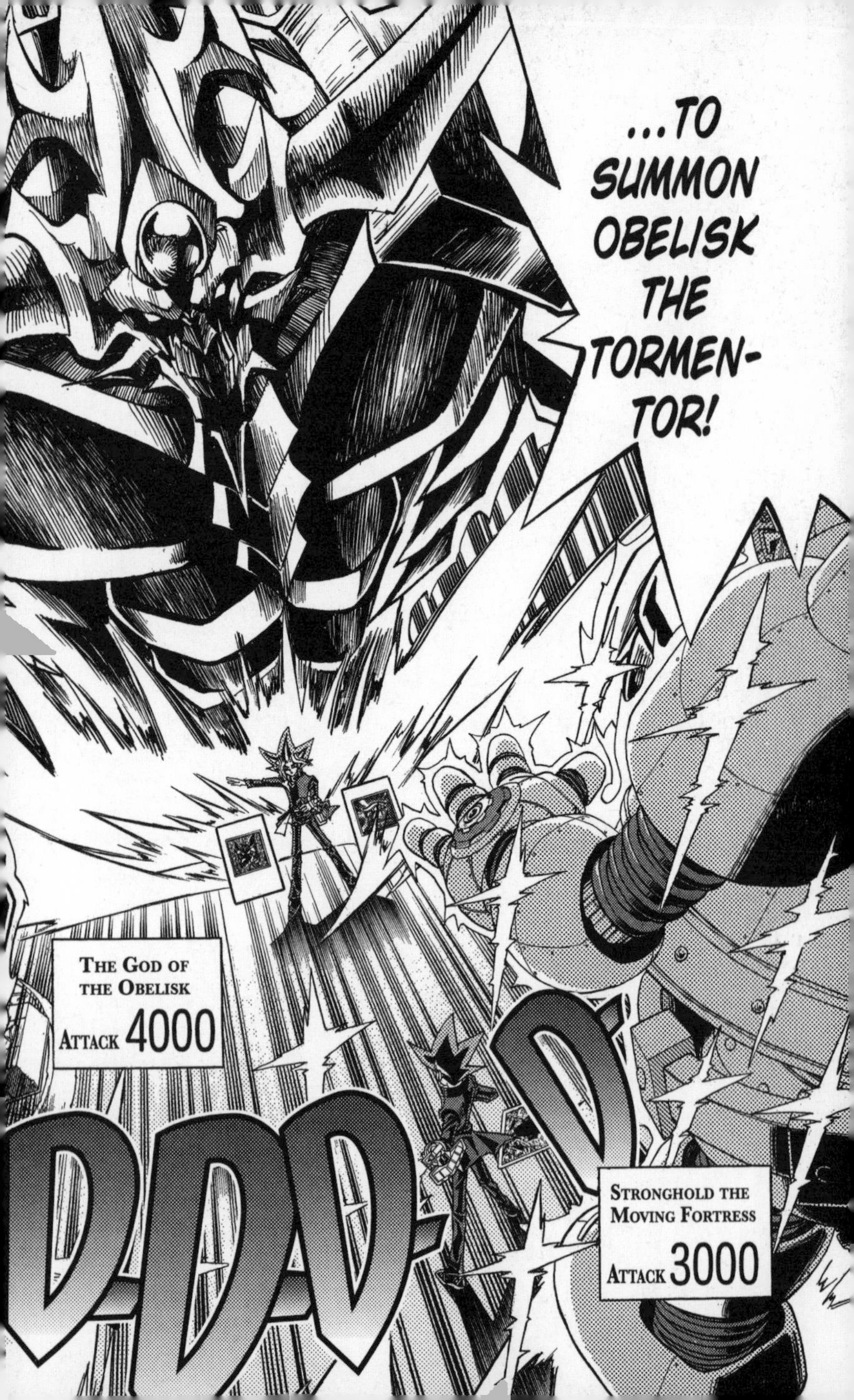
...TO SUMMON OBELISK THE TORMENTOR!
THE GOD OF THE OBELISK ATTACK 4000
STRONGHOLD THE MOVING FORTRESS ATTACK 3000

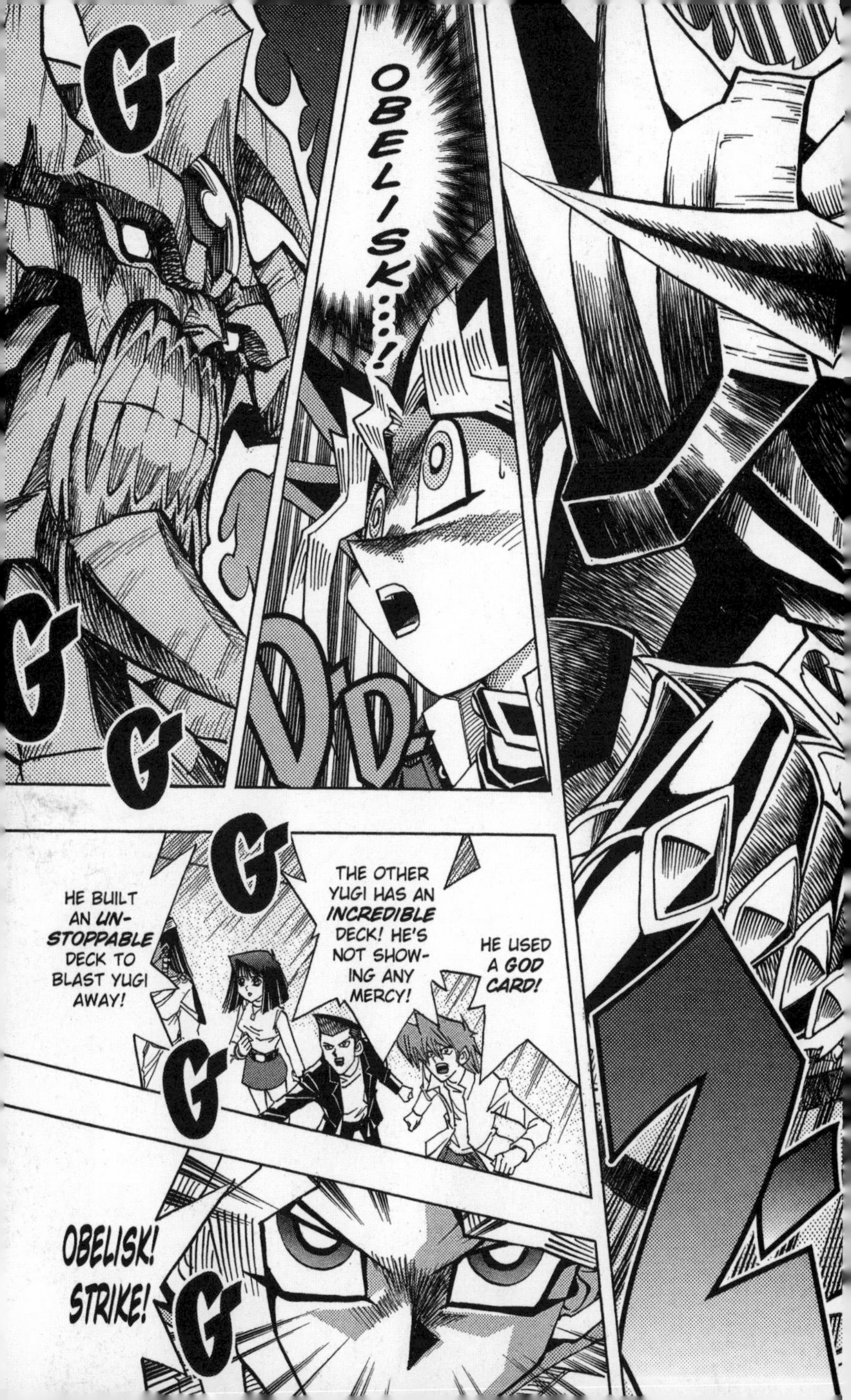
OBELISK...!
HE USED A GOD CARD!
THE OTHER YUGI HAS AN INCREDIBLE DECK! HE'S NOT SHOWING ANY MERCY!
HE BUILT AN UNSTOPPABLE DECK TO BLAST YUGI AWAY!
OBELISK! STRIKE!

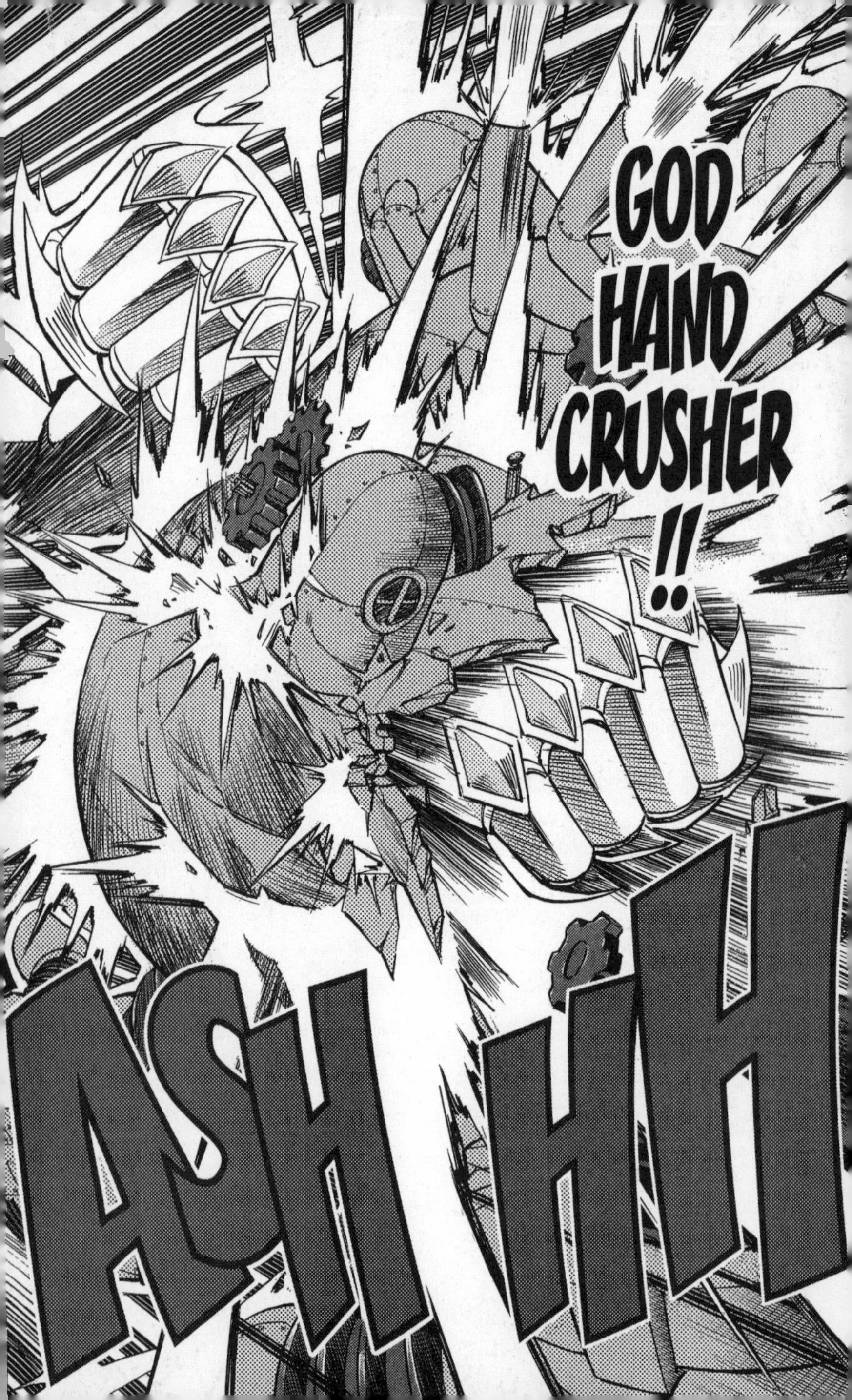
GOD HAND CRUSHER!!
ASH HH

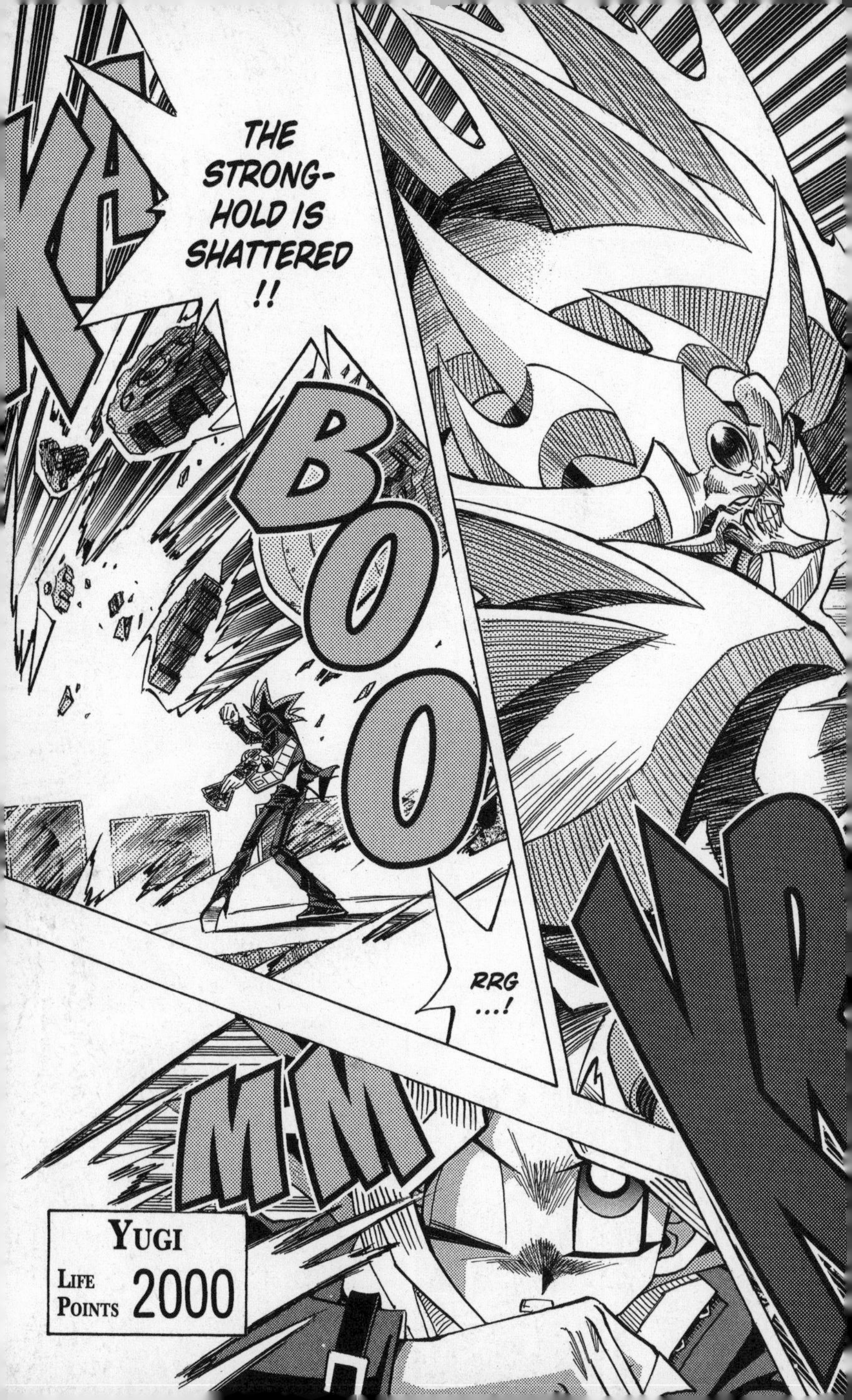
THE STRONG-HOLD IS SHATTERED !!
BOO
RRG ...!
MM
YUGI
LIFE POINTS 2000

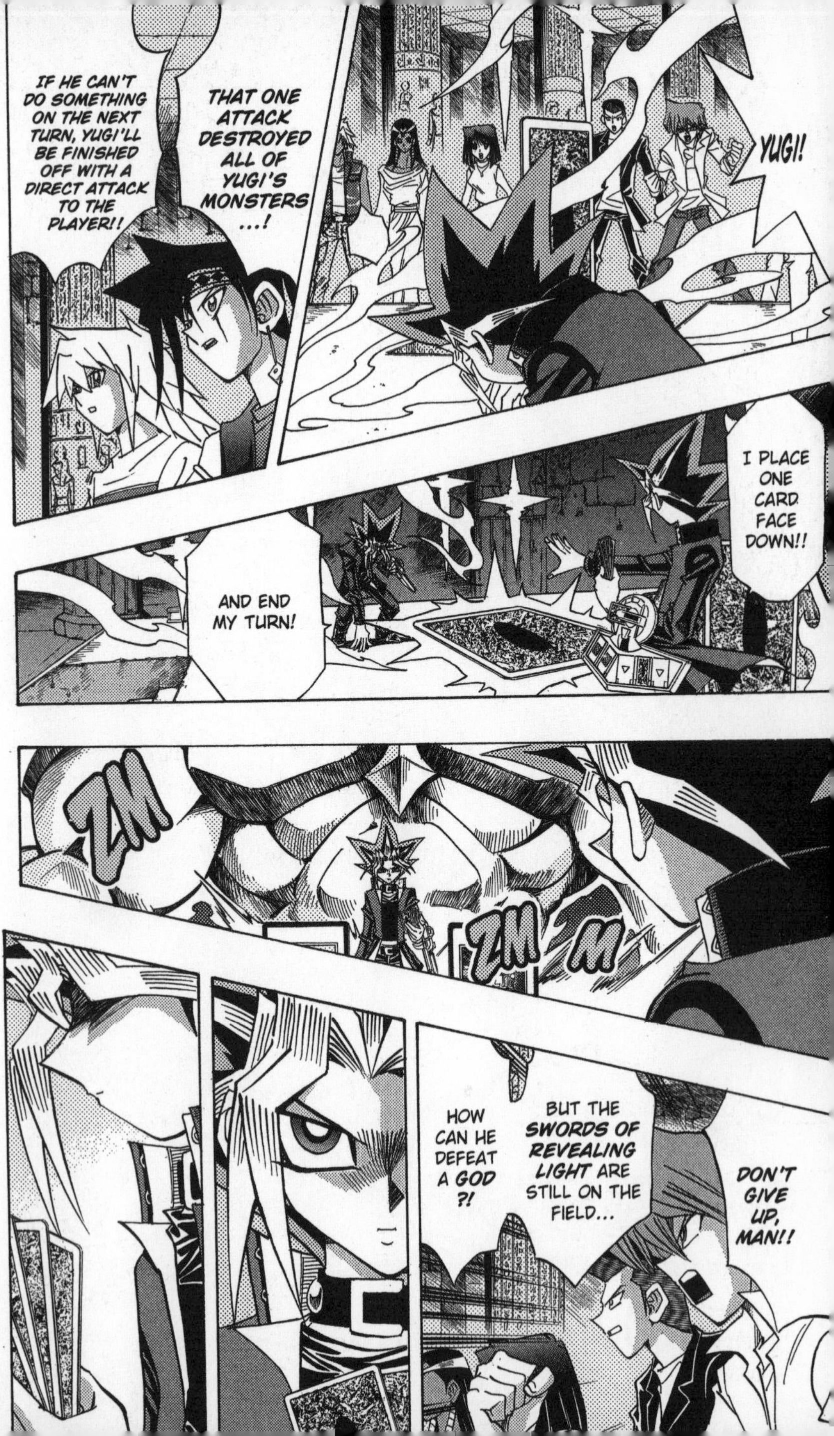
YUGI!
THAT ONE ATTACK DESTROYED ALL OF YUGI'S MONSTERS ...!
IF HE CAN'T DO SOMETHING ON THE NEXT TURN, YUGI'LL BE FINISHED OFF WITH A DIRECT ATTACK TO THE PLAYER!!
I PLACE ONE CARD FACE DOWN!!
AND END MY TURN!
ZM
ZM M
DON'T GIVE UP, MAN!!
BUT THE SWORDS OF REVEALING LIGHT ARE STILL ON THE FIELD...
HOW CAN HE DEFEAT A GOD ?!

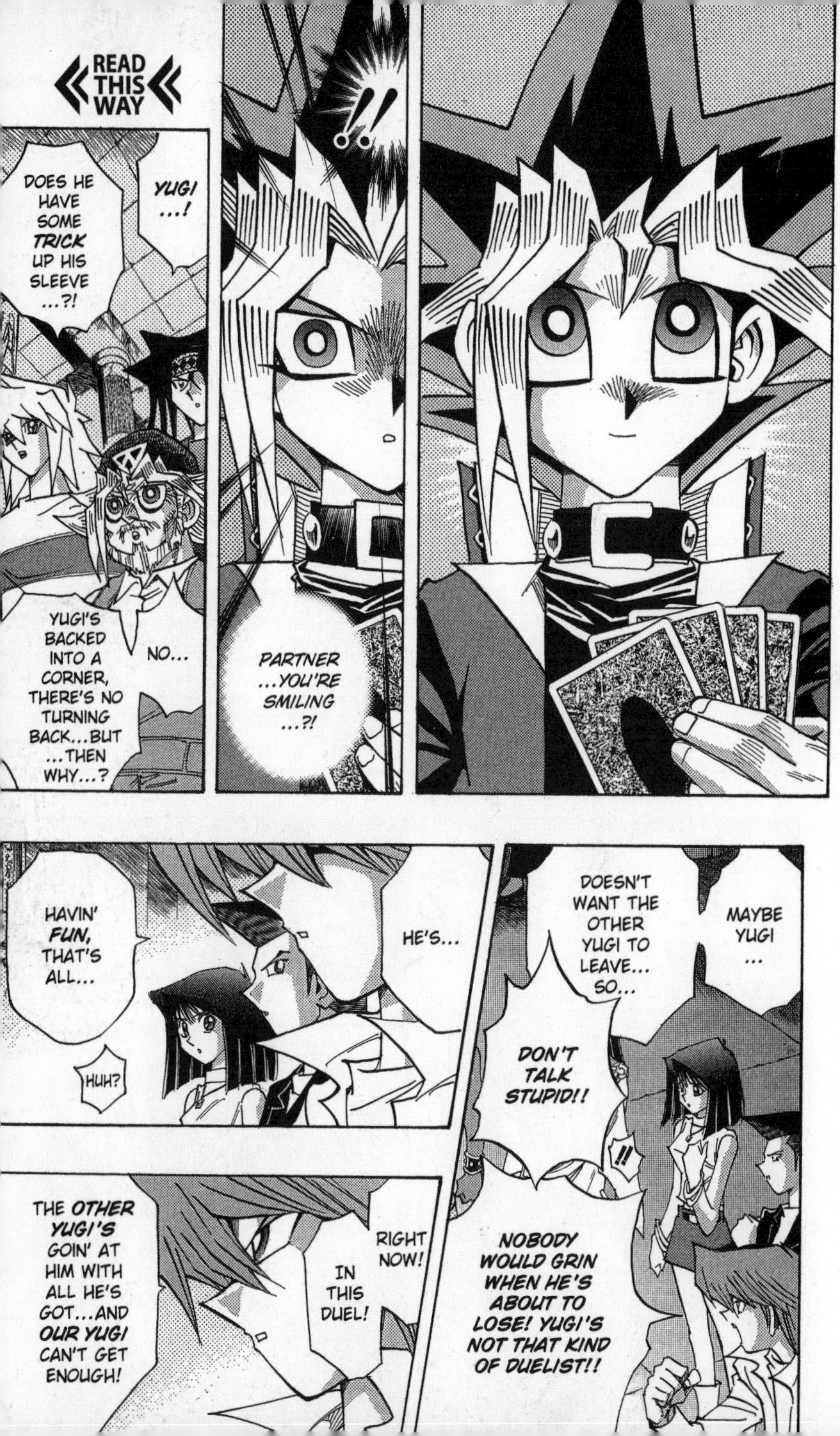
READ THIS WAY
!!
PARTNER ...YOU'RE SMILING ...?!
YUGI ...!
DOES HE HAVE SOME TRICK UP HIS SLEEVE ...?!
NO...
YUGI'S BACKED INTO A CORNER, THERE'S NO TURNING BACK...BUT ...THEN WHY...?
MAYBE YUGI ...
DOESN'T WANT THE OTHER YUGI TO LEAVE... SO...
DON'T TALK STUPID!!
!!
NOBODY WOULD GRIN WHEN HE'S ABOUT TO LOSE! YUGI'S NOT THAT KIND OF DUELIST!!
HE'S...
HAVIN' FUN, THAT'S ALL...
HUH?
RIGHT NOW!
IN THIS DUEL!
THE OTHER YUGI'S GOIN' AT HIM WITH ALL HE'S GOT...AND OUR YUGI CAN'T GET ENOUGH!

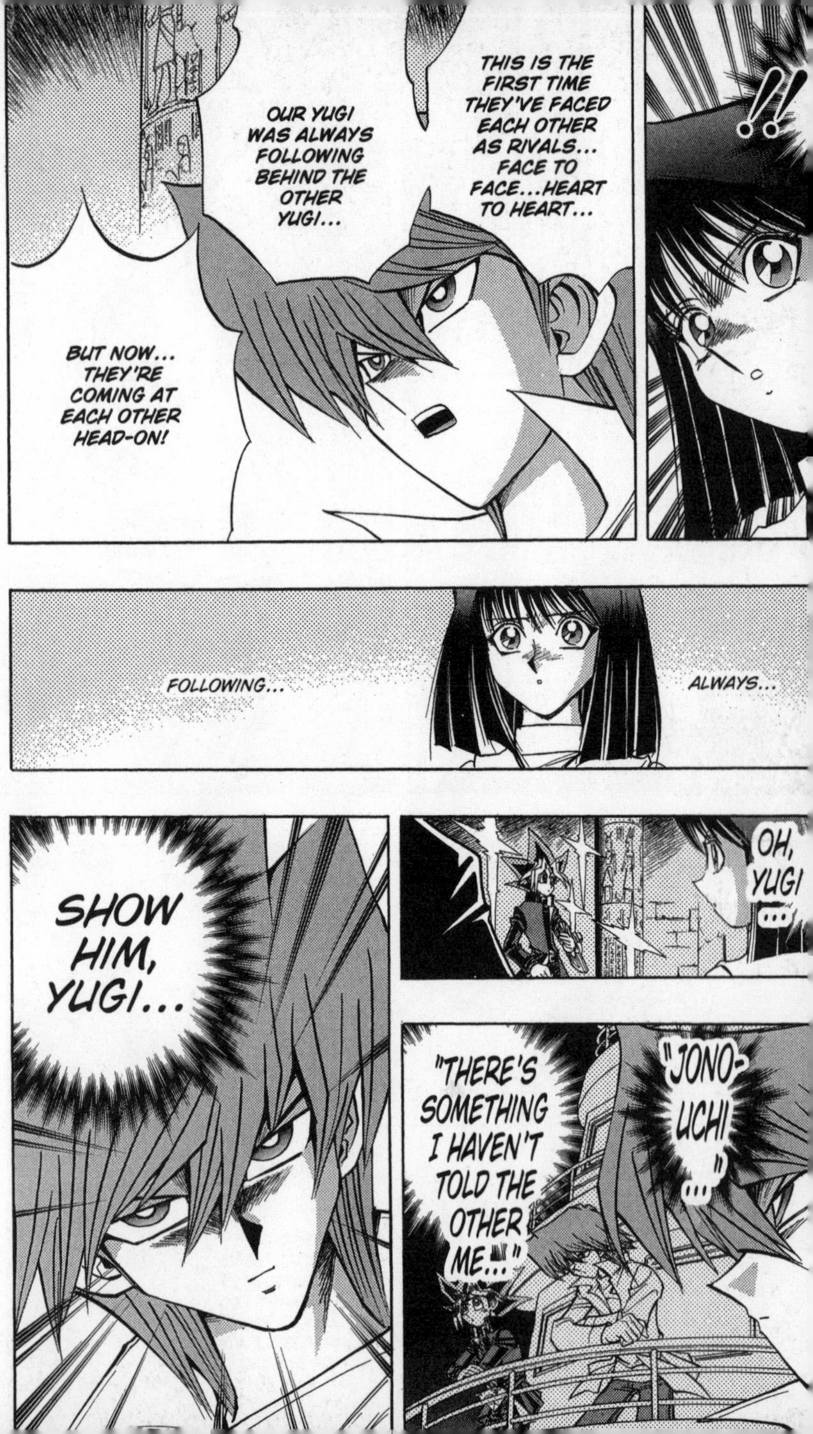
!!
THIS IS THE FIRST TIME THEY'VE FACED EACH OTHER AS RIVALS... FACE TO FACE...HEART TO HEART...
OUR YUGI WAS ALWAYS FOLLOWING BEHIND THE OTHER YUGI...
BUT NOW... THEY'RE COMING AT EACH OTHER HEAD-ON!
ALWAYS...
FOLLOWING...
OH, YUGI...
"JONO-UCHI..."
"THERE'S SOMETHING I HAVEN'T TOLD THE OTHER ME...!"
SHOW HIM, YUGI...

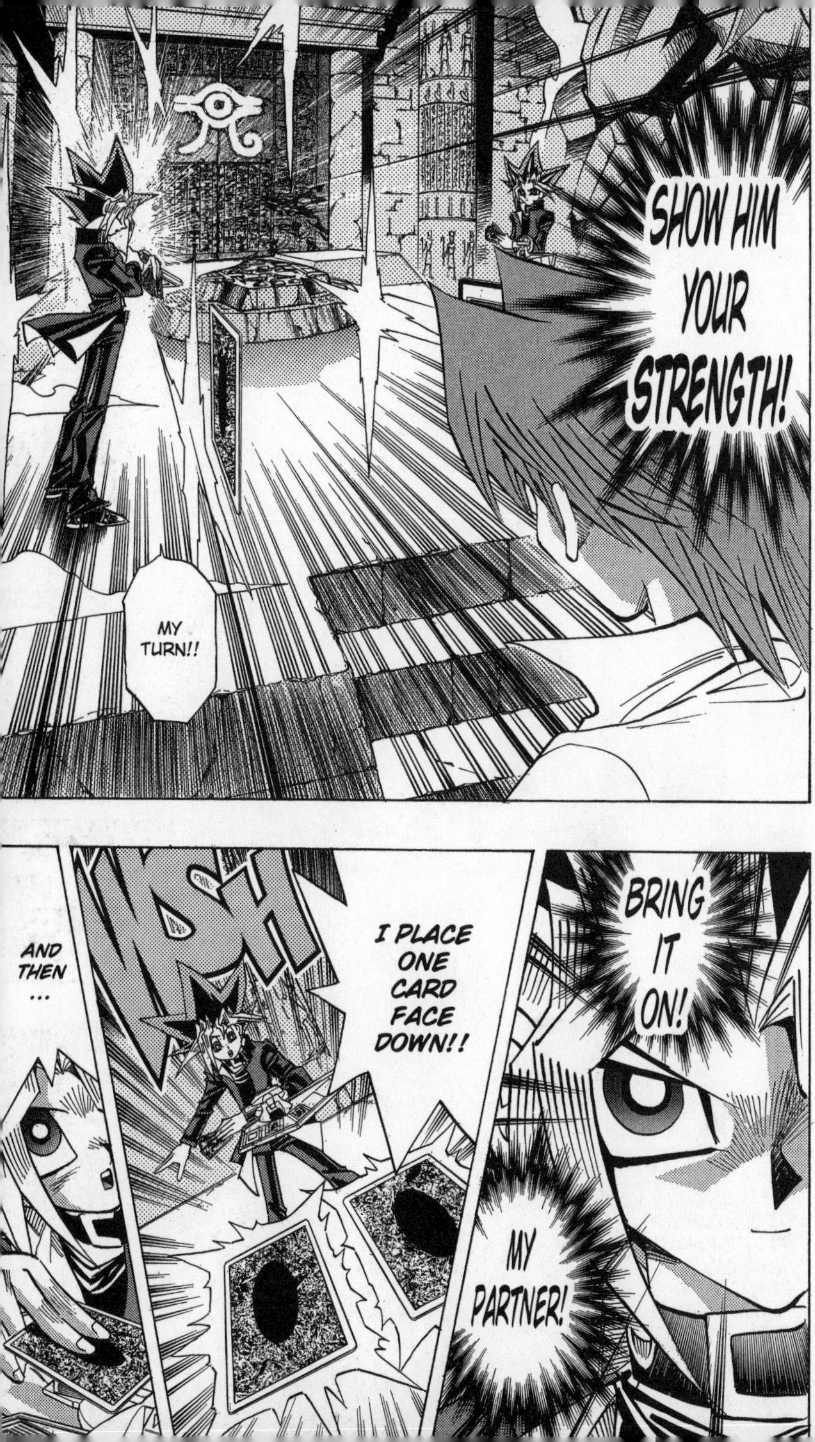
SHOW HIM YOUR STRENGTH!
MY TURN!!
BRING IT ON!
MY PARTNER!
I PLACE ONE CARD FACE DOWN!!
AND THEN ...

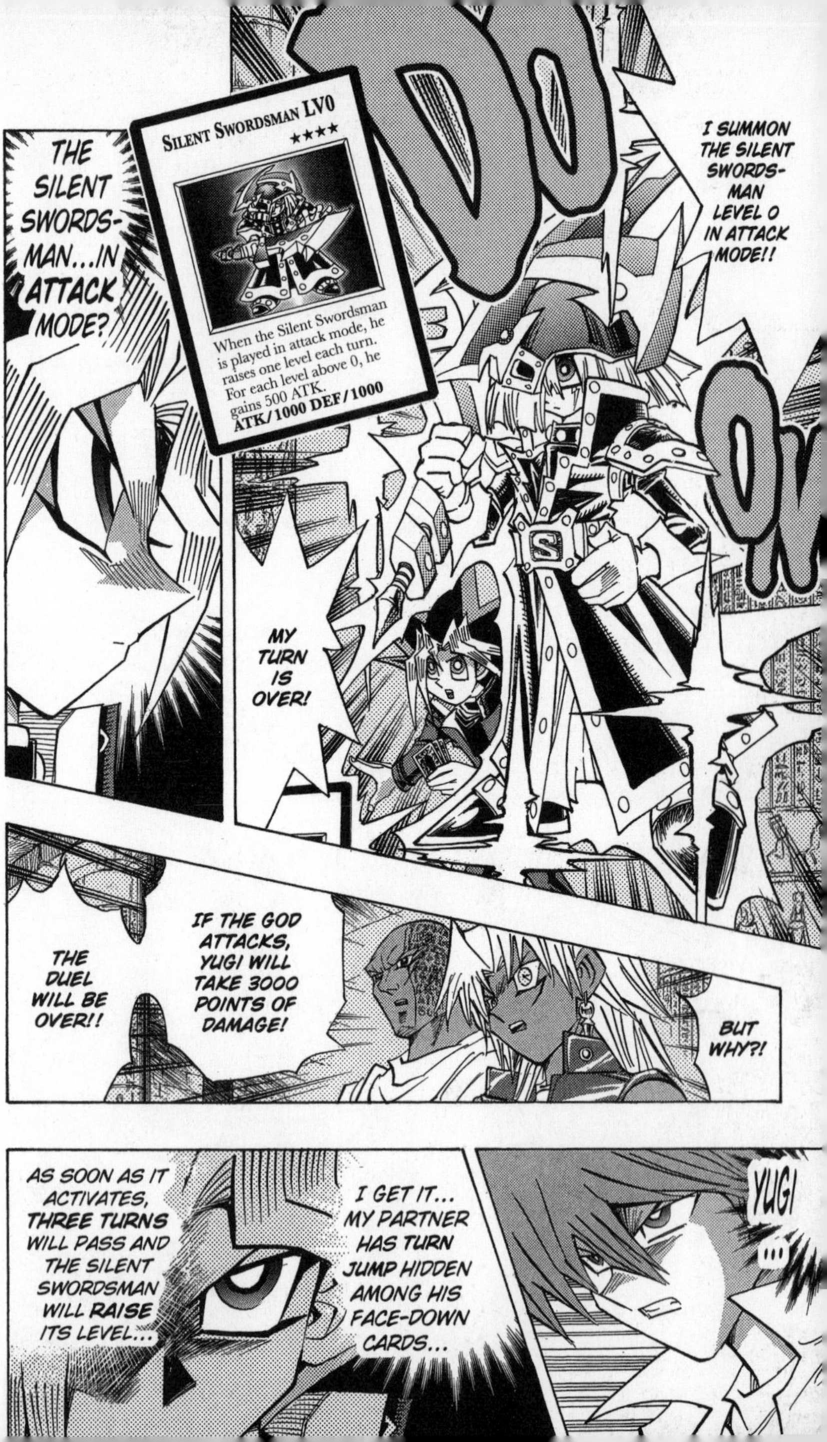
I SUMMON THE SILENT SWORDS-MAN LEVEL 0 IN ATTACK MODE!!
SILENT SWORDSMAN LV0
★★★★
When the Silent Swordsman is played in attack mode, he raises one level each turn. For each level above 0, he gains 500 ATK.
ATK/1000 DEF/1000
MY TURN IS OVER!
THE SILENT SWORDS-MAN...IN ATTACK MODE?
IF THE GOD ATTACKS, YUGI WILL TAKE 3000 POINTS OF DAMAGE!
THE DUEL WILL BE OVER!!
BUT WHY?!
YUGI ...
I GET IT... MY PARTNER HAS TURN JUMP HIDDEN AMONG HIS FACE-DOWN CARDS...
AS SOON AS IT ACTIVATES, THREE TURNS WILL PASS AND THE SILENT SWORDSMAN WILL RAISE ITS LEVEL...

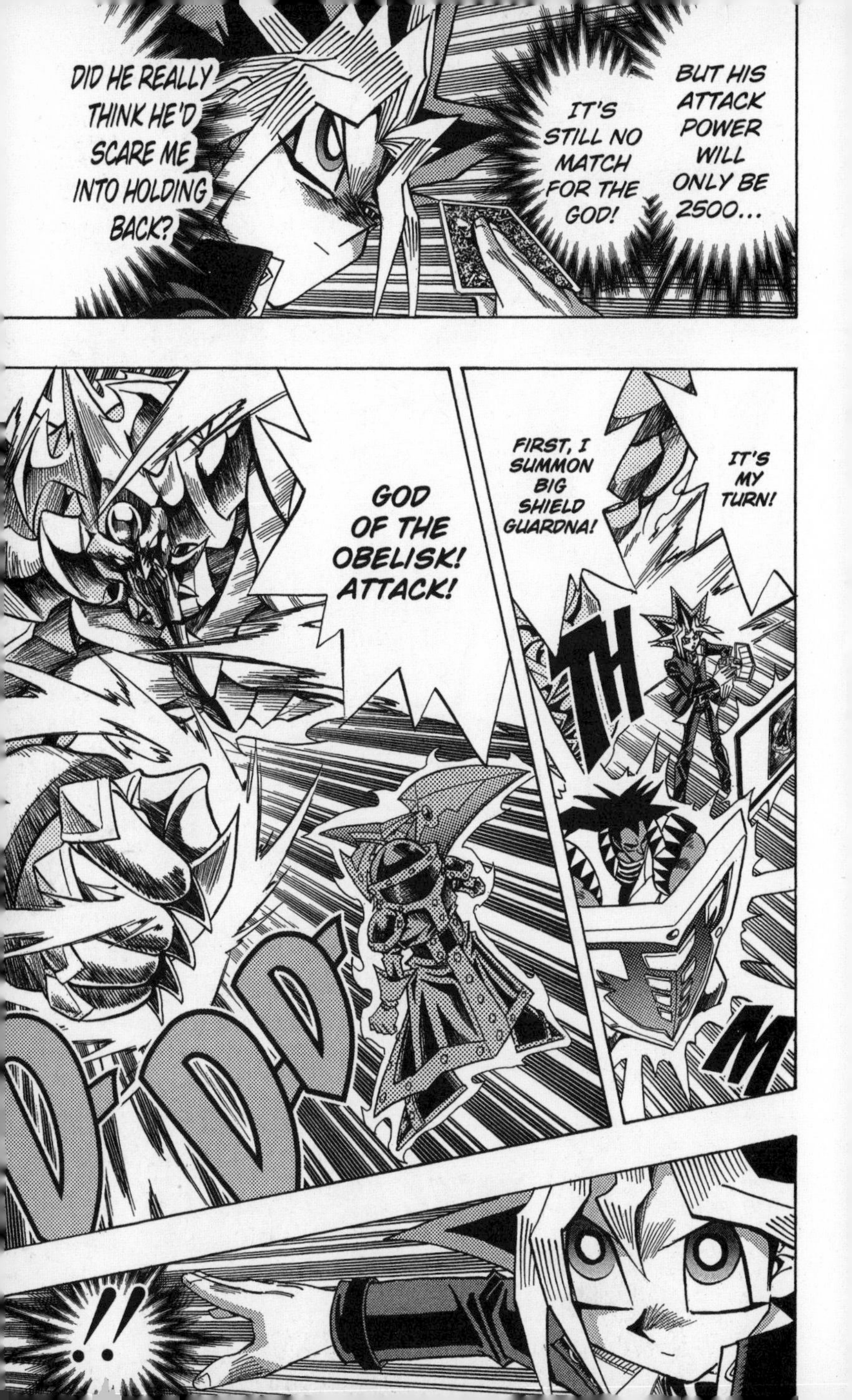
BUT HIS ATTACK POWER WILL ONLY BE 2500...
IT'S STILL NO MATCH FOR THE GOD!
DID HE REALLY THINK HE'D SCARE ME INTO HOLDING BACK?
IT'S MY TURN!
FIRST, I SUMMON BIG SHIELD GUARDNA!
TH
M
GOD OF THE OBELISK! ATTACK!
!!

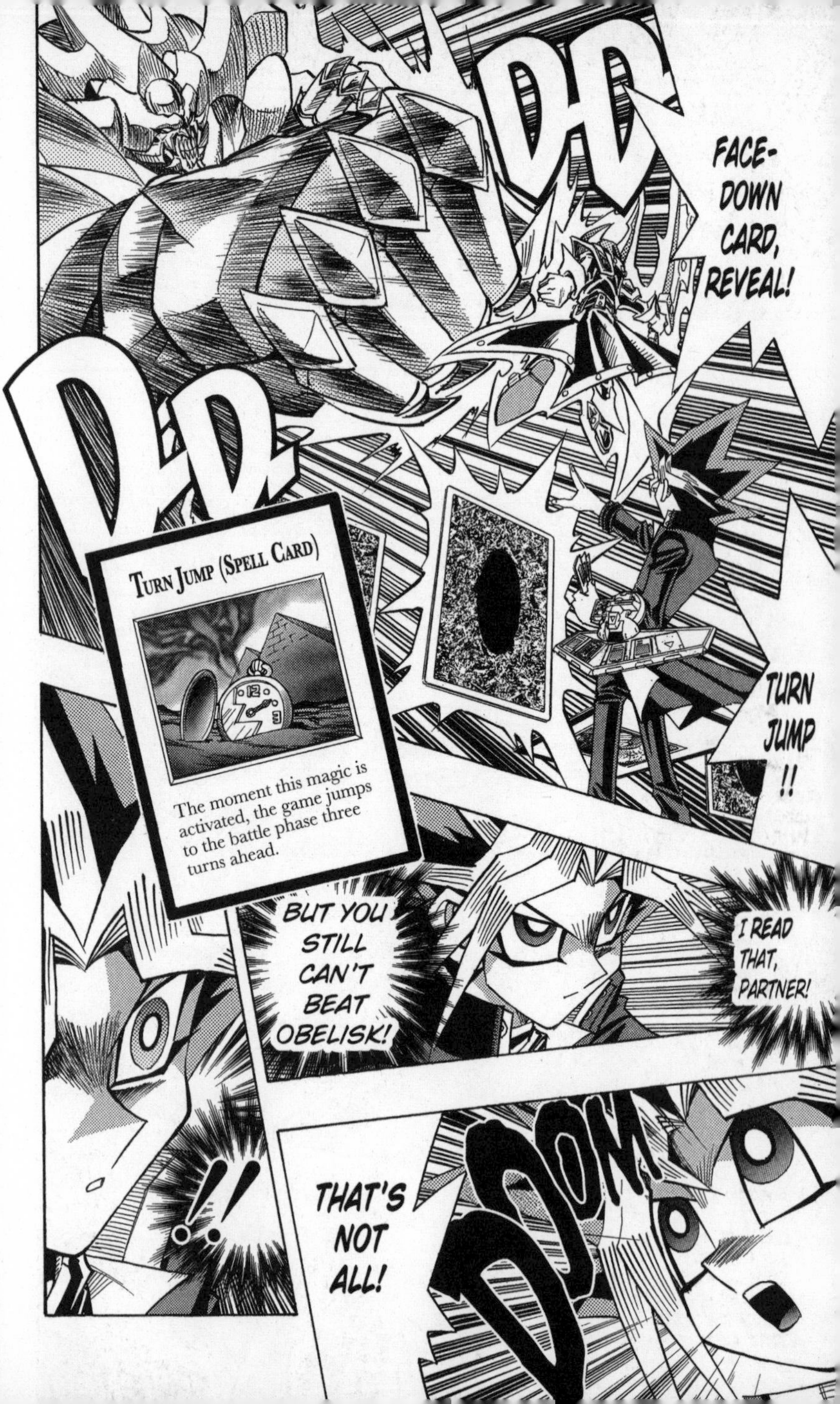
FACE-DOWN CARD, REVEAL!
TURN JUMP !!
TURN JUMP (SPELL CARD)
The moment this magic is activated, the game jumps to the battle phase three turns ahead.
I READ THAT, PARTNER!
BUT YOU STILL CAN'T BEAT OBELISK!
DOOM
THAT'S NOT ALL!
!!

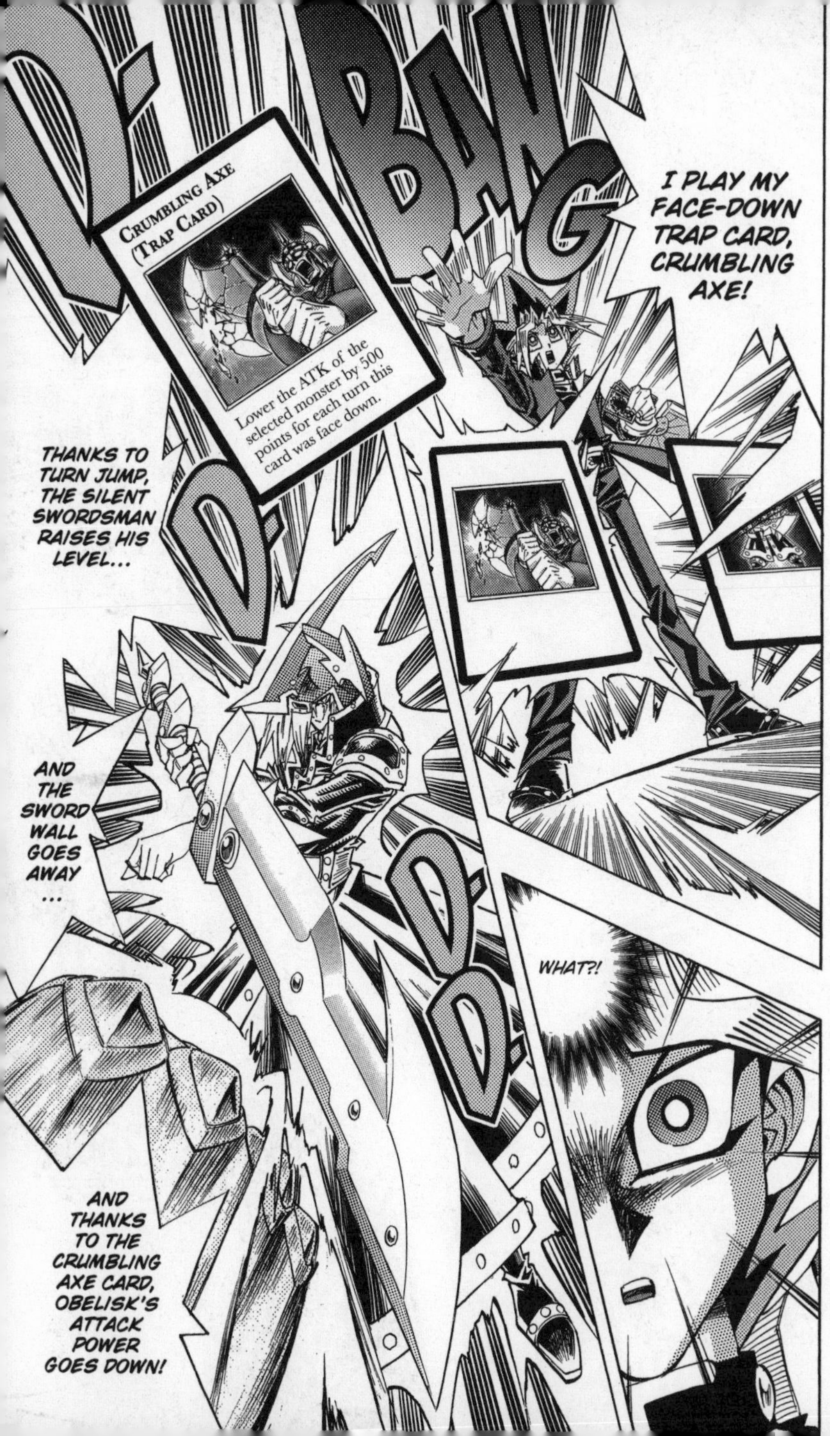
BAHG
I PLAY MY FACE-DOWN TRAP CARD, CRUMBLING AXE!
CRUMBLING AXE (TRAP CARD)
Lower the ATK of the selected monster by 500 points for each turn this card was face down.
THANKS TO TURN JUMP, THE SILENT SWORDSMAN RAISES HIS LEVEL...
AND THE SWORD WALL GOES AWAY ...
WHAT?!
AND THANKS TO THE CRUMBLING AXE CARD, OBELISK'S ATTACK POWER GOES DOWN!

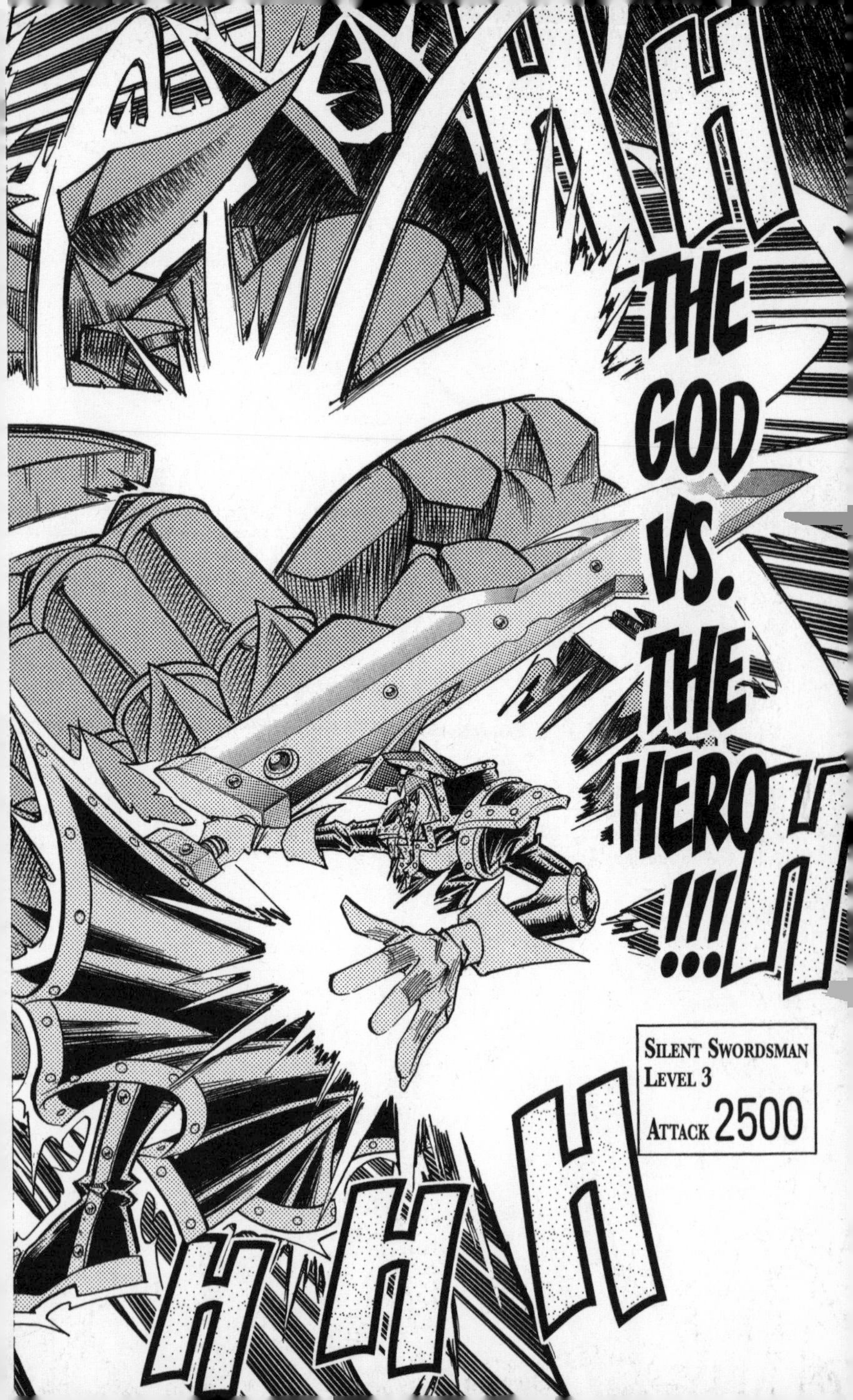
AAH
THE GOD VS. THE HERO!!!
HH
SILENT SWORDSMAN
LEVEL 3
ATTACK 2500
HHHH

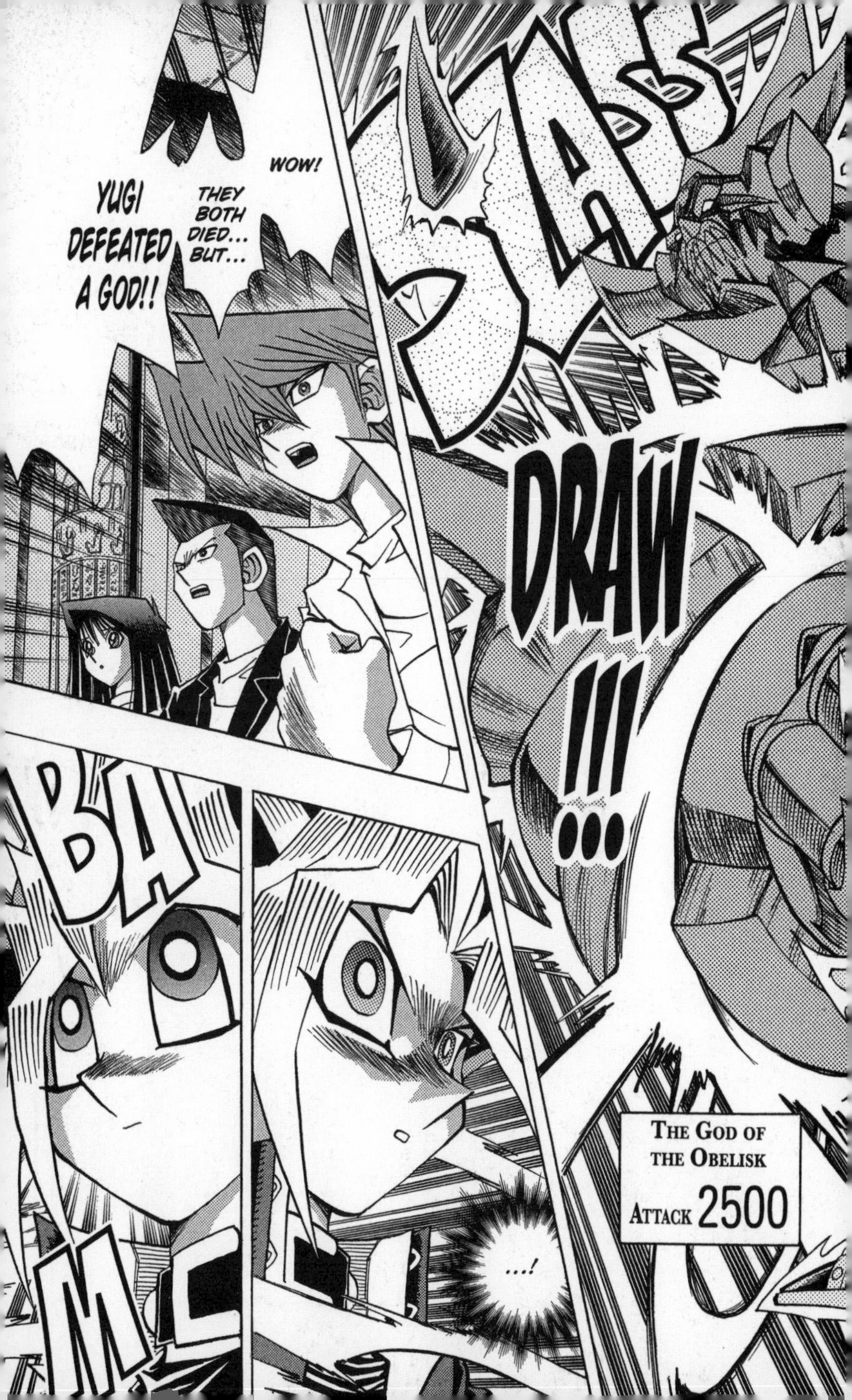
DRAW!!!...
WOW!
THEY BOTH DIED... BUT...
YUGI DEFEATED A GOD!!
THE GOD OF THE OBELISK
ATTACK 2500
...!

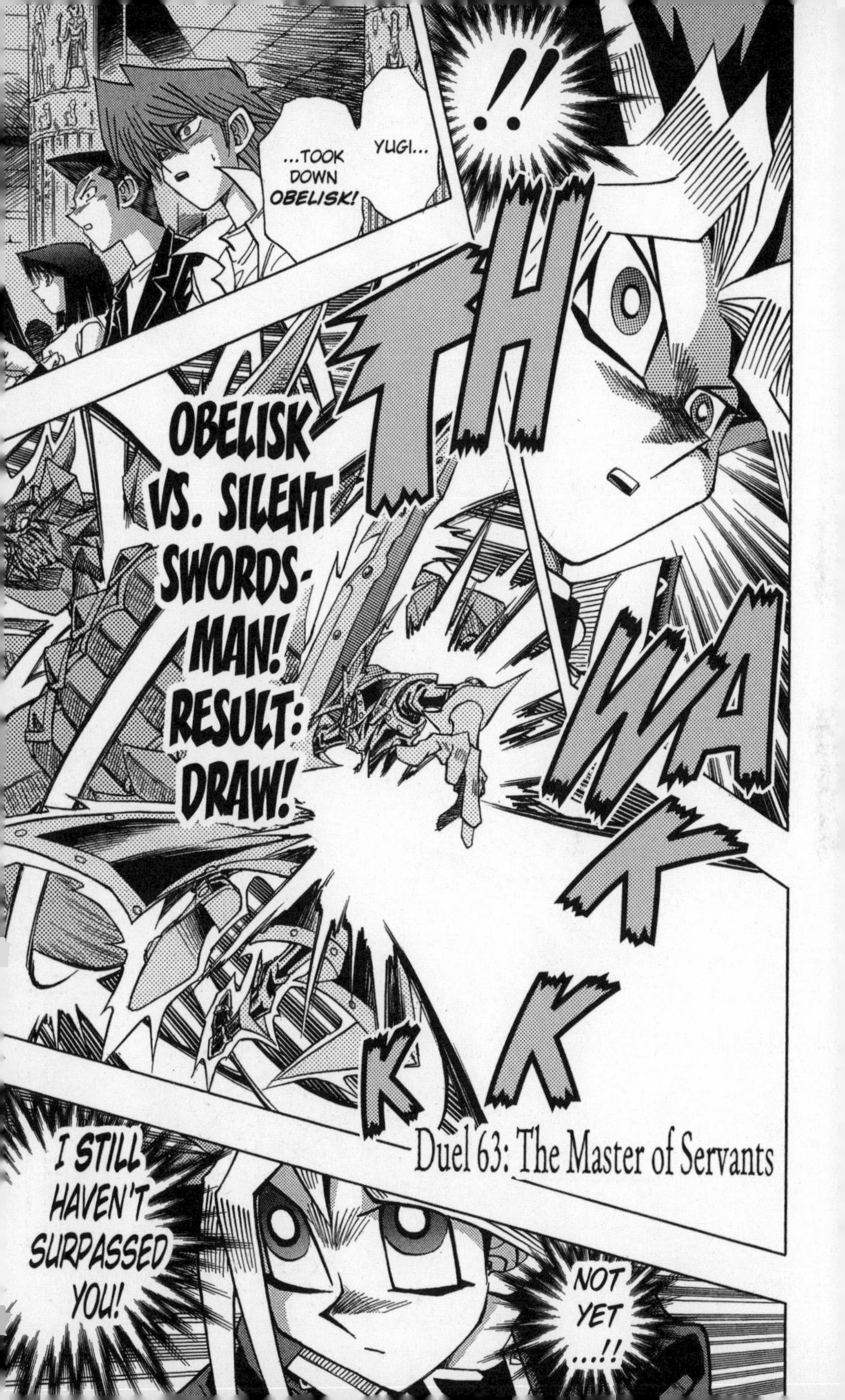
!!
YUGI...
...TOOK DOWN OBELISK!
THWAKK
OBELISK VS. SILENT SWORDS-MAN! RESULT: DRAW!
K
Duel 63: The Master of Servants
NOT YET ...!!
I STILL HAVEN'T SURPASSED YOU!

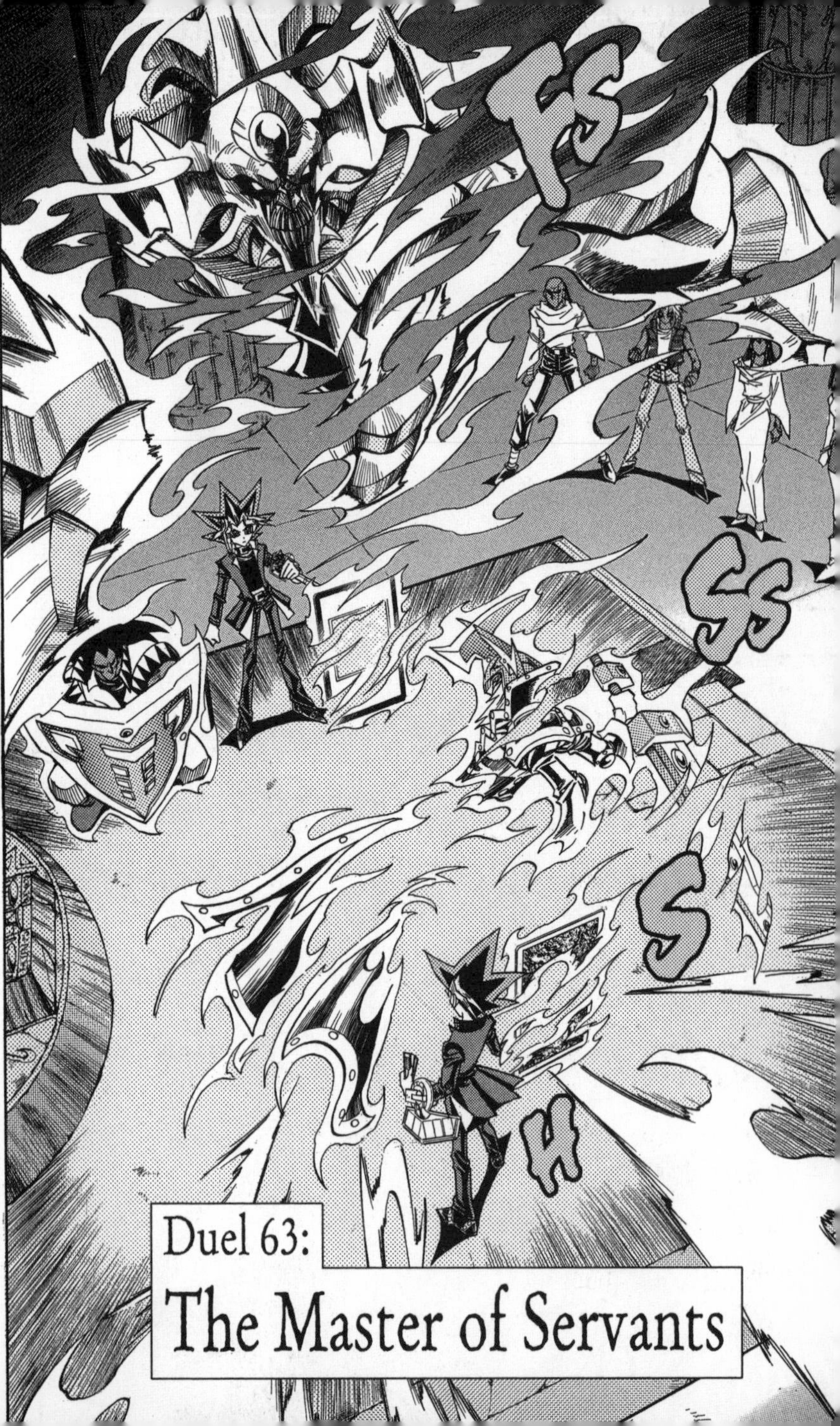
FS
SS
S
H
Duel 63:
The Master of Servants

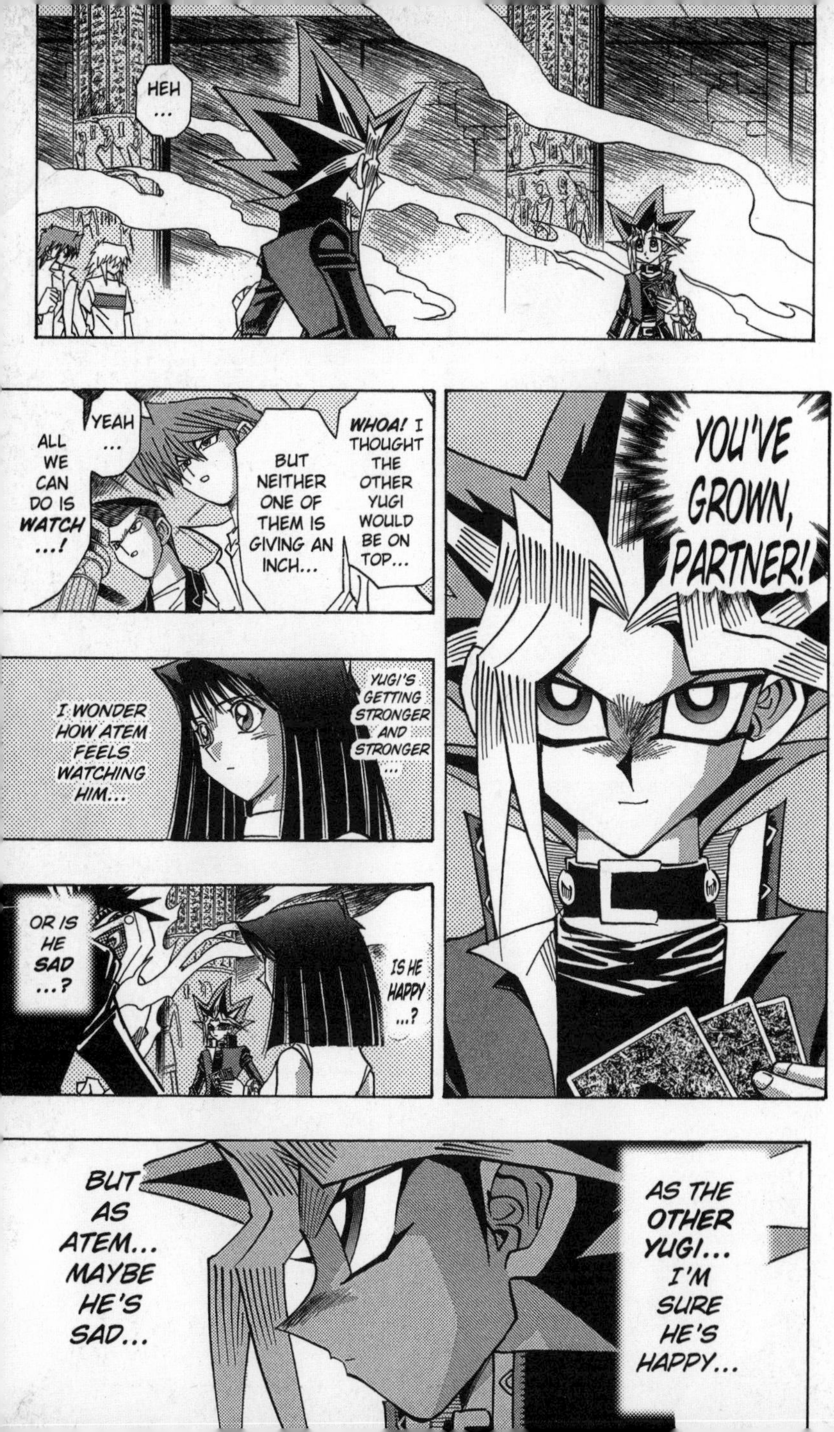
HEH ...
YOU'VE GROWN, PARTNER!
WHOA! I THOUGHT THE OTHER YUGI WOULD BE ON TOP...
BUT NEITHER ONE OF THEM IS GIVING AN INCH...
YEAH ...
ALL WE CAN DO IS WATCH ...!
YUGI'S GETTING STRONGER AND STRONGER ...
I WONDER HOW ATEM FEELS WATCHING HIM...
IS HE HAPPY ...?
OR IS HE SAD ...?
AS THE OTHER YUGI... I'M SURE HE'S HAPPY...
BUT AS ATEM... MAYBE HE'S SAD...

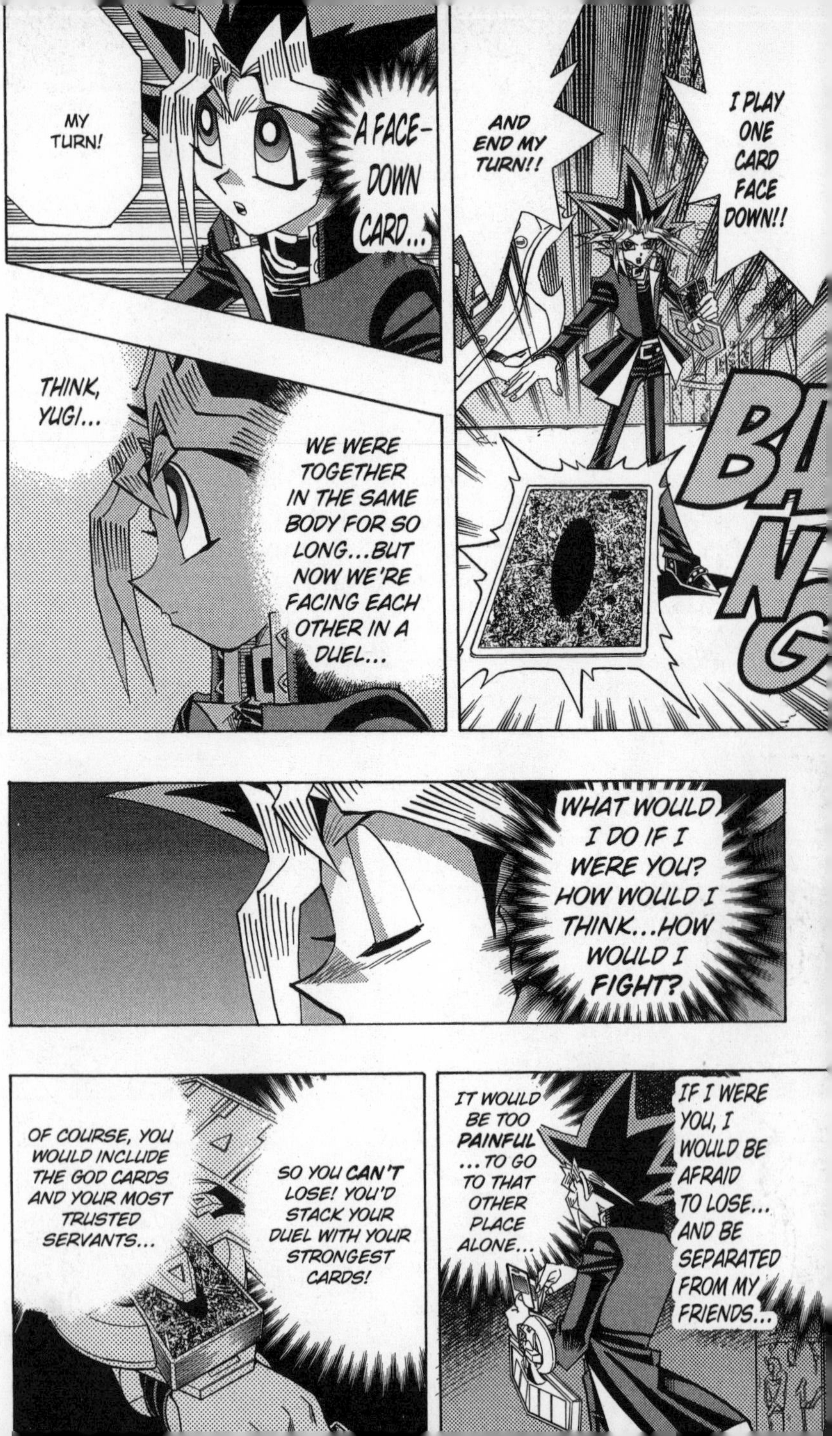
I PLAY ONE CARD FACE DOWN!!
AND END MY TURN!!
BANG
A FACE-DOWN CARD...
MY TURN!
THINK, YUGI...
WE WERE TOGETHER IN THE SAME BODY FOR SO LONG...BUT NOW WE'RE FACING EACH OTHER IN A DUEL...
WHAT WOULD I DO IF I WERE YOU? HOW WOULD I THINK...HOW WOULD I FIGHT?
IF I WERE YOU, I WOULD BE AFRAID TO LOSE... AND BE SEPARATED FROM MY FRIENDS...
IT WOULD BE TOO **PAINFUL** ...TO GO TO THAT OTHER PLACE ALONE...
SO YOU **CAN'T** LOSE! YOU'D STACK YOUR DUEL WITH YOUR STRONGEST CARDS!
OF COURSE, YOU WOULD INCLUDE THE GOD CARDS AND YOUR MOST TRUSTED SERVANTS...

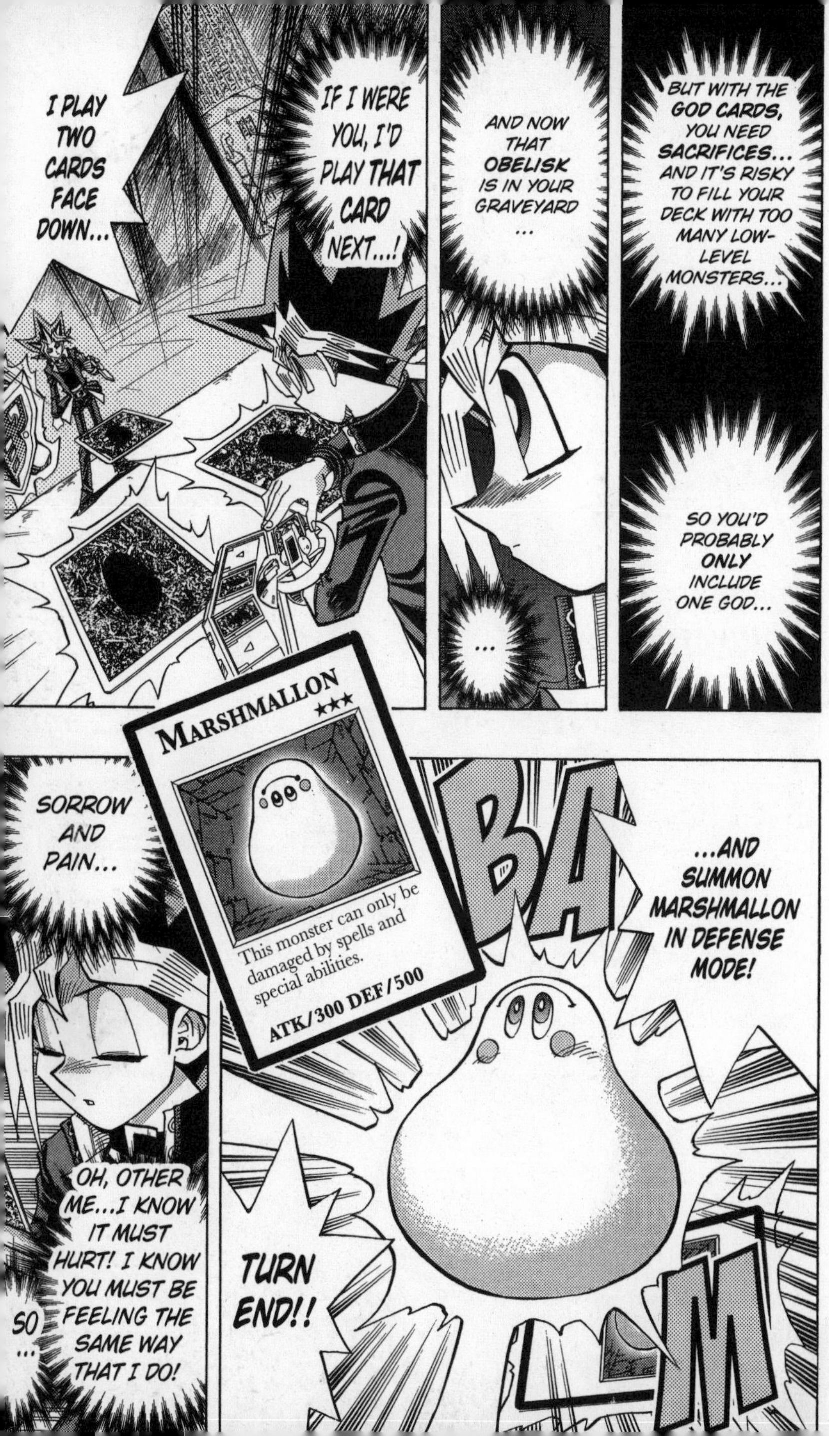
BUT WITH THE GOD CARDS, YOU NEED SACRIFICES... AND IT'S RISKY TO FILL YOUR DECK WITH TOO MANY LOW-LEVEL MONSTERS...
SO YOU'D PROBABLY ONLY INCLUDE ONE GOD...
AND NOW THAT OBELISK IS IN YOUR GRAVEYARD...
...
IF I WERE YOU, I'D PLAY THAT CARD NEXT...!
I PLAY TWO CARDS FACE DOWN...
...AND SUMMON MARSHMALLON IN DEFENSE MODE!
MARSHMALLON
★★★
This monster can only be damaged by spells and special abilities.
ATK/300 DEF/500
BAM
TURN END!!
SORROW AND PAIN...
OH, OTHER ME...I KNOW IT MUST HURT! I KNOW YOU MUST BE FEELING THE SAME WAY THAT I DO!
SO...

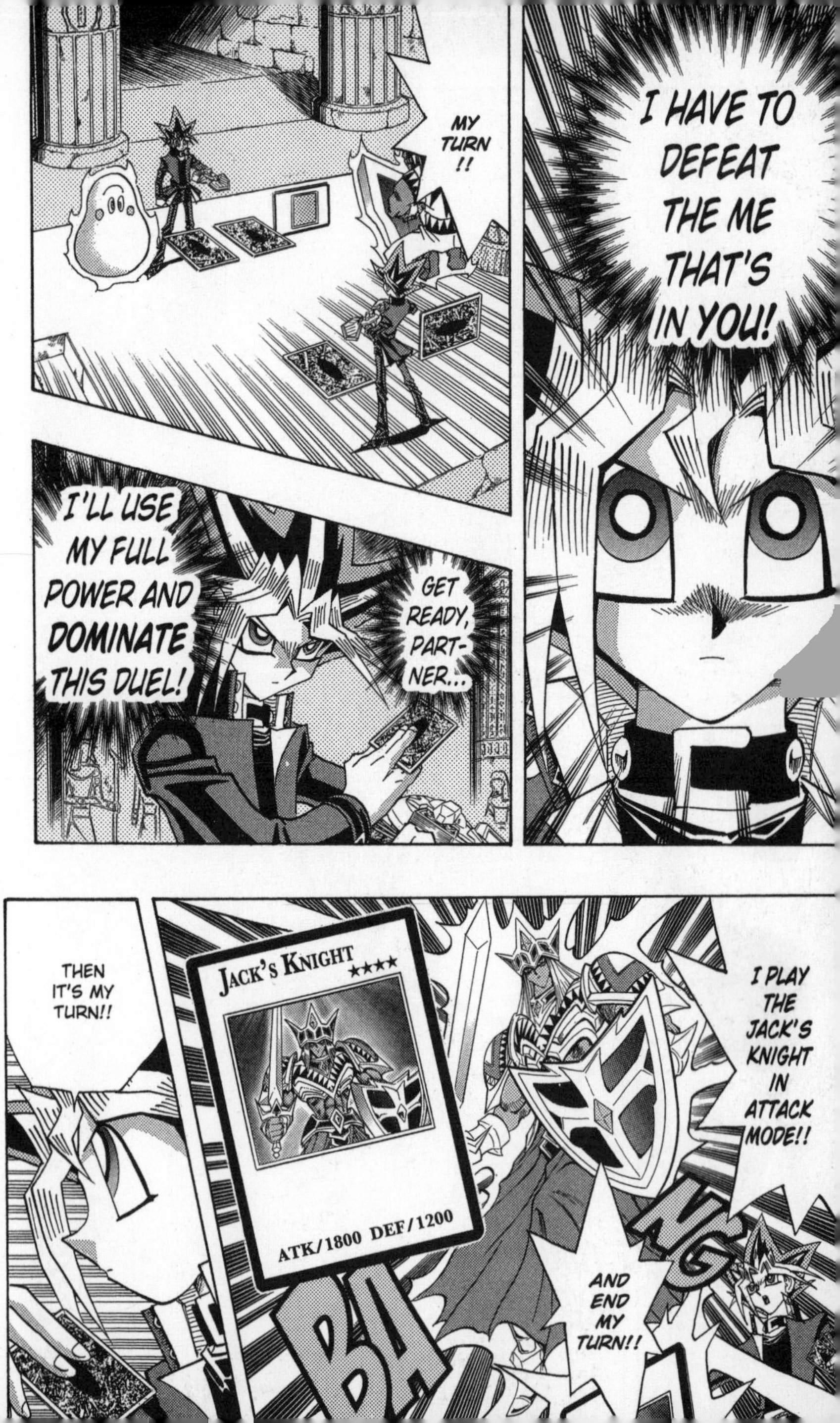
I HAVE TO DEFEAT THE ME THAT'S IN YOU!
MY TURN!!
GET READY, PARTNER...
I'LL USE MY FULL POWER AND DOMINATE THIS DUEL!
I PLAY THE JACK'S KNIGHT IN ATTACK MODE!!
AND END MY TURN!!
NG
JACK'S KNIGHT ★★★★
ATK/1800 DEF/1200
BA
THEN IT'S MY TURN!!

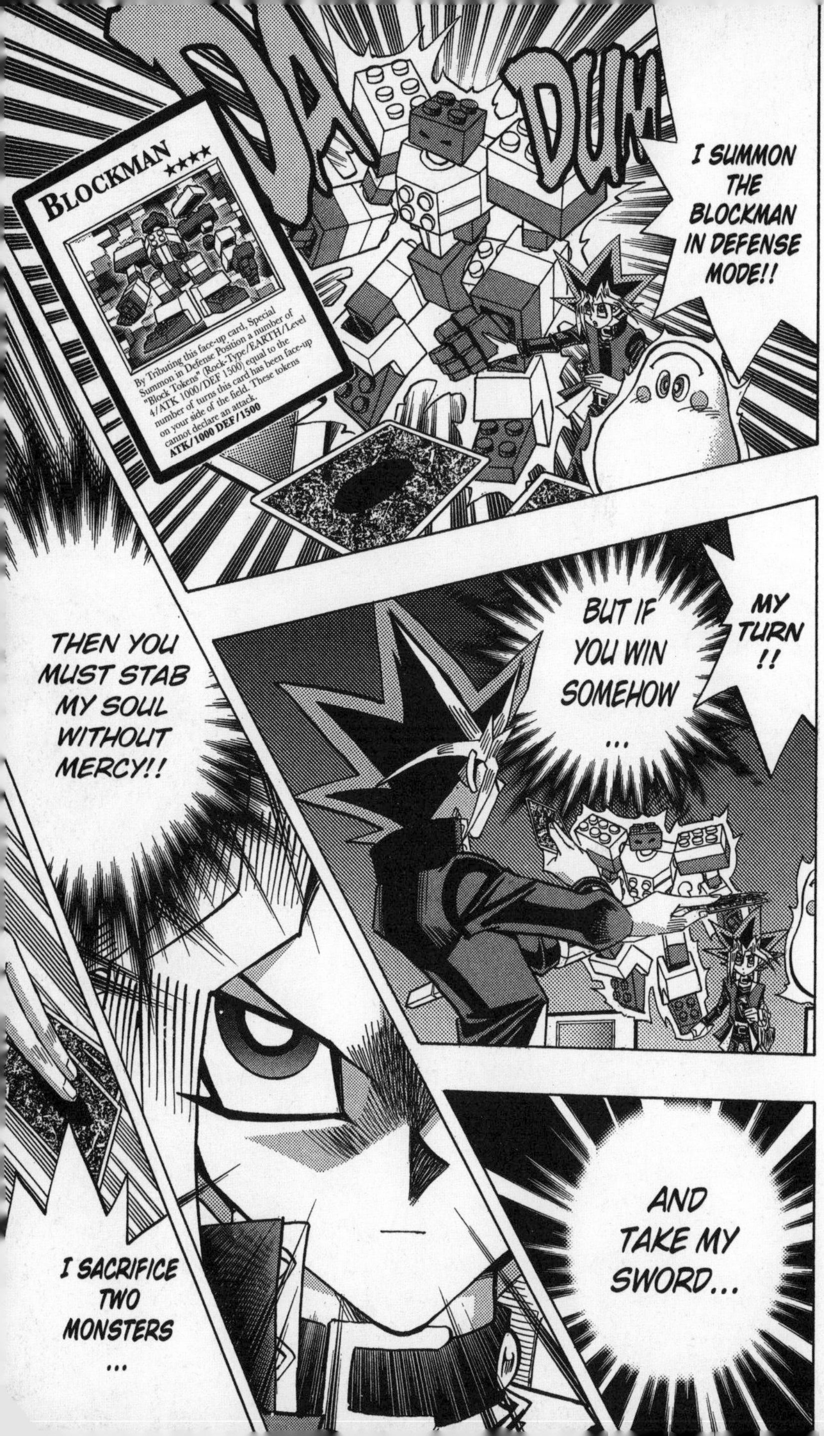
DA DUM
I SUMMON THE BLOCKMAN IN DEFENSE MODE!!
BLOCKMAN ★★★★
By Tributing this face-up card, Special Summon in Defense Position a number of "Block Tokens" (Rock-Type/EARTH/Level 4/ATK 1000/DEF 1500) equal to the number of turns this card has been face-up on your side of the field. These tokens cannot declare an attack.
ATK/1000 DEF/1500
MY TURN!!
BUT IF YOU WIN SOMEHOW ...
THEN YOU MUST STAB MY SOUL WITHOUT MERCY!!
AND TAKE MY SWORD...
I SACRIFICE TWO MONSTERS ...

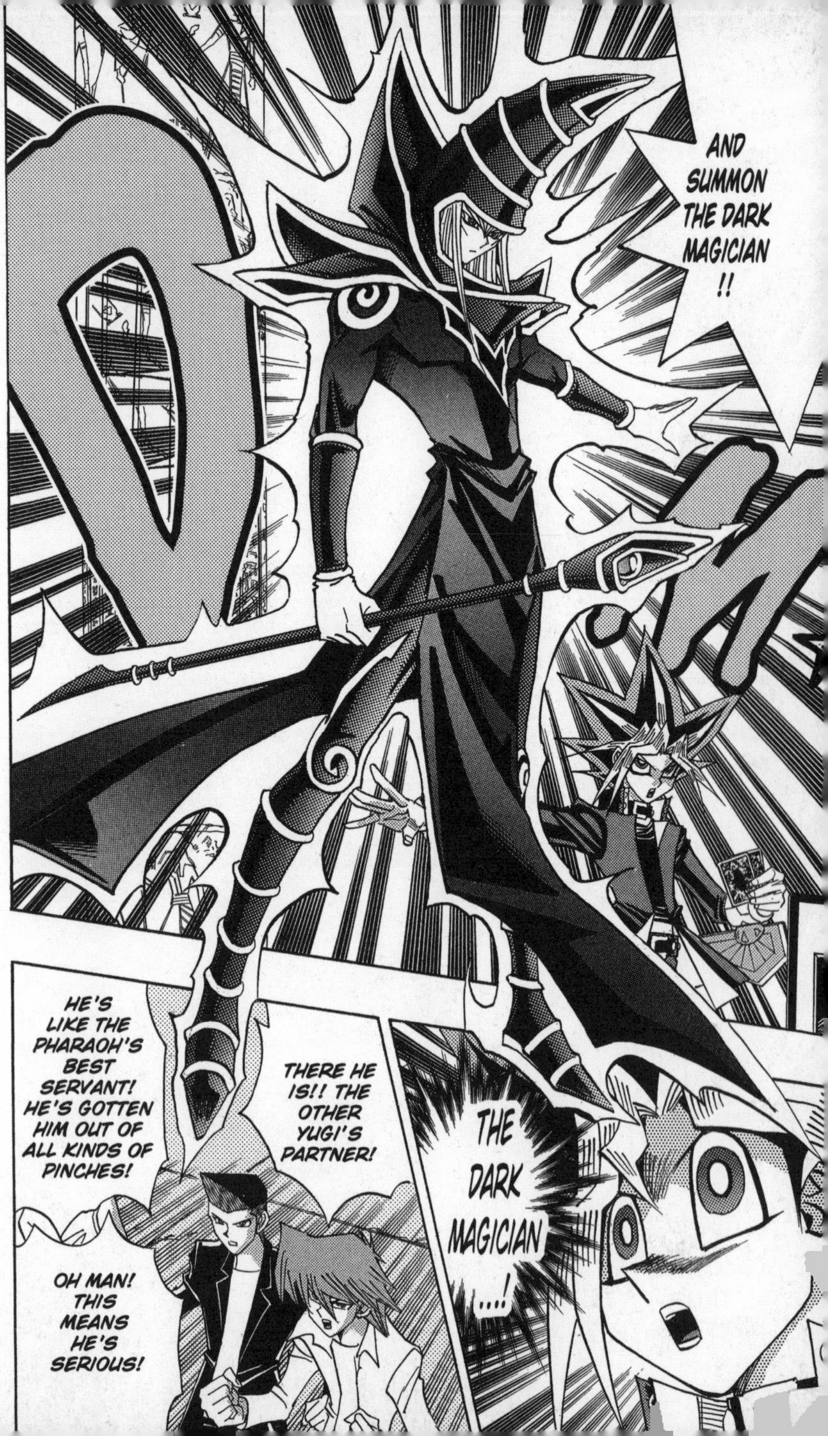
AND SUMMON THE DARK MAGICIAN !!
THE DARK MAGICIAN ...!
THERE HE IS!! THE OTHER YUGI'S PARTNER!
HE'S LIKE THE PHARAOH'S BEST SERVANT! HE'S GOTTEN HIM OUT OF ALL KINDS OF PINCHES!
OH MAN! THIS MEANS HE'S SERIOUS!

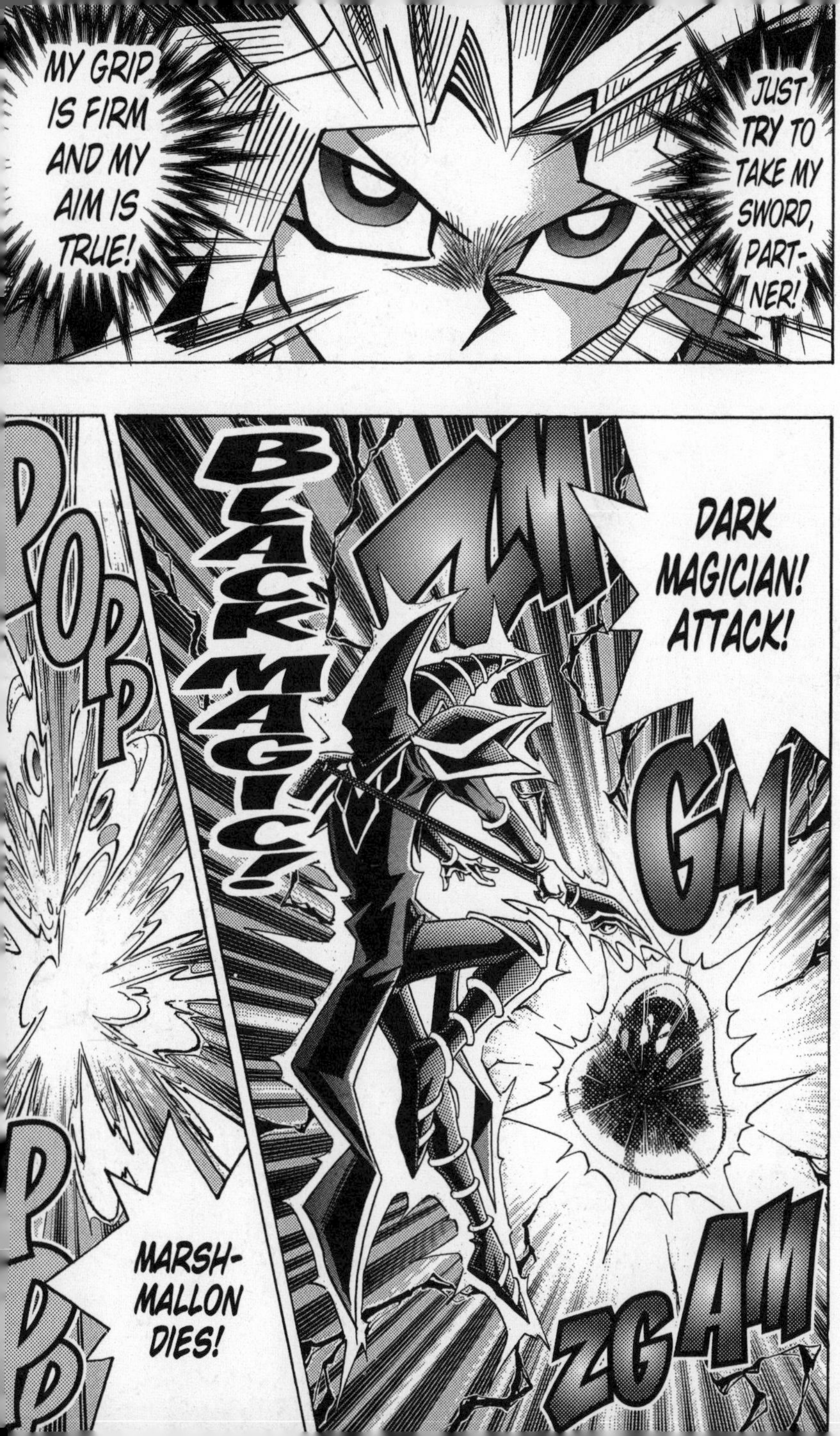
JUST TRY TO TAKE MY SWORD, PART-NER!
MY GRIP IS FIRM AND MY AIM IS TRUE!
DARK MAGICIAN! ATTACK!
ZM
GM
BLACK MAGIC!
POP
POP
ZGAM
MARSH-MALLON DIES!
POP

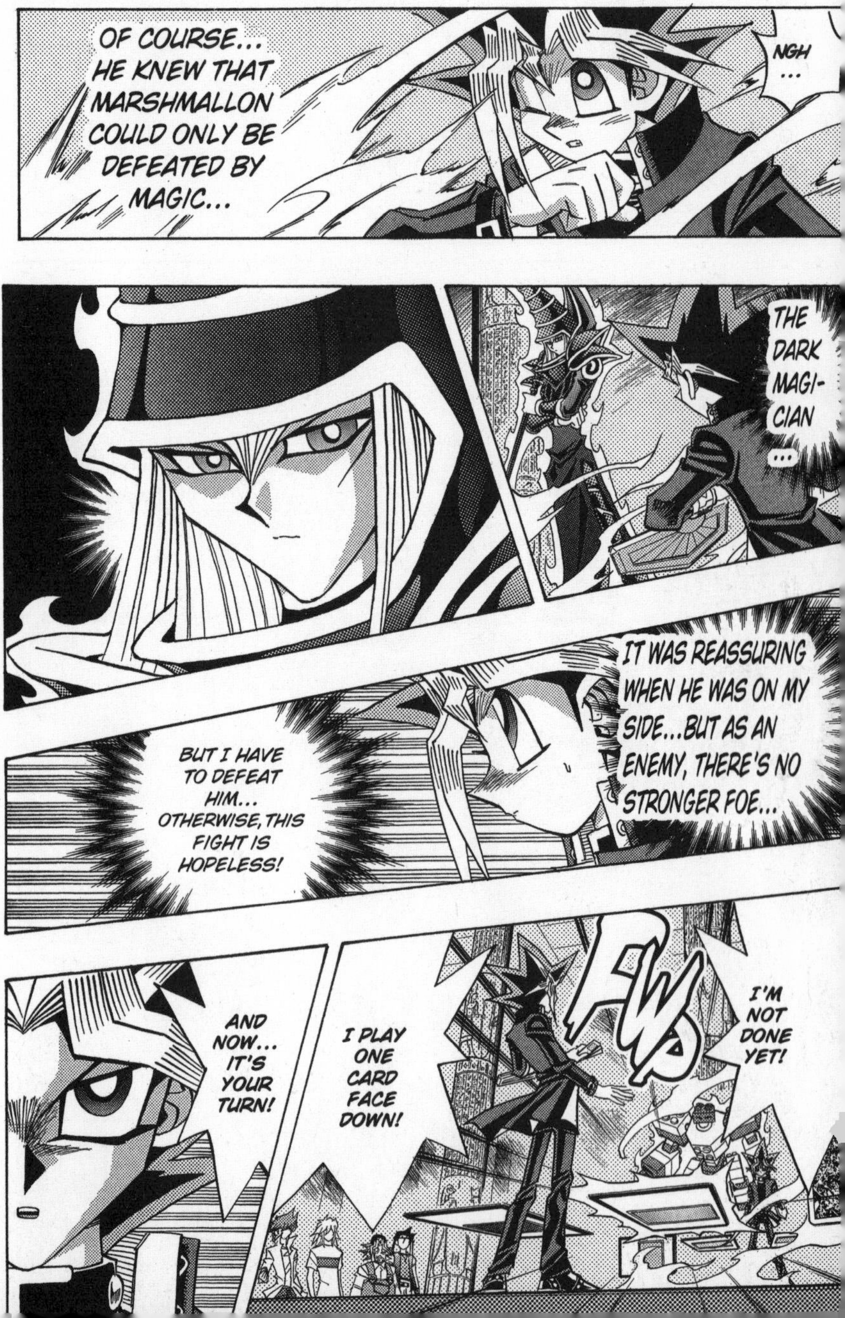
NGH...
OF COURSE... HE KNEW THAT MARSHMALLON COULD ONLY BE DEFEATED BY MAGIC...
THE DARK MAGICIAN...
IT WAS REASSURING WHEN HE WAS ON MY SIDE...BUT AS AN ENEMY, THERE'S NO STRONGER FOE...
BUT I HAVE TO DEFEAT HIM... OTHERWISE, THIS FIGHT IS HOPELESS!
I'M NOT DONE YET!
FWP
I PLAY ONE CARD FACE DOWN!
AND NOW... IT'S YOUR TURN!

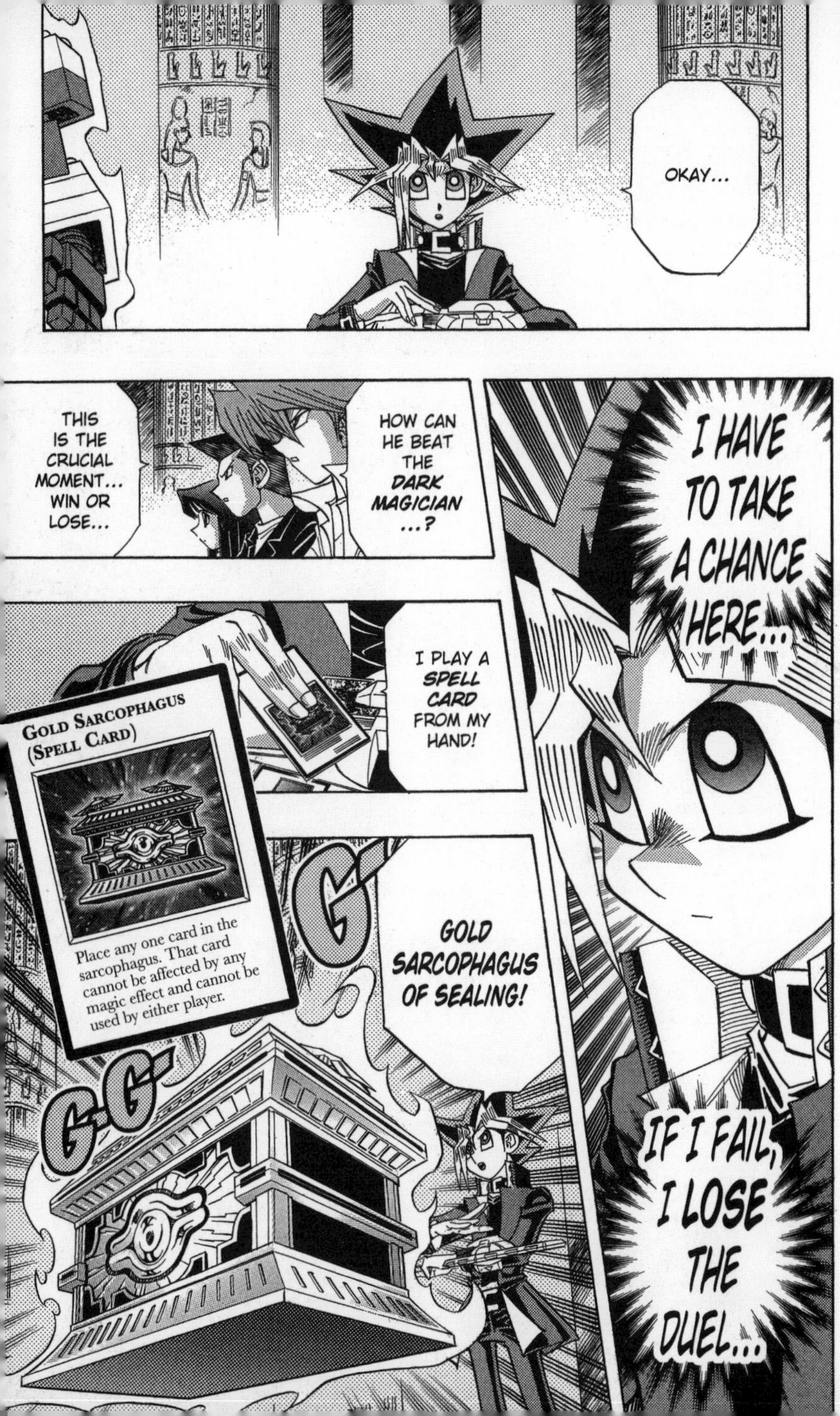
OKAY...
I HAVE TO TAKE A CHANCE HERE...
IF I FAIL, I LOSE THE DUEL...
HOW CAN HE BEAT THE DARK MAGICIAN ...?
THIS IS THE CRUCIAL MOMENT... WIN OR LOSE...
I PLAY A SPELL CARD FROM MY HAND!
GOLD SARCOPHAGUS OF SEALING!
G
Gold Sarcophagus (Spell Card)
Place any one card in the sarcophagus. That card cannot be affected by any magic effect and cannot be used by either player.
G-G

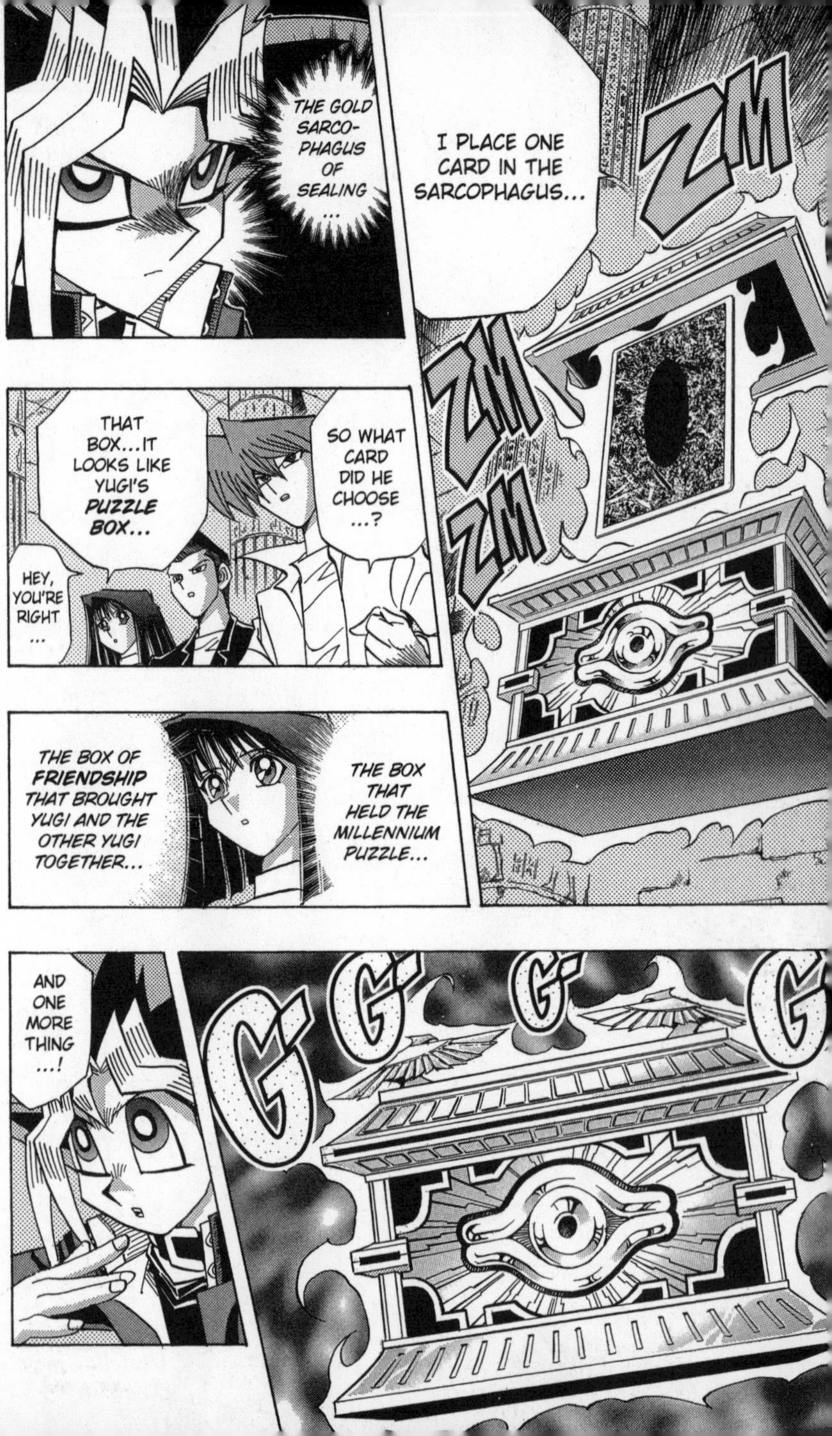
I PLACE ONE CARD IN THE SARCOPHAGUS...
ZM
ZM
ZM
ZM
THE GOLD SARCOPHAGUS OF SEALING...
SO WHAT CARD DID HE CHOOSE...?
THAT BOX...IT LOOKS LIKE YUGI'S *PUZZLE BOX*...
HEY, YOU'RE RIGHT...
THE BOX THAT HELD THE MILLENNIUM PUZZLE...
*THE BOX OF **FRIENDSHIP** THAT BROUGHT YUGI AND THE OTHER YUGI TOGETHER...*
G G G G
AND ONE MORE THING...!

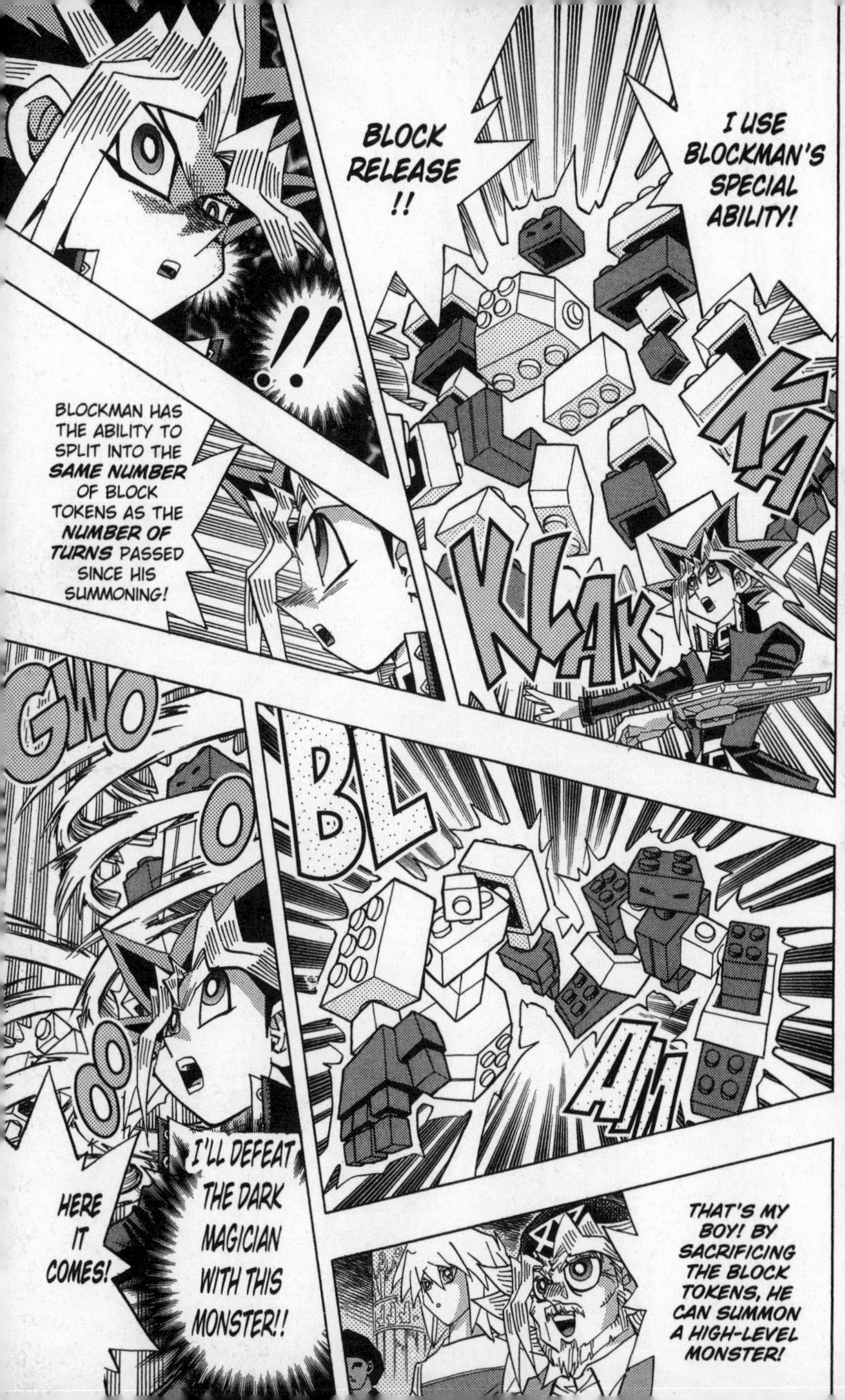
I USE BLOCKMAN'S SPECIAL ABILITY!
BLOCK RELEASE!!
KA
KLAK
!!
BLOCKMAN HAS THE ABILITY TO SPLIT INTO THE SAME NUMBER OF BLOCK TOKENS AS THE NUMBER OF TURNS PASSED SINCE HIS SUMMONING!
BL
AM
GWO
O
OO
THAT'S MY BOY! BY SACRIFICING THE BLOCK TOKENS, HE CAN SUMMON A HIGH-LEVEL MONSTER!
I'LL DEFEAT THE DARK MAGICIAN WITH THIS MONSTER!!
HERE IT COMES!

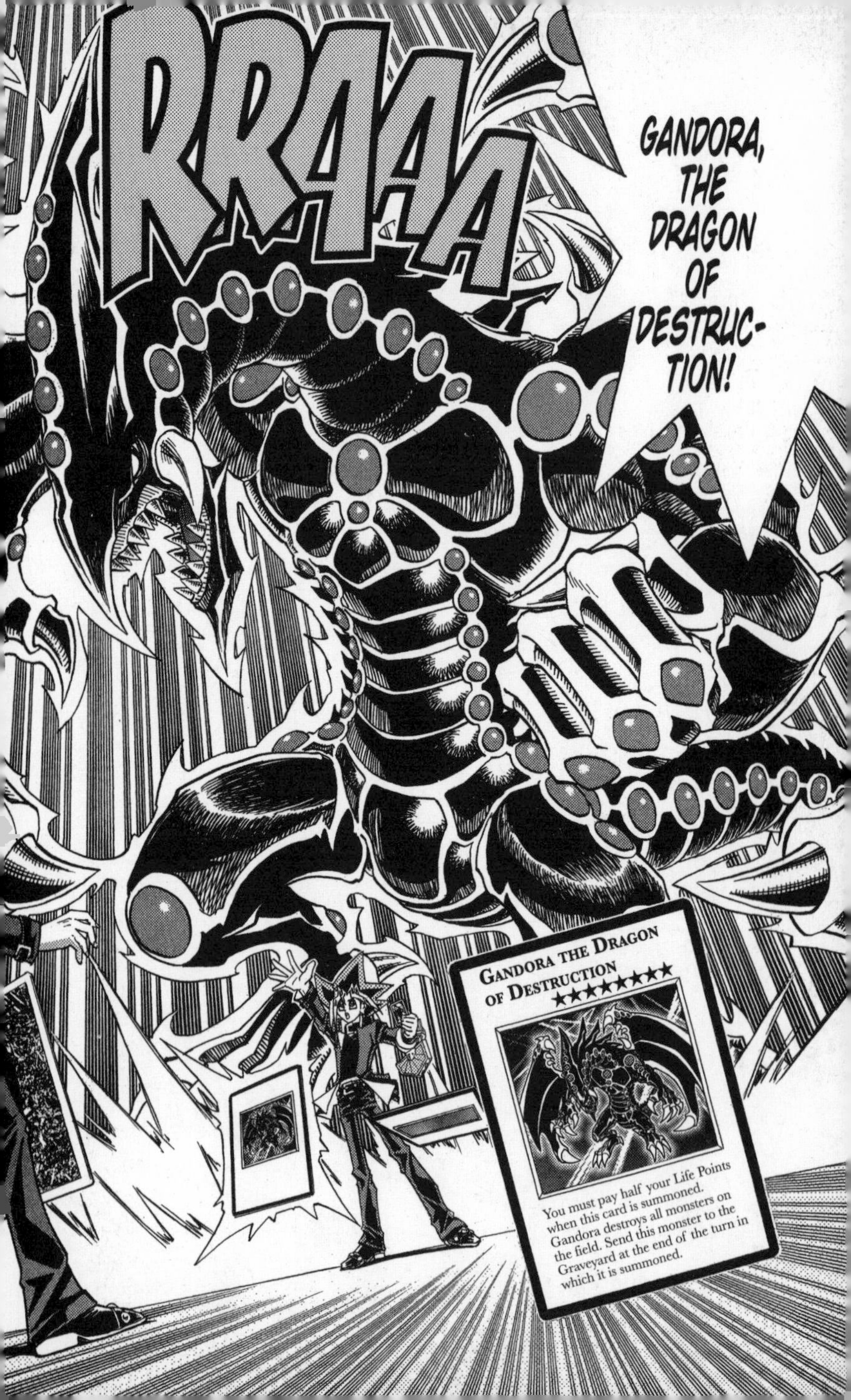
RRAAA
GANDORA, THE DRAGON OF DESTRUCTION!
GANDORA THE DRAGON OF DESTRUCTION
You must pay half your Life Points when this card is summoned. Gandora destroys all monsters on the field. Send this monster to the Graveyard at the end of the turn in which it is summoned.

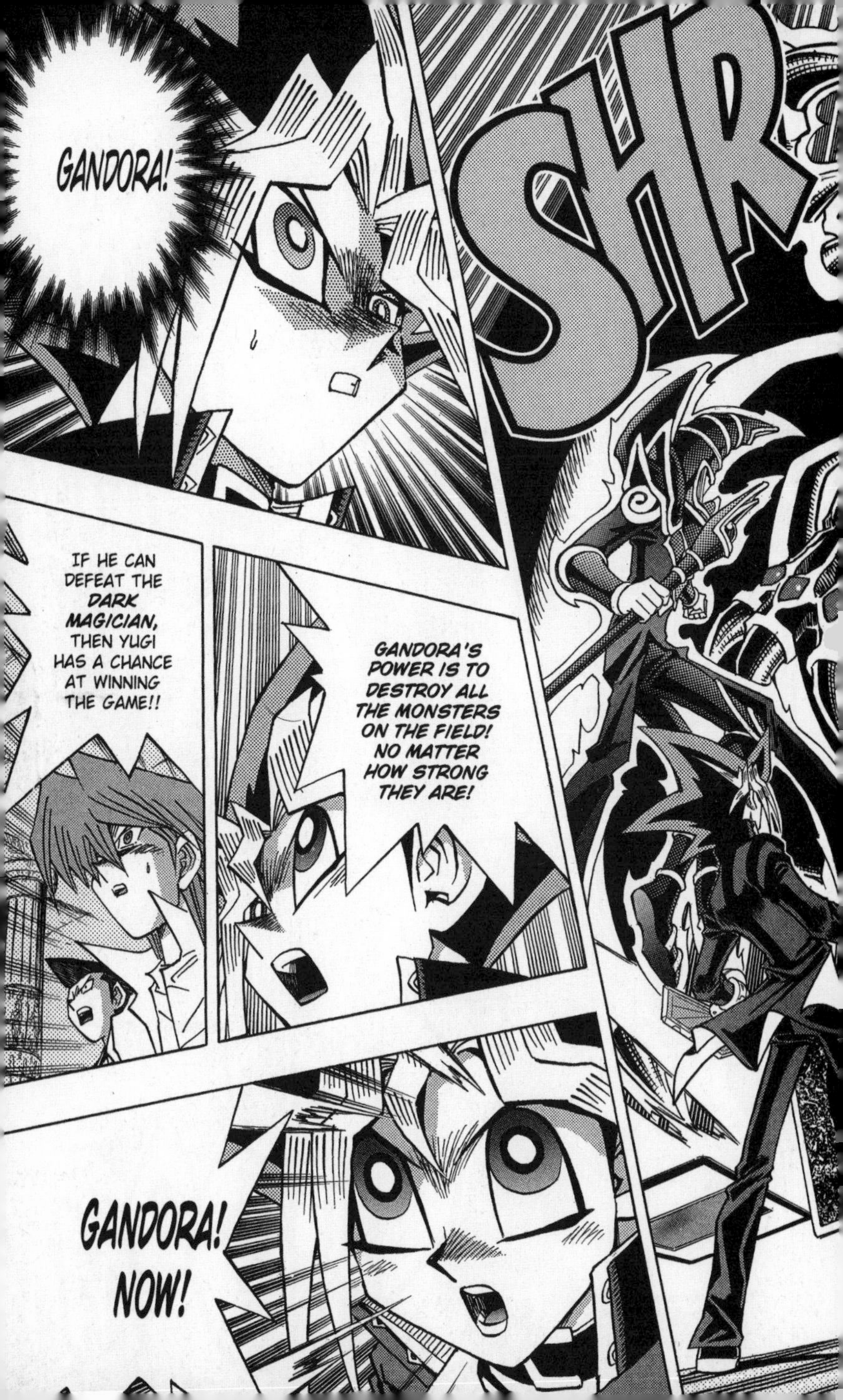
SHR
GANDORA!
GANDORA'S POWER IS TO DESTROY ALL THE MONSTERS ON THE FIELD! NO MATTER HOW STRONG THEY ARE!
IF HE CAN DEFEAT THE *DARK MAGICIAN,* THEN YUGI HAS A CHANCE AT WINNING THE GAME!!
GANDORA! NOW!

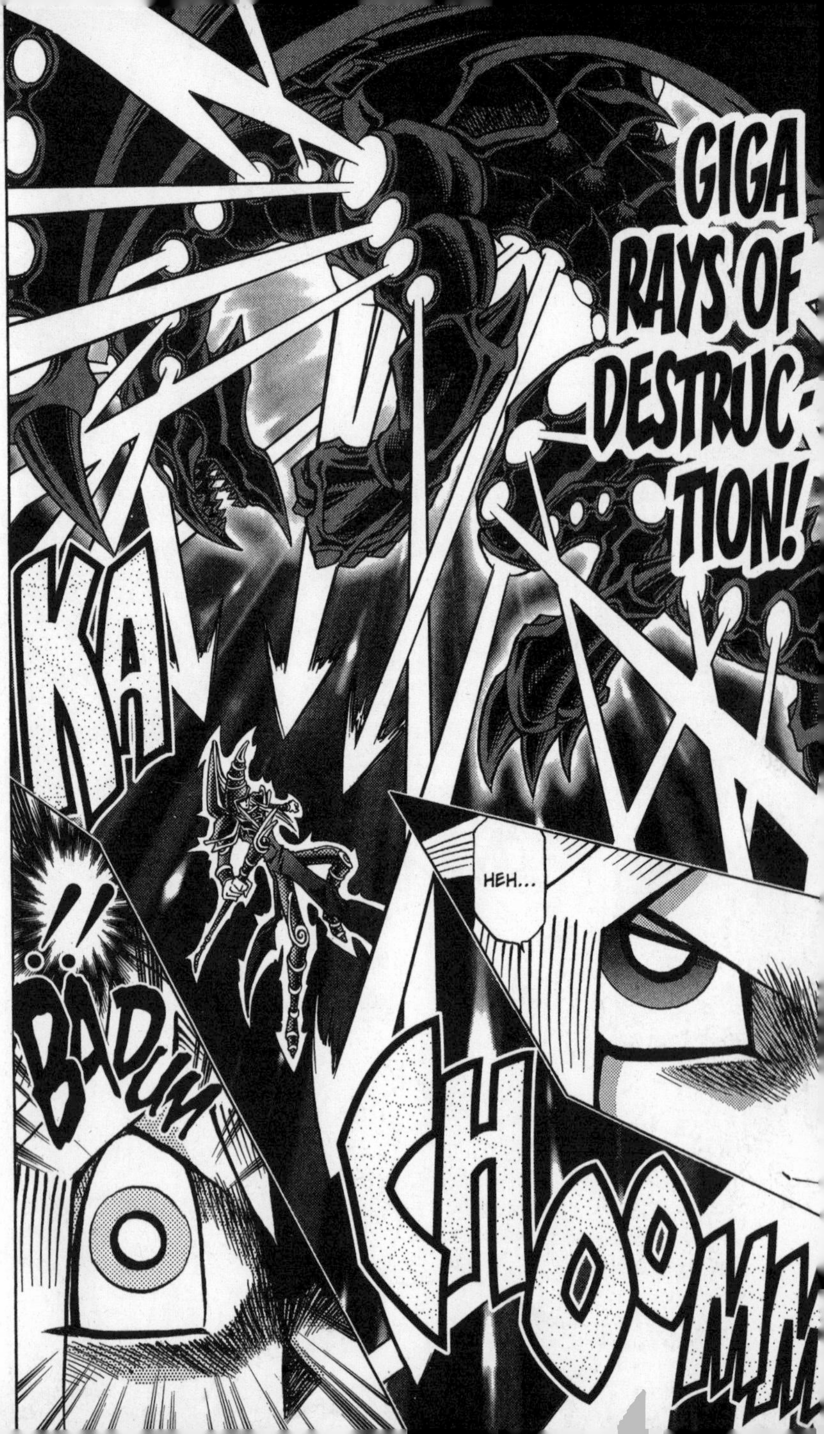
GIGA RAYS OF DESTRUC-TION!
KA
HEH...
CHOOMM
!!
BADUM

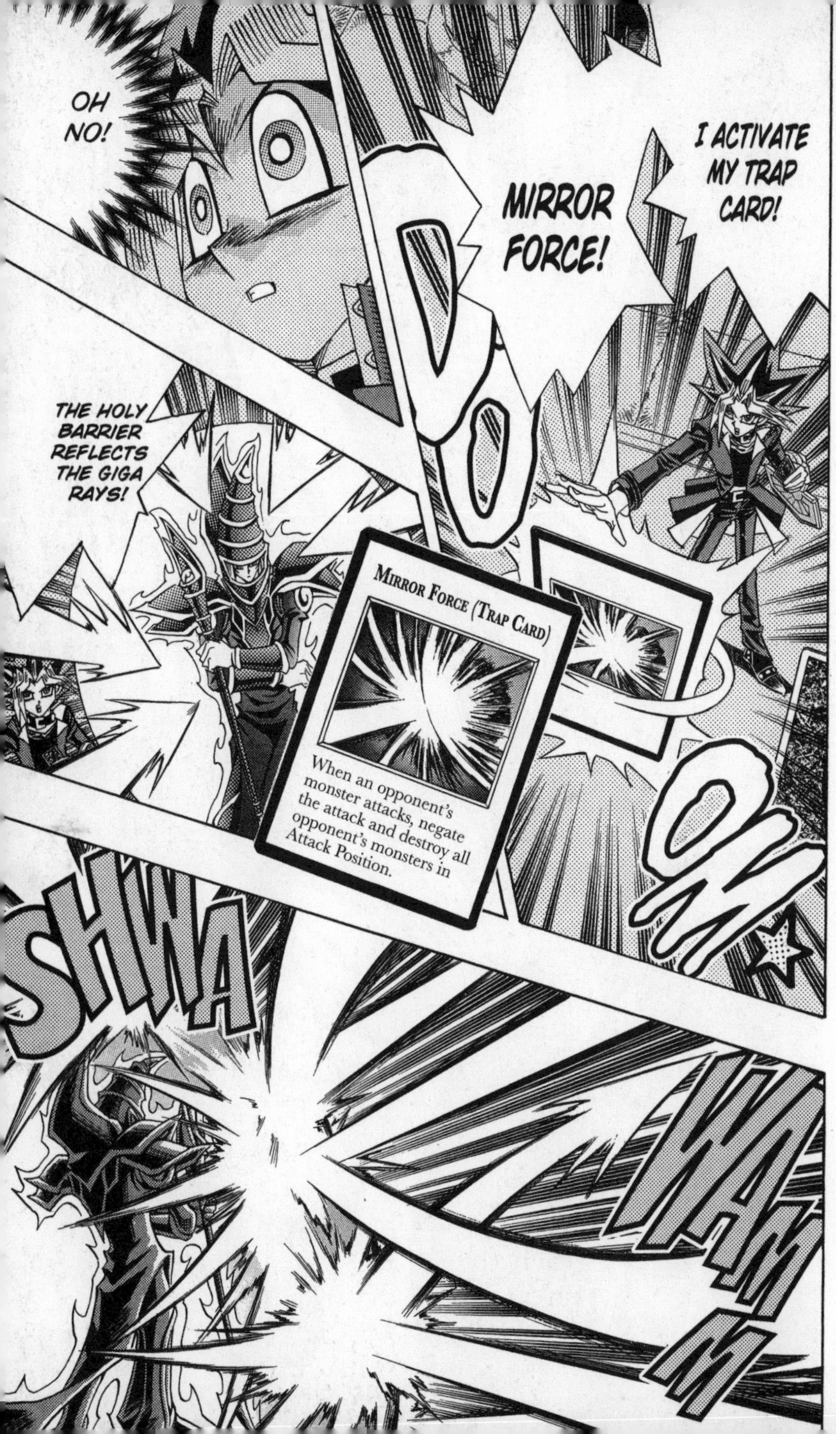
I ACTIVATE MY TRAP CARD!
MIRROR FORCE!
OH NO!
MIRROR FORCE (TRAP CARD)
When an opponent's monster attacks, negate the attack and destroy all opponent's monsters in Attack Position.
THE HOLY BARRIER REFLECTS THE GIGA RAYS!
SHWA

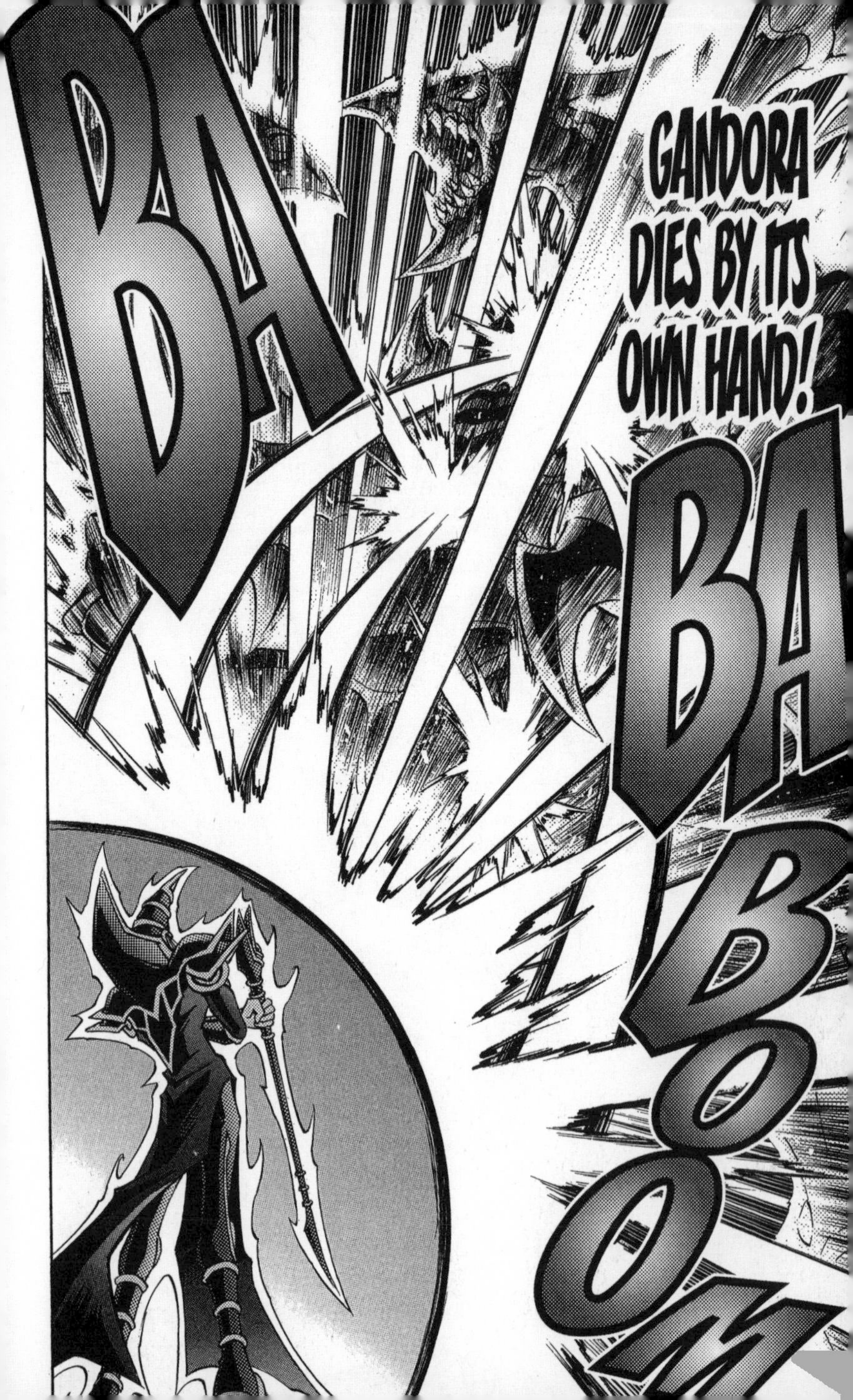
GANDORA DIES BY ITS OWN HAND!
BA
BABOOM

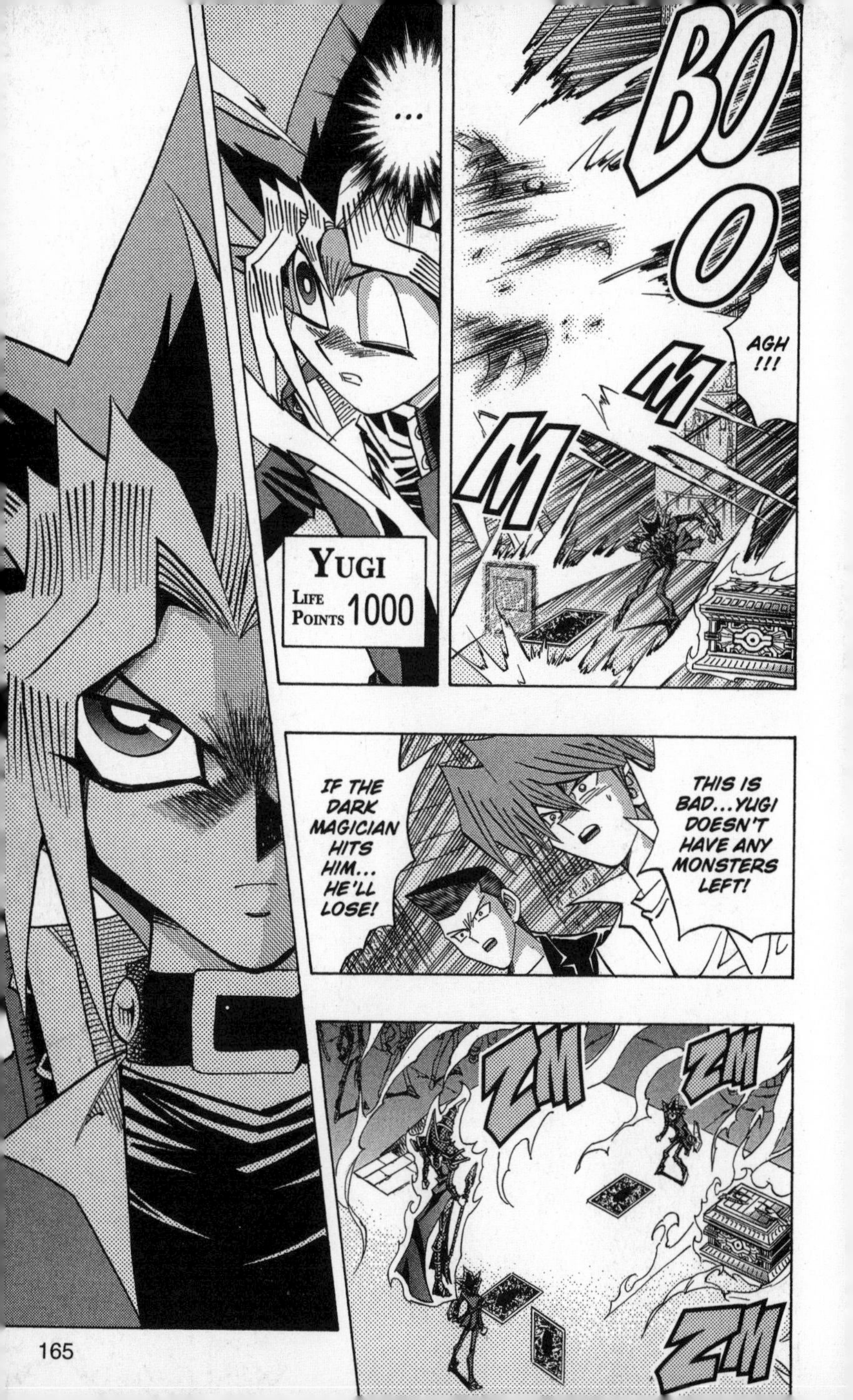
BOOOMM
AGH!!!
...
YUGI
LIFE POINTS 1000
THIS IS BAD...YUGI DOESN'T HAVE ANY MONSTERS LEFT!
IF THE DARK MAGICIAN HITS HIM... HE'LL LOSE!
ZM
ZM
ZM

Duel 64: The Last Gamble!!

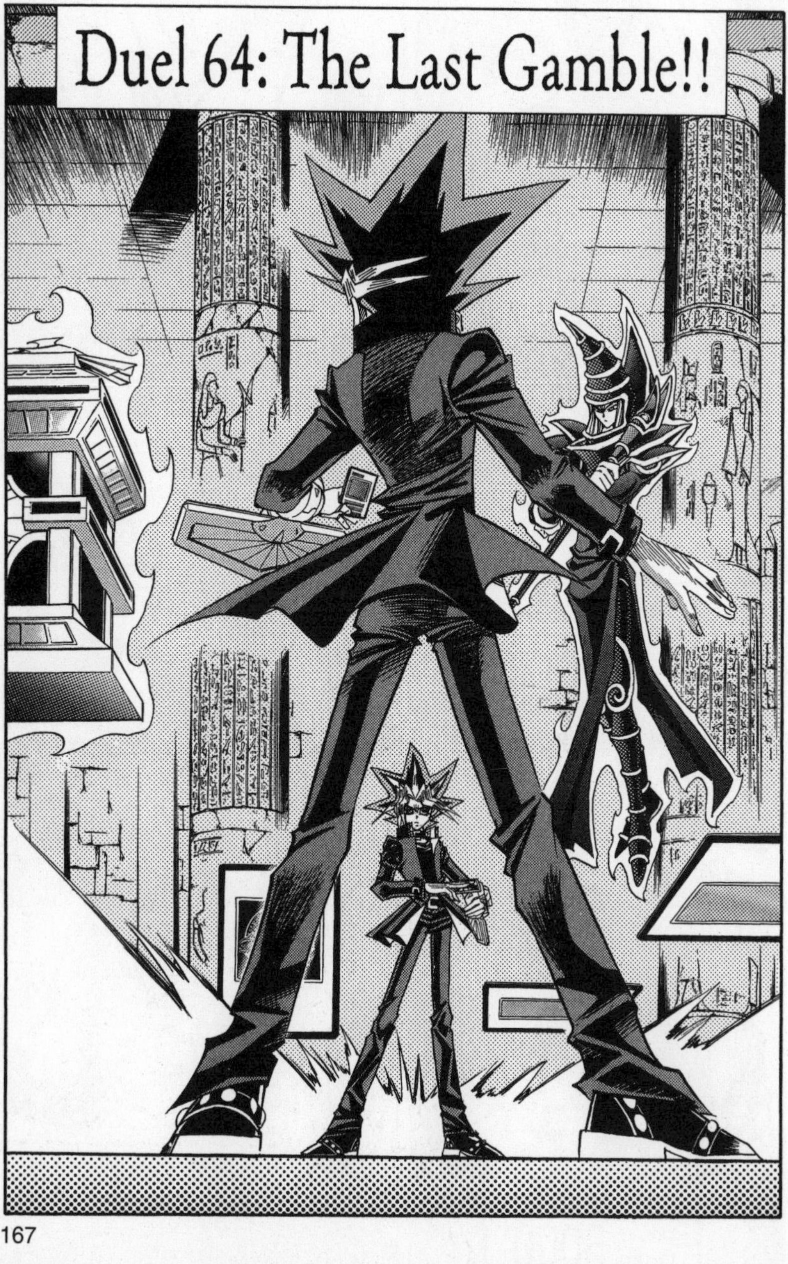

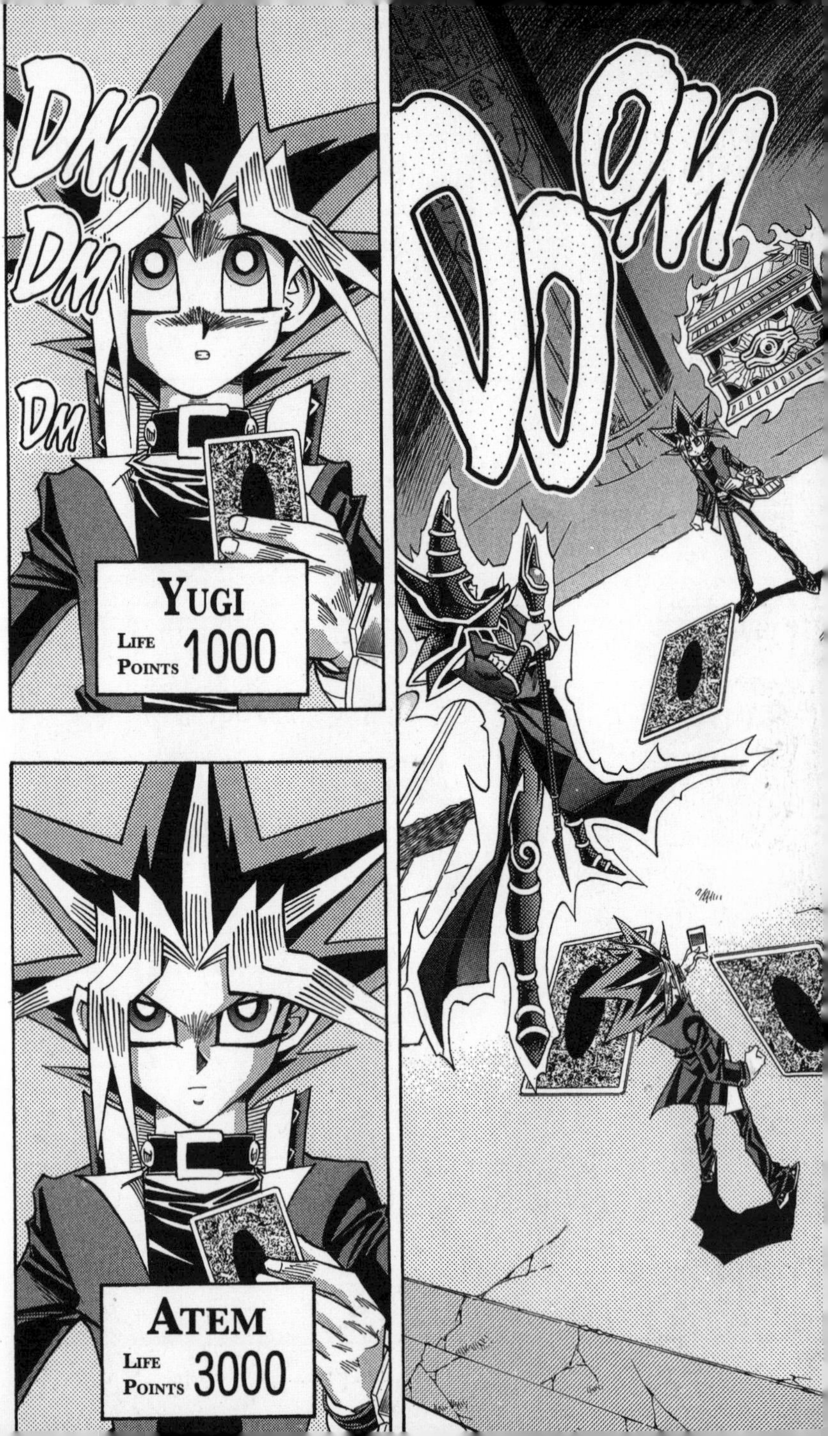
DOOOM
DM
DM
DM
YUGI
LIFE POINTS 1000
ATEM
LIFE POINTS 3000

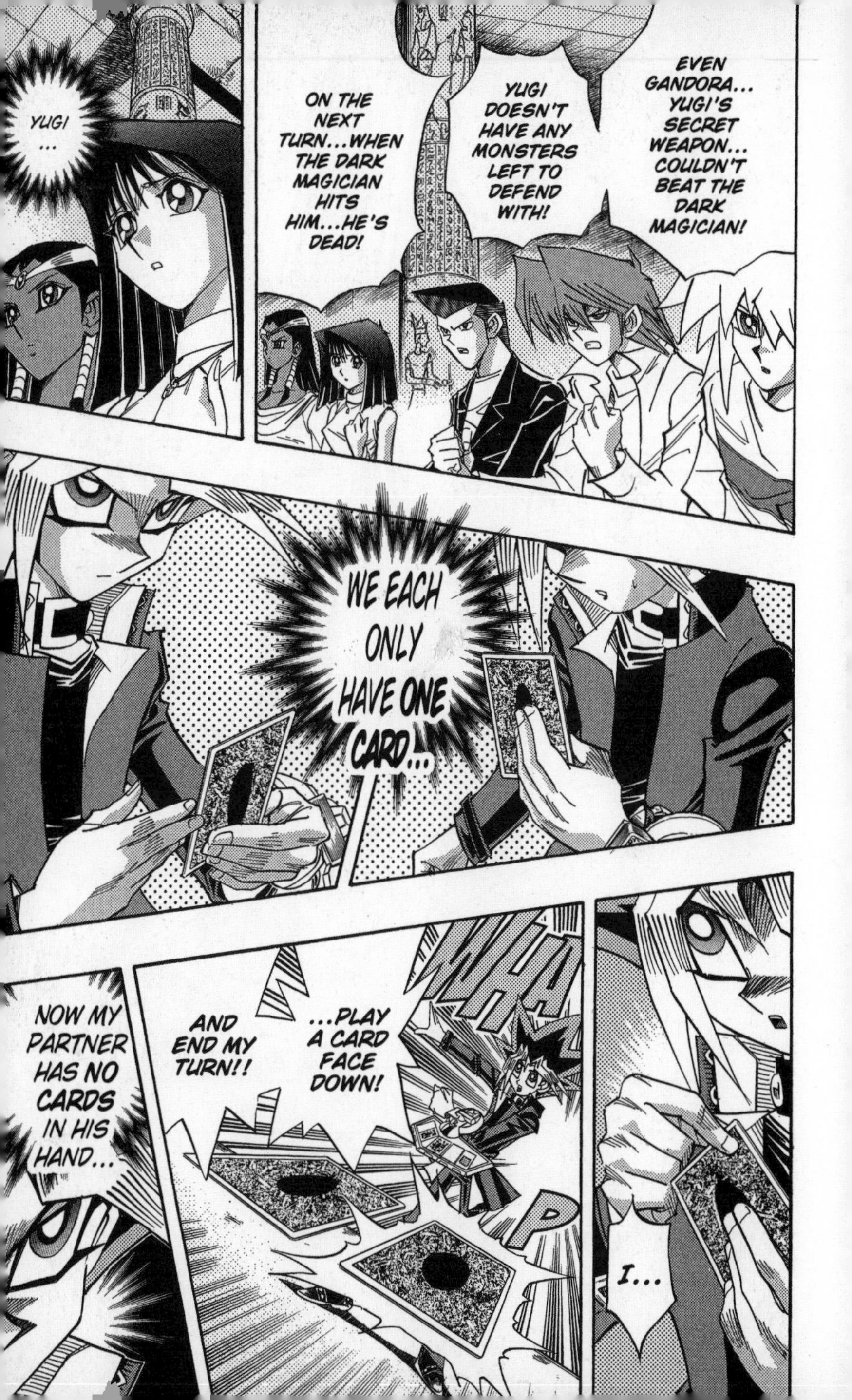
EVEN GANDORA... YUGI'S SECRET WEAPON... COULDN'T BEAT THE DARK MAGICIAN!
YUGI DOESN'T HAVE ANY MONSTERS LEFT TO DEFEND WITH!
ON THE NEXT TURN...WHEN THE DARK MAGICIAN HITS HIM...HE'S DEAD!
YUGI ...
WE EACH ONLY HAVE ONE CARD...
I...
...PLAY A CARD FACE DOWN!
AND END MY TURN!!
WHAP
NOW MY PARTNER HAS NO CARDS IN HIS HAND...

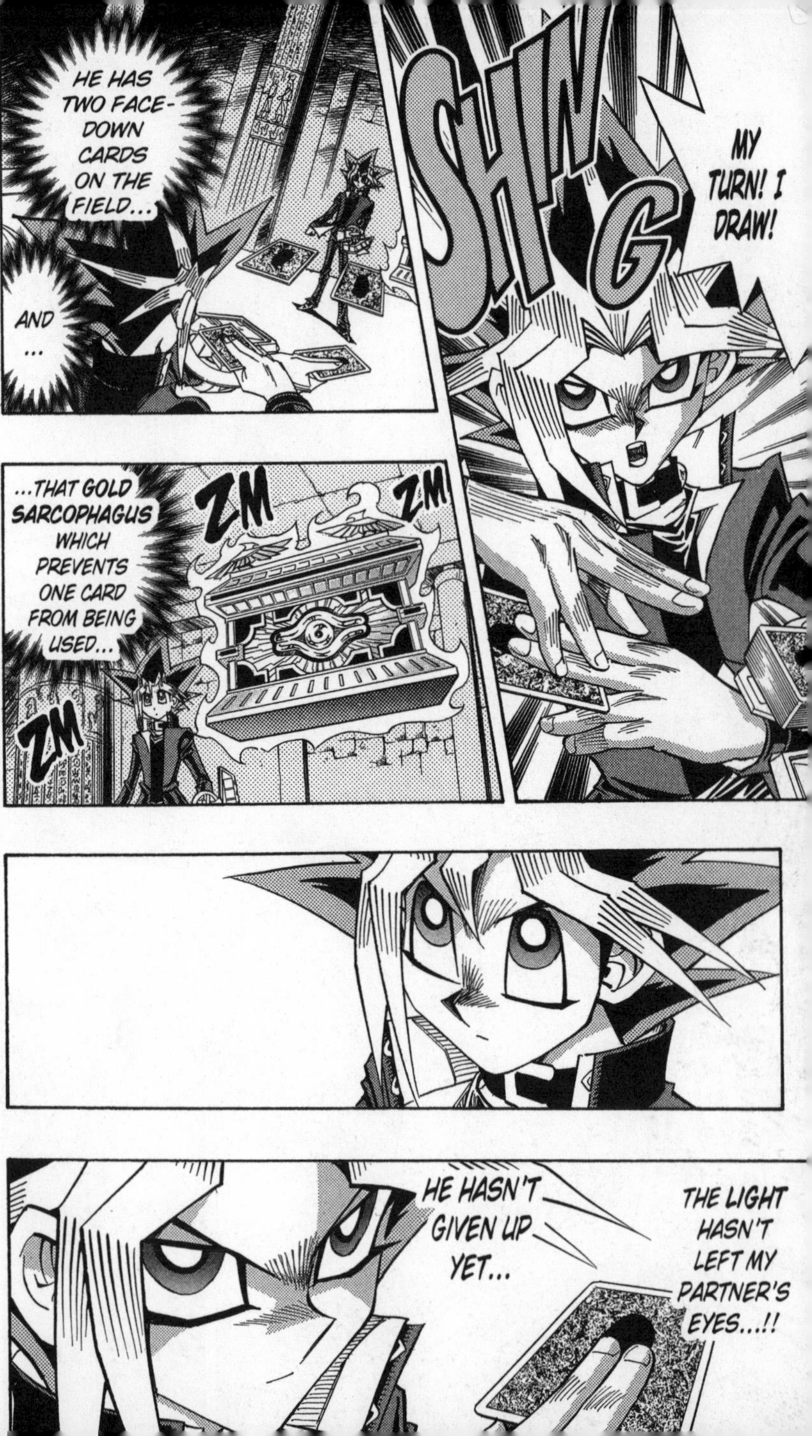
SHING
MY TURN! I DRAW!
HE HAS TWO FACE-DOWN CARDS ON THE FIELD...
AND ...
...THAT GOLD SARCOPHAGUS WHICH PREVENTS ONE CARD FROM BEING USED...
ZM
ZM
ZM
THE LIGHT HASN'T LEFT MY PARTNER'S EYES...!!
HE HASN'T GIVEN UP YET...

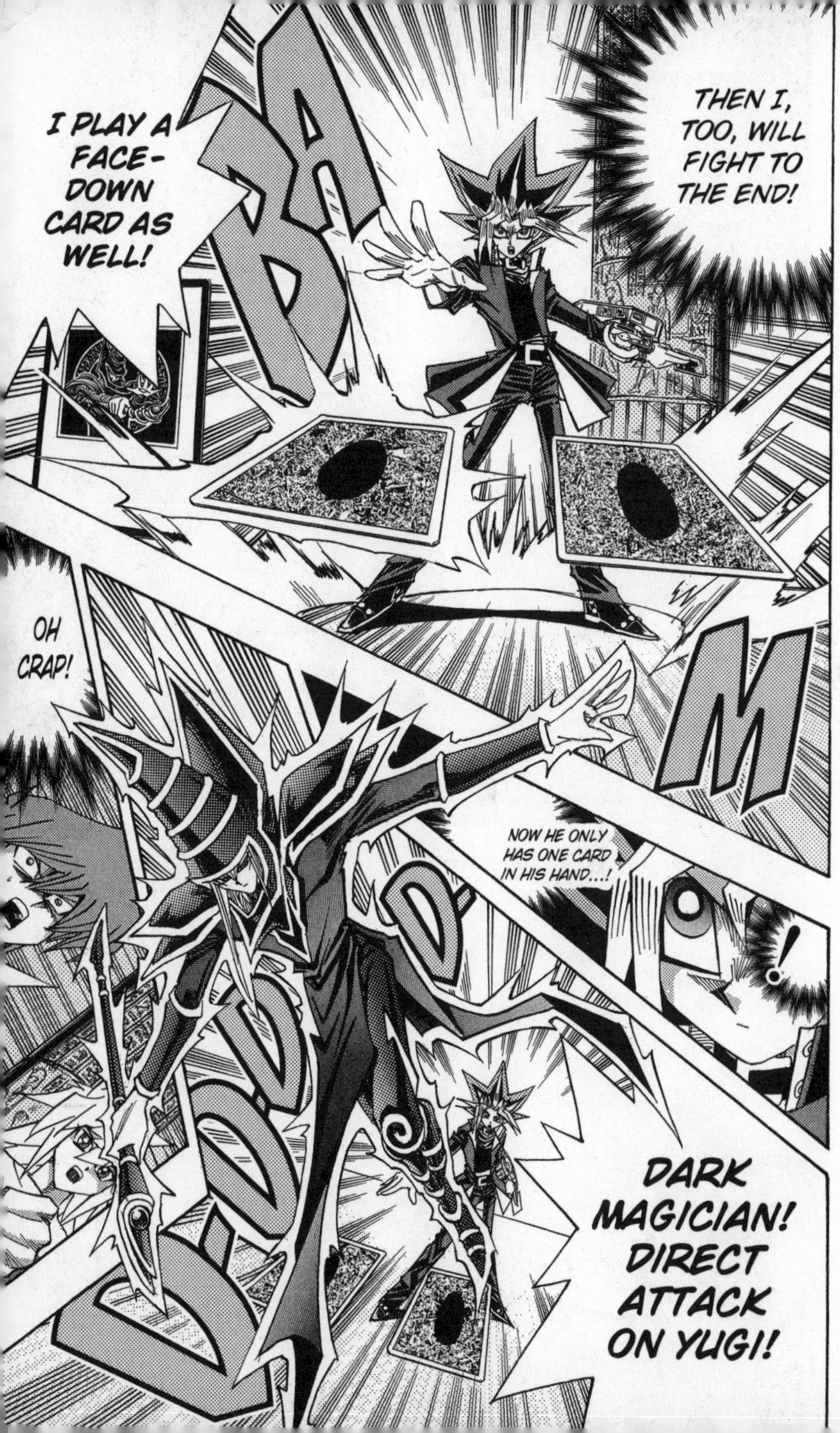
THEN I, TOO, WILL FIGHT TO THE END!
I PLAY A FACE-DOWN CARD AS WELL!
NOW HE ONLY HAS ONE CARD IN HIS HAND...!
!
OH CRAP!
DARK MAGICIAN! DIRECT ATTACK ON YUGI!

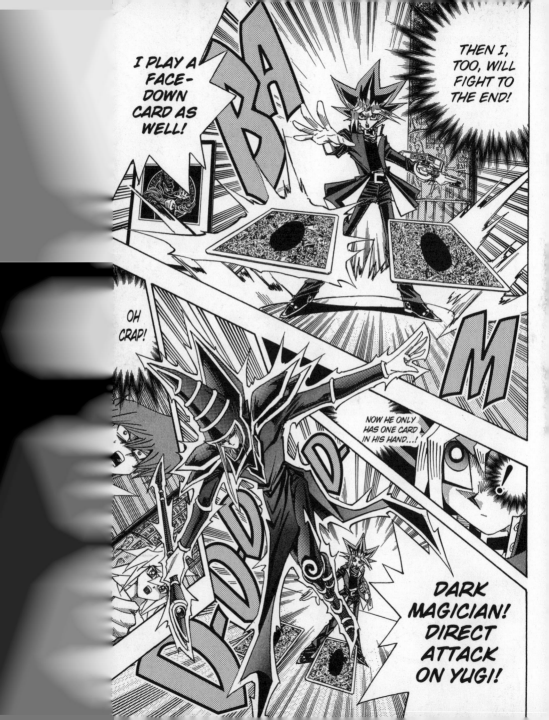

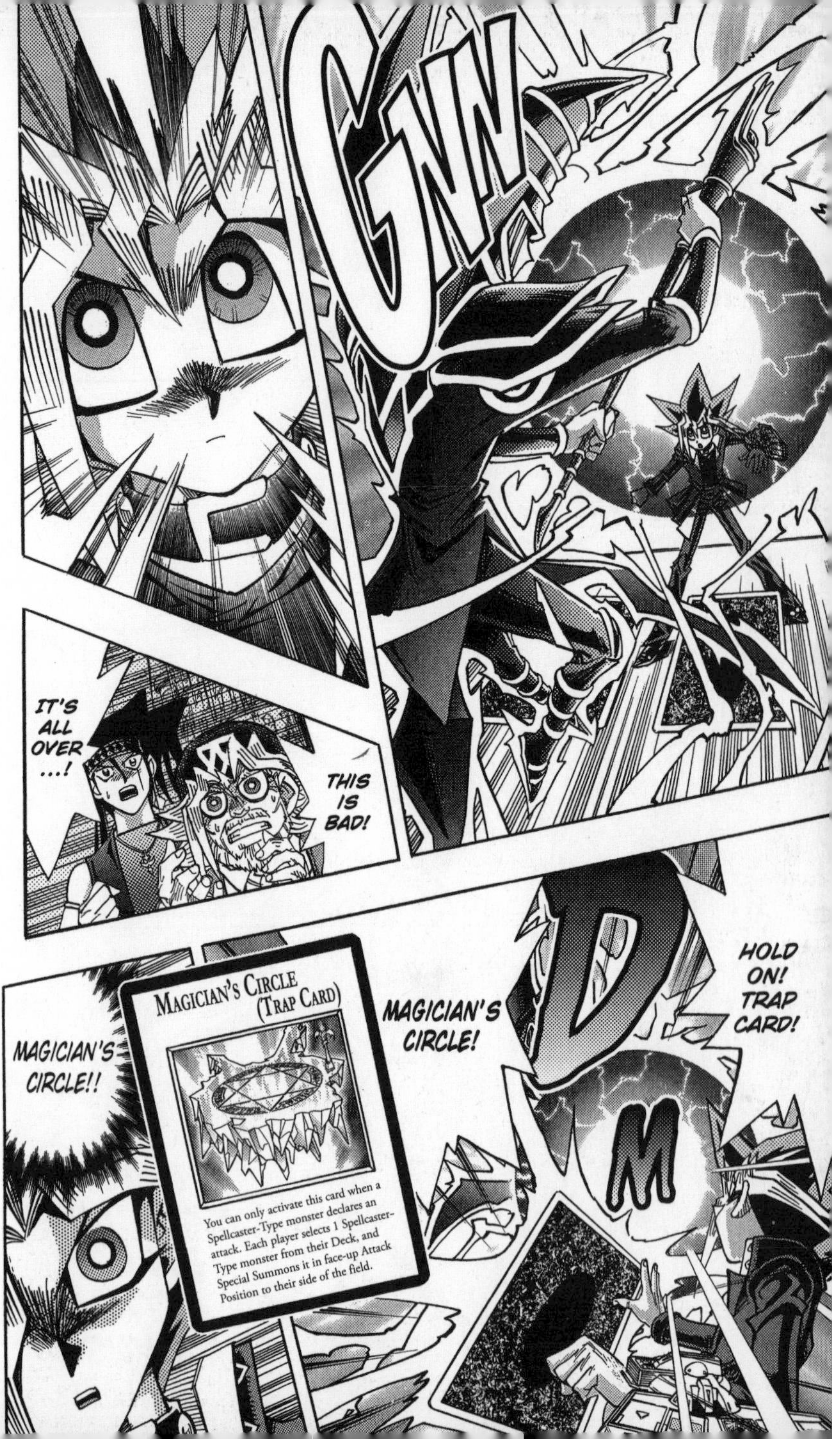
GNW
IT'S ALL OVER...!
THIS IS BAD!
HOLD ON! TRAP CARD!
MAGICIAN'S CIRCLE!
D
M
MAGICIAN'S CIRCLE!!
MAGICIAN'S CIRCLE (TRAP CARD)
You can only activate this card when a Spellcaster-Type monster declares an attack. Each player selects 1 Spellcaster-Type monster from their Deck, and Special Summons it in face-up Attack Position to their side of the field.

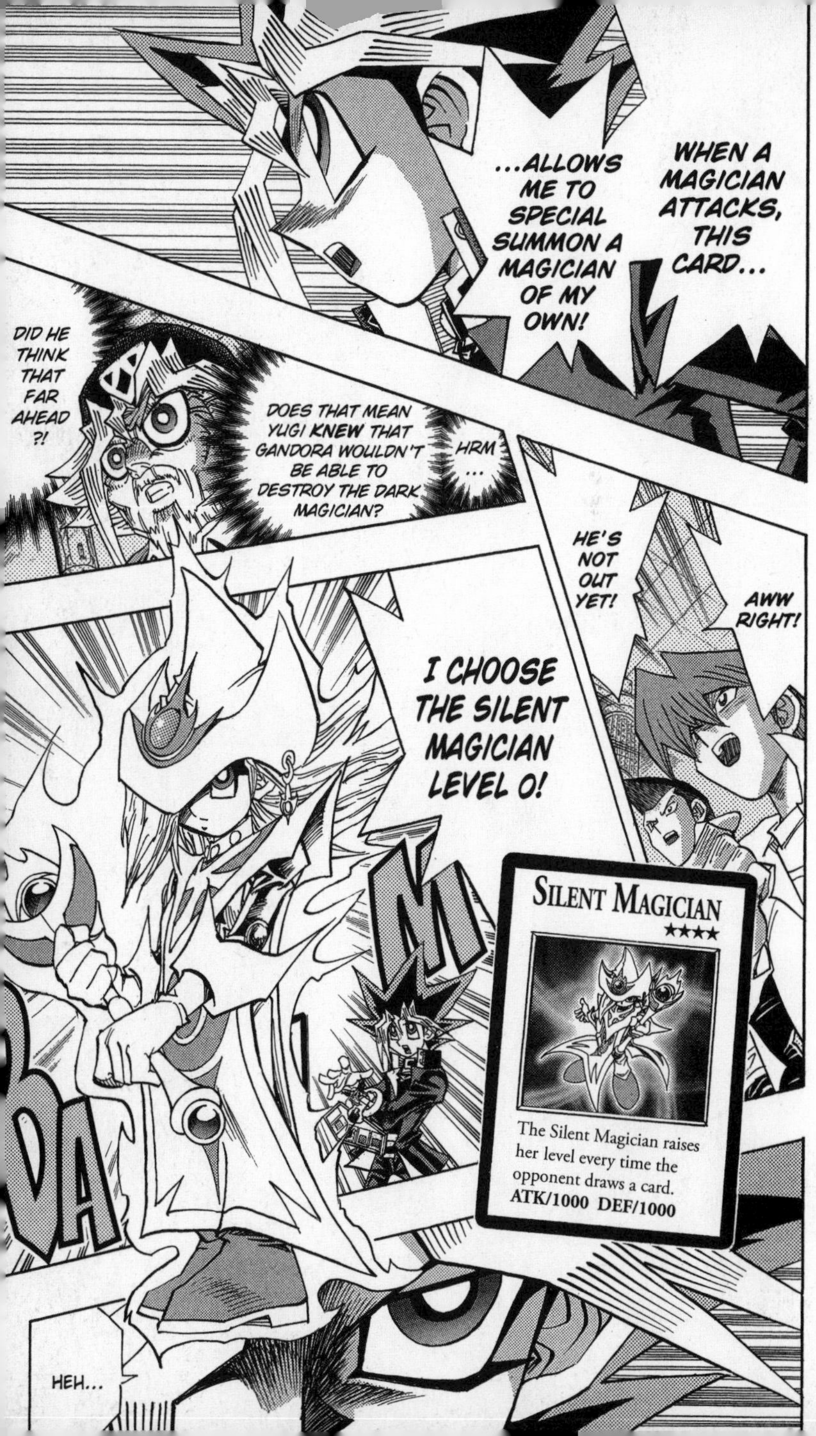
WHEN A MAGICIAN ATTACKS, THIS CARD...
...ALLOWS ME TO SPECIAL SUMMON A MAGICIAN OF MY OWN!
HRM...
DOES THAT MEAN YUGI KNEW THAT GANDORA WOULDN'T BE ABLE TO DESTROY THE DARK MAGICIAN?
DID HE THINK THAT FAR AHEAD ?!
AWW RIGHT!
HE'S NOT OUT YET!
I CHOOSE THE SILENT MAGICIAN LEVEL 0!
SILENT MAGICIAN
★★★★
The Silent Magician raises her level every time the opponent draws a card.
ATK/1000 DEF/1000
HEH...

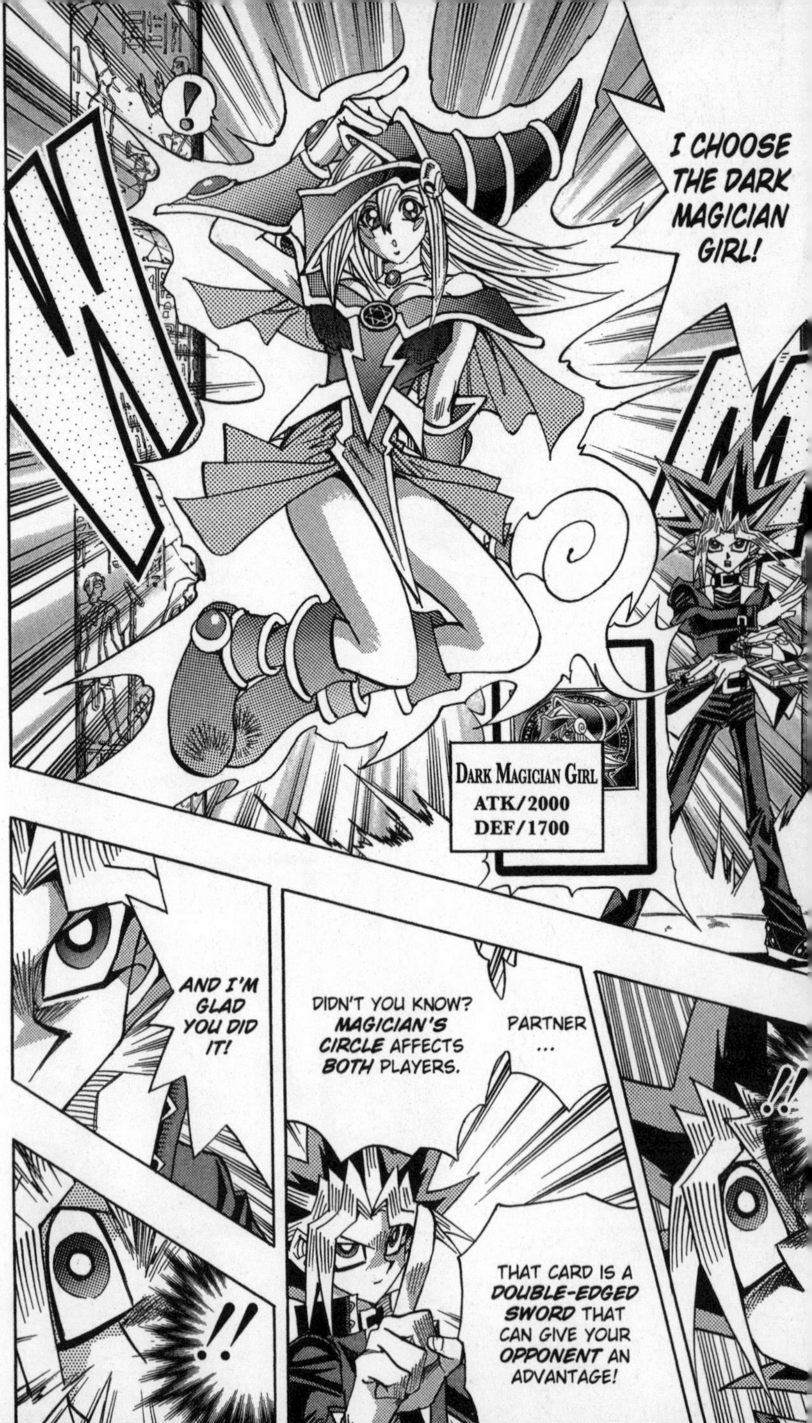

!
I CHOOSE THE DARK MAGICIAN GIRL!
DARK MAGICIAN GIRL
ATK/2000
DEF/1700
!!
PARTNER ...
DIDN'T YOU KNOW? MAGICIAN'S CIRCLE AFFECTS BOTH PLAYERS.
THAT CARD IS A DOUBLE-EDGED SWORD THAT CAN GIVE YOUR OPPONENT AN ADVANTAGE!
AND I'M GLAD YOU DID IT!
!!

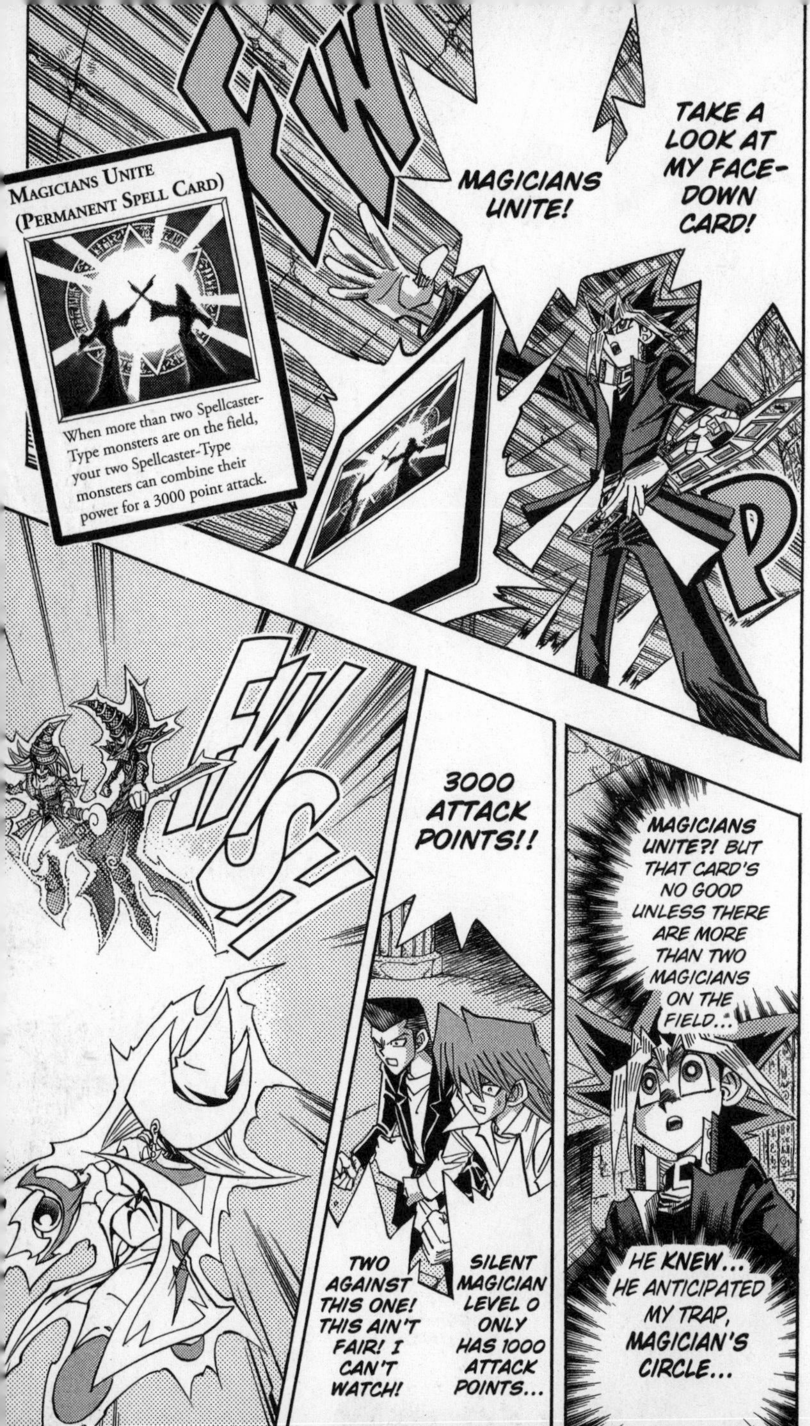
TAKE A LOOK AT MY FACE-DOWN CARD!
MAGICIANS UNITE!
MAGICIANS UNITE (PERMANENT SPELL CARD)
When more than two Spellcaster-Type monsters are on the field, your two Spellcaster-Type monsters can combine their power for a 3000 point attack.
MAGICIANS UNITE?! BUT THAT CARD'S NO GOOD UNLESS THERE ARE MORE THAN TWO MAGICIANS ON THE FIELD...
HE KNEW... HE ANTICIPATED MY TRAP, MAGICIAN'S CIRCLE...
3000 ATTACK POINTS!!
SILENT MAGICIAN LEVEL 0 ONLY HAS 1000 ATTACK POINTS...
TWO AGAINST THIS ONE! THIS AIN'T FAIR! I CAN'T WATCH!

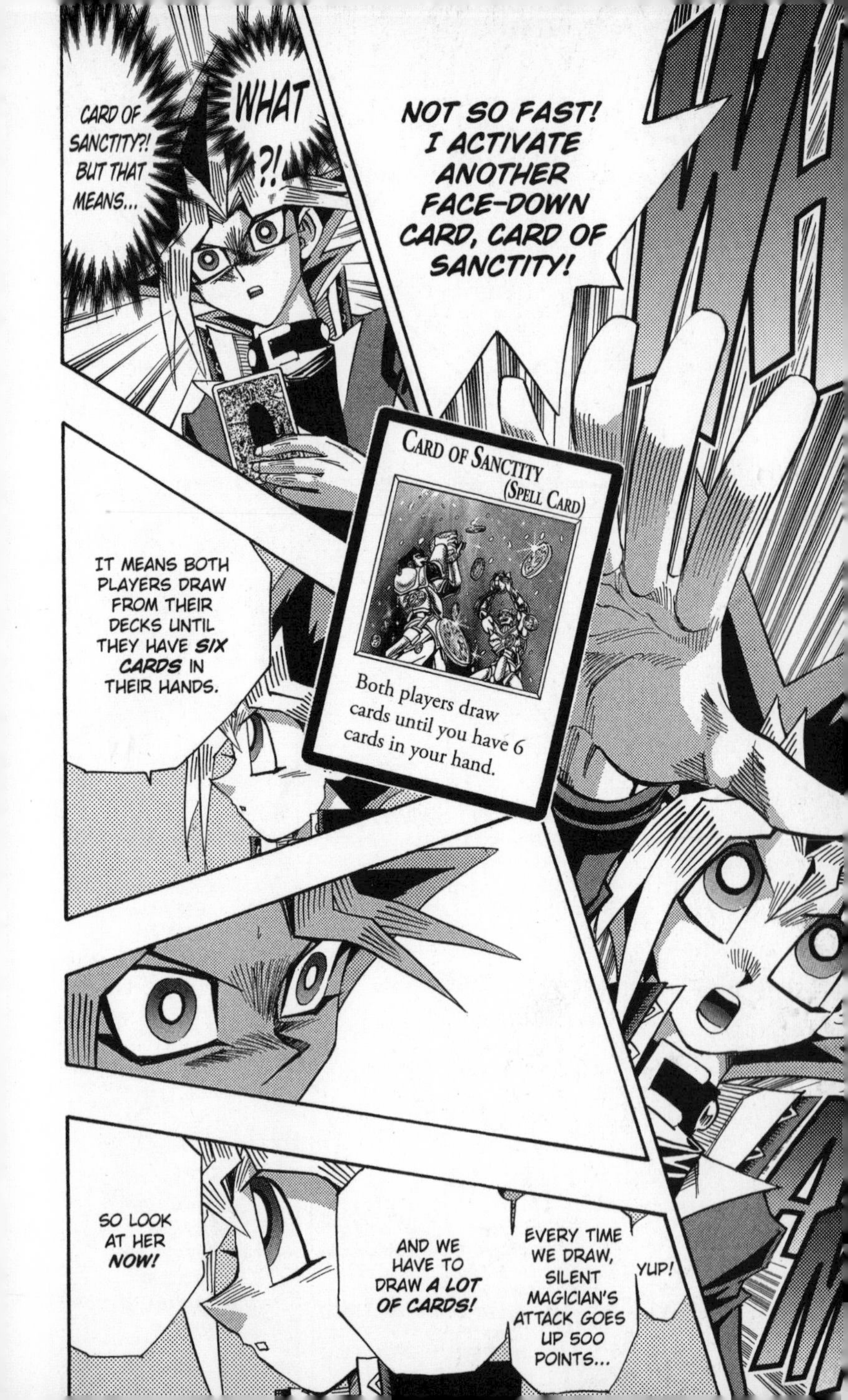
NOT SO FAST! I ACTIVATE ANOTHER FACE-DOWN CARD, CARD OF SANCTITY!
WHAT ?!
CARD OF SANCTITY?! BUT THAT MEANS...
CARD OF SANCTITY
(SPELL CARD)
Both players draw cards until you have 6 cards in your hand.
IT MEANS BOTH PLAYERS DRAW FROM THEIR DECKS UNTIL THEY HAVE SIX CARDS IN THEIR HANDS.
YUP!
EVERY TIME WE DRAW, SILENT MAGICIAN'S ATTACK GOES UP 500 POINTS...
AND WE HAVE TO DRAW A LOT OF CARDS!
SO LOOK AT HER NOW!

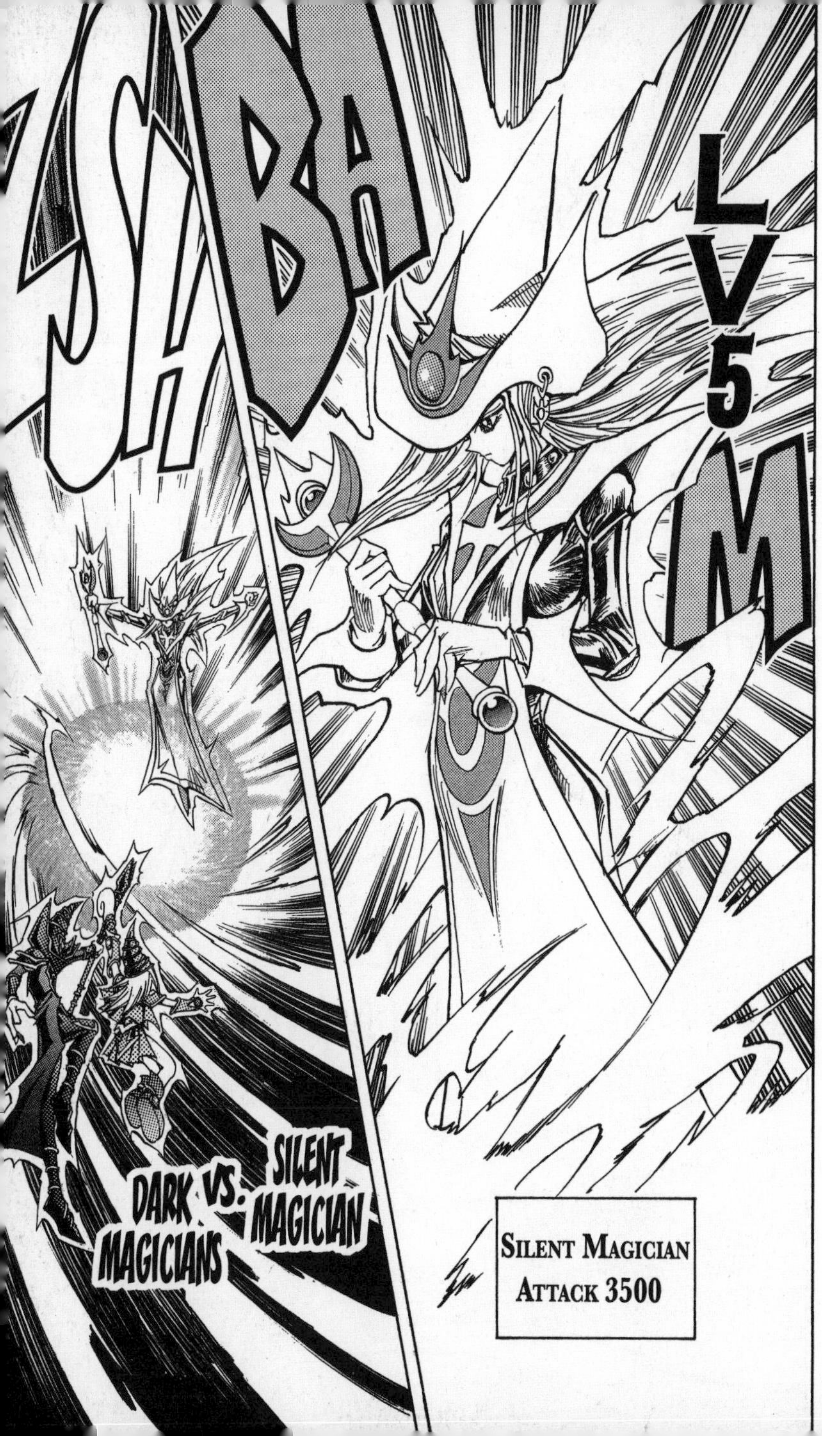
LV5
SILENT MAGICIAN
ATTACK 3500
DARK MAGICIANS VS. SILENT MAGICIAN

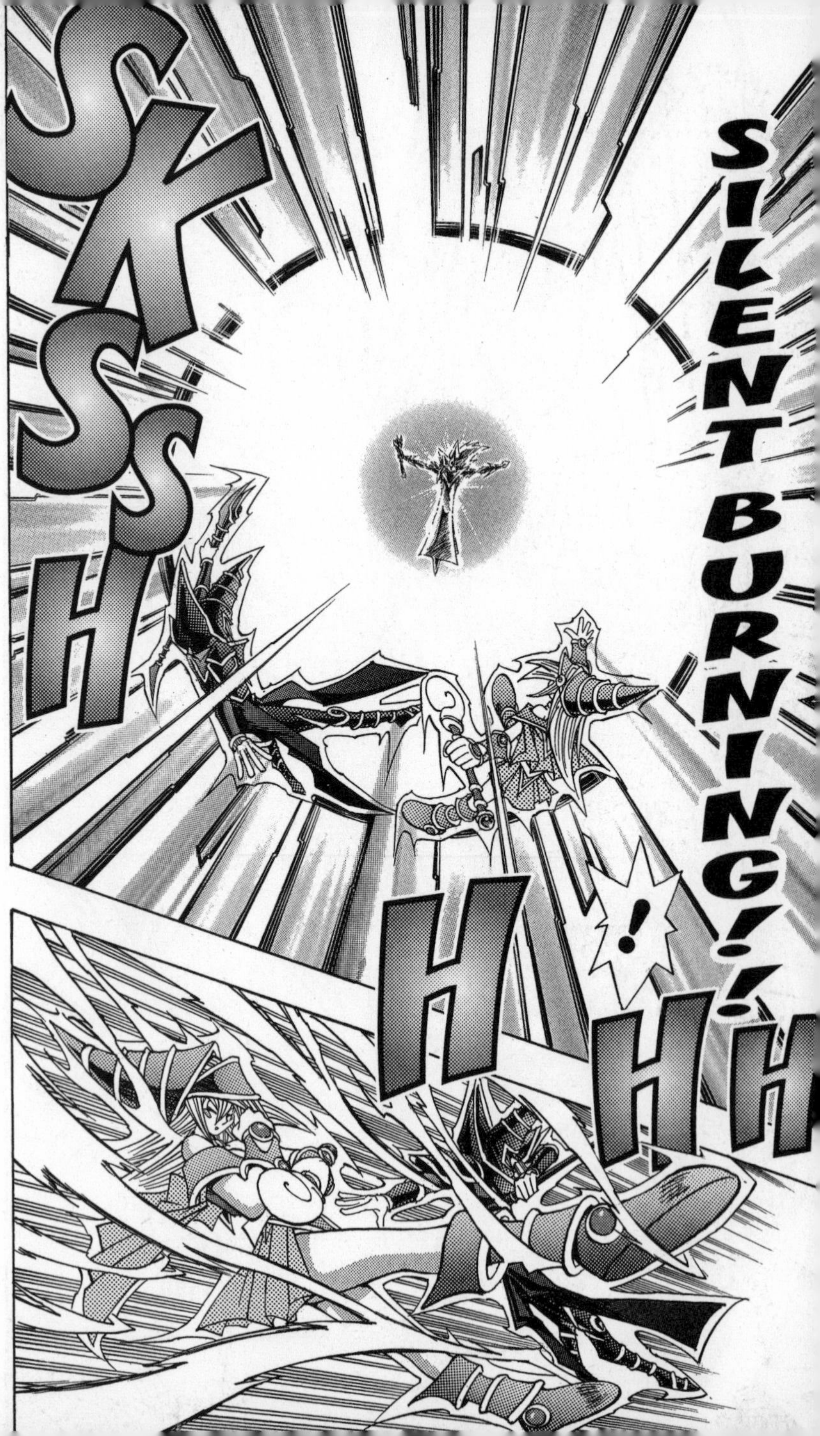
SILENT BURNING!!
SSSH
HHH
!

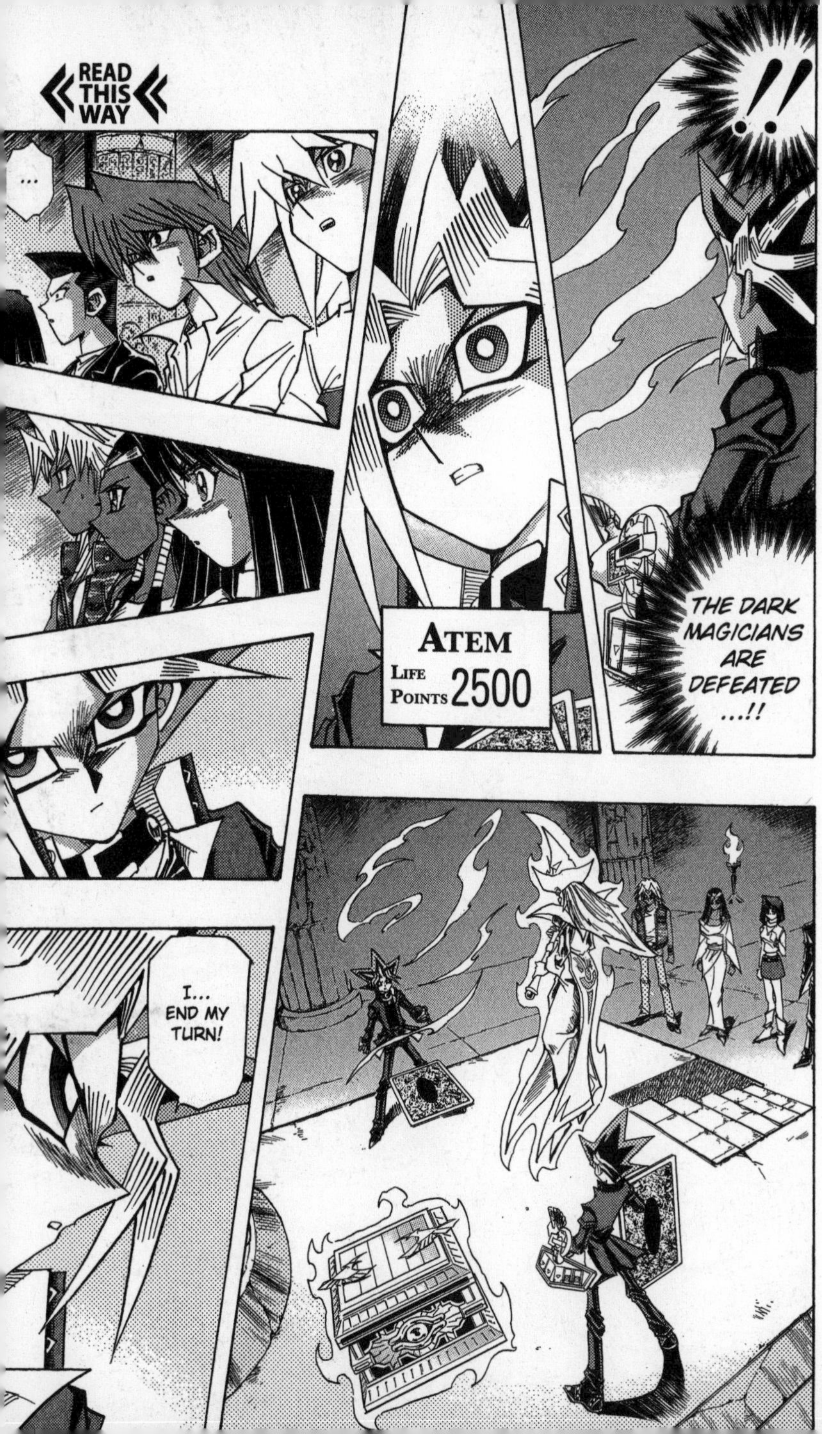
READ THIS WAY
!!
THE DARK MAGICIANS ARE DEFEATED ...!!
ATEM
LIFE POINTS 2500
...
I... END MY TURN!

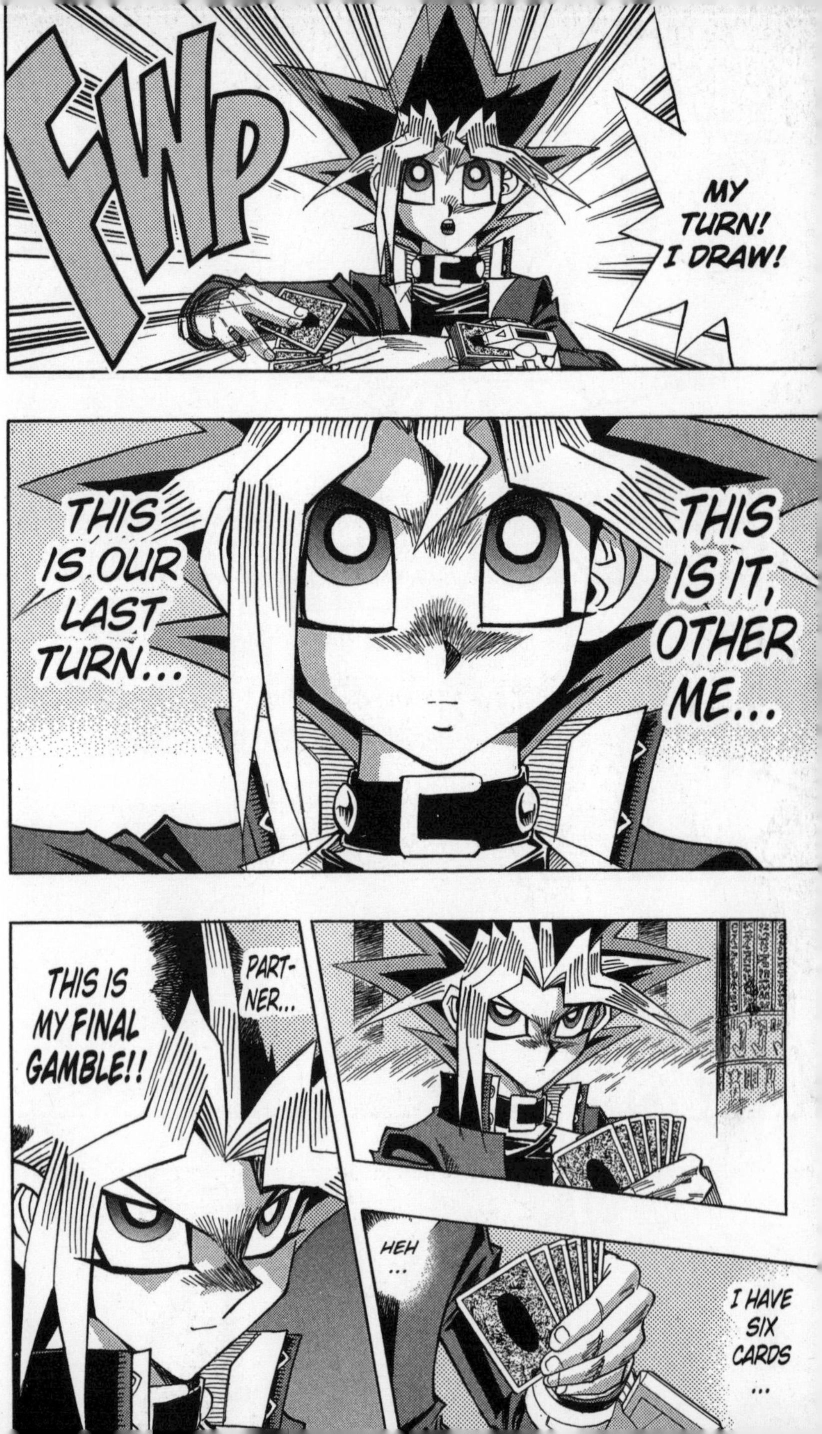
FWP
MY TURN! I DRAW!
THIS IS IT, OTHER ME...
THIS IS OUR LAST TURN...
HEH...
I HAVE SIX CARDS...
PART-NER...
THIS IS MY FINAL GAMBLE!!

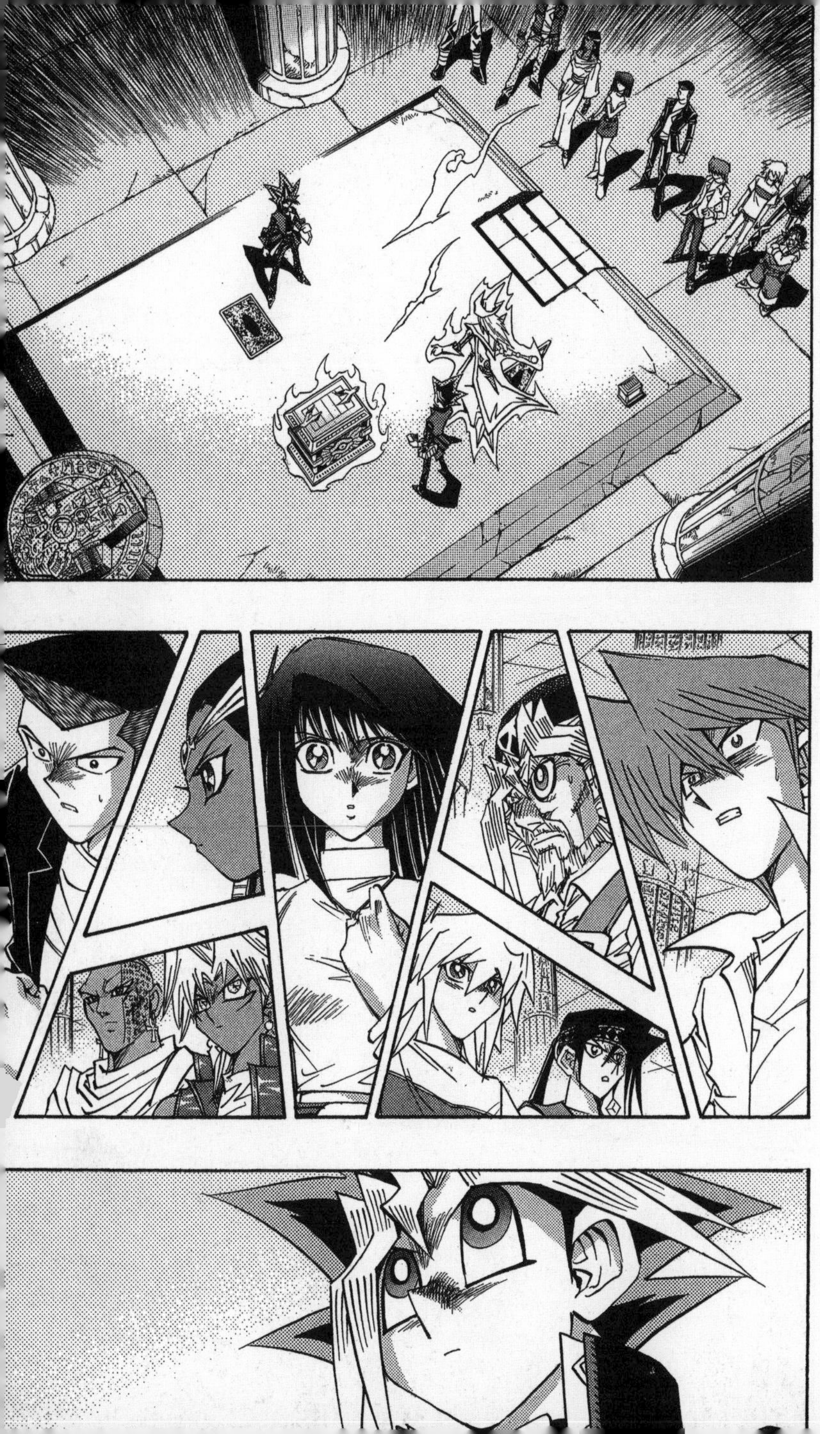

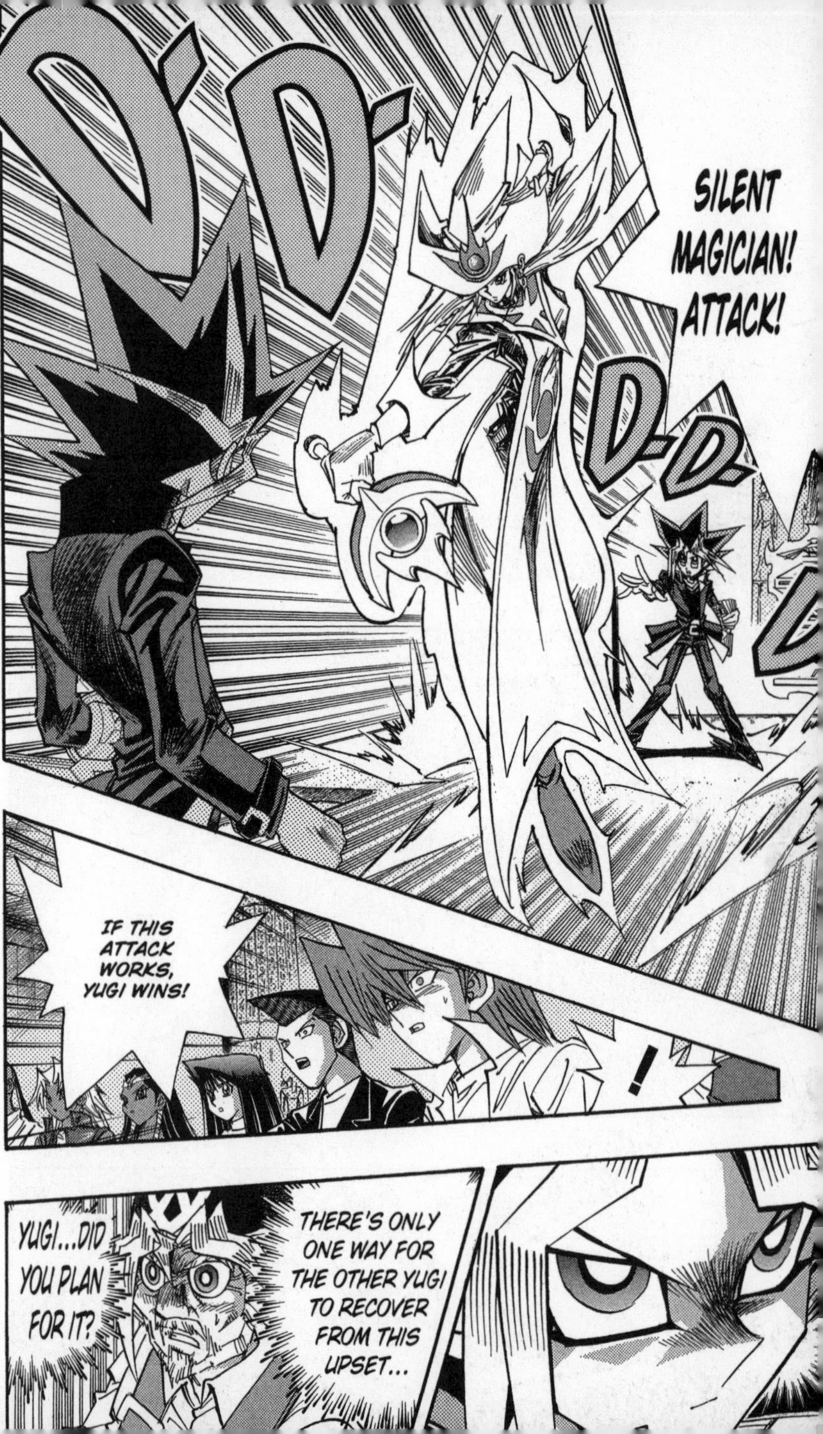
SILENT MAGICIAN! ATTACK!
D-D-D
D-D-D
!
IF THIS ATTACK WORKS, YUGI WINS!
THERE'S ONLY ONE WAY FOR THE OTHER YUGI TO RECOVER FROM THIS UPSET...
YUGI...DID YOU PLAN FOR IT?

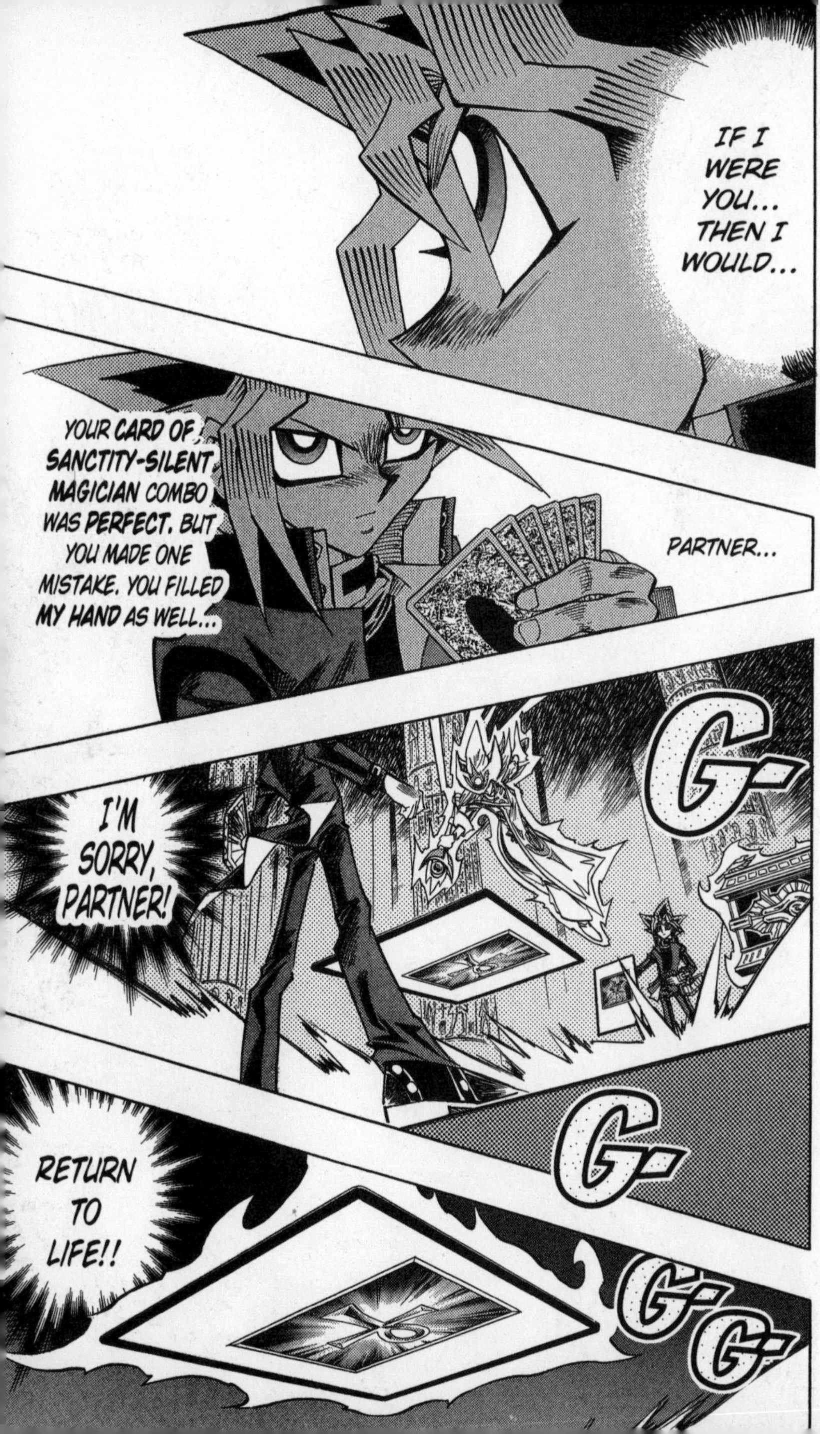
IF I WERE YOU... THEN I WOULD...
PARTNER...
YOUR CARD OF SANCTITY-SILENT MAGICIAN COMBO WAS PERFECT. BUT YOU MADE ONE MISTAKE. YOU FILLED MY HAND AS WELL...
G-
I'M SORRY, PARTNER!
G-
RETURN TO LIFE!!
G-G-

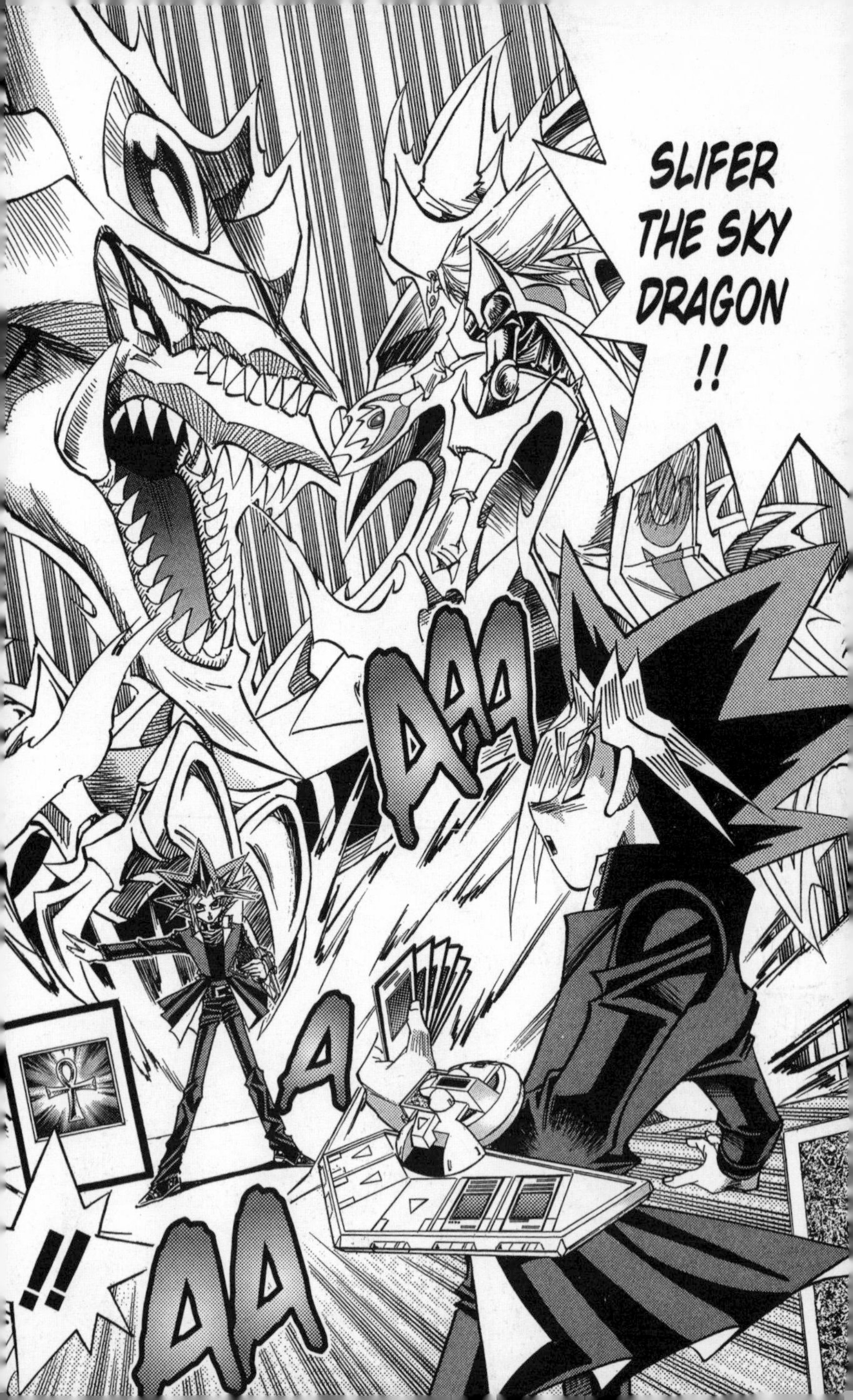
SLIFER THE SKY DRAGON !!
AAAAAA !!

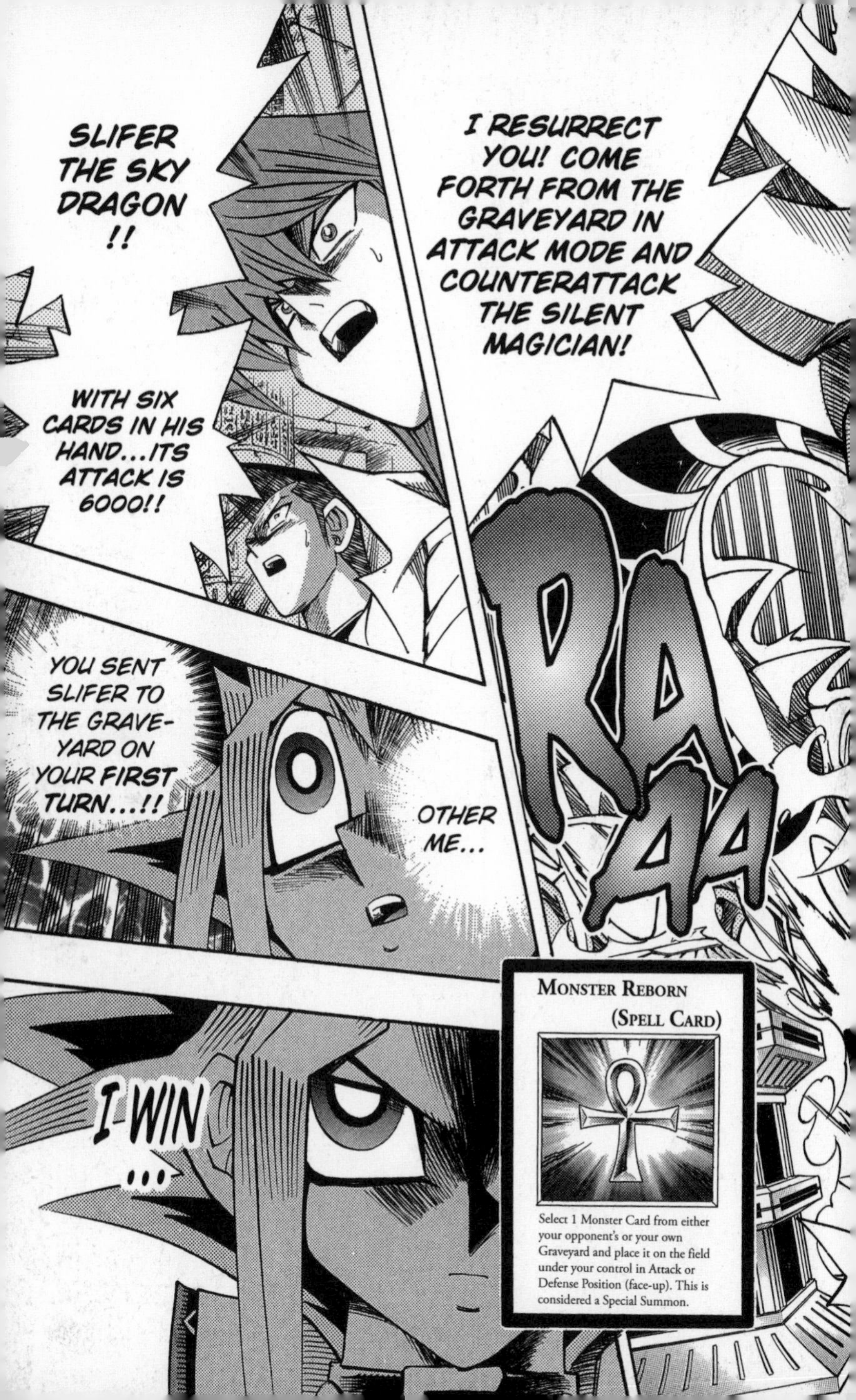
I RESURRECT YOU! COME FORTH FROM THE GRAVEYARD IN ATTACK MODE AND COUNTERATTACK THE SILENT MAGICIAN!
RAAA
SLIFER THE SKY DRAGON !!
WITH SIX CARDS IN HIS HAND...ITS ATTACK IS 6000!!
YOU SENT SLIFER TO THE GRAVE-YARD ON YOUR FIRST TURN...!!
OTHER ME...
MONSTER REBORN
(SPELL CARD)
Select 1 Monster Card from either your opponent's or your own Graveyard and place it on the field under your control in Attack or Defense Position (face-up). This is considered a Special Summon.
I WIN ...

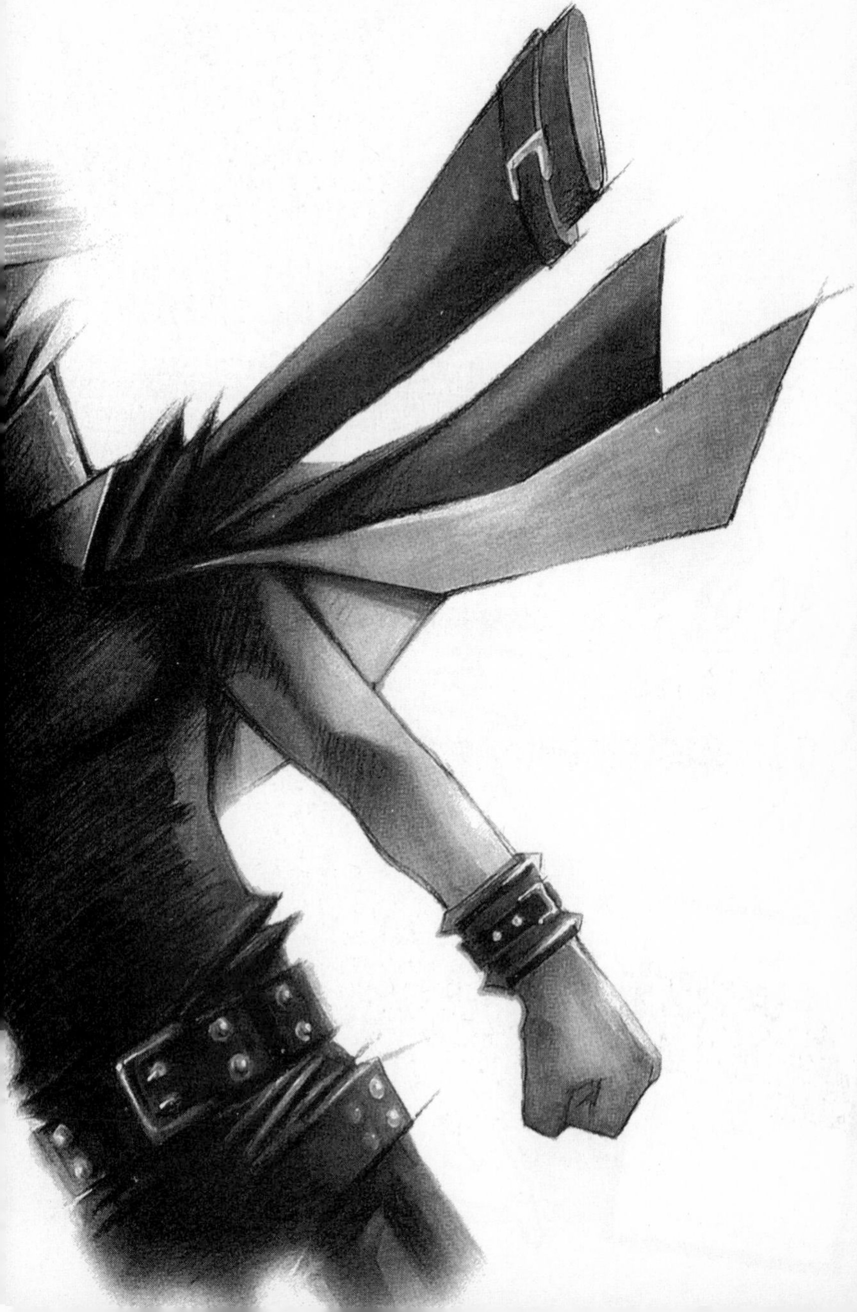

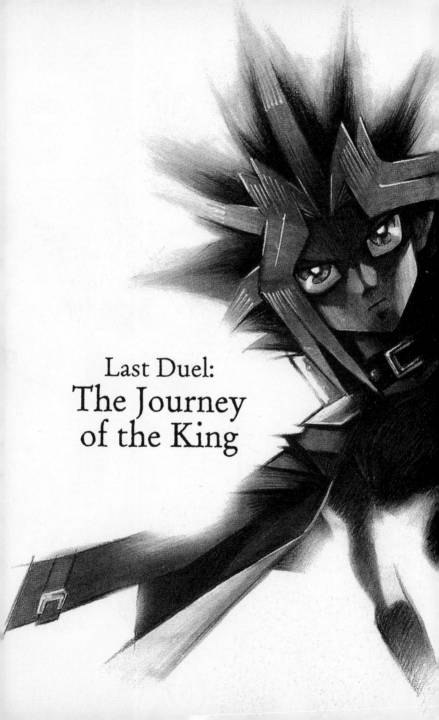

Last Duel:
The Journey
of the King

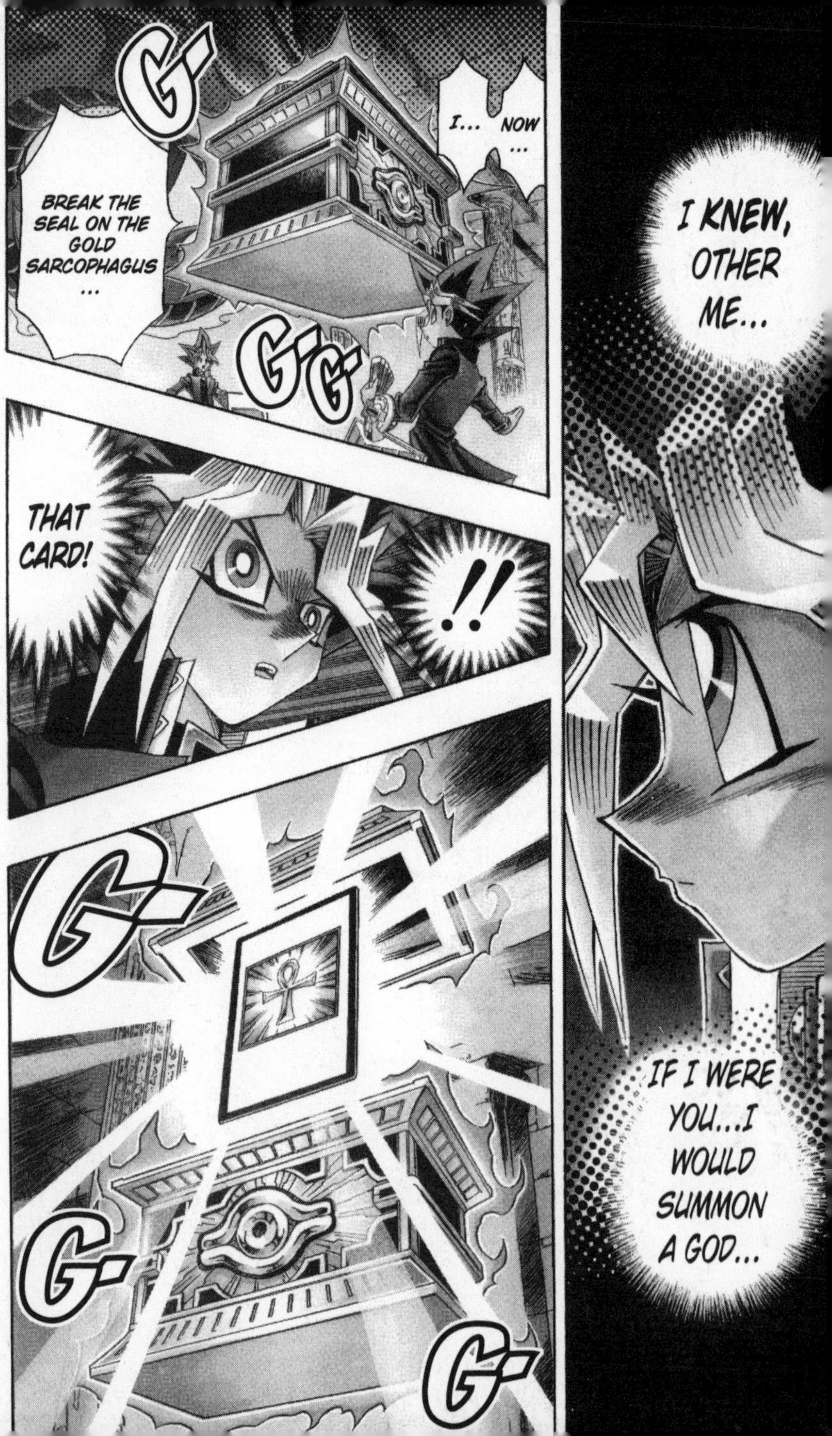
I KNEW, OTHER ME...
IF I WERE YOU...I WOULD SUMMON A GOD...
I... NOW ...
G-
BREAK THE SEAL ON THE GOLD SARCOPHAGUS ...
G-G-
!!
THAT CARD!
G-
G-
G-

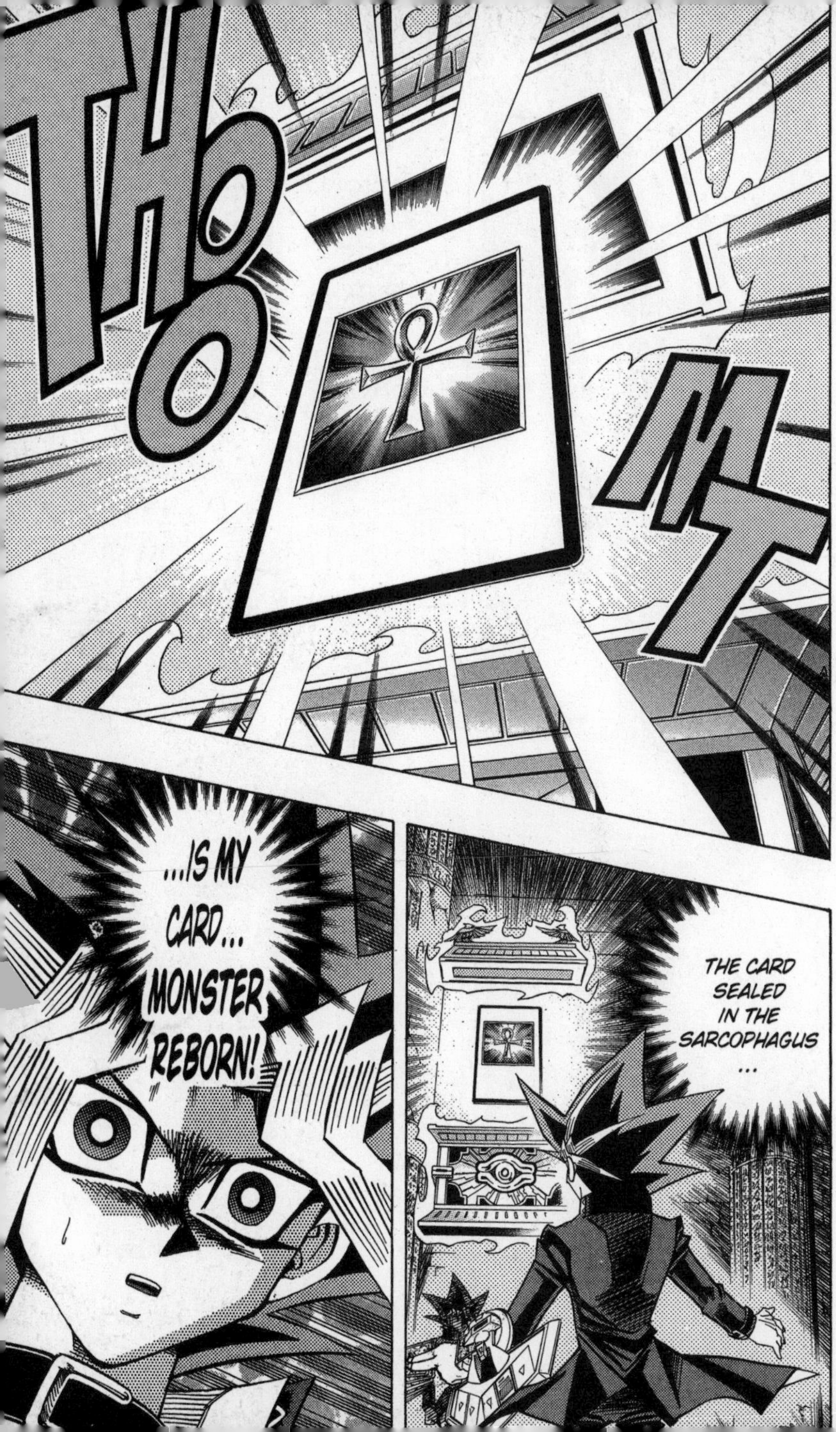
THOOMT
THE CARD SEALED IN THE SARCOPHAGUS ...
...IS MY CARD... MONSTER REBORN!

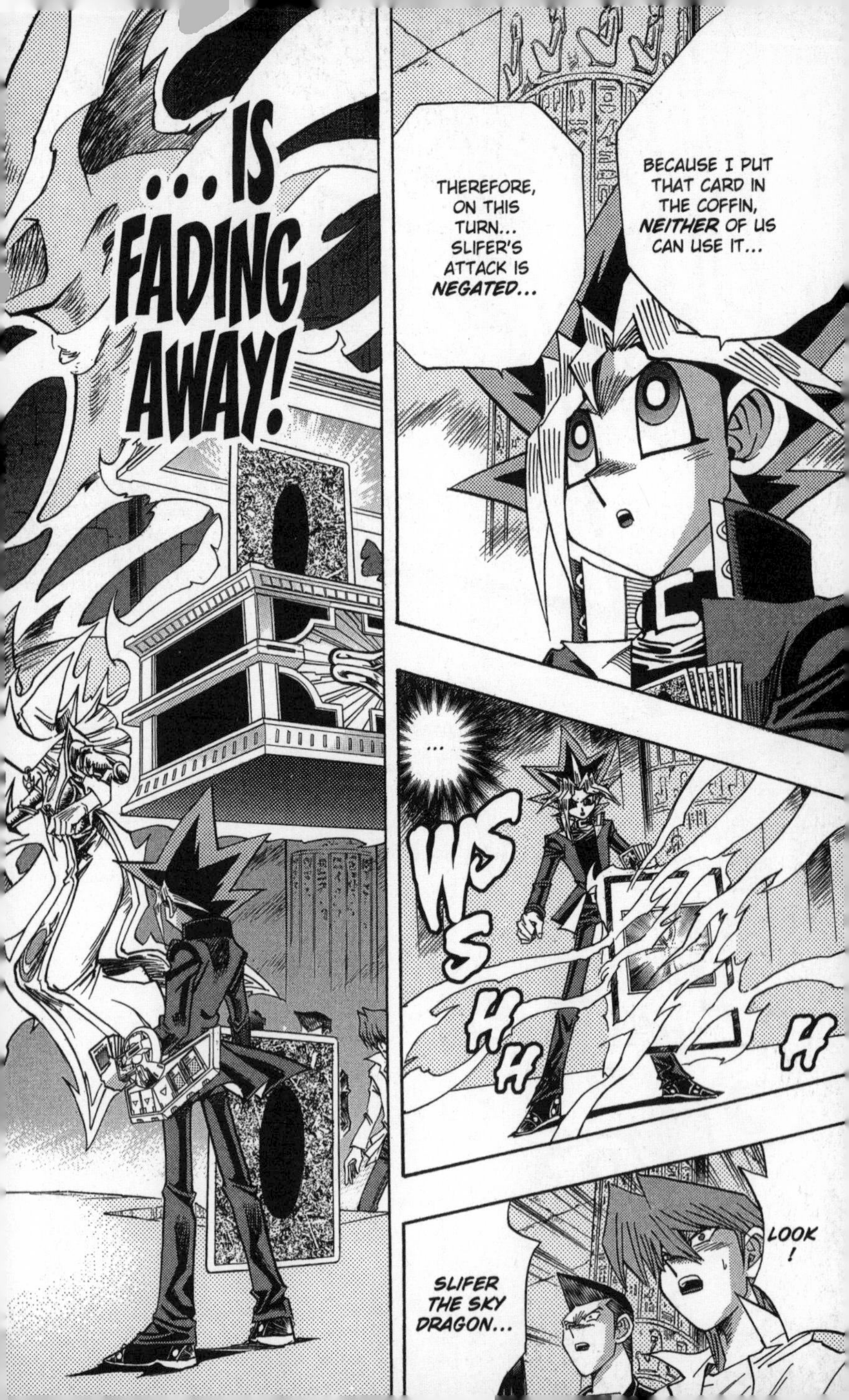
BECAUSE I PUT THAT CARD IN THE COFFIN, NEITHER OF US CAN USE IT...
THEREFORE, ON THIS TURN... SLIFER'S ATTACK IS NEGATED...
...
WSSHHHH
LOOK!
SLIFER THE SKY DRAGON...
...IS FADING AWAY!

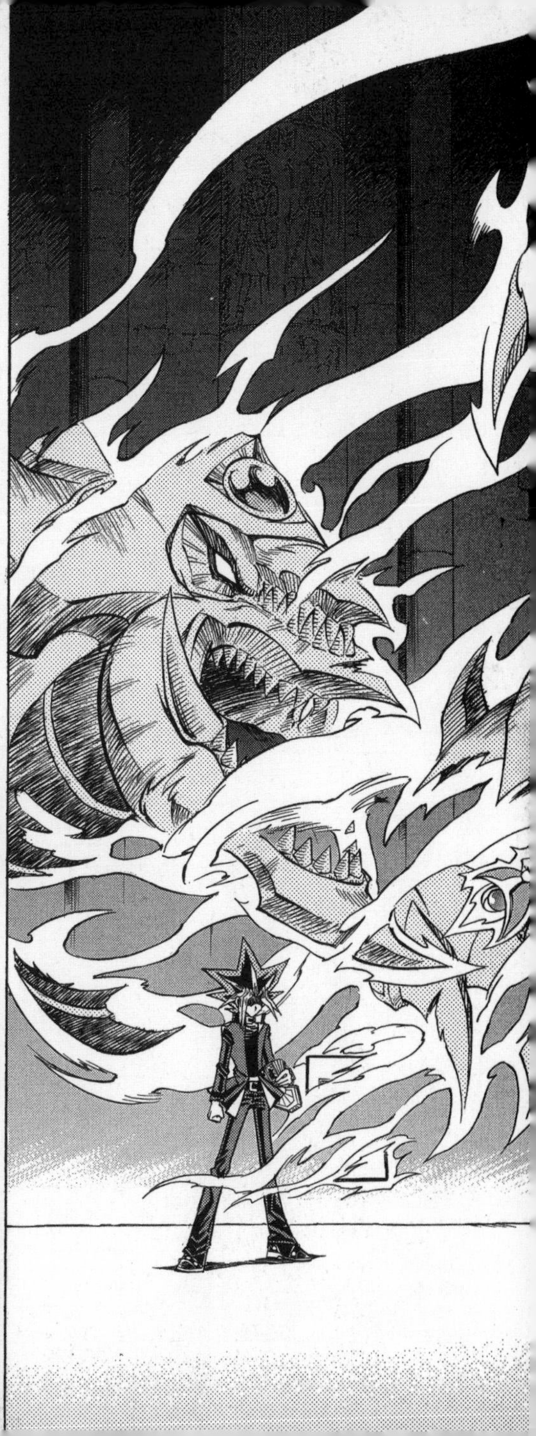
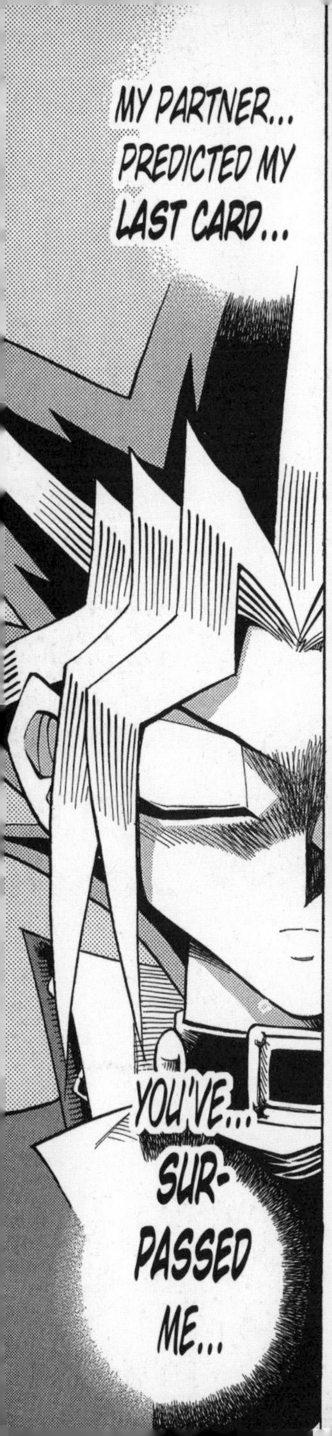
MY PARTNER... PREDICTED MY LAST CARD...
YOU'VE... SUR-PASSED ME...

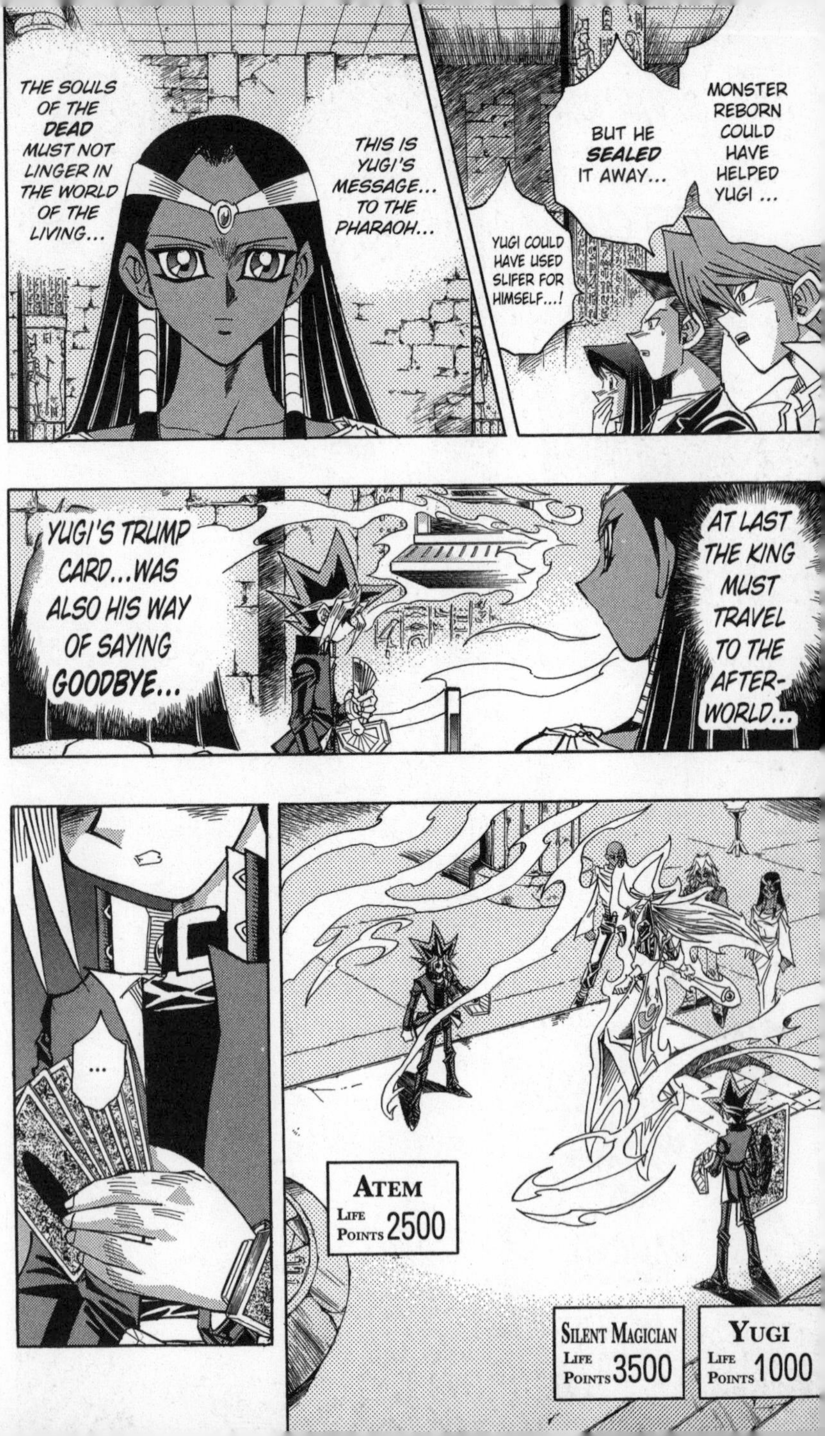
MONSTER REBORN COULD HAVE HELPED YUGI ...
BUT HE SEALED IT AWAY...
YUGI COULD HAVE USED SLIFER FOR HIMSELF...!
THIS IS YUGI'S MESSAGE... TO THE PHARAOH...
THE SOULS OF THE DEAD MUST NOT LINGER IN THE WORLD OF THE LIVING...
AT LAST THE KING MUST TRAVEL TO THE AFTER-WORLD...
YUGI'S TRUMP CARD...WAS ALSO HIS WAY OF SAYING GOODBYE...
ATEM LIFE POINTS 2500
SILENT MAGICIAN LIFE POINTS 3500
YUGI LIFE POINTS 1000
...

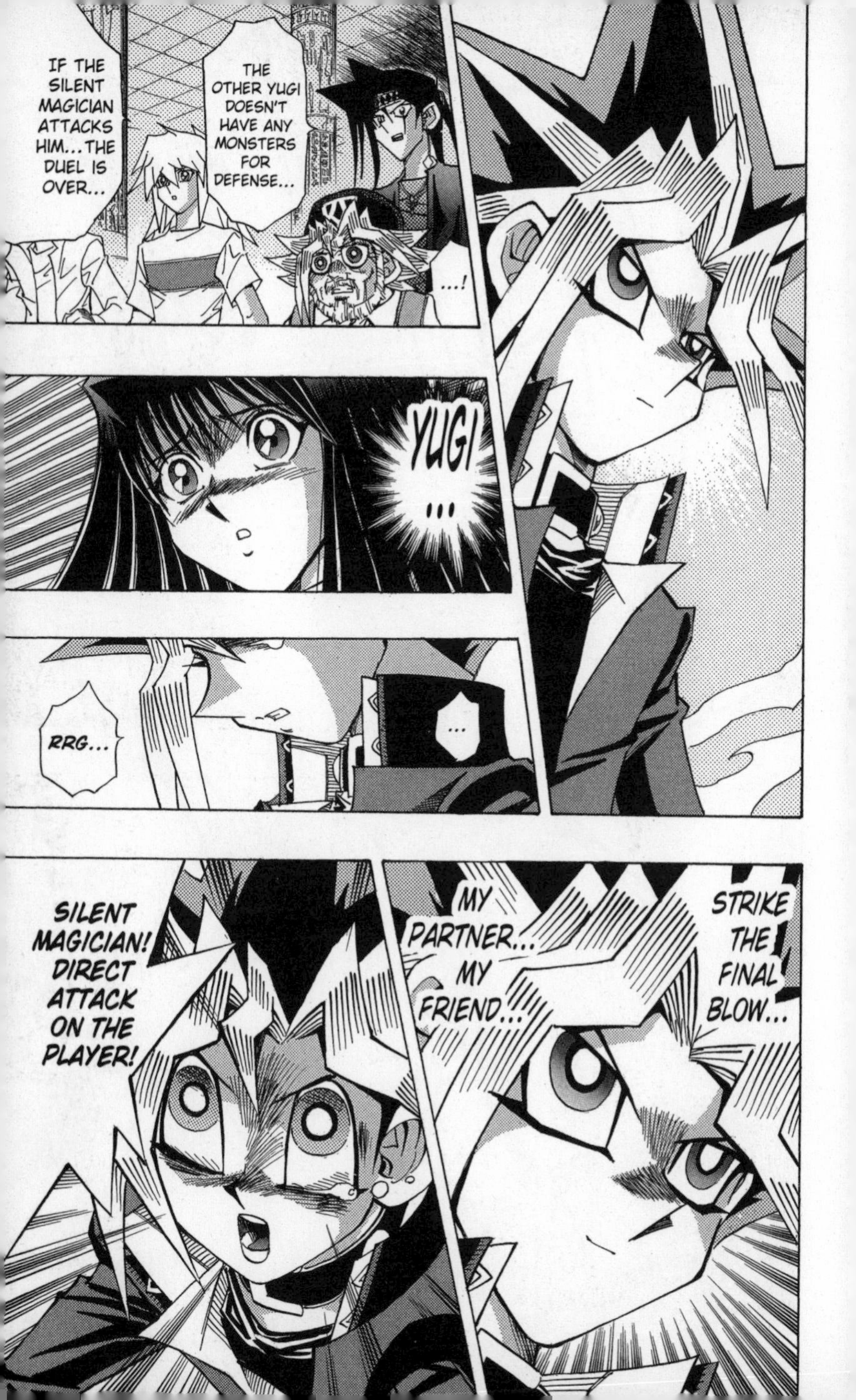
THE OTHER YUGI DOESN'T HAVE ANY MONSTERS FOR DEFENSE...
IF THE SILENT MAGICIAN ATTACKS HIM... THE DUEL IS OVER...
...!
YUGI...
...
RRG...
MY PARTNER... MY FRIEND...
STRIKE THE FINAL BLOW...
SILENT MAGICIAN! DIRECT ATTACK ON THE PLAYER!

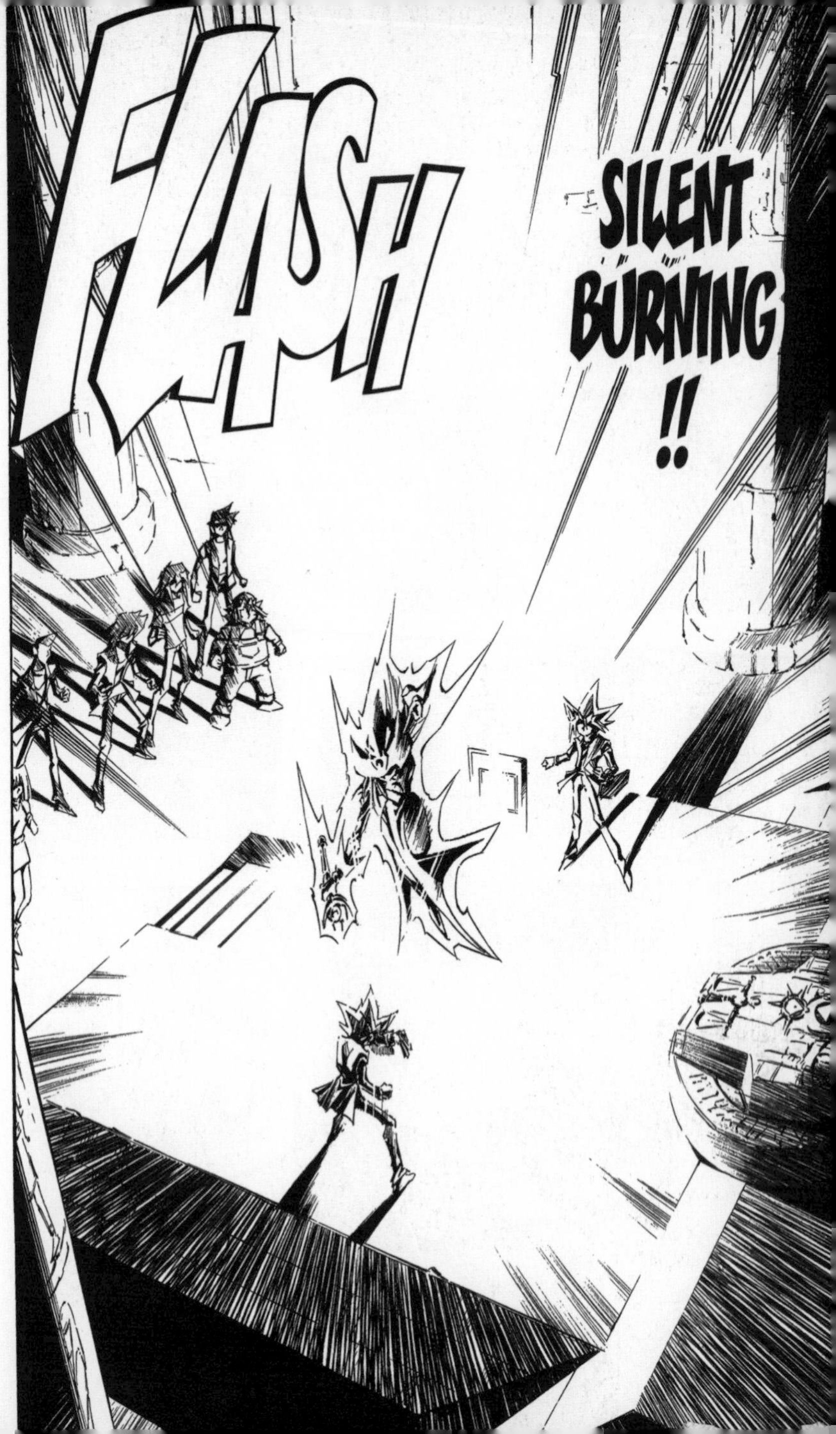
SILENT BURNING!!
FLASH

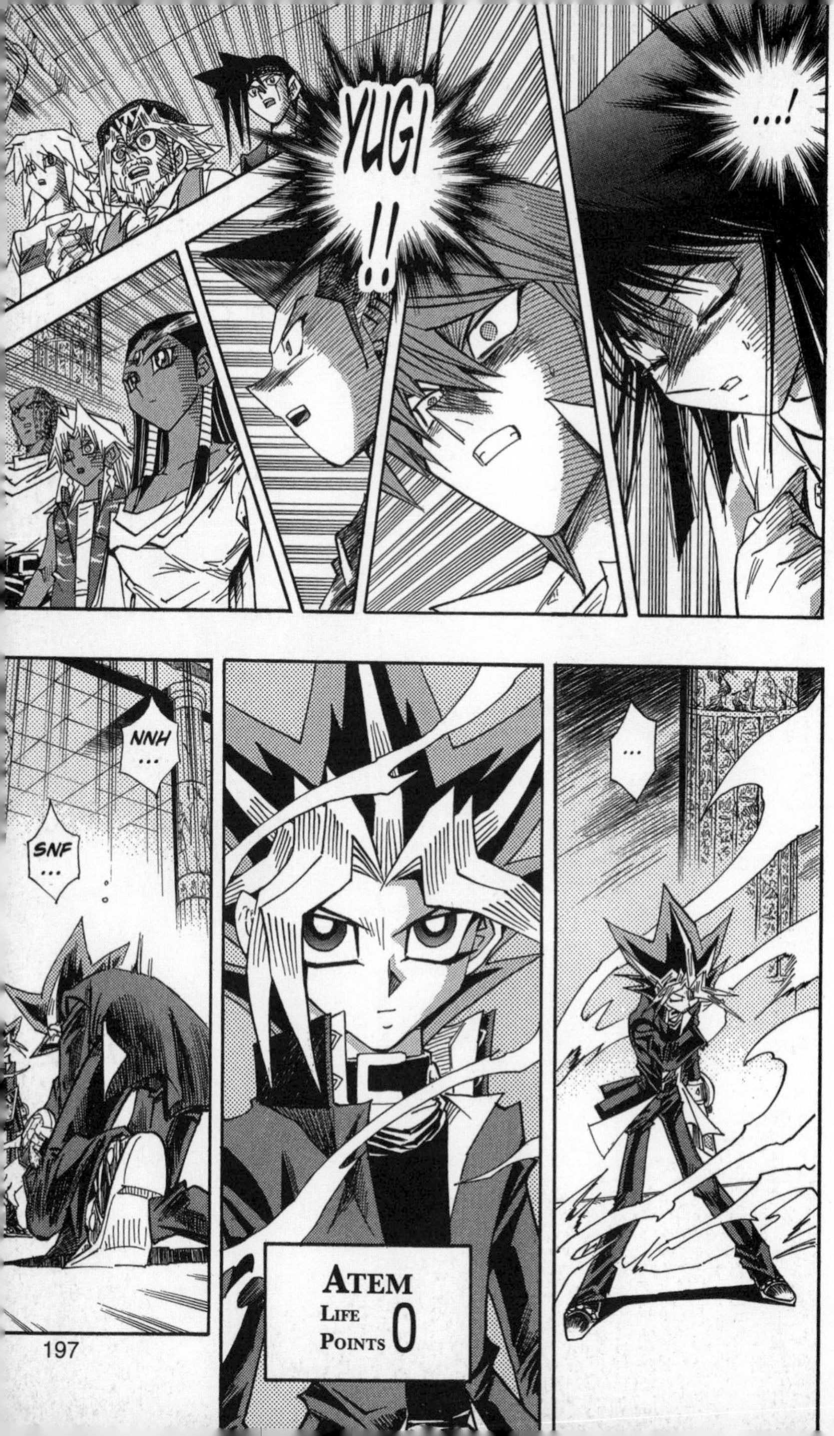
...!
YUGI !!
...
ATEM LIFE POINTS 0
NNH ...
SNF ...

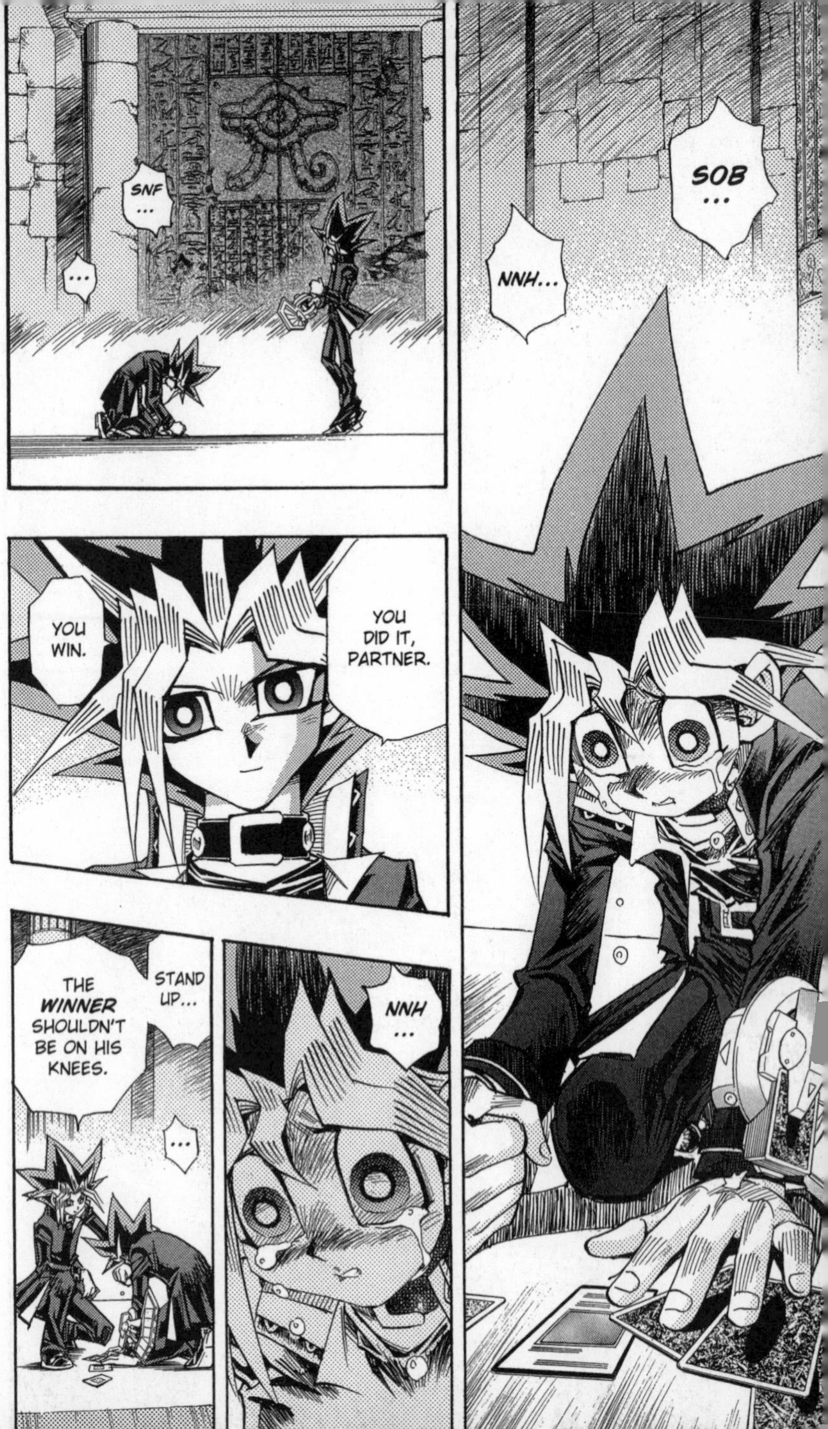
SOB ...
NNH...
SNF ...
...
YOU DID IT, PARTNER.
YOU WIN.
NNH ...
STAND UP...
THE WINNER SHOULDN'T BE ON HIS KNEES.
...

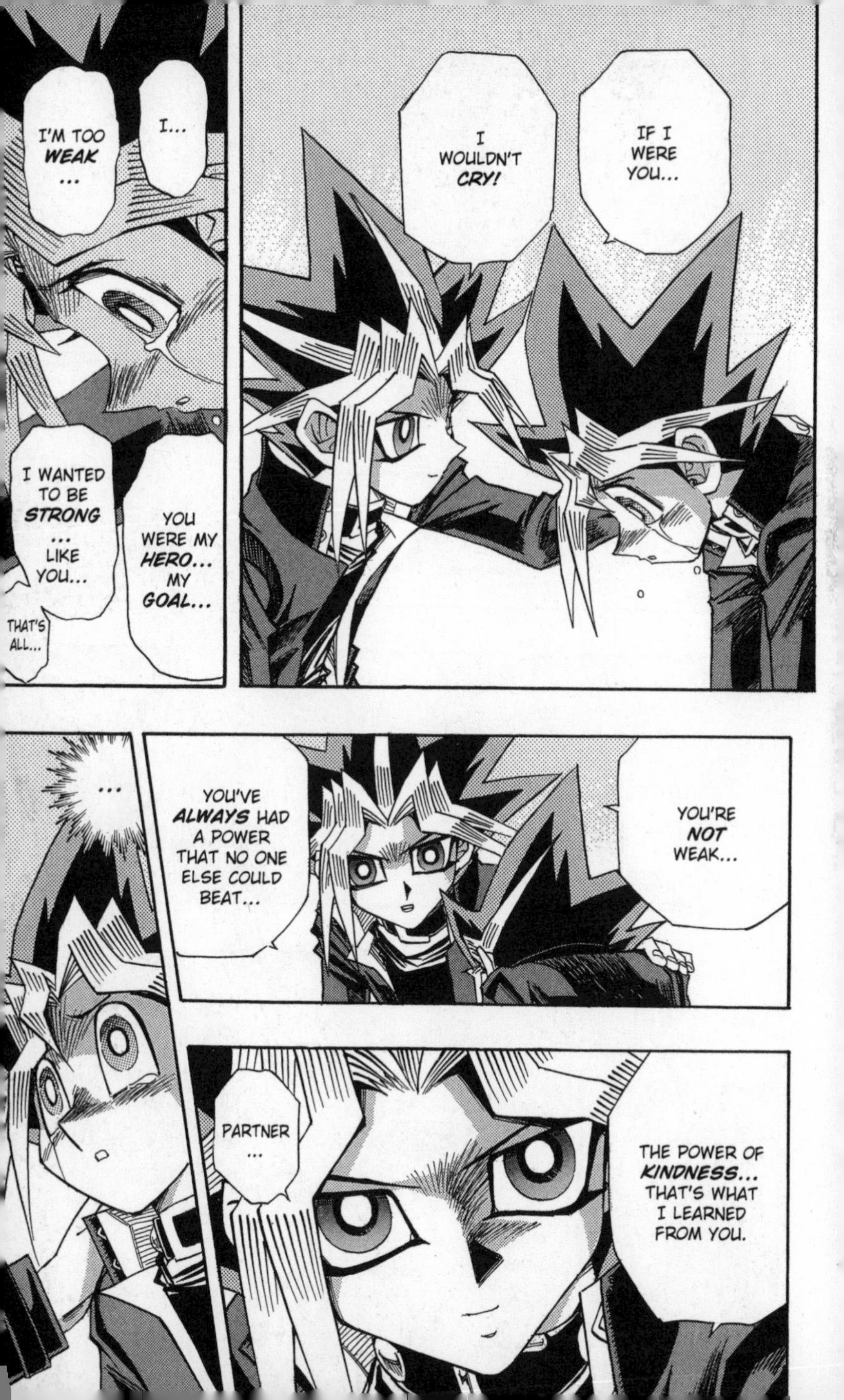

IF I WERE YOU...
I WOULDN'T CRY!
I...
I'M TOO WEAK ...
YOU WERE MY HERO... MY GOAL...
I WANTED TO BE STRONG ... LIKE YOU...
THAT'S ALL...
YOU'RE NOT WEAK...
YOU'VE ALWAYS HAD A POWER THAT NO ONE ELSE COULD BEAT...
THE POWER OF KINDNESS... THAT'S WHAT I LEARNED FROM YOU.
...
PARTNER ...

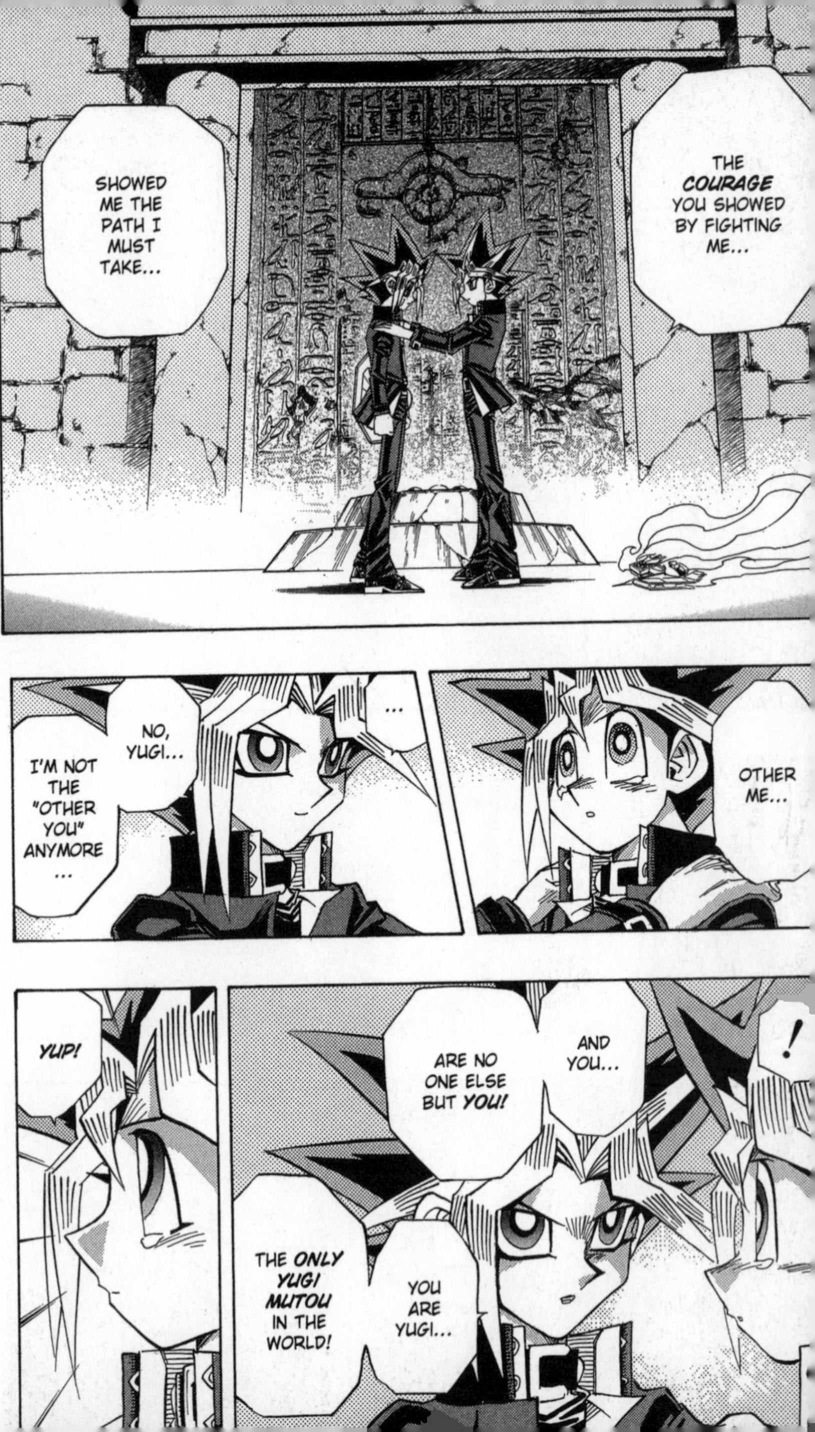
THE COURAGE YOU SHOWED BY FIGHTING ME...
SHOWED ME THE PATH I MUST TAKE...
OTHER ME...
...
NO, YUGI...
I'M NOT THE "OTHER YOU" ANYMORE ...
!
AND YOU...
ARE NO ONE ELSE BUT YOU!
YOU ARE YUGI...
THE ONLY YUGI MUTOU IN THE WORLD!
YUP!

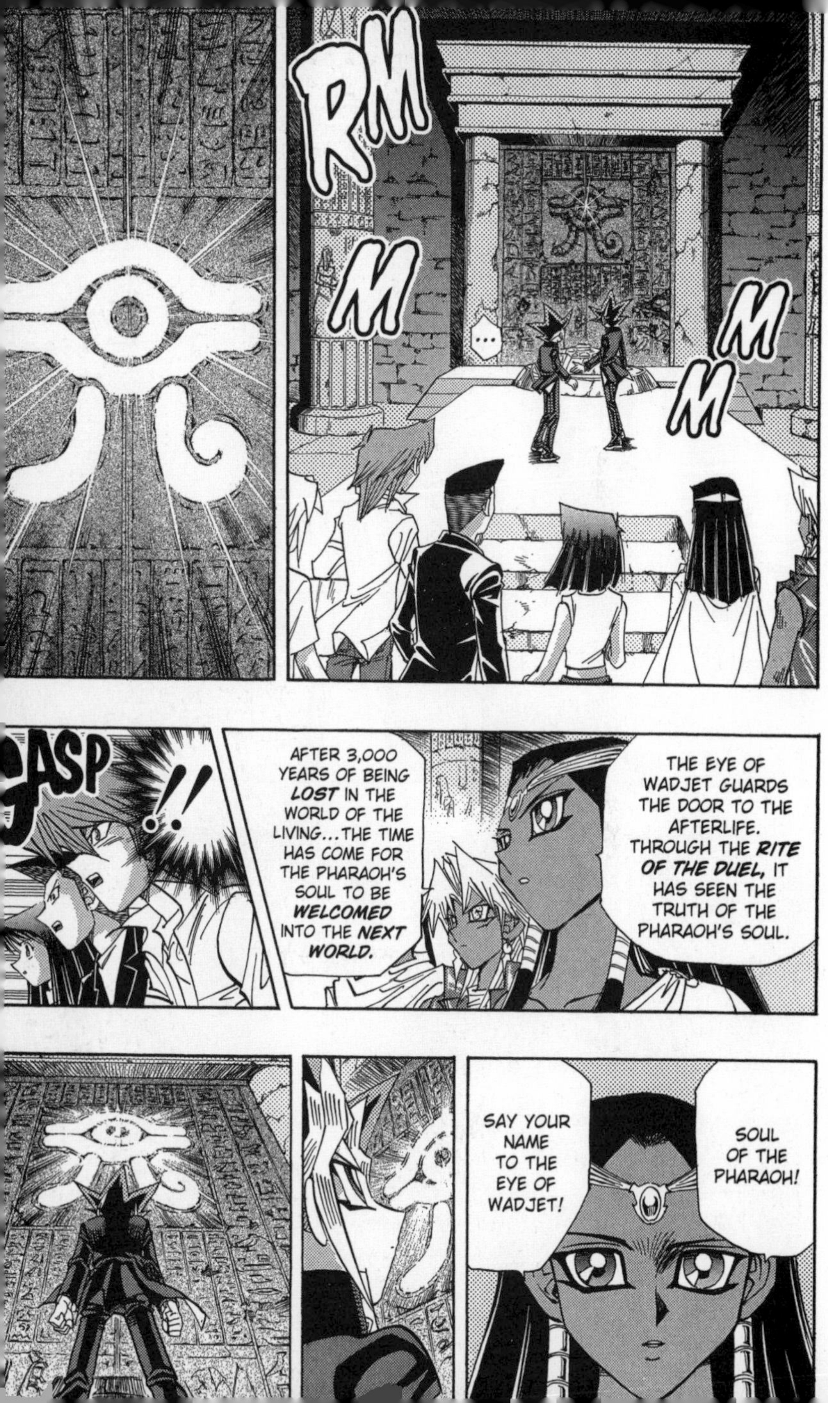
RM
M
M
M
...
THE EYE OF WADJET GUARDS THE DOOR TO THE AFTERLIFE. THROUGH THE ***RITE OF THE DUEL,*** IT HAS SEEN THE TRUTH OF THE PHARAOH'S SOUL.
AFTER 3,000 YEARS OF BEING ***LOST*** IN THE WORLD OF THE LIVING...THE TIME HAS COME FOR THE PHARAOH'S SOUL TO BE ***WELCOMED*** INTO THE ***NEXT WORLD.***
!!
GASP
SOUL OF THE PHARAOH!
SAY YOUR NAME TO THE EYE OF WADJET!

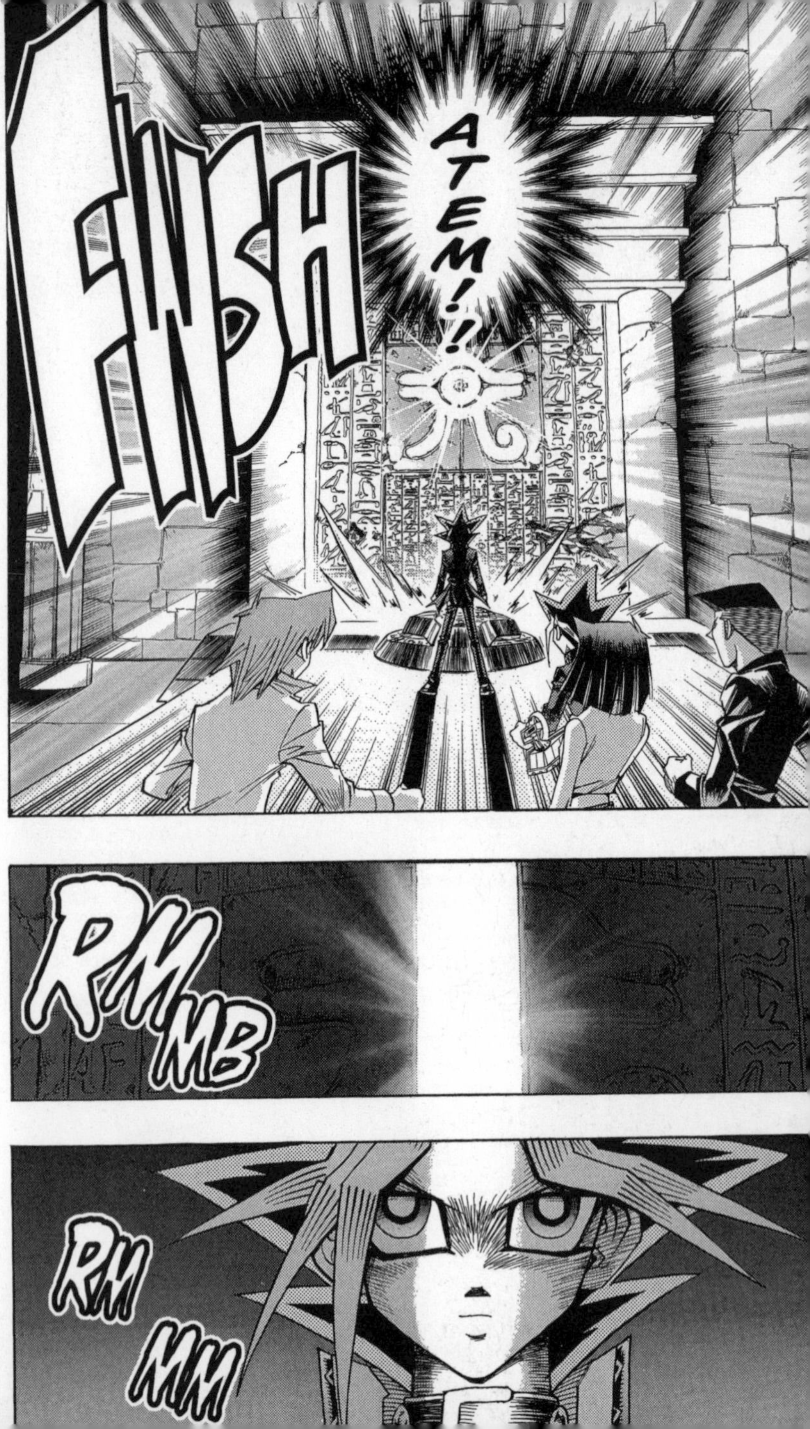
ATEM!!
FLASH
RMMB
RMMM

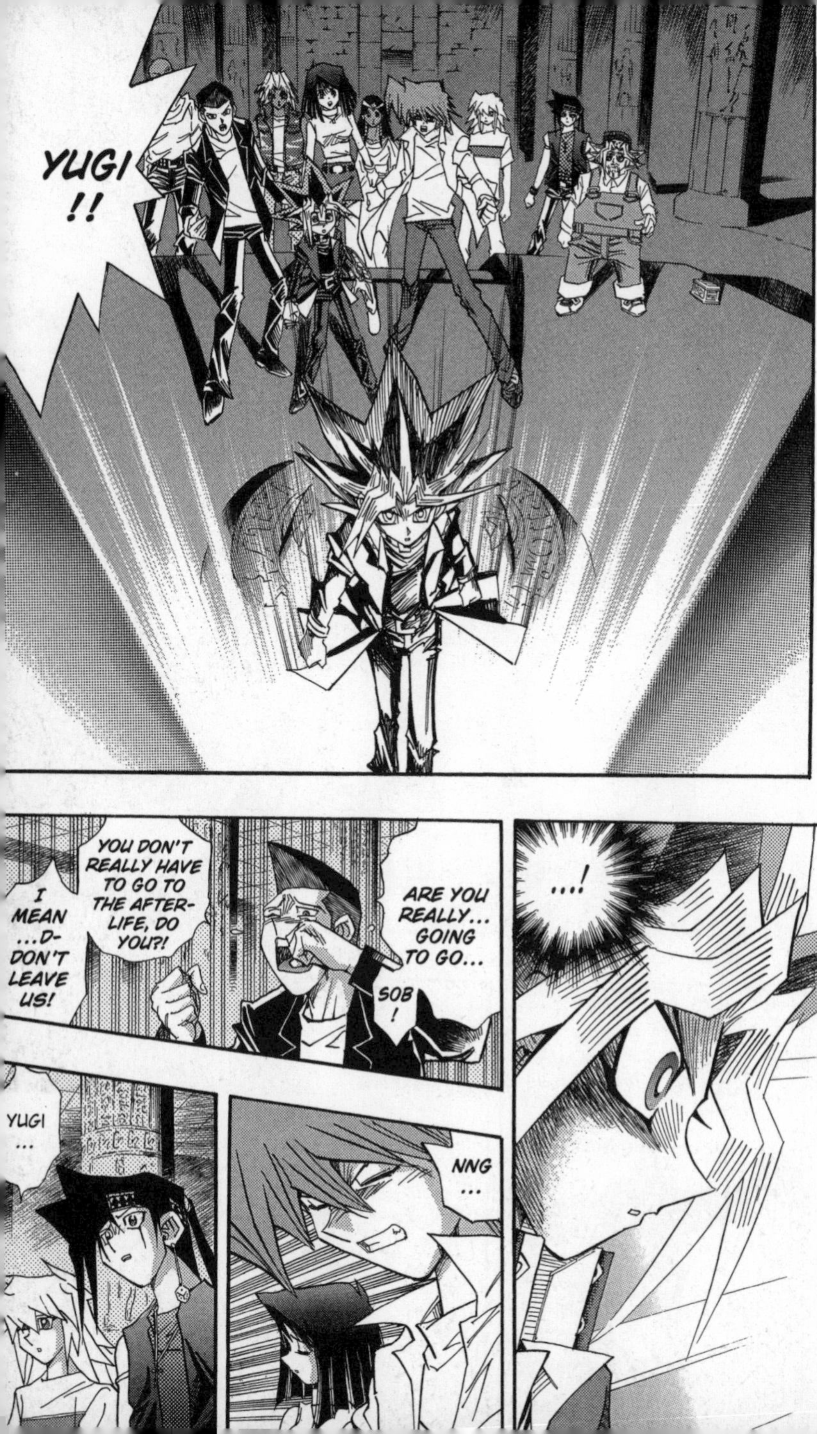
YUGI!!
...!
ARE YOU REALLY... GOING TO GO...
SOB!
YOU DON'T REALLY HAVE TO GO TO THE AFTER-LIFE, DO YOU?!
I MEAN ...D-DON'T LEAVE US!
NNG...
YUGI...

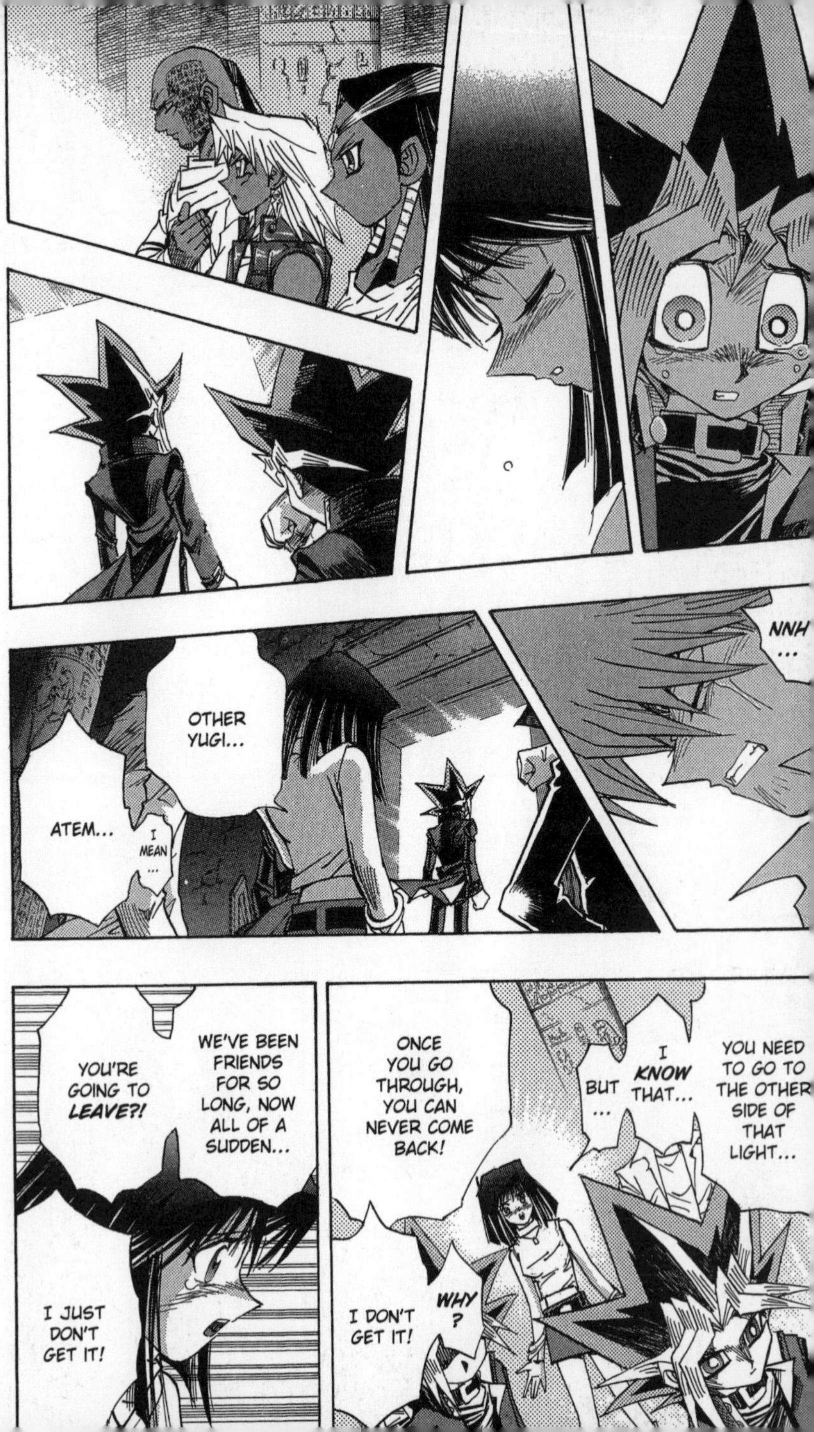
NNH...
OTHER YUGI...
I MEAN...
ATEM...
YOU NEED TO GO TO THE OTHER SIDE OF THAT LIGHT...
I *KNOW* THAT...
BUT...
ONCE YOU GO THROUGH, YOU CAN NEVER COME BACK!
WHY?
I DON'T GET IT!
WE'VE BEEN FRIENDS FOR SO LONG, NOW ALL OF A SUDDEN...
YOU'RE GOING TO *LEAVE?!*
I JUST DON'T GET IT!

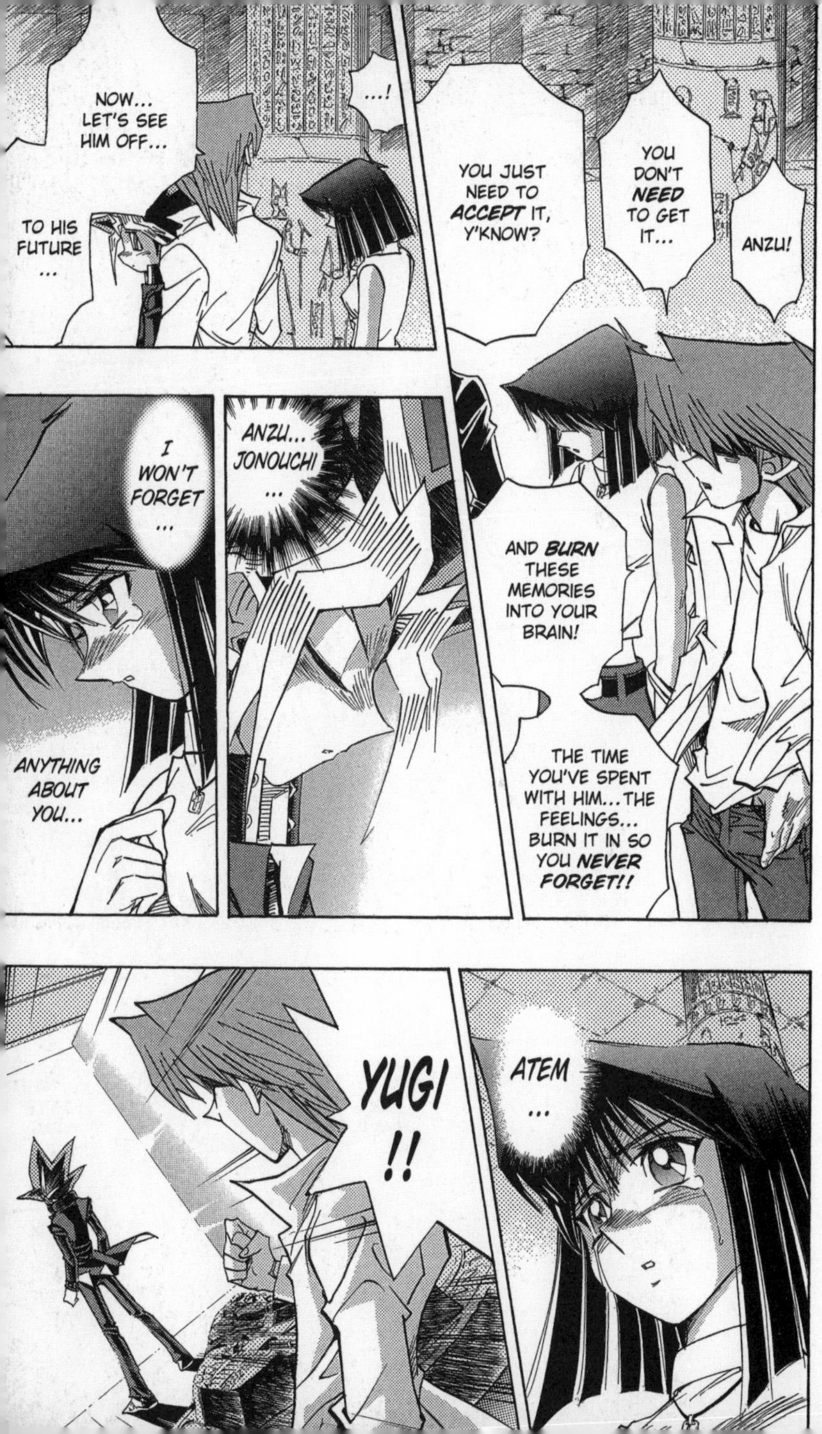
ANZU!
YOU DON'T NEED TO GET IT...
YOU JUST NEED TO ACCEPT IT, Y'KNOW?
AND BURN THESE MEMORIES INTO YOUR BRAIN!
THE TIME YOU'VE SPENT WITH HIM... THE FEELINGS... BURN IT IN SO YOU NEVER FORGET!!
...!
NOW... LET'S SEE HIM OFF...
TO HIS FUTURE...
ANZU... JONOUCHI...
I WON'T FORGET...
ANYTHING ABOUT YOU...
ATEM...
YUGI!!

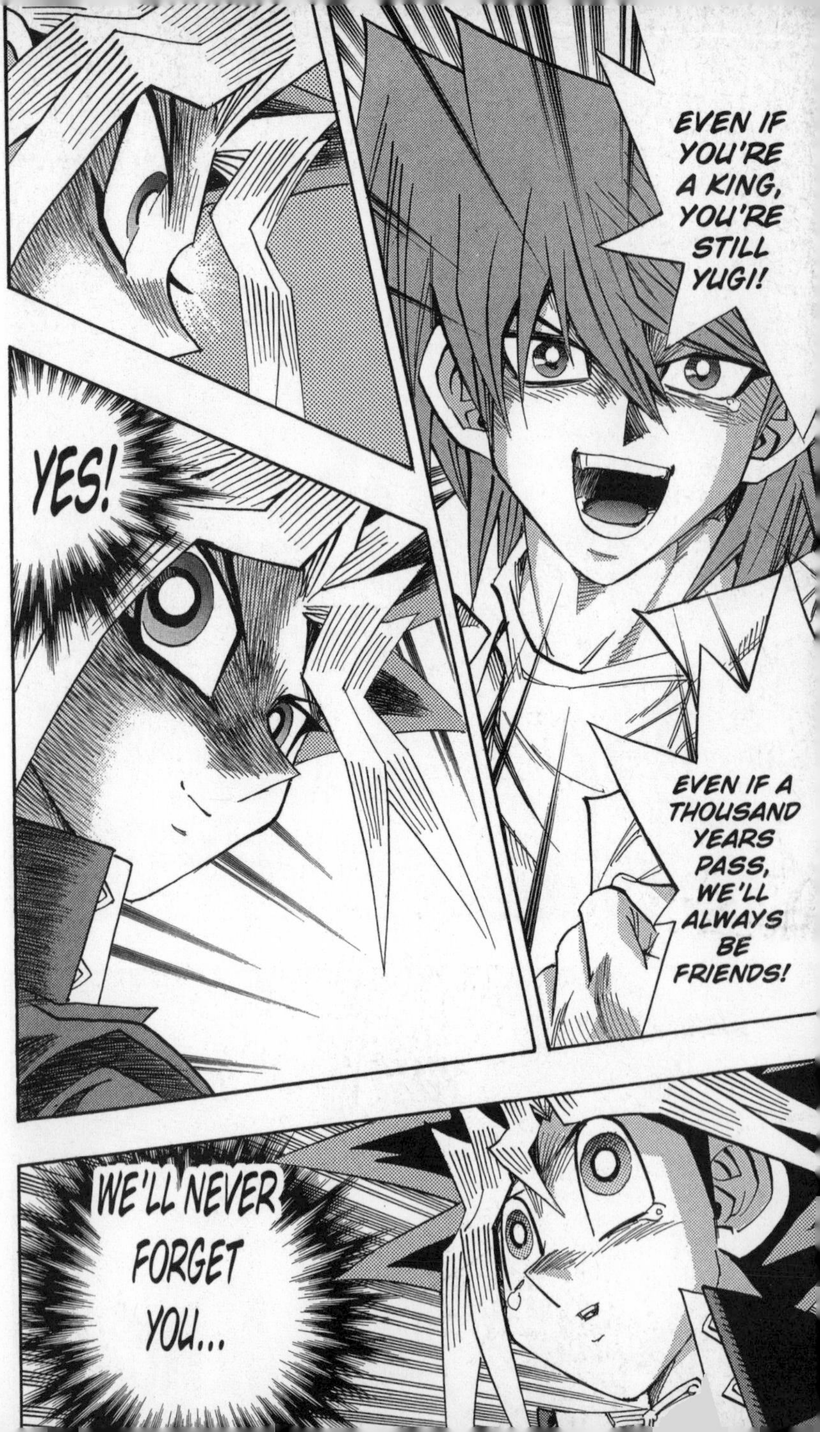
EVEN IF YOU'RE A KING, YOU'RE STILL YUGI!
EVEN IF A THOUSAND YEARS PASS, WE'LL ALWAYS BE FRIENDS!
YES!
WE'LL NEVER FORGET YOU...

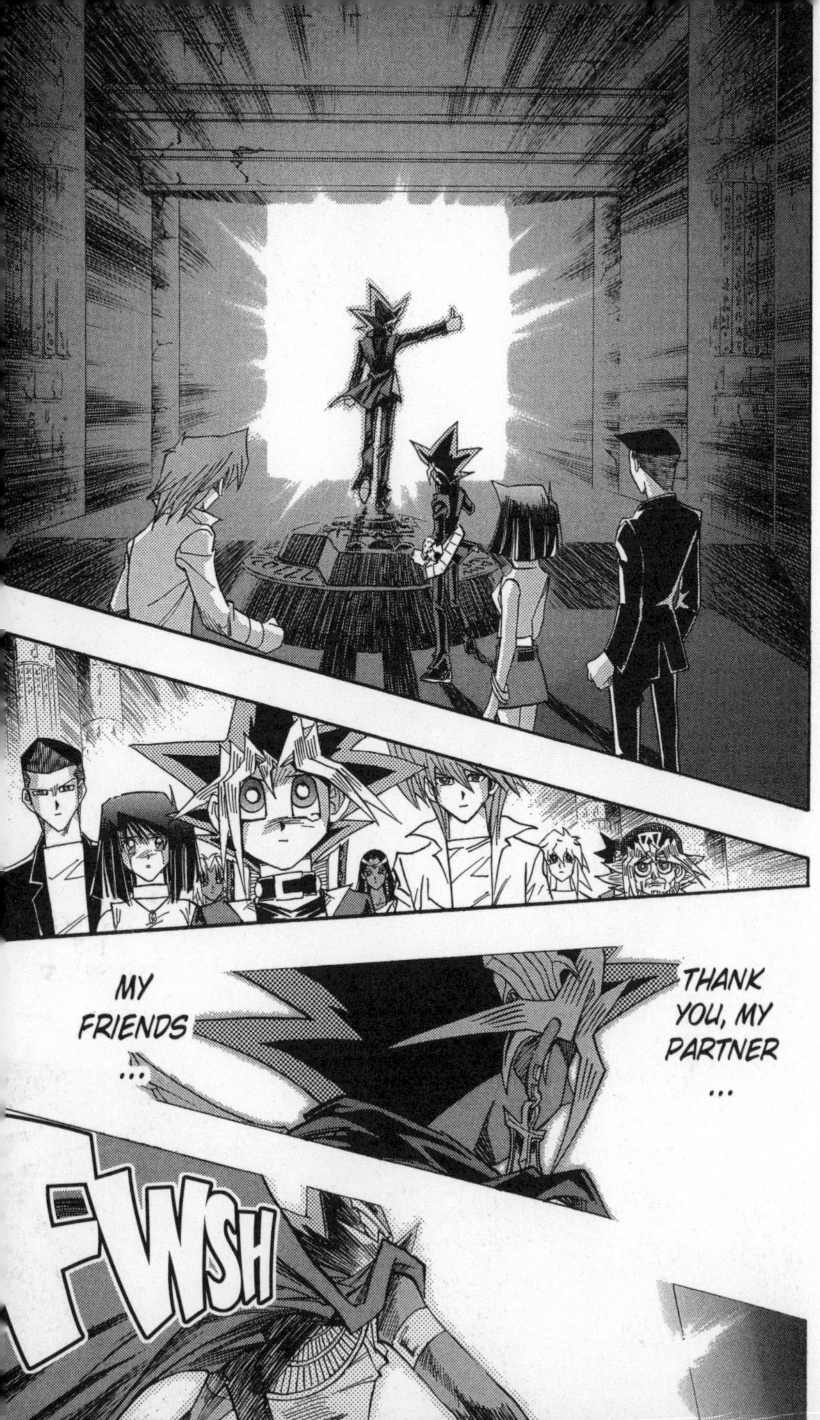
THANK YOU, MY PARTNER ...
MY FRIENDS ...
WSH

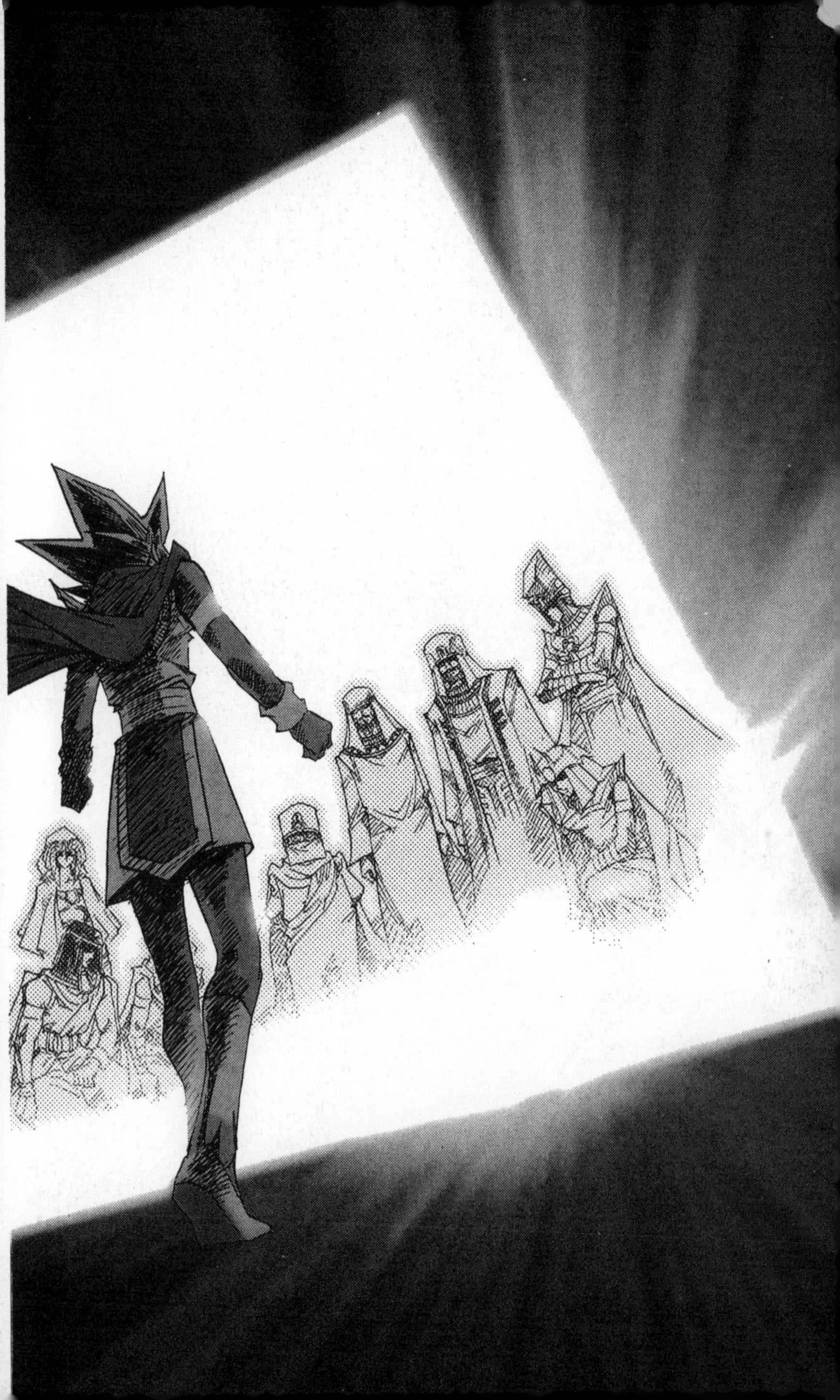

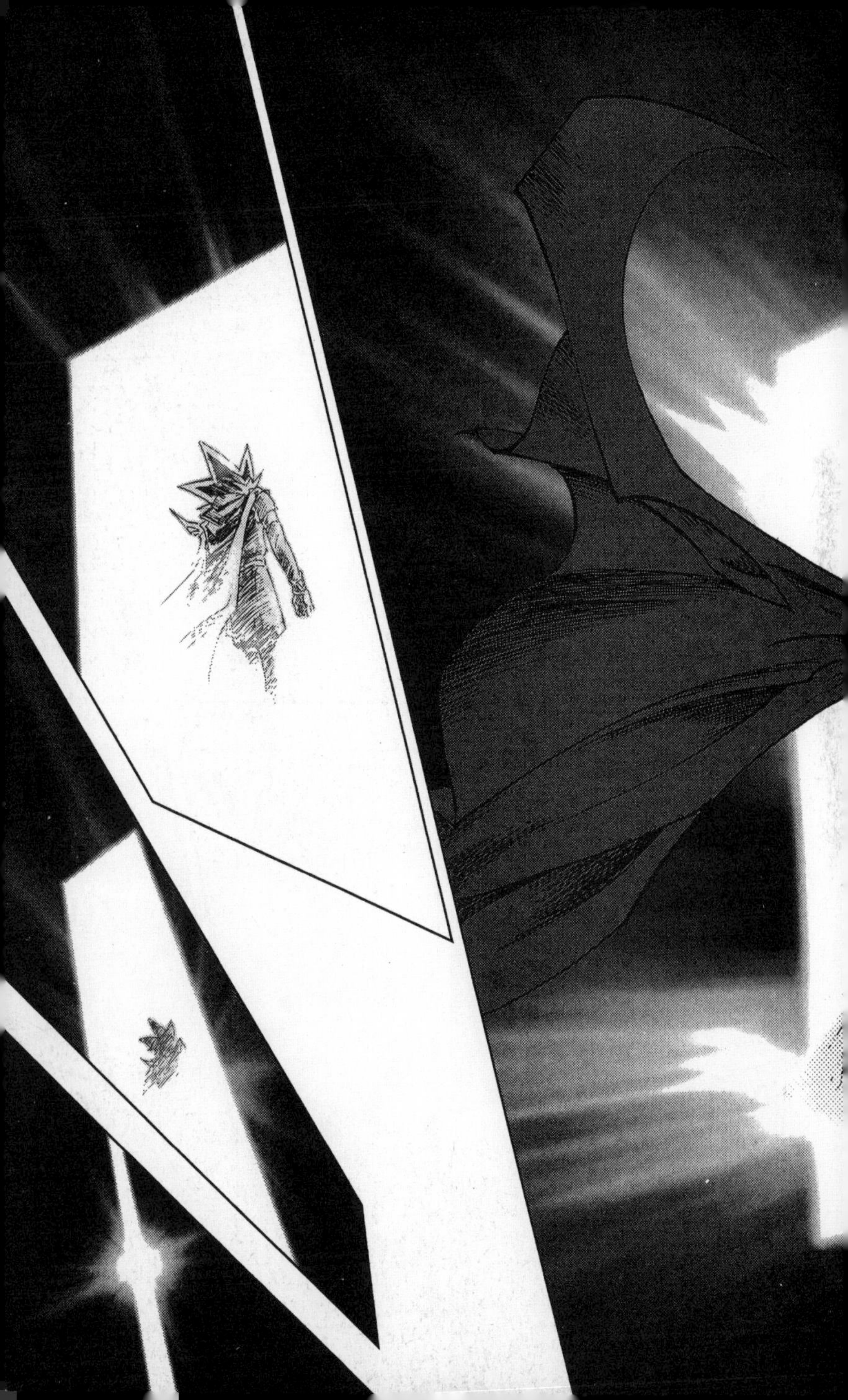

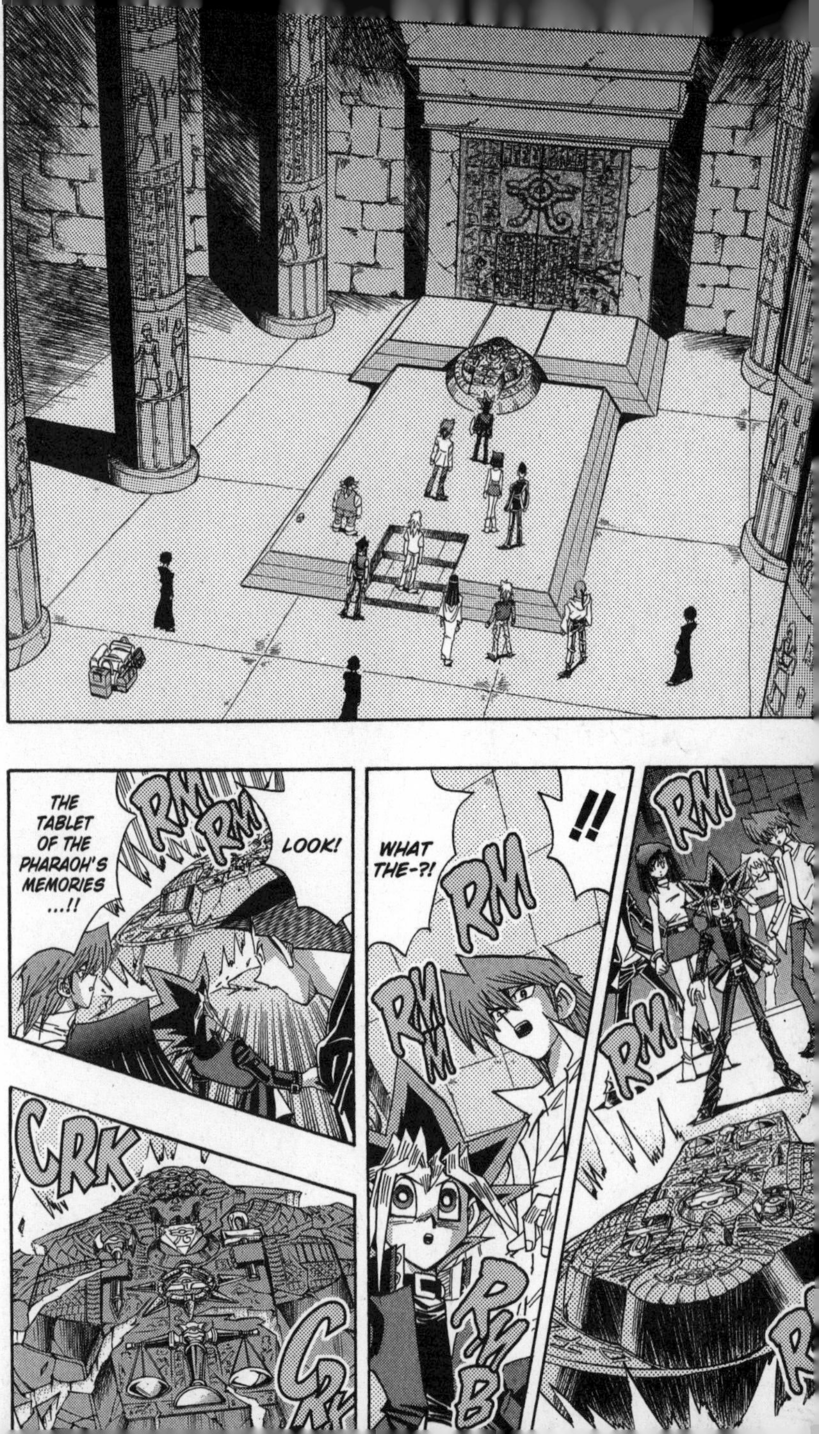
RM
RM
!!
WHAT THE-?!
RM
RM
RM
RM
LOOK!
THE TABLET OF THE PHARAOH'S MEMORIES ...!!
CRK

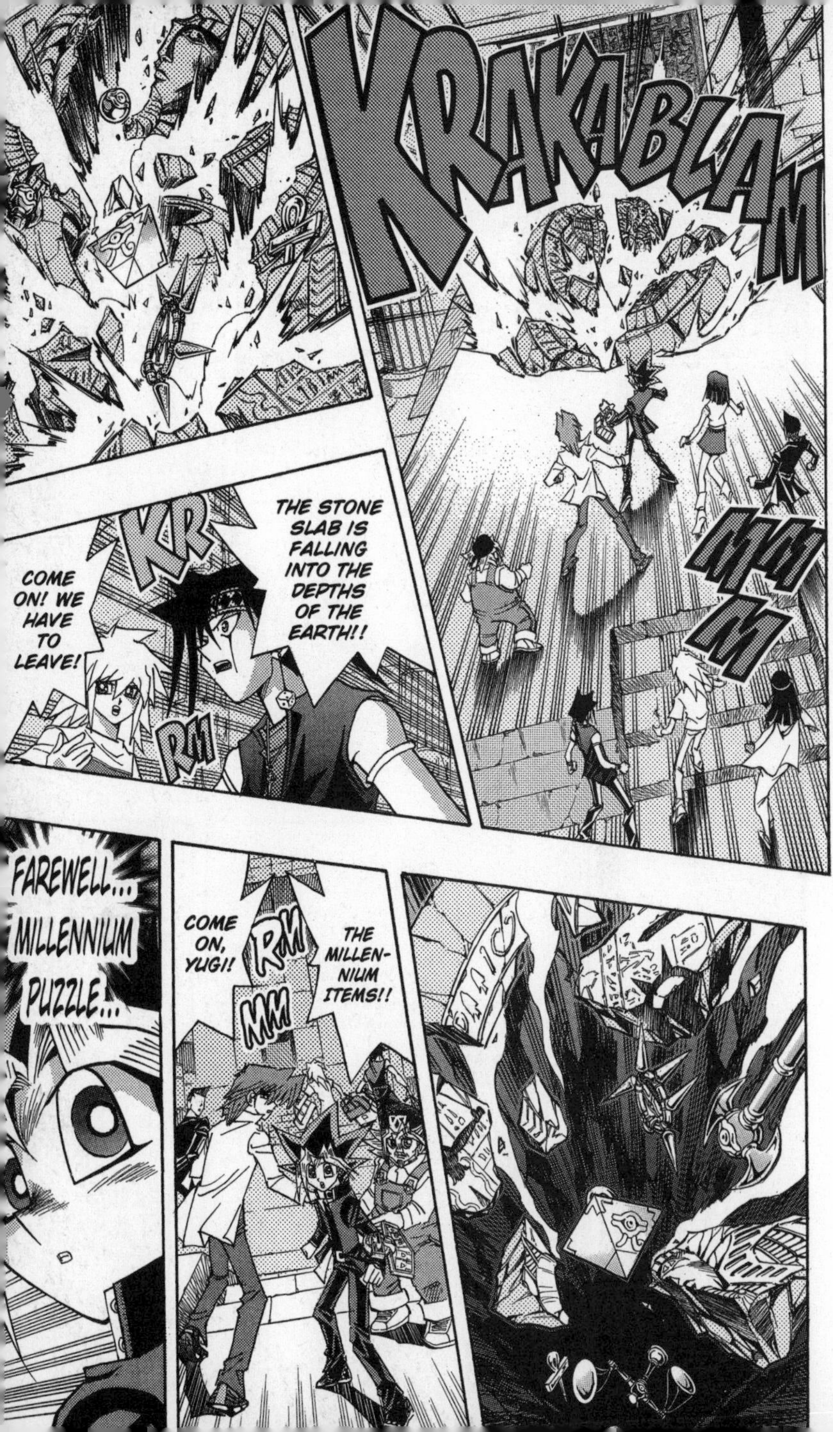
KRAKABLAM
MMMM
THE STONE SLAB IS FALLING INTO THE DEPTHS OF THE EARTH!!
KR
COME ON! WE HAVE TO LEAVE!
RM
THE MILLENNIUM ITEMS!!
COME ON, YUGI!!
RM
MM
FAREWELL... MILLENNIUM PUZZLE...

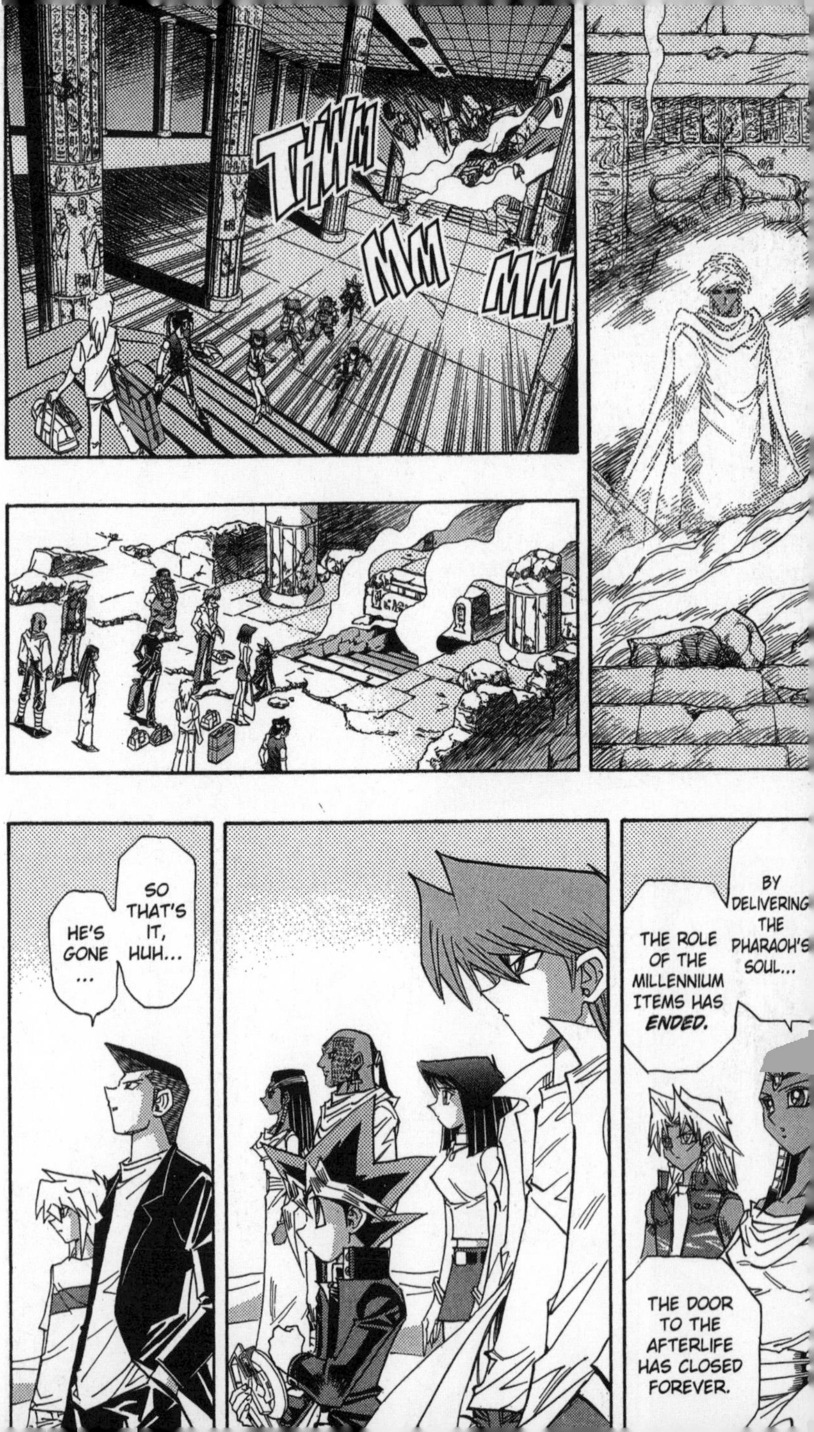
THWMMMMMM
BY DELIVERING THE PHARAOH'S SOUL...
THE ROLE OF THE MILLENNIUM ITEMS HAS *ENDED.*
THE DOOR TO THE AFTERLIFE HAS CLOSED FOREVER.
SO THAT'S IT, HUH...
HE'S GONE ...

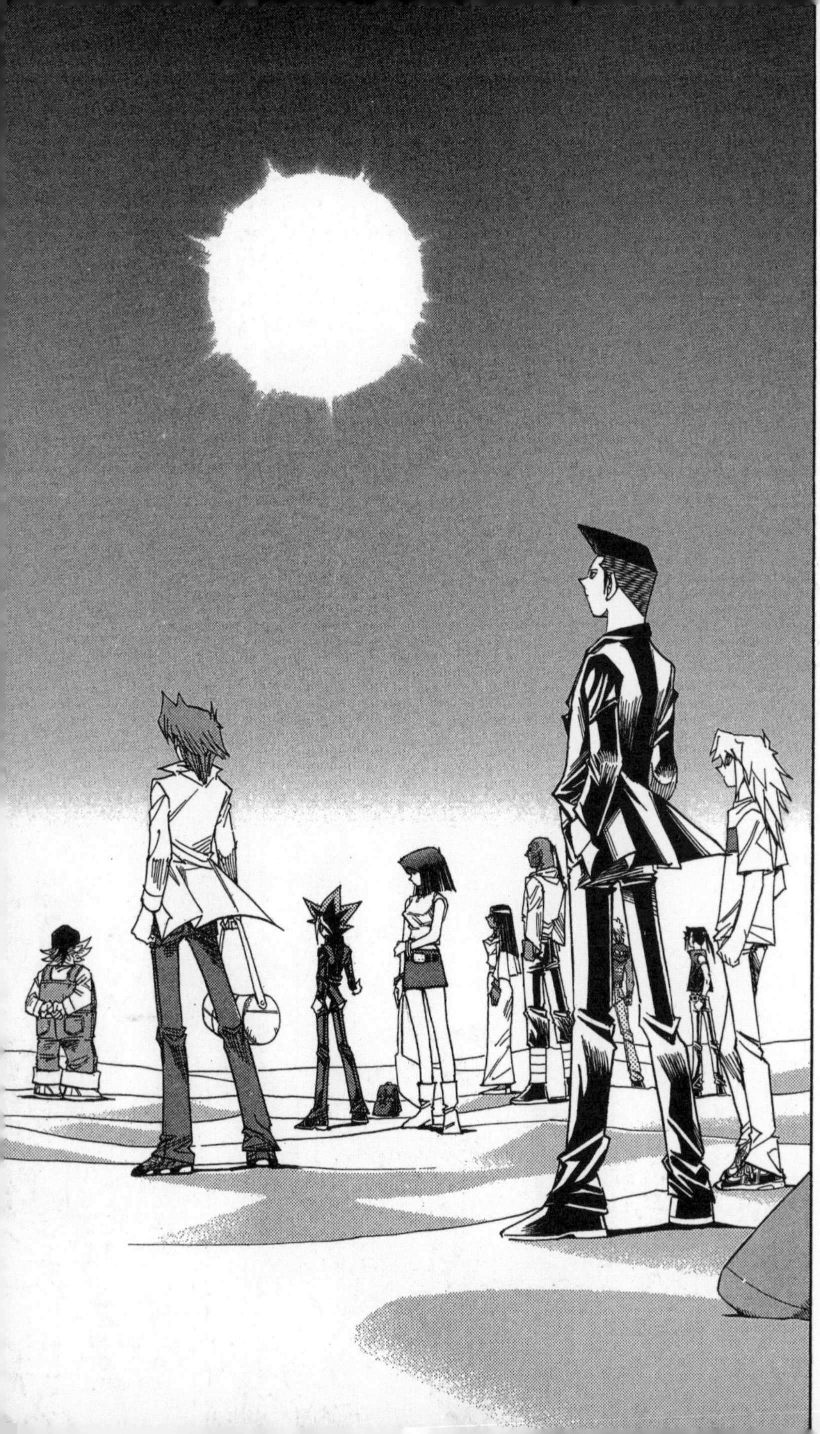

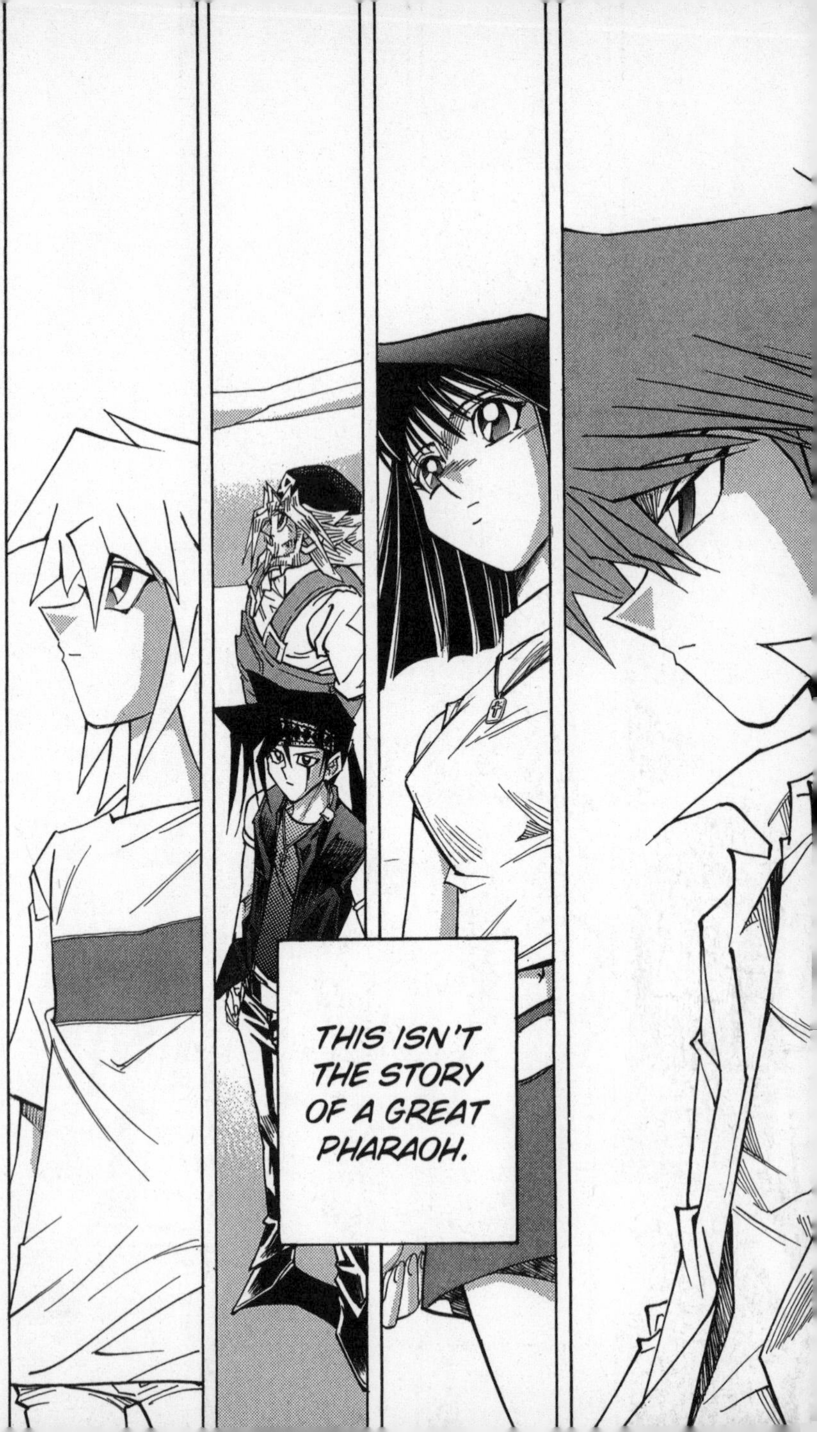
THIS ISN'T THE STORY OF A GREAT PHARAOH.

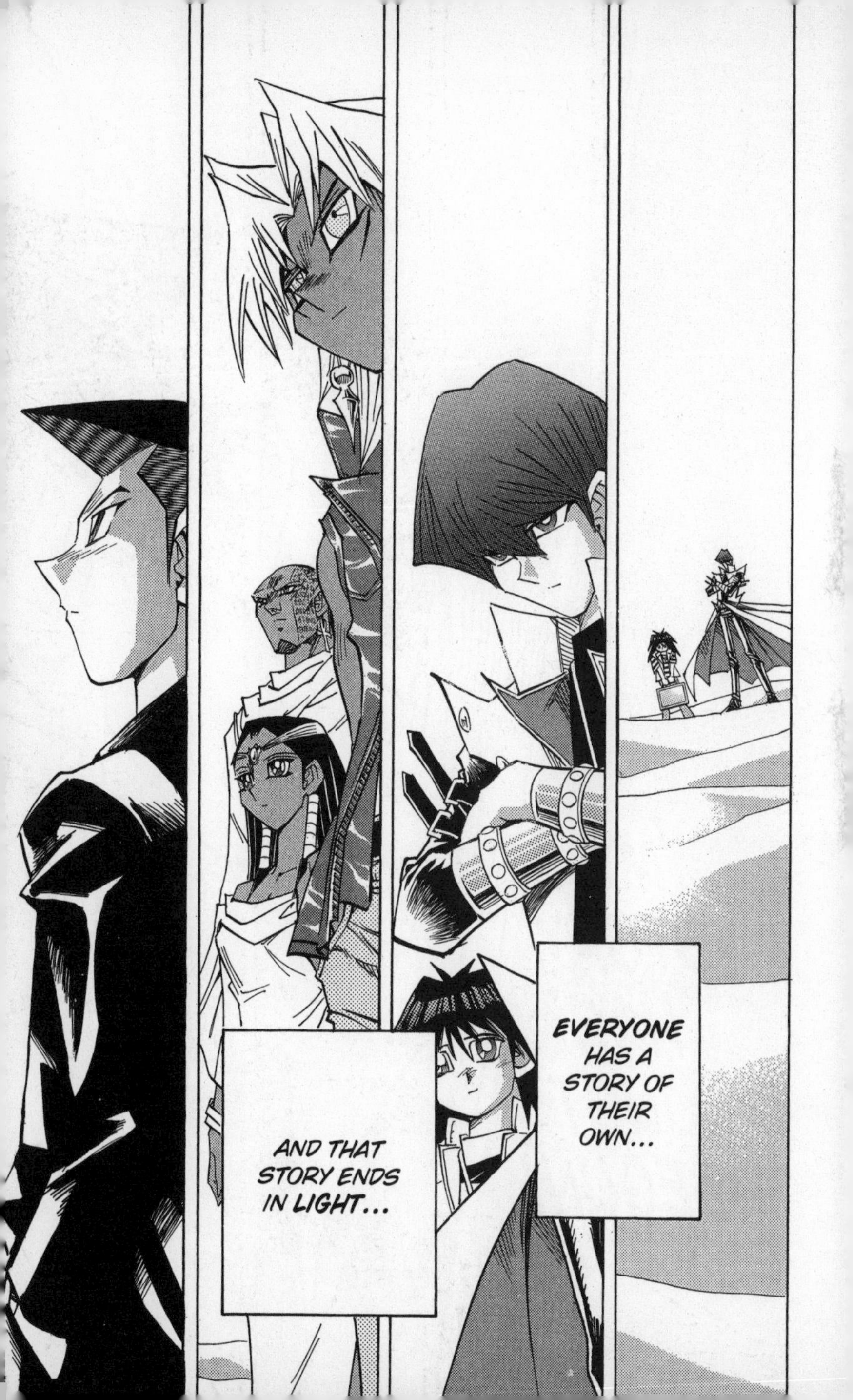
EVERYONE HAS A STORY OF THEIR OWN...
AND THAT STORY ENDS IN LIGHT...

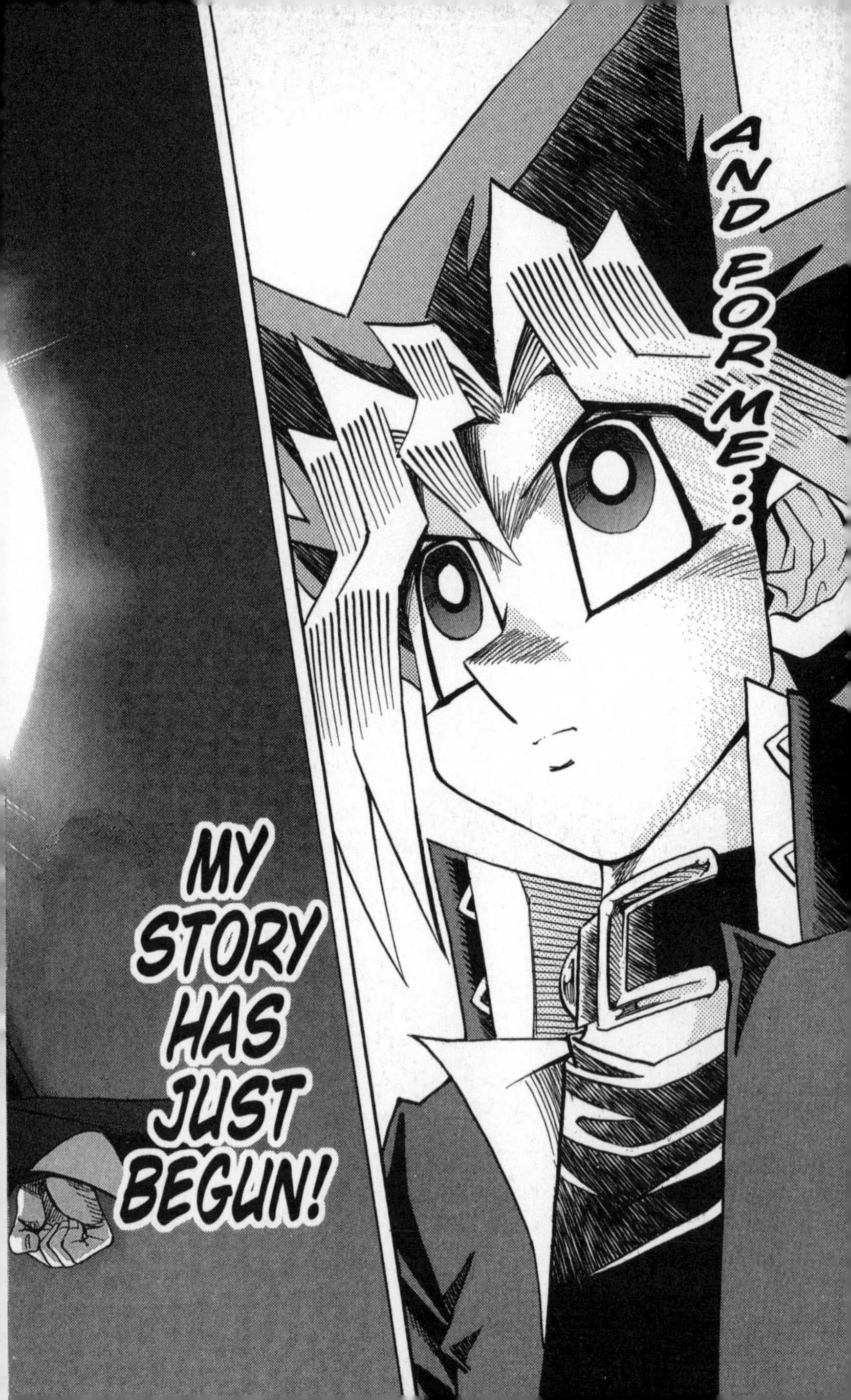
AND FOR ME...
MY STORY HAS JUST BEGUN!

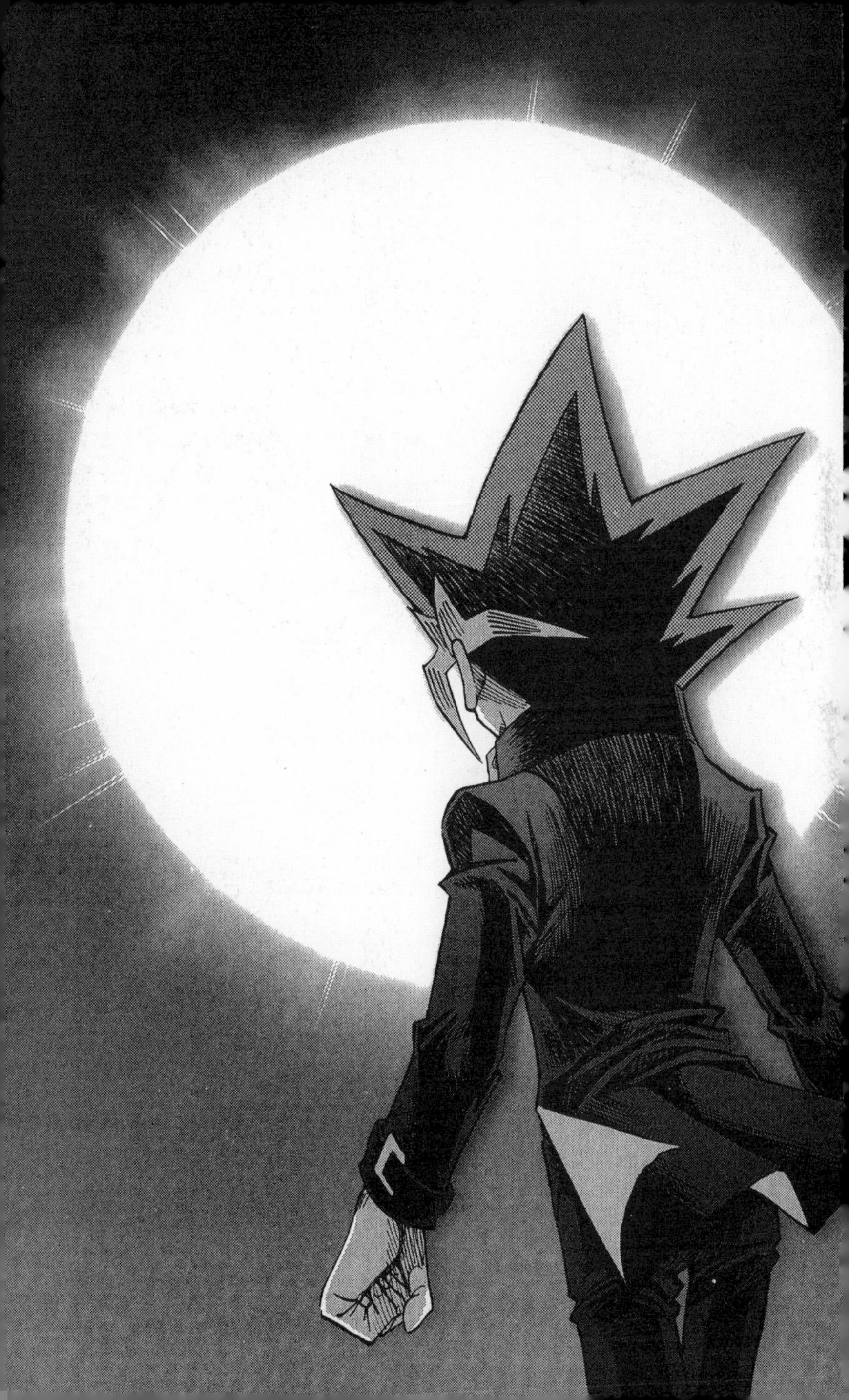

YU-GI-OH!

Presented by

KAZUKI TAKAHASHI

Staff

KEIYA KIYOTAKI

NAOYUKI KAGEYAMA

AKIRA ITO

MASASHI SATO

RYUJI GOTO

HIDENOBU ISAYAMA

AKIHIRO TOMONAGA

TOSHIRO ISHII

YOSHIO HIGASA

YOSHIAKI NISHIZAWA

YU MAEKAWA

Editor

YOSHIHISA HEISHI

HISAO SHIMADA

Special Thanks

TOSHIMASA TAKAHASHI

YU-GI-OH!

遊☆戯☆王

完

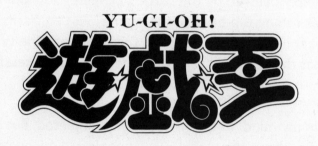

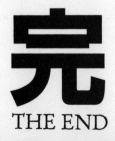

THE END

The games that the characters played were not played facing monitors, but facing other people. The opponents they played were the mirrors that reflected their hearts. In a basic sense, they fought each other's spirits. Because this was a manga, it was deeply colored by the battle between good and evil, but I think the basis of the "game" was to clarify what lies between people. I think this was the reason that the *Yu-Gi-Oh!* card game became so successful all over the world.

****

In my mind, *Yu-Gi-Oh!* has been completed. But throughout the world, many people are taking my work and the cards in their hands. In gratitude for that, I would like to prolong the world of *Yu-Gi-Oh!* for just a little while longer.

****

I borrow the end of this book to thank all of those who have participated in this world. Thank you from the bottom of my heart.

Kazuki Takahashi
April 14, 2004

AFTERWORD

For seven long years, I've traveled with *Yu-Gi-Oh!*. I think I've been able to draw the themes I've wanted to express, but as I end the series, my main concern is whether I've transmitted my message to my readers.

From the moment Yugi put together the Millennium Puzzle, the "other self" appeared in his heart. The time needed to explore two main characters turned this into a long series.

In our daily life, we never get to see ourselves except by standing in front of a mirror. But even a mirror won't reflect our hearts. The main characters of this work won the courage and strength of will to face each others' hearts.

✳✳✳✳✳✳✳✳✳✳✳✳✳✳✳✳✳✳✳✳✳✳✳

As we go about our lives, we touch people, we see people, and interact with them; and in doing so we feel and think many things. Sometimes we make others happy, sometimes we hurt them, we sympathize, and we disagree. In the midst of this, we learn that people's thoughts and feelings are not a one-way street. You may say that's something very basic and natural, but what I wanted to draw and write in this work was just that interaction between people, and in order to do that, I used "games."

You're Reading in the Wrong Direction!!

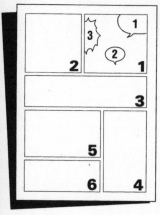

Whoops! Guess what? You're starting at the wrong end of the comic!

...It's true! In keeping with the original Japanese format, **Yu-Gi-Oh!: Millennium World** is meant to be read from right to left, starting in the upper-right corner.

Unlike English, which is read from left to right, Japanese is read from right to left, meaning that action, sound effects and word-balloon order are completely reversed... something which can make readers unfamiliar with Japanese feel pretty backwards themselves. For this reason, manga or Japanese comics published in the U.S. in English have sometimes been published "flopped"—that is, printed in exact reverse order, as though seen from the other side of a mirror.

By flopping pages, U.S. publishers can avoid confusing readers, but the compromise is not without its downside. For one thing, a character in a flopped manga series who once wore in the original Japanese version a T-shirt emblazoned with "M A Y" (as in "the merry month of") now wears one which reads "Y A M"! Additionally, many manga creators in Japan are themselves unhappy with the process, as some feel the mirror-imaging of their art alters their original intentions.

We are proud to bring you Kazuki Takahashi's **Yu-Gi-Oh!: Millennium World** in the original unflopped format. For now, though, turn to the other side of the book and let the games begin...!

—Editor